Mohamed Seedat • Shahna
Daniel J. Christie

Editors

Enlarging the Scope of Peace Psychology

African and World-Regional Contributions

Springer

Editors
Mohamed Seedat
Institute for Social and Health Sciences
University of South Africa
Johannesburg, South Africa

South African Medical Research Council-
  University of South Africa Violence,
  Injury and Peace Research Unit
Cape Town, South Africa

Shahnaaz Suffla
Institute for Social and Health Sciences
University of South Africa
Johannesburg, South Africa

South African Medical Research Council-
  University of South Africa Violence,
  Injury and Peace Research Unit
Cape Town, South Africa

Daniel J. Christie
Institute for Social and Health Sciences
University of South Africa
Johannesburg, South Africa

Department of Psychology
The Ohio State University
Columbus, OH, USA

ISSN 2197-5779   ISSN 2197-5787 (electronic)
Peace Psychology Book Series
ISBN 978-3-319-83258-6   ISBN 978-3-319-45289-0 (eBook)
DOI 10.1007/978-3-319-45289-0

Peace Psychology Book Series

Series Editor

Daniel J. Christie

Acknowledgments

Most of this volume draws on presentations and discussions that took place at the 14th Biennial Symposium on the Contributions of Psychology to Peace. Biennial symposia bring together local and international peace scholars to grapple with issues that bear on peace and human wellbeing. The 14th Biennial Symposium was held in Johannesburg and Pretoria, South Africa, in 2015.

Although symposia are sponsored by the Committee for the Psychological Study of Peace, the extent to which symposia engage in knowledge creation and social transformation has always depended primarily on Local Site Coordinators who take on the task of dealing with logistical matters and program development. Participants in the 14th Biennial Symposium were fortunate to have Mohamed Seedat and Shahnaaz Suffla serve as Site Coordinators. In addition to being extraordinarily gifted peace and community psychology scholars, they have a skill set that is well suited for the twin goals of Biennial Symposia—namely, to privilege voices from geohistorical contexts that are typically not included in dominant peace discourses and to build an international community that promotes peace-related research and action. Their leadership and example made it possible for international participants to see through the lens of critical dialogues centered on the conditions of marginalized people and the continued epistemic violence of contemporary global power configurations. Their openness, warmth, and generosity of spirit gave participants a glimpse of the meanings and manifestations of peace in South Africa while imparted a sense of urgency in efforts to disrupt global oppression and reconstitute an emancipatory agenda.

Like most Biennial Symposia, the number of delegates was small, only about 50 in all. And while the small number was well suited for meaningful interactions, delegates also had the unique privilege to learn from people who live in informal settlements. In particular, the people of Thembelihle, an informal settlement in Johannesburg, were generous in allowing delegates to be seated among them as they voiced their frustrations and concerns to political operatives. Their impassioned plea for better service delivery was an in vivo demonstration of a collective effort to disrupt oppression. Delegates were privileged to bear witness to the enactment of an emancipatory agenda in a settlement that could serve as a model for the potential of a liberation psychology taking root throughout South Africa.

The Institute for Social and Health Sciences of the College of Graduate Studies at the University of South Africa, and the South African Medical Research Council—University of South Africa Violence, Injury and Peace Research Unit served as institutional hosts of the symposium. Not surprisingly, symposia of this sort require the efforts of numerous staff from the host institutions whose largely invisible work makes it possible for delegates to focus and fully immerse themselves in the symposium content and processes as they unfold. Their efforts are acknowledged and greatly appreciated.

As usual, the ongoing support and, when necessary, the gentle prodding of Morgan Ryan, Editor of Behavioral Sciences, at Springer SBM, are very much appreciated. Through a dedicated staff at Springer, volumes in the *Peace Psychology Book Series* continue to help peace and community psychologists raise their collective voice in the pursuit of harmony and equity in human relations locally and globally.

Daniel J. Christie

Co-Chair, Committee for the Psychological Study of Peace

Series Editor, *Peace Psychology Book Series*

Contents

Contributors

Azeem Badroodien Centre for International Teacher Education, Cape Peninsula University of Technology, Cape Town, South Africa

Arvin Boller Ateneo de Manila University, Quezon, Philippines

Diane Bretherton University of Queensland, St Lucia, QLD, Australia

Hugo Canham Department of Psychology, University of the Witwatersrand, Johannesburg, South Africa

Daniel J. Christie Institute for Social and Health Sciences, University of South Africa, Johannesburg, South Africa

Department of Psychology, The Ohio State University, Columbus, OH, USA

James R. Cochrane International Religious Health Assets Programme (IRHAP), University of Cape Town, Cape Town, South Africa

Andrew Dawes Department of Psychology, University of Cape Town, Cape Town, South Africa

Norman Duncan Department of Psychology, University of Pretoria, Pretoria, South Africa

Donald Foster Department of Psychology, University of Cape Town, Cape Town, South Africa

Reeshma Haji Laurentian University, Barrie, ON, Canada

Akiko Hanaya Centre for International Teacher Education, Cape Peninsula University of Technology, Cape Town, South Africa

Teresa Lorena Jopson Coral Bell School of Asia Pacific Affairs, Australian National University, Canberra, ACT, Australia

Waheeda Khan Faculty of Behavioural Sciences, SGT University, Gurgaon, NCR-Delhi, India

Department of Psychology, Jamia Millia Islamia, New Delhi, Delhi, India

Richard N. Lalonde Department of Psychology, York University, Toronto, ON, Canada

Ursula Lau Institute for Social and Health Sciences, University of South Africa, Johannesburg, South Africa

South African Medical Research Council-University of South Africa Violence, Injury and Peace Research Unit, Cape Town, South Africa

Institute for Dispute Resolution in Africa, University of South Africa, Pretoria, South Africa

Siew Fang Law College of Arts Australia, Victoria University, Melbourne, Australia

Sandy Lazarus Institute for Social and Health Sciences, University of South Africa, Johannesburg, South Africa

South African Medical Research Council-University of South Africa Violence, Injury and Peace Research Unit, Cape Town, South Africa

Sramana Majumdar OP Jindal University, Hissar, India

Department of Psychology, Jamia Millia Islamia, New Delhi, Delhi, India

Shelley McKeown Graduate School of Education, University of Bristol, Bristol, UK

Cristina Jayme Montiel Ateneo de Manila University, Quezon, Philippines

Noraini M. Noor Department of Psychology, International Islamic University of Malaysia, Kuala Lumpur, Malaysia

Diana Rodríguez Teachers College, Columbia University, New York, NY, USA

Yusuf Sayed Centre for International Teacher Education, Cape Peninsula University of Technology, Cape Town, South Africa

University of Sussex, UK

Mohamed Seedat Institute for Social and Health Sciences, University of South Africa, Johannesburg, South Africa

South African Medical Research Council-University of South Africa Violence, Injury and Peace Research Unit, Cape Town, South Africa

Candice Simmons Institute for Social and Health Sciences, University of South Africa, Johannesburg, South Africa

South African Medical Research Council-University of South Africa Violence, Injury and Peace Research Unit, Cape Town, South Africa

Garth Stevens Department of Psychology, University of the Witwatersrand, Johannesburg, South Africa

Shahnaaz Suffla Institute for Social and Health Sciences, University of South Africa, Johannesburg, South Africa

South African Medical Research Council-University of South Africa Violence, Injury and Peace Research Unit, Cape Town, South Africa

Nora Sveaass Department of Psychology, University of Oslo, Oslo, Norway

Naiema Taliep Institute for Social and Health Sciences, University of South Africa, Johannesburg, South Africa

South African Medical Research Council-University of South Africa Violence, Injury and Peace Research Unit, Cape Town, South Africa

Laura K. Taylor School of Psychology, Queen's University, Belfast, UK

Michael Wessells Mailman School of Public Health, Columbia University, New York, NY, USA

Part I
Organizing Framework
and Summary of Chapters

Chapter 1
Toward a Socially Transformative Peace Psychology: Overview of the Symposium and Proceedings

Daniel J. Christie, Mohamed Seedat, and Shahnaaz Suffla

The chapters in this volume are based primarily on presentations and discussions that took place in 2015 at the 14th Biennial Symposium on the Contributions of Psychology to Peace. Twenty years earlier, the symposium was convened in Cape Town, just 1 year after the dismantling of Apartheid and the instantiation of a democratisation process that fully enfranchised the Black majority population. At that moment in history, the promise of reconciliation, both spiritually and materially, seemed within grasp and a climate of optimism was palpable. The 2015 symposium took place in a much more sombre climate as participants discussed the intractable problems of widespread poverty, economic inequality, political corruption, institutional intransigence, continued oppression, and a host of other structural and cultural problems (Bhorat & Van Der Westhuisen, 2010). The South Africa setting in 2015 was a stark reminder that political democracy and the adoption of a constitution that enshrines the principles of human rights do not ensure human well-being for all.

D.J. Christie (✉)
Institute for Social and Health Sciences, University of South Africa, Johannesburg, South Africa

Department of Psychology, The Ohio State University, Columbus, OH, USA
e-mail: christie.1@osu.edu

M. Seedat • S. Suffla
Institute for Social and Health Sciences, University of South Africa, Johannesburg, South Africa

South African Medical Research Council-University of South Africa Violence, Injury and Peace Research Unit, Cape Town, South Africa
e-mail: Seedama@unisa.ac.za; ssuffla@mrc.ac.za

© Springer International Publishing AG 2017   3
M. Seedat et al. (eds.), *Enlarging the Scope of Peace Psychology*,
Peace Psychology Book Series, DOI 10.1007/978-3-319-45289-0_1

Such was the context for the 2015 Biennial Symposium on the Contributions of Psychology to Peace, which took place in Johannesburg and Pretoria. The symposium's mandate has always been to privilege and bring forward "voices from cultures and situations that are typically not included in dominant peace discourses," a decree that calls for the amplification of epistemologies and ideologies that bear on liberatory praxis and originate in the Global South generally (Law & Bretherton, this volume), and in particular, in Latin America (Montero & Sonn, 2009), Asia (Montiel & Noor, 2009), and Africa (Seedat, Duncan, & Lazarus, 2001). Hence, the 2015 South Africa symposium, like many of those before, took place in a relatively middle-income country and consisted of delegates from around the world with about an even split between local and international scholars and practitioners.

Since their inception, biennial symposia have encouraged transdisciplinary understandings of the role of psychology in peace, conflict, and violence. And while psychological perspectives and concepts are focal, they are examined in the context of geohistorical developments. In the South Africa context, delegates generally appreciated that the political changes of 1994 did not fulfill the promise of advancing a social justice agenda that meets the needs of most South Africans. After the 1994 elections, the Truth and Reconciliation Commission moved swiftly and emphasised the urgency of forgiveness, reconciliation, and healing at the societal and political levels. At the psychological level, the compression of time and space for grieving and making meaning of personal losses were left wanting (Hamber, 2009; Stevens, Duncan, & Canham, this volume). In addition, the failure of the government to move forward on a social justice agenda can be observed today with even a cursory look at the enormous differences in the wealth and health of South Africans, differences that are in part fuelled by the confluence of an ethos venerating acquisitive motives along with neo-liberal institutional arrangements that privilege few at the expense of many (Seedat, van Niekerk, Suffla, & Ratele, 2014).

The lack of synchronicity between macro- and micro-level changes in the South Africa context underscores the importance of developing a peace psychology that shares with critical psychology the aim of scrutinising macro-level structures that have adverse effects on the psychosocial well-being of individuals and collectivities. Clearly, as a host of the symposium, the South African site offered a rich history from which to draw, particularly in light of the sequelae of Apartheid, the current wave of social unrest and the urgency of a research and praxis agenda that is psychologically driven and socially transformative.

Organisation and Chapters

In Part 1 of the book, which consists of two chapters, we provide an organising framework for the proceedings of the symposium and a brief overview of the chapters. Part II presents topics that originate primarily from conceptions in the Global North and can be regarded as traditional topics in peace psychology, while Part III provides a better representation of the approach to knowledge production that is underway in the Global South. The volume is distinguished by elaborating on an emerging perspective in peace psychology that seeks to promote epistemic peace, which is manifest in the production of knowledge about meanings of peace through the elicitation of voices from marginalised communities (cf. Lau & Seedat, 2015, this volume; Law & Bretherton, this volume; Law & Ramos, this volume; Lazarus, Cochrane, Taliep, Simmons, & Seedat, this volume; Stevens et al., this volume).

Part I: Organising Framework and Summary of the Chapters

In its earliest iteration, peace psychology was primarily a Western invention and did not advocate an emancipatory agenda that was concerned with the marginalisation of oppressed people. Instead, knowledge production in peace psychology was driven by the politics of the Cold War. For Western peace psychologists, the psychological underpinnings of the nuclear arms race and the prevention of nuclear war were the preeminent concerns. Emphasis was placed on the potential of psychologically informed analyses to deescalate tensions and promote constructive rhetoric and engagement in US–Soviet relations (Deutsch, 1983; Frank, 1967; Schwebel, 1965; White, 1984, 1986).

It was not until the beginning of the twenty first century that peace psychology adopted a more global perspective and fully embraced an emancipatory agenda (Christie, Wagner, & Winter, 2001). The conception of a more inclusive peace psychology was driven by developments outside the West where focal concerns were centred on structural violence, the systemic roots of violent episodes, and the promise of socially transformative activism (Butchart & Seedat, 1990; Dawes, 2001; Martín-Baró, 1994; Montiel, 2001). The South African context of the 2015 symposium was a reminder of the emancipatory agenda that is at the core and interstices of peace and critical psychology, as well as the most recent iteration of community psychology in South Africa (Seedat & Lazarus, 2011).

Today, it is generally recognised that sustainable peace requires the continuous crafting of both harmony and equity in human relations, the former of which was the focal issue of traditional research in peace psychology during the Cold War. In contrast, post-Cold War peace psychology foregrounds equity in tandem with harmony as indivisible and essential components in the pursuit of sustainable peace (Christie & Montiel, 2013). Accordingly, the full domain of peace psychology is presented within the covers of the current volume and organised in accordance with the (1) traditional concern of identifying psychological factors involved in the prevention and mitigation of violent episodes and the promotion of harmony in human relations; and (2) the more recent thrust of peace psychology concerning the mitigation of structural violence and enactment of emancipatory agendas that produce greater equity in human relations. These twin foci of peace psychology scholarship underscore the difference between episodic violence and structural violence, the former of which involves directly observable episodic events that physically harm another person or group. Given its observable and intermittent nature, episodic violence can be prevented and ameliorated. In contrast, structural violence occurs when there are enough resources for everyone's needs, yet some people are marginalised and systematically deprived of need satisfaction because of unequal patterns of resource distribution (Galtung, 1969). While episodic violence is often dramatic and can be prevented, structural violence is normalised, kills people slowly over time, and because of its ubiquitous nature, interventions most often are aimed at mitigation rather than prevention (Christie, 2006). At the same time, efforts to decrease episodic and structural violence can be complemented by countervailing efforts that effectively increase peaceful processes that promote harmony with equity (Taylor & Christie, 2015).

In the present chapter (Chap. 1), we use the term *peacemaking* when the primary goal is harmony. In contrast, when equity in human relations is at the centre of analytic and intervention efforts, we will refer to *peacebuilding*. While it seems reasonable to assume that both harmony and equity are essential for the pursuit of sustainable forms of peace, the chapters in the current volume will make it clear that these twin goals in peace psychology often sit uncomfortably with one another. Peacemaking interventions are based on theories and practices aimed at tension reduction, while peacebuilding praxis seeks to induce tension, agitate for change, and disrupt hierarchically organised structures and relations. In addition, peacemaking promotes harmony, while peacebuilding seeks to transform institutions and societies toward more equitable arrangements that open up spaces for expressions of voice and access to material resources for people who lack power. Moreover, the skills, competencies, and values involved in these twin components of peace are not always resonant. The current volume captures some of the tensions between these two different but overlapping approaches to sustainable peace.

Finally, because the symposia are designed to bring forward voices that are often unheard or silenced in peace discourses, the volume also raises the issue of epistemic violence, which can be viewed as a pernicious form of structural violence because voices from the Global South are seldom heard and often marginalised not only in peace discourses, but also in the knowledge generation process in peace psychology. Epistemic violence also intersects with the notion of cultural violence because the latter refers to the use of symbols to legitimise observable forms of episodic and structural violence (Galtung, 1990; Noor & Christie, 2015). Hence, the hegemony of Western concepts and themes in what is regarded as legitimate peace knowledge are manifestations of symbolic or cultural violence. As a methodological preliminary, the promotion of epistemic peace engenders a critical analysis of the semantic space occupied by peace psychology, a space traditionally reserved for scholarship originating in the Global North and not the Global South. Such a critical analysis scrutinises the legitimacy of the process and structure of knowledge in peace psychology, including epistemological assumptions and the very distinctions that are foundational to theory and praxis such as episodic, structural, and cultural violence and peace.

Following the present chapter, Chap. 2 in the volume by Law and Bretherton provides an organising framework, captures some of the tensions between peacemaking and peacebuilding, and casts these tensions within a larger framework of knowledge production in the Global North versus Global South. Recognising that simple North–South polarities mask a more complex reality, the authors use the dichotomy as a dialectical starting point to foreground differences in language, preferred methodologies, differential opportunities for participation in the knowledge generation process, the marginalisation of southern voices, and the privileging of Northern conceptions. In a sense, Law and Bretherton use a critical lens to view the knowledge generation process of peace psychology as practised in the Global North, and by so doing, they reiterate earlier work by scholars in South Africa and other geopolitical contexts who have characterised and problematised knowledge production in psychological research as ethno-science suffused with Euro-American individualism, classism, and patriarchy (Bulhan, 1993; Seedat, MacKenzie, & Stevens, 2004). Moreover, Law and Bretherton echo the concern most clearly enunciated by scholars in the Global South; namely, that knowledge production in the Global North supports dominant exclusionary social practices (Cooper, Nicholas, Seedat, & Statman, 1990). The overall thrust of the chapter supports the argument that systems of knowledge production and the construction of reality are embedded in culture and power relations. Law and Bretherton conclude by arguing for an inclusive approach in peace psychology that provides space for critical reflection in peace psychology and engages with epistemological pluralism rather than epistemic violence.

Following the organising framework of Law and Bretherton in Chap. 2, Part II of the volume consists of five chapters that draw on research from five different countries, all of which grapple with issues that comport with the traditional domain of peace psychology as framed largely in the Global North. Focal issues include intergroup conflict, violence, and peacemaking. The first two chapters examine the impact of violence on people who reside in Kashmir (Chap. 3) and Colombia (Chap. 4). While these two countries are positioned quite differently in a geopolitical sense, they share a recent history of protracted intrastate violence that has taken a toll on the populace. In these two cases, the reactions of people to protracted violence are described and some of the coping strategies they draw on are identified. Also examined is the role of social support in mitigating the effects of exposure to violence and promoting individual and collective well-being.

In the remaining three chapters of Part II, peacemaking research and practices in three countries are described: Northern Ireland, Canada, and Malaysia. Emphasis is placed on interventions designed to improve intergroup relations, prevent violent episodes, and promote harmonious relations. In short, chapters in Part II deal with research and practice on the effects of violence on individual and collective well-being (Chaps. 3 and 4) as well as research aimed at deepening our understanding of factors that prevent violence and generate harmony at the personal, interpersonal, and intergroup levels (Chaps. 5–7).

In Part III of the volume, six chapters (Chaps. 8–13) turn our attention to a more transformative form of peace psychology. Here the emphasis is on research and praxis that seeks to increase tension, agitate, and disrupt harmonious relations. The chapters in Part III challenge the status quo and move human interactions, relationships, institutions, and societal structures toward more equitable arrangements.

The notions of epistemic peace and violence undergird many of the chapters either implicitly or explicitly as questions are raised about Western hegemony and the value of moving the locus of knowledge production to marginalised communities. Many of the chapters originate in the South African context and focus a critical lens on matters of peace and social justice. In the remaining pages of this first chapter, we provide an overview of each of the chapters in Parts II and III.

Part II: Intergroup Conflict, Violence, and Peacemaking

Chapter 3 is situated in the Kashmir valley, a geohistorical context in which peace psychologists are seeking to more deeply understand the psychosocial impact of violence and prospects for peacemaking. While the beauty of the Kashmir valley is stunning, the people of the valley have had to endure three major wars between India and Pakistan since the partition of 1947. After more than 70,000 deaths, Kashmir remains highly militarised, wracked with violent political conflicts, and marked by economic hardships. In Chap. 3, Khan and Majumdar set out to more deeply understand how Kashmiri youth - who have spent their entire life in a war zone - perceive and experience violence. Previous research studies have used quantitative methods to explore the reactions of youth to stressful life conditions based in part on the usual assumption that the effects of exposure can be understood as an interaction between characteristics of the individual and the number and duration of specific events. The current research begins with the assumption that the experience of trauma is conditioned by social identities that operate within social contexts and are usefully explored through qualitative methods. Moreover, the authors suggest that a deeper understanding of the experiences of youth can shed light on the identity and future of the region as a whole.

Khan and Majumdar's research is consistent with previous research, indicating that young men are more likely to report being the victim of direct violence than young women; however, the experience of witnessing violence has strong emotional impacts for both young men and women. An important insight the authors share, based on their qualitative findings, is that young women often report that their witnessing of violence heightens their inhibitions to move about and speak freely.

Both men and women report being particularly impacted by policies that curtail their freedom, such as the banning of movie theatres, curfews on transportation, and periodic prohibitions on phone services. The qualitative approach identified a wide range of experiences that generally fall under the rubric of "mental torture", including feelings of harassment when having to prove one's identity and humiliation when being searched and interrogated or forcibly removed from one's home. Taken together, Khan and Majumdar's work demonstrates the value of a qualitative approach that takes into account the experiences of youth in war zones and draws attention to the unique social and political conditions that affect their well-being.

In Chap. 4, Taylor picks up on the theme of living in a violent and stressful environment, but in the context of the Caribbean coast of Colombia. In this geohistorical context, Taylor notes that members of paramilitary forces were demobilised beginning in 2005, but in recent years have been reconstituted as illegal armed groups involved in narcotrafficking and drug-related violence, thereby setting the stage for ongoing insecurity. Taylor examines how individuals respond to these stressful conditions, drawing on the conceptual distinction between destructive and constructive coping. While destructive coping is associated with internalising problems such as depression, anxiety, and post-traumatic stress, constructive coping is characterised by resiliency and engaging effectively with stressful situations. What is quite unique about Taylor's work is that two levels of analysis are examined; namely, individual coping responses at one level and community support at another level. Not surprisingly, constructive coping was associated with lower levels of depression, while destructive styles predicted higher levels of depression. Community support also mattered: individuals who perceived their communities to be more cohesive and engaged in constructive coping reported fewer symptoms of depression than individuals who perceived their social environment as less supportive. In addition to clarifying the likely dynamics in play at the individual and community levels, Taylor's research offers mental health and policy implications.

In Chap. 5, McKeown presents contact theory, a framework that provides the intellectual scaffolding for applications of one of the most powerful interventions designed to improve intergroup relations. Contact theory is based on the proposition that bringing conflicted groups in contact with one another can improve intergroup attitudes, particularly when groups are working cooperatively and equitably toward a common goal and their activities are sanctioned by authorities (Pettigrew & Tropp, 2006). Situated in the context of Northern Ireland, McKeown examines some of the intergroup tensions that pit Catholics against Protestants and points out that, while partitioning the problem along religious lines is convenient, the conflict is far more complex and has roots in competing national and political ideologies. Notwithstanding the oversimplified dichotomy of Catholic versus Protestant, it is clear that intergroup relations have improved to some extent since the signing of the Good Friday/Belfast peace agreement more than 15 years ago. However, segregation and negative intergroup attitudes remain part of the psychosocial landscape.

The protracted nature of the Northern Ireland conflict makes it clear that peacemaking efforts call for transgenerational projects with much of the hope for a more harmonious future invested in youth and educational initiatives as potential agents and institutions of change. McKeown reviews the educational system in Northern Ireland with particular attention given to the small percentage of integrated schools at elementary and secondary levels. These schools meet some of the conditions that favour the effective use of intergroup contact as a means of improving intergroup attitudes.

In addition to discussing the potential role of education in promoting positive intergroup relations in Northern Ireland, McKeown presents the results of survey research on changes in attitudes among 16-year-olds over an 11-year period from 2003 to 2013. Results demonstrated that integrated schools were associated with a number of outcomes indicative of improved intergroup relations when compared to segregated schools. More specifically, youth in integrated schools were more likely than youth attending other schools to prefer having their children live, work, and attend school in a mixed-religion setting. These results are consistent with contact theory and provide a platform for McKeown to draw implications of the research for peacemaking and policymaking in the North Ireland context.

In Chap. 6, Haji and Lalonde pick up on an important proposition derived from contact theory; namely, intergroup contact can be an exceptionally effective means of improving intergroup relations if the contact situation leads to the formation of friendships. Previous research indicates friendships contribute to the improvement of inter-racial attitudes above and beyond mere contact effects. The central question raised in the current chapter is whether having a friend who is a member of another religious group increases one's openness toward members of that particular religious group as well as other religions. To test these hypotheses, Haji and Lalonde recruited participants for a study in two Canadian cities: Toronto, a culturally diverse city in terms of religion and ethnicity, and Berrie, a much less diverse city. Participants who indicated they had an outgroup religious member among their five closest friends were more likely to exhibit positive attitudes toward outgroup members on a variety of measures. These findings occurred in both cities suggesting the findings are robust. The effects occurred not only in relation to the particular religion of a friend, but also generalised to interfaith relationships. In short, Chaps. 5 and 6 underscore the value of intergroup contact and friendships as a peacemaking intervention.

Chapter 7 by Christie and Noor shifts the emphasis from contact to intergroup rhetoric and the power of language in fueling conflict and peace between ethnic groups. The research is situated in Malaysia, a multi-ethnic society in which rival ethnic groups have been engaged in a protracted political conflict since independence in 1957. Based on the assumption that perceiving the ethnic other as a human being is a precondition for creating, maintaining, and restoring harmonious relations between groups, Christie and Noor used a coding scheme to identify patterns of humanisation and dehumanisation in the rhetoric of political elite in Malaysia. The deep divide between Malays and Chinese Malaysians has taken the centre stage in their analyses, which yielded ample evidence for the kind of dehumanising rhetoric that generally clusters around references to the other as either subhuman and animal-like or robotic and mechanistic. The particularised features of dehumanising rhetoric varied depending on the source and target, but as a broad generalisation Chinese tended to characterise Malays in animalistic terms, while Malays more often used mechanistic references when referring to Chinese.

Some instances of humanising the other also were found in the rhetoric of Malays and Chinese Malaysians; however, these rhetorical statements did not neatly fit the coding scheme that was used and required a reconceptualisation of what it means to humanise the other in the context of Malaysia. Taken together, the results provide guidelines for the kind of rhetoric that could shift the political landscape in a more constructive direction in order to mitigate some of the harmful features of identity politics, thereby improving the working relationships between political elite who occupy rival political parties.

Part III: Toward a Socially Transformative Peace Psychology

Part III answers the call of Law and Bretherton (Chap. 2) to enlarge the semantic space in peace psychology in order to accommodate knowledge production processes that originate in experiences of the Global South. In Chap. 8, Lazarus et al. enlarge the traditional domain of peace psychology by reaching out to members of an informal settlement in South Africa and engaging in a multi-year Community-Based Participatory Research (CBPR) programme. Like many CBPR programmes, emphasis is placed on researchers and community members working and learning together as they co-construct knowledge and take actions to transform living conditions. Situated in the Helderberg Basin of the Western Cape province of South Africa, the central thrust of the programme is an effort to reduce episodic and structural violence in tandem with the promotion of peace and social justice.

A unique feature of the programme is its exploration of the potential of religious assets and spiritual capacity to promote both harmony and socially transformative processes. Community members conceptualised religious assets in two forms: tangible (e.g. a mosque, church, prayer, religious leaders) and intangible (e.g. compassion, empathy). In addition, a new construct, spiritual capacity, was invented to denote "creative freedom" or the ability to "imagine something that does not exist and bring it into being." As such, spiritual capacity is manifest in the creation of a wide range of human inventions including religious assets, which, the authors note, can be a force for peacemaking and peacebuilding if accompanied by a moral imperative to promote harmony and equity in relationships.

The authors draw on systems theory to conceptualise the programme, thus recognising the usefulness of deploying peace-promoting interventions at and across various levels of a system, including the individual, interpersonal, and larger social units and interactions, all interlinked and embedded in a dynamic system. The programme is noteworthy because community members and researchers are co-constructing knowledge that bears on the role of religious assets and spiritual capacity in promoting peace using a critical methodology with socially transformative aspirations. As such, the programme deals head on with the problem of epistemic violence—the marginalisation of knowledge production in the Global South—and seeks to enlarge the scope of knowledge that is considered legitimate in peace psychology.

In Chap. 9, Stevens, Duncan, and Canham introduce a methodology employed in the Apartheid Archive Project. The Project picks up on a central theme of the symposium, *Engaging Invited and Invented Spaces for Peace* (Suffla, 2015). Invited spaces are official spaces for the practice of citizenship that derive their authority from local and international donors, governmental structures, and other formal entities (Cornwall, 2002, 2004). In the South Africa context, negotiations between Nelson Mandela and then president, F.W. de Klerk, as well as the formal institutional mechanisms and instruments that were in play during the transition to democratic structures all took place within an invited space. While dramatic political and social changes have taken place in a relatively peaceful way through invited spaces in South Africa, formal institutional mechanisms have not been able to create the kind of society in which everyone enjoys harmony and material equity. In contrast to invited spaces, invented spaces of citizenship are created from below and operate outside of hegemonic spaces claimed through formal legal mechanisms. Invented spaces effectively seize and expand the space for social change (Miraftab, 2004).

Stevens, Duncan, and Canham discuss the philosophical underpinnings and potentially transformative power of the invented space occupied by the Apartheid Archive Project. The Project is a repository of stories of race and racism based on the experiences of "ordinary" South Africans. Recognising that the political economy of South Africa was not able to synchronise democratising impulses with inclusive economic development, the Project is designed to foreground the everyday experiences of South Africans who lived under the old Apartheid system and identify ways in which the system continues to have an impact on individuals and groups in contemporary South Africa. While the Truth and Reconciliation Commission has contributed to the construction of grand and dramatic narratives of Apartheid atrocities, the archive includes stories of people who occupy marginalised social categories in society, thereby yielding narratives of perpetration, victimisation, complicity, trauma, resilience, contestation, and resistance to oppression. From the authors' perspective, peacebuilding requires the disruption of stable elements of the status quo through a process of *interrogatory destabilisation,* which involves the repetition of critical deconstructions of hegemonic assumptions and regimes of truth. The authors contend that interrogatory destabilisation can open spaces for an *insurgent politics* in which people internalise a sense of agency, contest narratives that normalise structure-based inequalities and power differentials, and engage in transformative actions that yield more equitable social arrangements.

Continuing with the theme of providing invented spaces for the stories of people who occupy marginalised social categories in society, in Chap. 10, Lau and Seedat describe a community-based action research project designed to elicit *Community Storylines* from people who live in Thembelihle, a marginalised township in South Africa. The storylines reflect the ongoing struggles of people who express concerns about unmet basic needs and echo the same kind of issues that were salient during Apartheid. The storylines reflect on poverty, inequality, geospatial deprivation, oppression, lack of voice, media colonisation, helplessness, and a limited sense of agency in the face of institutional intransigence and shortcomings of the State. These narratives of poverty and struggle for recognition comport with a human needs analysis in peace psychology (Christie, 1997; Pilisuk, 1998; Schwebel, 1997) and highlight the desirability of peacebuilding efforts that result in social recognition and the kind of epistemic justice that values community voice and knowledge production. The authors highlight the liberatory potential of an elicitive methodology that fosters individual and collective awareness and agency, and provides a safe space for the expression of rage that otherwise could be misdirected toward loved ones or culminate in symbolic and ineffectual burnings of state property.

Chapter 11 by Jopson extends some of the same themes of structural violence and social justice to gender issues, with emphasis on the marginalisation of women in formal peace negotiations throughout Southeast Asia. Jopson notes that women's participation and voice is minimal, and even though there are indications that women are increasingly being included in formal peace processes, there remain barriers to moving gender justice to the centre of peace agendas. Jopson surveys women's involvement in peace efforts in Southeast Asia and highlights in particular the role of women in negotiations taking place in the Southern Philippines. The current peace negotiations between the insurgent Moro Islamic Liberation Front, which operates in the poorest region of the country, and the Government of the Philippines are designed to address the structural roots of conflict. Under consideration are the creation of a Bangsamoro government and the adoption of a Bangsamoro Development Plan, which places economic development and governance among the highest structural priorities, but also recognises gender gaps as a cross-cutting issue in education, politics, and workforce involvement. Drawing on discourse analysis, Jopson finds that gender is used in the development plan as synonymous with women and argues that if women's issues are conflated with gender issues, the development process will fail to appreciate how gender operates and presume that women will always be able to speak for all genders with respect to gender-based oppression. Central to the chapter is the contention that peace discourses need to be gendered to promote sustainable peace in the Southern Philippines.

The potential role educational policy could play in redressing the social injustices visited upon marginalised people whose voice is submerged and who lack material resources is addressed in Chap. 12, by Sayed, Badroodien, Rodrigues, and Hanaya. In particular, the authors argue that the educational system in South Africa could serve as a catalyst to promote social cohesion and sustainable peace. The contested meanings of "social cohesion" are discussed in the context of international organisations, some of which equate social cohesion with solidarity and trust, while others highlight the notion of inclusion. Rather than resolving the definitional issue, the authors tacitly assume a broad definition of social cohesion and focus their chapter on propositions they believe contribute to social cohesion.

Among the propositions advanced are the following: social cohesion is enhanced when inequalities in socio-cultural, political, and economic systems are reduced; inequalities are also at the root of violent episodes; teachers can be key agents in the transformation of society toward more equitable human relationships and systems by promoting a redistribution of resources, recognising diversity, dealing with grievances through reconciliation processes, and increasing the representation of those who are marginalised in matters that affect their well-being. The authors suggest that the enactment of these propositions results in the kind of good quality education that produces greater social cohesion and a durable kind of peace.

The authors conclude with a review of some education policies that have emerged in the wake of Apartheid and argue that the notion of "social cohesion" was given short shrift in these policies. Reference to "social cohesion" did not appear very frequently until 2009, and even then, the emphasis was and continues to be on the reduction of violence rather than addressing the roots of social divisions. In short, according to the authors, in the South Africa context the promotion of social cohesion and a sustainable form of peace should be central to educational policy, and to this end, it is essential for policies to enumerate principles to guide actions that effectively address the contemporary and historical roots of structural violence.

In Chap. 13, Montiel and Boller grapple with the issue of macro-level tranformations that take place when repressive governments are challenged by prodemocracy movements. While large-scale social movements are typically the subject of socio–political analysis, Montiel and Boller flesh out some of the psycho-collective substrates of non-violent democratic transitions. Drawing on a wide range of people power movements, the authors begin by describing the features and stages of successful democratisation movements that give way to more open and pluralistic political system of governance. Two stages are central to their analysis: a vertical set of dialectics that take place as people power topples repressive government structures and a lateral dialectic phase in which democratic structures become consolidated.

The role of individual and collective subjectivities and actions in both stages are identified and the emotional dynamics and narratives that are in play during each of these stages are proposed. The authors note the importance of individual anger and courage when confronting oppressive political structures and institutions, and they emphasise the imperative and power of collective emotions which originate in group-shared histories and collective memories of oppression. Although vertical pressures may topple repressive regimes and open space for just political arrangements, consolidation turns on the ability of prodemocracy movements to shift toward lateral dialectics and transition to the process of within-group peacemaking.

Many movements have failed to consolidate more pluralistic arrangements, a problem the authors attempt to address by underscoring the importance of individuals and collectivities exhibiting respect and tolerance for psycho-social skills and competencies involved in lateral moves that are necessary for the instantiation of participatory political structures and the reduction of tension in relationships and governing systems. Clearly, Montiel and Boller argue for politically transformative actions that privilege voice and representation in matters that affect people's well-being, actions driven by the interplay of emotional processes that operate at multiple levels within a larger dynamic psycho-socio-political system.

Finally, Chap. 14, by Wessells, Sveaass, Foster, and Dawes, calls for transformation in the practice of psychology to fully embrace the principle of "do no harm" even when the State implores psychologists to set aside professional ethics and engage in behaviour that harms others for national security purposes. The call for changes in psychology institutions worldwide is issued against the backdrop of two historical cases in which psychologists allowed national law to supersede international law and human rights: (a) the actions of psychologists in South Africa during the Apartheid era and (b) recent reports of US psychologists' involvement in torture following the 9/11 attacks. In recounting the case of South Africa, the authors describe how psychological research revealed the mistreatment of some detainees, subjecting them to isolation, sleep deprivation, beatings, and other forms of torture during the Apartheid era. These findings were made available to the South African Psychological Association and the Association took no action to stop torture. There is no evidence that South African psychologists participated in torture. In the US case, however, documents recently have been released indicating that psychologists were responsible for writing the manual for administering torture and actually engaged in torture at various sites around the world. Moreover, the American Psychological Association in collaboration with the US Department of Defense amended the ethical code for psychologists to include a provision that allowed psychologists to effectively jettison the ethical code if the code was in conflict with the expectations of a governing authority, which included national security and legal entities that fall under the rubric of the State (Hoffman et al., 2015).

In addition to reconstructing some of the history of psychologists' actions during the Apartheid era in South Africa and more recently in the United States, the authors address pragmatic issues and cite research that debunks the myth that harsh interrogation methods yield actionable intelligence (Senate Select Committee, 2015) and caution against the potential blowback that such methods can engender as a recruitment tool for violent actors who seek retribution, thereby continuing the cycle of violence. On ethical grounds, two problems are apparent: harsh interrogations (1) are inconsistent with the "right to not be tortured" and (2) weaken global efforts to build strong norms against unethical actions by psychologists and other professionals.

The authors recommend a number of specific national laws that are consistent with the United Nations Convention against Torture and Other Cruel, Inhuman or Degrading Treatment or Punishment (UNCAT). These include the right to a speedy trial, legal limits on the length of solitary confinement, and provisions for independent human rights bodies to monitor detention and interrogation sites. For sub-state actors such as psychological associations, licensure should be contingent upon psychologists' allegiance to UNCAT principles; in addition, psychologists should receive training to mitigate the bystander effect when faced with violations of human rights. In short, national laws and psychological associations should be aligned with the international standards of UNCAT.

Taken together, the thrust of Part III of the volume reinforces one of the central objectives of biennial symposia; namely, to bring forward voices that are often marginalised in peace discourses. The epistemic violence of a peace psychology dominated by the Global North is on full display in the chapters that populate Part III of the volume as authors privilege the voice of those who are typically excluded in peace discourses. These voices can be heard in the CBPR programme situated in the Helderberg Basin of the Western Cape (Chap. 8), the Apartheid Project of South Africa (Chap. 9), the Storylines Project in the South African township of Thembelihle (Chap. 10), the women who are making headway in peace negotiations in Southeast Asia (Chap. 11), efforts to promote social cohesion and justice in South Africa through education policies (Chap. 12), and people power movements that have taken place around the world (Chap. 13). Psychologists' violation of the professional ethic to "do no harm" is on display in Chap. 14. Among the most glaring violations was the involvement of psychologists in state-sanctioned torture against detainees, thereby placing national interest and power politics above human rights. Such a breach of morality calls for the Global North and South to join together and take action to position the field of peace psychology at the centre of an emancipatory agenda for all.

References

Bhorat, H., & Van Der Westhuisen, C. (2010). Poverty, inequality and the nature of economic growth in South Africa. In N. Misra-Dexter & J. February (Eds.), *Testing democracy: Which way is South Africa going* (pp. 46–70). Oxford, UK: African Books Collective.

Bulhan, H. A. (1993). Imperialism in studies of the psyche: A critique of African psychological research. In L. J. Nicholas (Ed.), *Psychology and oppression: Critiques and proposals* (pp. 1–34). Johannesburg: Skotaville.

Butchart, A., & Seedat, M. (1990). Within and without: Images of community and implications for South African psychology. *Social Science & Medicine, 31,* 1093–1102.

Christie, D. (1997). Reducing direct and structural violence: The human needs theory. *Peace and Conflict: Journal of Peace Psychology, 3,* 315–332.

Christie, D. J. (2006). What is peace psychology the psychology of? *Journal of Social Issues, 62,* 1–17.

Christie, D. J., & Montiel, C. J. (2013). Contributions of psychology to war and peace. *American Psychologist, 68,* 502–513.

Christie, D. J., Wagner, R. V., & Winter, D. D. (2001). *Peace, conflict, and violence: Peace psychology for the 21st century.* Upper Saddle River, NJ: Prentice-Hall.

Cooper, S., Nicholas, L. J., Seedat, M., & Statman, J. M. (1990). Psychology and apartheid: The struggle for psychology in South Africa. In L. J. Nicholas & S. Cooper (Eds.), *Psychology and apartheid* (pp. 1–21). Johannesburg: Vision.

Cornwall, A. (2002). *IDS working paper 170.* Brighton: Institute of Development Studies.

Cornwall, A. (2004). Spaces for transformation? Reflections on issues of power and difference in participation in development. In S. Hickey & G. Mohan (Eds.), *Participation: From tyranny to transformation* (pp. 75–91). London: ZED Books.

Dawes, A. (2001). Psychologies for liberation: Views from elsewhere. In D. J. Christie, R. V. Wagner, & D. D. Winter (Eds.), *Peace, conflict, and violence: Peace psychology for the 21st century* (pp. 295–306). Upper Saddle River, NJ: Prentice-Hall.

Deutsch, M. (1983). The prevention of World War III: A psychological perspective. *Political Psychology, 4,* 3–31.

Frank, J. D. (1967). *Sanity and survival in the nuclear age.* New York: Random House.

Galtung, J. (1969). Violence, peace, and peace research. *Journal of Peace Research, 6*(3), 167–191.

Galtung, J. (1990). Cultural violence. *Journal of Peace Research, 27*(3), 291–305.

Hamber, B. (2009). *Transforming societies after political violence: Truth, reconciliation and mental health.* New York, NY: Springer.

Hoffman, D. H., Carter, D. J., Viglucci, C. R., Heather, L. B., Guo, A. X., Latifi, S. Y., et al. (2015). *Report to the special committee of the board of directors of the American Psychological Association: Independent review relating to APA ethics guidelines, national security interrogations, and torture.* Chicago: Sidley Austin LLP.

Lau, U., & Seedat, M. (2015). The community story, relationality and process: Bridging tools for researching local knowledge in a peri-urban township. *Journal of Community & Applied Social Psychology, 25*(5), 369–383.

Martín-Baró, I. (1994). *Writings for a liberation psychology.* Cambridge: Harvard University Press.

Miraftab, F. (2004). Invited and invented spaces of participation: Neoliberal citisenship and feminists' expanded notion of politics. *Wagadu, 1,* 1–7.

Montero, M., & Sonn, C. C. (2009). *Psychology of liberation.* New York: Springer.

Montiel, C. J. (2001). Toward a psychology of structural peacebuilding. In D. J. Christie, R. V. Wagner, & D. D. Winter (Eds.), *Peace, conflict, and violence: Peace psychology for the 21st century* (pp. 282–294). Upper Saddle River, NJ: Prentice-Hall.

Montiel, C. J., & Noor, N. M. (2009). *Peace psychology in Asia*. New York: Springer.

Noor, N., & Christie, D. J. (2015). Themes in peace psychology research. In D. Bretherton & S. F. Law (Eds.), *Methodologies in peace psychology: Peace research by peaceful means* (pp. 43–70). New York: Springer.

Pettigrew, T. F., & Tropp, L. R. (2006). A meta-analytic test of intergroup contact theory. *Journal of Personality and Social Psychology, 90*, 751–783.

Pilisuk, M. (1998). The hidden structure of contemporary violence. *Peace and Conflict: Journal of Peace Psychology, 4*, 197–216.

Schwebel, M. (1965). *Behavioral science and human survival*. Palo Alto, CA: Science and Behavior Books.

Schwebel, M. (1997). Job insecurity as structural violence: Implication for destructive intergroup conflict. *Peace and Conflict: Journal of Peace Psychology, 3*, 333–352.

Seedat, M., Duncan, N., & Lazarus, S. (Eds.). (2001). *Theory, method and practice in community psychology: South African and other perspectives*. Johannesburg: Oxford University Press.

Seedat, M., & Lazarus, S. (2011). Community psychology in South Africa: Origins, developments, and manifestations. *Journal of Community Psychology, 39*(3), 241–257.

Seedat, M., MacKenzie, S., & Stevens, G. (2004). Trends and redress in community psychology during 10 years of democracy (1994–2003): A journal-based perspective. *South African Journal of Psychology, 34*, 595–612.

Seedat, M., van Niekerk, A., Suffla, S., & Ratele, K. (2014). Psychological research and South Africa's violence prevention responses. *South African Journal of Psychology, 44*(2), 136–144.

Senate Select Committee. (2015). *The senate intelligence committee report on torture: Committee study of the central intelligence agency's detention and interrogation program*. New York: Melville House.

Suffla, S. (2015, May). *Engaging invited and invented spaces for peace*. Paper presented at the 14th Biennial Symposium on the Contributions of Psychology to Peace. Johannesburg, South Africa.

Taylor, L. K., & Christie, D. J. (2015). Promoting harmonious relations and equitable well-being: Peace psychology and "intractable" conflicts. In K. Sharvit & E. Halperin (Eds.), *The social psychology of intractable conflicts* (pp. 203–212). New York: Springer.

White, R. K. (1984). *Fearful warriors: A psychological profile of U.S.-Soviet relations*. New York: Free Press.

White, R. K. (1986). *Psychology and the prevention of nuclear war*. New York: New York University Press.

Chapter 2
The Imbalance Between Knowledge Paradigms of North and South: Implications for Peace Psychology

Siew Fang Law and Diane Bretherton

Introduction

Peace psychology develops theories, methodologies, and practical approaches to address issues of conflict and violence and to promote peace. Grounded in the discipline of psychology, those who are identified as peace psychologists often find themselves having to navigate and negotiate multiple competing and, at times, contradictory demands and priorities. In particular, peace psychologists are expected to function within certain structures and systems. While knowledge making is one of their key contributions as peace psychologists, discussion of how peace psychologists are situated in systems of knowledge making is rare. Similarly, literature on how these systems of knowledge making might conflict with core values of peace is sparse.

Given that the 2015 Symposium on the Contributions of Psychology to Peace was held in the Southern part of the world, and much of the research literature in psychology comes from the North (Arnett, 2008), we used this opportunity to reflect on and examine knowledge domains and influences of the North and the South. We explored imbalances in knowledge that exist: what are some of the dilemmas and paradoxes confronting peace psychology in the past and present? How can we as peace psychologists address the imbalance as individuals and in our professional capacities?

This chapter addresses four themes. Firstly, recognising that peace psychology is grounded in the discipline of psychology, we deconstruct and problematise power inherent in the discipline. Secondly, through unpacking some of the history of

S.F. Law (✉)
College of Arts Australia, Victoria University, Melbourne, Australia
e-mail: Siewfang.law@vu.edu.au

D. Bretherton
University of Queensland, St Lucia, QLD, Australia
e-mail: d.bretherton@uq.edu.au

© Springer International Publishing AG 2017
M. Seedat et al. (eds.), *Enlarging the Scope of Peace Psychology*,
Peace Psychology Book Series, DOI 10.1007/978-3-319-45289-0_2

dominant psychological institutions, we explore how psychological knowledge from the North has impacted on and continues to influence the rest of the world. Thirdly, we examine the systems of knowledge making. We argue that systems perpetuate this power imbalance. Finally, we will discuss what peace psychologists might do, at personal and professional levels, to address the imbalances.

Power, Privilege, and Prestige Within Psychology

Unlike other disciplines, such as social work and community development, psychology has long been established as a "profession" and a "science" (Hergenhahn, 2009; Oshodi, 1996). The institutionalisation of psychology as a discipline has granted the psychologists a "brand" that comes with certain privileges, power, and prestige.[1] The American Psychological Association (APA)'s strategic plan goals are to "maximize the association's organizational effectiveness, expand psychology's role in advancing health and increase recognition of psychology as a science" (APA, 2015).

Being "scientists", psychologists are expected to operate under a set of stringent expectations, regulations, and frameworks that are governed by organisations such as the APA and, in the Australian context, the Australian Psychological Society. The regulations aim to ensure a standardised high quality of ethical practice for all psychologists. While the protection of clients meets a genuine need, the creation of one dominant normative form can function to exclude other perspectives and marginalise psychologists from other regions.

Peace psychology, as recognised by the APA as Division 48s "Society for the Study of Peace, Conflict and Violence" in the USA, often finds itself confronted by various ideological, theoretical, methodological, and practical dilemmas and paradoxes. While aspiring to promote peace using non-competitive, collaborative, equal, and fair approaches, members of Division 48 need to fulfil certain requirements in order to obtain institutional support, formal recognition and credentials, and career opportunities. Gaining greater institutional recognition has direct implications for peace psychology. Establishing formally recognised course offerings, attracting student enrolments, and publishing research in recognised journals are important to the progress of the field of peace psychology. Without sufficient institutional support and formal recognition, peace psychology may not be considered to be "real" psychology. There is a dilemma in that processes of gaining institutional recognition and support might require psychologists to operate in ways that are competitive, economically-driven, hierarchical, and at times imperialistic.

---

[1] These are evidenced in advertisements of psychology courses and career paths. For example, http://psychcentral.com/diff.htm; http://studyassist.gov.au/sites/studyassist/mytertiarystudyoptions/providers-that-offer-commonwealth-assistance/pages/heproviderprofile?title=The%20Cairnmillar%20Institute%20School%20of%20Psychology%20Counselling%20and%20Psychotherapy.

A number of studies have reported that psychological research is dominated by North American scholarship (Cole, 2006; Denmark, 1998). Arnett's (2008) study found that some of the most influential psychological journals owned by the APA overwhelmingly reflect North American perspectives: 73 % of the first authors live and work in USA (an additional 14 % from other English-speaking countries and 11 % from Europe). A narrow range of humanity is being studied—most samples were USA undergraduate psychology students (Arnett, 2008). Taking into consideration the fact that Americans living in the USA only represent 5 % of the world's population, and that their way of life, social and political environment, culture, and economy are vastly different from the 95 % that constitutes the rest of the world's population, raises questions as to whether mainstream psychological theories apply to the entire human population. The claim that discipline of psychology is the "science of humanity" is therefore debatable.

The flagship journal of peace psychology, *Peace and Violence: Journal of Peace Psychology*, was not included in Arnett's (2008) review. Unlike the journals reviewed by Arnett, the *Journal of Peace Psychology* has a diverse representation of editors, reviewers, and authors and publishes international articles that look at a wide range of geo-locational contexts. Nevertheless, it remains the case that, because the field of peace psychology is situated in a structurally unequal playing field, peace psychologists are often confronted with ideological and practical dilemmas when producing and publishing their work.

Systems of Knowledge Making

Historically, psychological theory has been developed and influenced by affluent, educated scholars in the Northern part of the world, with roots in Europe and then predominately in the USA (Arnett, 2008). Mainstream psychology is often considered to be Eurocentric (Naidoo, 1996) and derived from a White middle-class value system (Katz, 1985). Key theorists from Europe and the USA, such as B. F. Skinner, Sigmund Freud, Erik Erikson, and Jean Piaget, appear on reading lists of psychology courses all over the world (Hergenhahn, 2009). While acknowledging their important contributions to the field of psychology, psychological knowledge from the North penetrates and dominates the work and imaginations of psychologists in the rest of the world.

Peace psychology has a similar historical pattern: notable scholars, such as William James, referred to by Morton Deutsch as the first peace psychologist (cited in Hergenhahn, 2009), Konrad Lorenz, Theodor Adorno, Irving Janis, Gordon Allport, John Burton, and Stanley Milgram, have contributed to psychological understandings of peace, conflict, and violence. Their work has been included in many peace and conflict studies curricula in North American and Western European institutions of higher education (Webel & Sotakova, 2012). Their knowledge has been used in teaching and cited in writing in other parts of the world.

Knowledge and mental models from societies of the Southern periphery exist, but are less well-known. In this chapter, the descriptions of "North" and "South" are used not as fixed sets of propositions, nor do they refer to physical geographical locations. They are used to signify the geopolitical systemic and structural inequality that exists across the globe. Connell (2007) describes Southern communities as those marginalised in the global sphere, including, but not limited to, people from Africa, South and Latin America, the Middle-East, South and South-West Asia, and Aboriginal Australia. These communities in the South share commonalities such as a history of colonisation. Their culture and societies are highly plural and hybridised. They represent some of the communities most impacted upon by colonisation, postcolonisation, and globalisation. They are often misunderstood and labelled as "other" and their intellectual work is under-represented in the mainstream media and the research literature.

Hence, knowledge is unequally and unfairly produced. It both reflects and creates privilege for some and is oppressive of others. Connell asserted that:

> [t]he effects of a world economy of knowledge are structured by the history of colonialism and current north-south global inequalities. The differentiation of knowledge rests on the very different histories and situations of metropolitan, creole, colonized and postcolonial intelligentsias. Different knowledge projects have been constructed in global space, which feed back on our understanding of knowledge itself. Less recognized, but increasingly important, are uses of southern and post-colonial perspectives in applied social science (Connell & Dados, 2014, p. 117).

Systems of knowledge making (epistemologies) and of the way we construct reality (ontologies) are not only culturally bound in time and space, but are also embedded in power relations. Within such systems, knowledge is considered to be a "controlled substance" as it "is protected and manipulated by individuals and groups" (Leitko & Peterson, 1982, pp. 447–448). To maintain power and control, structures of knowledge making and knowledge dissemination are established. Increasingly, *credible* knowledge becomes something that can be possessed, patented, traded, ranked, and measured. These processes require governance of much larger and powerful regulatory groups or institutions. Through institutionalised incentives and disincentives, academics are now engaging in new subjectivities that are defined by a market-driven discourse. These neoliberal systems of knowledge production force academics to make *knowledge* that fits in the systems and structures that produce and reproduce prestige, power, and privilege (Cornell, 2014).

Knowledge systems of the North emphasise structure, logic, rationality, and linear thought processes (Trompenaars, 1993). These mental modalities are evidenced in many social and psychological practices, research approaches, and publication systems. This thinking orientation has been valued as "better" than approaches that have other structures and emphases.

In the competitive system of knowledge production, credentials from Northern universities are often accorded greater credibility and economic worth. Coupled with the rise and spread of English as a language of international communication (Harris, 2001), knowledge from the Anglophone regions, mainly from the USA, Canada, and the United Kingdom has greater circulation in the literature and remains predominantly influential in disseminating psychological constructs, concepts, and approaches, compared to literature published in other languages.

Through promoting "psychology as a science", the APA, for instance, established that certain knowledge, such as empirical findings, has greater value and economic worth than other forms of knowledge, such as Aboriginal dreaming and storytelling. A review of the history of psychology by Hergenhahn (2009) suggested that, since the APA was founded in 1892, pure, scientific psychology has been valued more than less-scientifically oriented psychology. Many forms of knowledge in the South, such as traditional folklore and spiritual rituals that are richly expressed in oral, visual, or ceremonial forms, receive lesser credence in mainstream psychology (Walker, 2015).

Language has a significant role in the functionality, communication, and dissemination of knowledge. Since the English language is a global language (Crystal, 2003; Graddol, 1997), academics in the English-speaking regions have been accorded greater prestige, power, and privilege than academics in non-English speaking regions. Knowledge produced in the English-speaking, White-dominated societies has dominated knowledge produced in non-English speaking regions. There are pockets of English speaking countries in the South, for example, in South Africa, Australia, and New Zealand, which can compete with their Northern counterparts to meet the "world standard" and achieve recognition in the "world ranking systems".

Languages other than English have a unique intellectual tradition. The structure and functions of a native language do bear upon the ways in which some philosophical problems are posed and some ontological insights are shaped (Mou, 1996). Further discussion on the implications of language and the theory of language in the context of philosophy will be explored and examined in the next section of the chapter.

North–South Imbalance of Psychology Knowledge Making and Distribution

Contemporary, neoliberal approaches to knowledge production create, as Cornell (2007, 2014) suggests, a form of white-collar labour or workforce. Using a metaphoric example, she illustrates that indigenous knowledge from peripheral sites is usually treated as *raw data*. Once raw data has been *extracted* from the periphery and made into the form of knowledge projects, it is then *exported* and *processed* using the methods, theories, and assistance of *modern* technology invented and used by the knowledge workers in the North. *Processed* knowledge is then written in the language of the workers, *tested* (undergoes the scrutiny of peer reviews and feedback from editors, mostly in the North), then given credit as "quality knowledge". The credence given to the processed knowledge gives greater status and prestige to the knowledge workers and manufactures (publishers and universities) than to those who provide the *raw data*. *New* knowledge is then disseminated in *reputed* publications that may or may not reach or gain feedback from the South. At times, the "new" knowledge, which may be so processed that it is unrecognisable to the indigenous society, is imposed on the global South (Connell & Dados, 2014). This cycle essentially enriches and privileges a particular group of knowledge workers and their institutions, establishes a hegemonic practice, and in the process disempowers the South. The rise of corporate control over publishing and profit-making results in a concentration of influential topics and authors, situated in the North. Furthermore, credible knowledge requires a systematic and structured intellectual workforce and institutions to control space and manage its economic structure (i.e. income and ranking) and regulate production (i.e. accreditation and standardisation).

De Sousa Santos (2007), a critical theorist from the Southern periphery, echoes this sentiment and argues that the systems of knowledge making are products of colonisation and imperialism. Within this history of knowledge inequality, local and indigenous work produced in the Southern periphery, especially articles published in languages other than English, continue to be marginalised from the dominant knowledge systems. Despite the importance and relevance of local knowledge, their publications rarely meet the *standard* set by those in the North. As a result, much of the literature of the Global South remains largely unknown in the North, further widening the North–South imbalance (Maluf, 2014; Mellor, 2015).

"There has been certainly, and unfortunately—for colonialist reasons and legacies—a disproportion of white scholars on many levels of study fields, African studies included" (Hassan, 2015, n.p.). At the time of writing this chapter, we found very little literature that covered psychology from Africa. Among the references, we found the term "African Psychology" or "Black Psychology", which is essentially referring to African American Psychology (Belgrave & Allison, 2010; Holliday, 2009; Oshodi, 1996). Journals such as *Journal of Modern African Studies* are dominated by editors from the North (of the 26 members on the Editorial Boards, 22 are in the USA, UK and Europe, only four editors are from Africa). The *Journal of Psychology in Africa* is no longer published in Africa. Instead, for the last decade, it has been published in the USA. Once we came to South Africa (as part of the Peace Psychology Symposium), we found there is a vibrant critical psychology footprint. However, the local (to South Africa) journals, such as the *South African Journal of Psychology*, the *South African Journal of Industrial Psychology,* and the *African Safety and Peace Promotion Journal of Injury and Violence Protection* did not receive adequate recognition from the North. The *Journal of Black Studies* loudly asserts that it "offers important and intellectually provocative articles exploring key issues facing African Americans" (Journal of Black Studies website) and its main publications are articles focusing on the African–American context.

At the time of writing the chapter, we heard the protests of a collective Somali academics on Facebook and Twitter to a newly launched Somali journal entitled *Somaliland Journal of African Studies* (SJAS), a peer-reviewed scholarly journal that claims a particular focus on East Africa, but has no Somali acting as an editor, advisory board member, or contributor. Somalian academics turned to the social media to voice their discontent. As Hassan (2015) notes, "twitter activism is nothing new…people used social media to deconstruct the privilege within academia while connecting communities internationally, strengthening the message that black voices will no longer be undervalued in African and Black studies" (n.p.). Markus Hoehne, a White German anthropologist and a co-editor of *SJAS*, responded to the critique of his academic journal on social media. Hassan (2015) reports that Hoehne insisted "there is a general absence of Somalis in academia because they don't seem to value scholarship. He went on to claim that this issue would subside if Somalis were willing to do the work" (Hassan, n.p.).

We have focused our discussion of the South on Africa, but of course the arguments apply equally to other parts of the South, such as South and Latin America. Maluf, a prominent educational psychologist from Brazil, who publishes her work in the Portuguese language, called for greater balance between the Global North and South (2014). In one of her recent studies that involved interviews with prominent psychology academics across South America, she found that, due to the cost of accessing literature and academic databases, many academics in South America have limited access to international academic literature and research materials. Moreover, due to English not being their first language, many academics find it difficult to get their work accepted and published in English language journals. Most of their research findings were published in their first language and non-English publications that are not widely distributed to and accessed by academics and students across the globe (Maluf, 2014). This has direct implications for the ways they contribute to new knowledge. Through measurements of citations, impact factors, and rankings, their work would be considered to be less rigorous, influential, and significant than their English-language colleagues in the North.

Due to geopolitical and historical differences, psychology from the South has unique and different, but equally important, knowledge as the North. Montero (2015) asserts that a number of key philosophers from the South America region could contribute to the understanding of Peace Psychology. For example, Enrique Dussel's concept of analectic (1985, 1988) is a vital philosophy in diversity and inclusion of "others". It "expands and enriches one's totality, with aspects coming from beyond what one considers as our usual reality" (Montero, 2015, p. 159). The 'Others' include those rejected or ignored or marginalised from society's benefits. Analectic theory emphasises the co-existence of "I", "you", and "they" in a balanced ecosystem. The exclusion of "others" impoverishes the "I" as well as the relationship. According to Montero,

> Analectic is a method working for equality, promoting the rights of people and constructing balance in society. Those conditions mean the right observation of two of the most violated aspects regarding peace. This method by putting aside privileges and searching the respect of others, also produce liberating ways of living, opposing exclusions (2015, p.n.).

Neoliberal,[2] market-driven, globalisation of knowledge production (Cornell, 2014; Epstein & Morrell, 2012) reinforces the domination of privilege and exclusivity in the urban culture of the North. Increasingly, contemporary psychologists operate to maintain their exclusive and privileged status through adopting statistics

---

[2] Neoliberalism is generally understood as "a system of ideas circulated by a network of right-wing intellectuals, or an economic system mutation resulting from crises of profitability in capitalism. Both interpretations prioritize the global North" (Connell & Dados, 2014, p. 117).

as a main tool of analysis and by considering only that which is quantifiable. Situated in the space and place of knowledge production superiority, academics often have little option but to continue re-producing knowledge toward the "unshakable hegemony of the historical, philosophical and sociological" privilege (De Sousa Santos, 2009, p. 103). The problem is not that academics do not try to be peaceful, but that they themselves are trapped in a Northern mind-set and unable to see beyond its limitations. Because science functions on the assumption that reduction of the complexities of natural phenomena is a necessary condition for conducting scientific research, the system distrusts the evidence of immediate experience which is based on common knowledge—the "others". Knowledge from the Southern peripheries continues to be considered as rough, derivative, and inferior and, therefore, excluded.

Psychologists, in particular peace psychologists, need to rethink and be conscious of the limitations and exclusivity of paradigms we are operating within. If we continue operating within superior, privileged, and exclusive paradigms, we will no longer have sufficient criticality to fully understand the increasingly complex world, where boundaries are blurred and cultures are hybrid. De Sousa Santos (2009) cites Goody who asserts that it is only through understanding global history that academics are able to unveil the unequal intellectual playing field in contemporary societies and avoid falling in the trap of postcolonialism and postmodernism. It is only to the extent that Eurocentrism is superseded that scholars will be able to produce knowledge more accurately on the epistemological level, and more progressively on the social, political, and cultural levels. Only this kind of history will allow the world to recognise itself in its indefinite diversity, which includes the infinite diversity of similarities and continuities as well.

Worldviews. While history prescribes contemporary world politics, James (1892–1985) once said that the single most informative thing one could know about oneself or an individual is understanding his or her *Weltanschauung* (worldview) (Lamberth, 1999). This epistemological question has been explored by many scholars, including Foucault (1972). Different worldviews present different "realities" and "truths" to individuals and groups.

> A worldview is a way of describing the universe and life within it, both in terms of what is and what ought to be. A given worldview is a set of beliefs that includes limiting statements and assumptions regarding what exists and what does not...what objects or experiences are good or bad, and what objectives, behaviours and relationships are desirable or undesirable... (Koltko-Rivera, 2004, p. 4).

Our worldviews and belief systems profoundly define the nature of reality (ontology), the nature of knowing reality (epistemology), the role of belief systems in the inquirers, and the types of tools that are used to obtain knowledge (methodology) (Guba & Lincoln, 1994). As Koltko-Rivera (2004) suggests, "worldviews include assumptions that may be unproven, or even unprovable, but these assumptions are superordinate, in that they provide epistemic and ontological foundations for other beliefs within a belief system" (p. 4).

Realities are "mental constructions, socially and experientially based, local and specific, dependent for their form and content on the persons who hold them" (Guba, 1990, p. 27). In this notion, realities are relative or emic as opposed to universal or etic. As the values of participants are part and parcel of their reality construction, excluding participants from the Southern peripheries could be a form of structural violence in knowledge production.

Worldviews are expressed in discourses that have particular formation of language, conveyance of meaning, and use of knowledge. Therefore, language is essential to the imposition, establishment, and functioning of the cultural hegemony that influences what and how people think about themselves and their place in a society.

The concept of an ecology of knowledge was introduced by De Sousa Santos (2007, 2009). This ecology describes the inter-dependent nature of different spheres within the knowledge ecosystem. The ecological approach to knowledge offers a unique perspective to understand unequal power relations and hierarchy. It highlights the importance of having, supporting, and maintaining plurality and diversity of knowledge as keys for global–local sustainable development.

Language. Foucault (1972) states that language and power play significant roles in constructing realities, rather than thinking of reality as something that is there, waiting to be discovered. English has often been portrayed as a global language (Crystal, 1998; Jambor, 2007). Already influential from the British Empire from the seventeenth to mid-twentieth Century, the dominance of English language has been extended by American media and technology (Graddol, 1997). The growing economic and cultural influence of the USA and its status as a global superpower since the Second World War has significantly accelerated the spread of the language around the world (Graddol, 1997). It is also accepted that English is the global *lingua franca*, or a language most utilised for international communication between and among language communities (Jambor, 2007). Nevertheless, the notion that English is the language of all the people of the globe is flawed; English is not the official language of the world. English is the third most spoken native language in the world, after Mandarin Chinese and Spanish (Crystal, 1998).

With approximately 2500 languages (or 30 % of the world's living languages), Africa is one of the most linguistically diverse continents (Ndhlovu, 2008). "All the languages of Africa invoke ontological and epistemological" realities (Zelena, 2006; cited in Ndhlovu, 2008). As Zelena noted, "language is the carrier of a people's culture, it embodies their system of ethics and aesthetics, and it is a medium for producing and consuming knowledge, a granary of their memories and imaginations" (cited in Ndhlovu, 2008, p. 20). In the context of Africa, it was known that knowledge is conveyed using proverbs, symbolisms, metaphors, and poetic expressions (Oshodi, 1996; White, 1970). Their practices of psychology and psychotherapy predate the Greek, Roman, and Hebrew traditions in which much of the contemporary psychology has been rooted (Oshodi, 1996; Tay, 1984).

Nevertheless, there is a lack of academic research that recognises the values of Africa's rich language resources (Ndhlovu, 2008). Mainstream academic literature tends to associate the plurality of African languages with problems, such as socio-economic backwardness, ethnic conflicts, civil unrest, political tensions, under-development, and poverty. Often, literature links one-language policy with economic prosperity and political stability (Ndhlovu, 2008). The denial of African literature goes so far that some scholars from the North have claimed "there is no ethics in Africa" (Murove, 2014, p. 36).

What is absent in mainstream discourse is the understanding that multilingualism could be an asset as well as a fundamental human right:

> [w]hen one looks at language, one would see hundreds, perhaps, thousands of years of experience; a people experiencing life on earth where they interacted among themselves, with outsiders and with the environment. These forms of interactive engagements among themselves and with nature allow people to develop an array of wisdoms, ways of coping with the environment and strategies of survival, all of which are preserved and transmitted through the medium of language (Ndhlovu, 2008, p. 143).

Ubuntu

Hence, when denying and rejecting the plurality of languages in Africa, "it is the accumulated wisdoms that die" (Ndhlovu, 2008, p. 143). One of the fundamental, age-old African philosophies for ethics and peace—*Ubuntu*—has, after many years of marginalisation, surfaced in English language academic literature of mainstream ethical discourses.*Ubuntu* is based on the worldview of rationality. It describes the essence of being human, or humanness, that human beings cannot function in isolation. Instead, human beings thrive in communities. Ubuntu suggests that people must live with others in a spirit of respect, generosity, and trust; treat other people with kindness, compassion and care; and live in a way that improves the community around them. The concept of Ubuntu inspires sharing and co-operation between individuals, cultures, and nations, instead of possessiveness, competitiveness, and self-interest (Murry, 2013)."Ubuntu is part and parcel of the post-colonial quest for a rebirth of an African identity" (Murove, 2014, p. 37). Language is fundamental to one's identity and thought systems, and African logic is interwoven with religious, socio-cultural, and metaphysical worldviews. African thought processes and languages are largely embedded with myths, metaphors, proverbs, and idioms.Tragically, the Ubuntu virtue of collaboration and collectivism has been denied and rejected by a number of scholars based in the global North. For example, Wim van Binsbergen, a Dutch anthropologist, trivialised Ubuntu and reduced it to "a remote etic reconstruction" (Murove, 2014, p. 37). A scholar in African Philosophy, at the University of Münster, Germany, Stephen Theron, condemns Ubuntu as primitive, tribalism, a formula for under-development of society for its lack of emphasis on individual responsibility. The colonised, individualist approach to humanness has been equated to self-interest, social–economic and capitalist models of humanness, which is incompatible with Ubuntu. "Colonisation uses distortion and destruction to achieve total occupation and exploitation" through neoliberalism, colonisation of language and value systems, human relations, and thought processes of the Global South

(Murove, 2014, p. 41).Until today, African notions of ethics remain marginalised in most of the education systems in South Africa and modules on ethics have largely been sourced from Eurocentric literature (Murove, 2014). Tension between the traditional African wisdom of communal relations and the colonial "scientific" understanding of individualistic human relations is an echo of the colonisation of Africa:

> The ethic of Ubuntu was denigrated by colonial scholarship as an ethic that was mainly a phenomenon of human primitivity, as an expression of infantile behaviour, and equally a manifestation of an infliction of dependency complex syndrome. The conviction amongst colonial scholars who were too excited and intoxicated by Charles Darwin's theory of evolution was based on the idea that communal ethic and communal existence was nothing else but an expression of primitivism which ought to be conquered by an ethic of individualism which has been the main reason behind the rise of western civilization (Murove, 2014, p. 38).

The status quo of psychology has been increasingly contested by field practitioners around the world (Katz, 1985; Naidoo, 1996) who have "appealed to the profession to re-examine and re-evaluate the theory and practice base of psychology and its sub-disciplines" (Naidoo, 1996, p. 16).

Implications for Peace Psychology

The conceptual implications for peace psychology and peace psychologists are profound. Epistemology, the study of the nature of knowledge, is fundamental to the endeavour to build the discipline of psychology. It casts a light on the essence of what we do, whether we are researchers, teachers, students, or practitioners of psychology. Many peace psychologists will have experienced criticism from colleagues to the effect that peace values water down the rigour of the discipline, or that advocacy has no place in science. However, the discussion of knowledge paradigms points to the way in which even positivist psychology is being restricted by a Northern worldview, with cultural and economic, rather than scientific boundaries. The fundamental belief in the nature of science as being open to new discoveries and perspectives is being lost to a market-driven discourse. The schism between peace values and academic excellence can be reconciled. Peace values push us to be more open to other paradigms and ways of looking at the world, which expand our knowledge paradigm and increase the sample of the human population that is being investigated. Hence, what peace psychologists can do about the imbalance of North and South is to continue with their efforts, and be encouraged to know that they have a strong epistemological rationale, as well as an ideology of peace to provide a solid ground for their work. They can be more sensitive and mindful in the partnerships they create across the North-South divide. Peace psychology has begun to use more diverse methods that are open to other voices, knowledge paradigms, forms of data, and interpretation (Bretherton & Law, 2015). Also, technological advances are helping to provide data from different parts of the world, which meet scientific standards, such as reliability and validity, but are less "framed" by the researcher than was the case in earlier studies. Examples of such methods would be the use of Photovoice (Seedat, Suffla, & Bawa, 2015) or data mining (Montiel, Boller, & Galvez, 2015).

When examining peace in a global–local context, it is necessary for peace psychologists to do some hard thinking about our own acquired knowledge, the way we produce and reproduce knowledge, and what other forms of knowledge have been marginalised and relegated to "non-existence". We need to begin by deconstructing knowledge and systems of knowledge and actively engage in critical thinking, reflexivity, and action, so we do not become passive recipients and re-producers of colonial values.

For many years, psychological contributions to peace and conflict studies have incorporated various psychological theories, methods, and research findings. To promote peace through the work we do, peace psychologists call for the need to conduct research peacefully and to be sensitive to local, cultural, and geopolitical context (e.g. Bretherton & Balvin, 2012; Christie, 2006). Peace psychology researchers are encouraged to enact peaceful values such as respect, listening to understand, and embodying peace values in the design, implementation, and evaluation of practical interventions and research projects. Field projects often attempt to address the inherent privilege and power of psychologists and its impact on those they work with (e.g. Balvin, 2015; Wessells, 2015). Peace psychologists are encouraged to explore and use unconventional psychological theoretical frameworks and paradigms to fully understand peace, conflict, and violence (Mellor, 2015; Walker, 2015). They have also called for more critical, reflective, and integrated methodological approaches (Onwuegbuzie & Tashakkori, 2015). Research methods and data analysis approaches often consider plural perspectives and link multiple levels (Mellor, 2015; Webel & Sotakova, 2012).

Through a conscious effort by peace psychologists from the North to reach out to psychologists from other parts of the globe, the community of peace psychologists has become increasingly diverse and has grown to include more psychologists and psychological knowledge from the South. Peace psychology is at the forefront advocating for different paradigms, models, and methods to represent reality from the vantage point of the oppressed (Soon, Smith, & Meyers, 2015). This has been echoed in the literature as: postcolonial psychology (Duran & Duran, 1995), decolonisation (Fanon, 1952, 1964), humanistic psychology (Schneider, Pierson, & Bugenta, 2014), and a call to contextualise and indigenise psychology (Kim & Berry, 1993; Kim & Park, 2004).

To counter the force of unequal knowledge making, peace psychologists need to be reflexive and aware of our own socio–political positioning, worldviews and, hence, our own assumptions and practices. It is through continually unpacking and de-constructing ideas that we can become more aware of the "knowns" and "unknowns", as well as the subjective and objective implications of our actions and contributions to the complex world. To do this, peace psychologists could employ analectic methods to detect our deep-seated subjectivities and the biases in our consciousness. Processes, such as naturalisation, habituation, and alienation, have implications for privilege and oppression (Montero, 2015). These processes are about engaging in dialogue, openness to others, asking critical questions, and problematising ideas and situations that are taken for granted.

There are a number of small and practical actions that peace psychologists can take to bridge the gap. As we have said, the first and most important implication is the need for peace psychologists to be aware of the power imbalances that exist and to reflect on their own position in the knowledge making system. By being part of a diverse community, they can work together to build a better understanding of different paradigms and expand their knowledge of the world.

Secondly, we should put in greater effort into engaging in dialogue with a diverse group of people. It is easier to have dialogue with people who are similar to us, in terms of age, language, culture, religion, politics, school of thought, or ideology. Individuals who are more similar to us are usually closer, easier to work with, and more accessible than individuals who are more different or foreign, such as our enemies, competitors, and those who simply may not "exist" in our cognition. We could learn a lot about ourselves, "them", and the relationships between "I" and "them" when we are prepared to open and shared spaces, ideas and worldviews, and address questions that we may be unable to answer in separate silos. Due to a history of distrust, engaging in dialogue with the others may require patience, time, and effort. Hence, we could be conscious of any feeling of superiority, put aside our sense of entitlement, and approach others with humility, humbleness, and respect. We could visit places, spaces, and cultures that differ from our own. We should not limit our imagination only to travelling to foreign countries; we could also explore places within our own neighbourhoods. Most societies have pockets of communities that have a congregation of newly arrived migrants, refugees, gays and lesbians, indigenous and religious backgrounds, as well as disadvantaged communities such as the homeless and disabled communities. The embodied experience in places and spaces of vulnerability and less-in-control contexts could provoke thinking, openness, flexibility, and critical reflections. Through "forging professional and personal links with committed individuals and associations in the diaspora may provide important sources of support and research collaboration" (Naidoo, 1996, p. 19).

Thirdly, we could learn another language. Acquiring another language could help us better understand different worldviews and perspectives. Language and semantic grammar show different logical structures and priorities in society. Moreover, learning to write in another language gives us an embodied experience of being in a less powerful position—as a learner, rather than an expert. Writing and publishing in a second, less fluent language could be challenging, but this experience allows us to understand and embody the perspectives of the vulnerable. It forces us to think outside the square and operate beyond our comfort zone. The experience of learning another language could also make us better, more effective, and more humble teachers, writers, reviewers, and editors.

In the fourth place, we could be more proactive in embracing the qualities of peacemakers (Bretherton & Bornstein, 2003), such as optimism, recognising the contradictions in nature, valuing the interconnectedness of humanity and the world, and being less egocentric in our work. Individually and collectively (as a community of peace psychologists), we need to be resilient when confronted by ongoing forces and pressures that promote inequality and injustice in the macro systems and structures.

At a professional level, we could, in the fifth place, initiate more collaborative projects that consist of team members across disciplines, school of thoughts, regions, cultures, languages, and ages. Diversity brings new knowledge and creativity. It gives a more balanced perspective to ideas and approaches to problems. While science has dominated psychological research and thinking, perhaps peace psychologists could consider also embracing other modalities and approaches, including philosophy, spirituality, religion, cultural studies, anthropology, arts, and language in peace psychology research. Examples of collaborations include co-teaching, co-researching, co-authoring, and co-editing work.

In the sixth place, we could encourage greater representation of academics in the South in editorial and reviewing processes. Editors determine the types of knowledge and define the quality of knowledge to be accepted in publications. Taking into consideration that editors have authority and power as gatekeepers in publishing, they could ensure reviewing and editing processes that have reviewers and editors who represent different regions as well as different language groups.

In the seventh place, we could continue to encourage and promote the creation of broader avenues for academic publication, including open source journals. Market-driven academic publishers dominate the knowledge-sharing systems of the Northern hegemony. Often, academics are forced to publish with narrowly defined "recognised" publishers. At times, authors are required to pay fees in order to get their articles published. Hard copies of psychology textbooks are extremely costly, yet, the electronic copies of books and articles are charged per download. Knowledge is, hence, for sale at a price that many cannot afford. We could also initiate publications that consider diverse expressions, such as writing genre (i.e. use of first-person voice, reflections, poems, creative, and metaphoric expressions), languages (i.e. in languages other than English), and art forms. These diverse approaches to expressing knowledge and ideas should be recognised at institutional levels. As academics who produce work in this way are not regarded and promoted in the same way as conventional, English-language academics, we, peace psychologists, need to be active in advocating for structural changes in academia.

As an eighth point, organising symposia and conferences in the less-represented regions can help address the imbalance. The Committee for the Psychological Study of Peace (CPSP) does very well in ensuring that its biennial symposia are held in places and regions that have rich knowledge and cultures, but are less well-represented in the academic world. Due to different economic and political opportunities, the theorists from the Southern periphery often do not have the same opportunities to engage and contribute knowledge and exchange ideas through attending and participating at international conferences. CPSP has hosted Symposia on the Contributions of Psychology to Peace not only in the Northern, but also in the Southern peripheries. There is a norm to ensure regional participation and a balanced and equitable representation from the world of peace psychology.

Ninth, while many conventional academic conferences are useful for academics in sharing research findings and knowledge and for networking purposes, conference topics are often narrowly defined and programmes are highly structured. We could more fully embrace the concept of social entrepreneurship in the work we do. This would entail being proactive in hosting and running more innovative knowledge-sharing spaces and places; professional development seminars that focus on how to support academics and early career researchers to deal with undesirable systemic and structural academic pressures; and workshops, modelled on the community café, that promote the use of alternative avenues of publishing academic research findings (e.g. legitimate open source journals, short-listing of publishers that promote social justice and equality).

Lastly, recognition should be given to innovative social entrepreneurs, activists, and academics who have made positive change in the field. They are the unsung heroes of academia. Their achievements and successes are focused on supporting others and are not measured using the individualistic mainstream academic indexes and ranking systems. They may not be those recognised psychology researchers with long lists of first-authored publications. They are those who resist the systemic and structural pressures, are willing to put in extra time and effort to assist, and empower and give opportunities to students and colleagues who otherwise would be marginalised or pushed out in the competitive field. Many of these are excellent educators and mentors and have qualities that are of utmost value to all academicians and students, yet unfortunately they do not receive a well-deserved amount of recognition in the mainstream systems. In the process of addressing North–South imbalances, we should not forget to recognise and acknowledge the work of individuals who have "worked behind the scenes" for many years.

Conclusion

The experience of the 2015 Peace Symposium in South Africa was a reminder that peace psychologists from across the world share experiences and that global trends and events play an important role in shaping human thought and action. Peace psychology has moved from considering only individuals and concerns itself with collective bodies such as communities and societies. Thinking more globally, contrasting the role of North and South in the generation of knowledge also reminds us that peace psychologists need to be more aware of global dynamics. Working within an ecology of knowledge, the different levels of understanding and intervention need to be linked to each other, rather than considered in isolation.

Peace psychologists have been proactive in promoting peace at different levels and in various ways. Due to our psychological training, backgrounds, identities, and socio-political positioning, many peace psychologists carry historical baggage and need to take care to not reproduce colonial processes. Through interrogating the notions of unequal knowledge production and distribution as structural violence, and critical reflection on our roles as researchers and knowledge producers, peace psychologists can move forward in a way that meets the values of sound scholarship and effective peace. Small but powerful actions can give peace psychologists an extra edge and perspective. It is through consciousness, deliberation, and strategic activism that contemporary scholars can swim against the currents of inequality in knowledge-making systems and reach a more comprehensive understanding of humanity.

References

American Psychological Association (APA). (2015). Retrieved November 2, 2014, from http://www.apa.org/about/index.aspx

Arnett, J. (2008). The neglected 95%: Why American psychologists need to become less American. *American Psychologist, 63*(7), 602–614.

Balvin, N. (2015). Translating psychological research into policy, advocacy and programmes in international development. In D. Bretherton & S. F. Law (Eds.), *Methodologies in peace psychology: Peace research by peaceful means* (pp. 361–380). New York: Springer.

Belgrave, F. Z., & Allison, K. W. (2010). Introduction to African American psychology. In F. Z. Belgrave & K. W. Allison (Eds.), *African American psychology: From Africa to America* (2nd ed., pp. 1–25). Thousands Oak, CA: Sage.

Bretherton, D., & Balvin, N. (2012). *Peace psychology in Australia.* New York: Springer.

Bretherton, D., & Bornstein, J. (2003). The qualities of peacemakers: What can we learn from Nobel Peace Prize Winners about managing conflict? In W. J. Pammer & J. Killian (Eds.), *Handbook of conflict management* (pp. 33–49). New York: Marcel Dekker.

Bretherton, D., & Law, S. F. (2015). *Methodologies in peace psychology: Peace research by peaceful means.* New York: Springer.

Christie, D. J. (2006). What is peace psychology the psychology of? *Journal of Social Issues, 62,* 1–18.

Cole, M. (2006). Internationalization in psychology: We need it now more than ever. *American Psychology, 61,* 904–917.

Connell, R. (2007). *Southern theory: Social science and the global dynamics of knowledge.* Crows Nest, NSW, Australia: Allen & Unwin.

Connell, R., & Dados, N. (2014). Where in the world does neoliberalism come from? The market agenda in southern perspective. *Theory and Society, 43*(2), 117–138.

Crystal, D. (1998). *English as a global language.* Cambridge: Cambridge University Press.

Crystal, D. (2003). *English as a global language.* Cambridge: Cambridge University Press.

De Sousa Santos, B. (2007). Beyond abyssal thinking: From global lines to ecologies of knowledges. *Review (FernandBraudelCenter), 30*(1), 45–89.

De Sousa Santos, B. (2009). A non-occidentalist west? Learned ignorance and ecology of knowledge. *Theory, Culture & Society, 26*(7–8), 103–125.

Denmark, F. L. (1998). Women and psychology: An international perspective. *American Psychologist, 53,* 465–473.

Duran, E., & Duran, B. (1995). *Native American postcolonial psychology.* New York: SUNY Press.

Epstein, D., & Morrell, R. (2012). Approaching southern theory: Explorations of gender in South African education. *Gender and Education, 245,* 469–482.

Fanon, F. (1952). Black skin white mask: The experience of a black man in a white world (C. Markmann, Trans.). New York: Grove Press.

Fanon, F. (1964). Wretched of the earth: A Negro psychoanalysts study of the problem of racism and colonialism in the world today (C. Farrington, Trans.). New York: Grove Press.

Foucault, M. (1972). *The archaeology of knowledge.* New York: Pantheon Books.

Graddol, D. (1997). *The future of English? A guide to forecasting the popularity of the English language in the 21st century.* London: British Council.

Guba, E. G. (1990). *The paradigm dialog.* Newbury Park, CA: Sage.

Guba, E. G., & Lincoln, Y. S. (1994). Competing paradigms in qualitative research. In N. K. Denzin & Y. S. Lincoln (Eds.), Handbook of qualitative research (pp. 105-117). Thousand Oaks, CA: Sage.

Harris, D. G. (2001). English as international language in geography: Development and limitations. *Geographical Review, 91*(4), 675–689.

Hassan, H. (2015). A Somali journal launched without any Somali editors, igniting a debate on white privilege. Retrieved April 20, 2015, from https://www.vice.com/read/somali-journal-launches-without-any-somali-voices-highlighting-another-case-of-white-privilege-in-academia

Hergenhahn, B. R. (2009). *An introduction to the history of psychology* (6th ed.). Belmont: Wadsworth Cengage Learning.

Holliday, B. G. (2009). The history and vision of African American psychology: Multiple pathways to place, space, and authority. *Cultural Diversity and Ethnic Minority Psychology, 15*(4), 317–337.

Jambor, P. Z. (2007). English language imperialism—Points of view. *Journal of English as an International Language, 2,* 103–123.

Katz, J. (1985). The sociopolitical nature of counselling. *The Counselling Psychologist, 13,* 615–624.

Kim, U., & Berry, J. W. (1993). *Indigenous psychologies: Experience and research in cultural context.* Newbury Park, CA: Sage.

Kim, U., & Park, Y. S. (2004). Indigenous psychologies. In C. Spielberger (Ed.), *Encyclopedia of applied psychology* (pp. 263–269). Oxford: Elsevier Academic Press.

Koltko-Rivera, M. E. (2004). The psychology of worldviews. *Review of General Psychology, 8,* 3–58.

Lamberth, D. C. (1999). William James and the metaphysics of experience: James's radically empiricist Weltanschauung. In D. C. Lamberth (Ed.), *Cambridge studies in religion and critical thoughts* (pp. 9–60). Cambridge: Cambridge University Press.

Leitko, T. A., & Peterson, S. A. (1982). Social exchange in research: Toward a 'new deal'. *Journal of Applied Behavioral Science, 18,* 447–462.

Maluf, M. R. (2014, July 10). Psychology in Latin-American countries: Innovation, trends and barriers. Transversal keynote lecture. In *28th International Congress of Applied Psychology, Paris.*

Mellor, D. (2015). Postcolonial research. In D. Bretherton & S. F. Law (Eds.), *Methodologies in peace psychology: Peace research by peaceful means* (pp. 177–198). New York: Springer.

Montero, M. (2015). Philosophies of participation: Analectic and consciousness methods. In D. Bretherton & S. F. Law (Eds.), *Methodologies in peace psychology: Peace research by peaceful means* (pp. 223–236). New York: Springer.

Montiel, C., Boller, A., & Galvez, F. L. (2015). Using the internet and social media in peace psychology research. In D. Bretherton & S. F. Law (Eds.), *Methodologies in peace psychology: Peace research by peaceful means* (pp. 345–357). New York: Springer.

Mou, B. (1996). The structure of the Chinese language and ontological insights: A collective-noun hypothesis. *Philosophy East and West, 49*(1), 45–62.

Murove, M. F. (2014). Ubuntu. *Diogenes, 59*(3–4), 36–47.

Murry, P. (2013). *260 fingers and the philosophy of Ubuntu.* Retrieved June 8, 2015, from http://www.paulamurray.ca/wp-content/uploads/2013/08/260-Fingers-and-the-Philosophy-of-Ubuntu.pdf

Naidoo, A. V. (1996). Challenging the hegemony of Eurocentric psychology. *Journal of Community and Health Sciences, 2*(2), 9–16.

Ndhlovu, F. (2008). Language and African development: Theoretical reflections on the place of languages in African studies. *Nordic Journal of African Studies, 17*(2), 137–151.

Onwuegbuzie, T., & Tashakkori, A. (2015). Utilizing integrated methods for research in peace psychology. In D. Bretherton & S. F. Law (Eds.), *Methodologies in peace psychology: Peace research by peaceful means* (pp. 115–138). New York: Springer.

Oshodi, J. E. (1996). The place of spiritualism and ancient Africa in American psychology. *Journal of Black Studies, 27*(2), 172–182.

Schneider, K. J., Pierson, J. F., & Bugenta, J. F. T. (2014). *The handbook of humanistic psychology: Theory, research, and practice*. Thousand Oaks, CA: Sage.

Seedat, M., Suffla, S., & Bawa, U. (2015). Photovoice as emancipatory praxis: A visual methodology towards critical consciousness and social action. In D. Bretherton & S. F. Law (Eds.), *Methodologies in peace psychology: Peace research by peaceful means* (p. 309). New York: Springer.

Soon, C., Smith, K., & Meyers, K. (2015). Challenging structural violence through community drama: Exploring theatre as transformative praxis. In D. Bretherton & S. F. Law (Eds.), *Methodologies in peace psychology: Peace research by peaceful means* (pp. 293–308). New York: Springer.

Tay, A. L. (1984). Psychology in black Africa. *UNESCO Courier, 37*, 11–14.

Trompenaars, F. (1993). *Riding the waves of culture*. London: Nicholas Brealey.

Walker, P. (2015). Indigenous research paradigms. In D. Bretherton & S. F. Law (Eds.), *Methodologies in peace psychology: Peace research by peaceful means* (p. 159). New York: Springer.

Webel, C., & Sotakova, V. (2012). *Psychological contributions to peace studies, the encyclopedia of peace psychology*. West Sussex: Wiley-Blackwell.

Wessells, M. (2015). Program evaluation: Why process matters? In D. Bretherton & S. F. Law (Eds.), *Methodologies in peace psychology: Peace research by peaceful means* (p. 381). New York: Springer.

White, J. E. M. (1970). *Ancient Egypt: Its cultures and history*. New York: Dover.

Zelena, P. T., (2006). The inventions of African Identities and Languages: The Discursive and Developmental Implications. Selected Proceedings of the 36th Conference on African Linguistics, pp. 14–26. Somerville, MA: Cascadilla Proceedings Project.

Part II
Intergroup Conflict, Violence, and Peacemaking

Chapter 3
A Qualitative Exploration of Salient Incidents of Violence Exposure Among Youth in Kashmir: Beyond Direct Violence

Waheeda Khan and Sramana Majumdar

Introduction

Exposure to violence is a popular topic of interest in political and social psychology, often used as an independent variable and affecting outcomes like PTSD, depression, resilience, and other psychosocial variables (Barber, 2009a). Most of these studies use Exposure to Trauma questionnaires or scales that are based on a general understanding of traumatic events like physical violence, sexual violence, destruction of home and property, death of loved ones, and other factors that may affect an individual's well-being. The understanding of trauma and violence, however, is culture-, context- and individual-specific and needs to be understood in terms of the varied experiences, memories, perceptions, and evaluations of the individuals within the community exposed to it (Bikmen, 2013).

Though limited, there have been efforts to map the political identity, ideology, attitudes, and perceptions of youth over the years. What is missing though is how these perceptions relate to the experience of violence and differences that exist within the broad category of youth. In a population where the youth were born into an era of violence and have been actively engaged in the politics surrounding the conflict, their experiences become prominent in shaping the history and identity of the region.

W. Khan (✉)
Faculty of Behavioural Sciences, SGT University, Gurgaon, NCR-Delhi, India

Department of Psychology, Jamia Millia Islamia, New Delhi, Delhi, India
e-mail: profwkhan@gmail.com

S. Majumdar
OP Jindal University, Hissar, India

Department of Psychology, Jamia Millia Islamia, New Delhi, Delhi, India
e-mail: sramana06@gmail.com

© Springer International Publishing AG 2017   39
M. Seedat et al. (eds.), *Enlarging the Scope of Peace Psychology*,
Peace Psychology Book Series, DOI 10.1007/978-3-319-45289-0_3

With this background, the current paper explores how a population that is exposed to various forms of violence understands the forms and meanings of this exposure. The main objective is to highlight context-specific understandings of violence and trauma through a qualitative, exploratory analysis of incidents that are perceived as being violent by the individuals experiencing them. By exploring salient aspects of violence exposure and recording the likelihood of these experiences being reported by the participants themselves, we hope to shed light on diverse understandings of violence and trauma within a particular historical, political, and social context. Moreover, such an approach has the potential of identifying some aspects of violent experiences that are often ignored, thereby better informing diagnostic and measurement criteria. The dominant theoretical framework in psychiatric/trauma work that guides the understanding of exposure to violence is based on perspectives and knowledge of how violent phenomena are experienced and therefore measured (Stevens, Eagle, Kaminer, & Higson-Smith, 2013). Exploring the perceptions about violence exposure and how they are related to specific contextual aspects of a conflict can therefore expand the theoretical framework for explaining individual and group perceptions and behaviour in conflict situations.

The Expanding Framework of Violence Exposure

The realisation that exposure to violence as a construct is not monolithic and may be diverse and complex in the way individuals experience, process, and remember the events is supported by an array of contemporary research that is increasingly drawing attention to the complexities involved in evaluating contexts of political violence. Barber (2009b) has worked extensively on the qualitative complexities of youth's experiences with violence. Barber discusses how the interaction between a violent environment and youth can differ on many accounts. The nature of violence, perceptions about it as well as youth's engagement in the politics surrounding the conflict are all important factors that need to be considered. The author calls attention to the tendency of researchers and practitioners to follow overarching theories and assumptions about the experiences of violence among populations enduring conflicts. He points out that 'to presume (explicitly or implicitly) that the violence of war is experienced uniformly across conflicts, and further, that it automatically has debilitating effects (moreover of the same type and severity) on those who endure it misses much critical texture and variation that is essential to the basic goals of understanding and providing assistance' (p. 288).

Muldoon and Lowe (2012) in an attempt to understand the experience of traumatic events from a social identity approach point out that these experiences can no longer be seen as an interaction between individual and a specific event, rather it is the experience of an individual operating within a social context, who is trying to reintegrate into a system post the traumatic experience. Hammack (2010) follows a similar interpretative approach towards understanding youth experiences of violence in which he draws upon the contradictory narratives of identity in the context of the Palestinian conflict. Recchia and Wainryb (2011) found distinct dominant trends in how youth who are exposed to violence make sense of the violence. They conclude that some of the youth perceive these experiences as personally or culturally significant, while others see them as incongruent, frightening, and so challenging to their sense of self that they remove the aspect of agency completely from these memories.

Similar findings have been reported in studies on the experience of trauma in a non-conflict setting. Rasmussen, Karsberg, Karstoft, and Elklit (2013) conducted an evaluation study on a sample of Indian male and female youth and found that Indian males were more likely to report experiences of sexual trauma than women and suggested many cultural factors that may be responsible for this non-normative evidence.

In long drawn protracted conflicts, the meaning making process is even more detailed and extended because of the involvement of multiple parties, time lapses, escalating, and deescalating phases of violence as well as changes in the very nature of violence. Previous literature has reported on the normalising and distancing strategies employed by individuals who are exposed to violence for a prolonged period of time and have to deal with consistent symbols of fear and threat (De Jong et al., 2011; Muldoon, Cassidy, & McCullough, 2009; Palmberger, 2010). Jones (2002) discusses a peculiar finding in light of its socio-cultural context, wherein the nature of the conflict and the perceived end and possibility of action influenced the relationship between search for meaning and psychological well-being among Bosnian adolescents. The same author also reported on similar context-based differences in another study, where the youth's perceptions of war and experiences of it differed significantly according to the meaning given to them (Jones & Kafetsios, 2005). Keeping in mind the growing emphasis on comprehensive approaches towards the understanding of violence, and exposure to it among youth in political conflicts, and because of the lack of similar initiatives in Kashmir, the present study was conducted to explore the nature and type of events that were perceived as violent by Kashmiri youth and analyse the same within the socio-cultural and political context of the conflict in Kashmir.

Contextualising the Study: The Kashmir Conflict

Kashmir has historically been a multi-ethnic society that experienced a number of wars for the occupation of this picturesque land. The political conflict that culminated into the present era of violence has its roots in the colonisation of India and its subsequent partition into Hindu dominated Hindustan (present India) and Pakistan, the latter with a Muslim majority. The failure to take into account the opinions of Kashmiris during the partition and the following wars between India and Pakistan (1947, 1965, 1998–1999) has created lines of division across the landscape of Kashmir that has resulted in the militarisation of the Valley and a situation of terror, insecurity, and political strife. Duschinki (2009) narrates that since independence from British colonial rule, the Kashmir Valley has experienced 'militarisation, repression, economic deprivation and indiscriminate violence' along with 'the denial of democratic processes' (p. 696). The author goes on to describe the nature of separatist militancy that emerged in Kashmir in the 1980s and various developments in the nature and form of resistance adopted by different factions of the population since then, including pro-separation politicians, Kashmiri youth, and others.

The violence has had phases of guerrilla type warfare, psychological terror, and large scale political resistance and movements questioning the legitimacy of state power (Behera, 2006; Duschinski, 2009). Ganguly and Bajpai (1994) view the conflict in Kashmir as a 'mix of ethnic religious and territorial battles, irredentism, hypernationalism, and economic reform and turbulence leading to protracted interstate and intrastate conflict'. Khan (2009) points out that the political violence in Jammu and Kashmir has its roots in the acts of the political elites and the weaknesses of institutions, both in the bureaucracy and in party organisations. According to Jha (1996), militancy in Kashmir is not born out of poverty or economic deprivation, but of the despair of a small, select group of young people who form a new but disinherited middle class sector; a class that was trained to wield power, but denied the opportunity to do so.

The conflict is now more than three decades old, with interrelated issues of human rights violations, displacement, and confrontations between opposing parties based on ideology, territory, and identity. The protracted low intensity conflict involving multiple parties has created a stagnant political state where the average Kashmiri person's right to self-determination has emerged as the basis for separatist ideologies that dominate the present Kashmiri discourse. Simultaneously, the loss to life and property as a consequence of the protracted conflict has been severe.

Conflict-related violence in Kashmir is reported to have taken more than 70,000 lives (Kashmir: Conflict Profile, South Asia's Longest War, 2013), since the onslaught of armed militancy in the late 1980s. The conflict has adversely affected every sphere of the Kashmiri society, crippling the normal lives of people. The wounds inflicted on Kashmir society are deep and go well beyond the socio-economic problems of neglect and poverty. Unnatural deaths, kidnappings, extra judicial killings, curfews, bomb blasts, mine blasts, and the presence of a large number of armed security personal in every nook and corner of Kashmir have led to the unprecedented growth of psychiatric disorders in the region. As per assessment of the International Committee of the Red Cross (ICRC), after the physical health part of a human being, mental well-being is the most stressed area in conflict situations and violent emotional reactions are manifest mainly among children and women. Those who are victims of violent situations suffer psychological stress and trauma. A traumatic event is defined by its capacity to evoke terror, fear, helplessness, or horror in the face of a threat to life or serious injury (APA, 1994). Such traumatic events are quite common in the lives of Kashmiri children and youth. Exposure to the dead and mutilations in situations, especially when these events occur in relation to the family, close friends, or the neighbourhood, increases the risk of adverse psychiatric events. Armstrong and Boothroyd (2008) in their study on 125 adolescent girls concluded that stressful life events were a significant predictor of emotional problems and other psychological problems. Like individuals, the society and the community may also get traumatised if it happens to pass through violent situations on a sustained basis. Communities exposed to disasters experience a number of traumatic events including threat to life, loss of property, exposure to death, and economic devastation. In this environment, high perceived threat, lack of predictability, and high loss and injury are quite common, which in turn are associated with the highest risk of psychiatric morbidity (Zatzick et al., 2001).

Rather (2013) presents a brief on the health situation in Kashmir where the increase in cases of psychological disability and health-related issues, coupled with the disruption to economy and society as a consequence of the conflict, has created an urgency, which requires immediate attention. Parlow (2013), on the other hand, suggests that the degree of disruption in Kashmir has been less when compared to more extreme conflicts, and most of the cases of exposure to violence have been related to the constant state of 'living in fear of the military', which has had marked health effects on the children of the region.

Exposure to violence in Kashmir. The extent of violence exposure among the civilian population in Kashmir Valley is staggering, as can be seen from the findings of the following two reports that were based on studies targeted specifically at gauging the extent of trauma exposure in the Valley. The first is a survey conducted by De Jong et al. (2008), which found high levels of direct and indirect exposure to violence with more than 80% exposed to crossfires and roundups, 44% having witnessed some form of mental or physical harassment, and as many as 70% of respondents reporting that they witnessed some form of mental or physical torture. The second report comes from a study by Margoob, Khan, Mushtaq, and Shaukat (2006), where the authors were attempting to get an overall picture of the extent of trauma exposure in the Kashmiri population. They found a high lifetime prevalence of trauma (>50%), which was comparable between men and women with more than half of the sample having experienced explosions and firings. More recently, Paul and Khan (2014) and Bhat (2014) found very high rates of mental distress and related symptoms of anxiety and depression among children and adolescents of the Kashmir Valley, which was seen as an outcome of the experiences with political conflict. Both studies found that direct experiences with violence, where the participant was the victim or witnessed violence on a family member, was significantly related to distress symptoms, anger, and depressive mood. Paul and Khan (2014) in their study on school children in Kashmir reported that direct exposure to violence is a significant risk factor (OD = 1.81) for behavioural and emotional problems. The most commonly found mental disorders were anxiety (8.5%), followed by mood disorders (6.3%) and then behavioural disorders (4.3%).

Amin and Khan (2009) evaluated the prevalence of depression among the civilian population in Kashmir and found that more than 55% of the participants reported significant symptoms of depression, which was highest among young adults in the age group of 15–25 years. According to Shoib, Dar, Bashir, Qayoom, and Arif (2012), suicidal attempts in Kashmir have increased by 250% in the last 18 years, when compared to pre-conflict times.

Youth in the Kashmir conflict. The conflict in Kashmir has affected the lives of everyone, irrespective of age, gender and class. However, the young adults of today, who were born and raised during the most tumultuous phase of violence in the history of Kashmir, have become the most politically active, volatile and violent segment of the Kashmiri civilian population. Contrastingly, they continue to lead the non-violent struggle for self-determination and have been found to advocate tolerant and peaceful steps towards social change and conflict resolution in the Valley (Dar, 2011).

A large faction of the student population has been involved in the anti-state movements in the last decade. While exact data on the percentage of young people attending universities across Kashmir is not available, the state overall has a literacy rate of about 70% for males and 50% for females. There are about two hundred thousand students enrolled in Kashmir University alone, which has its main campus in the city of Srinagar.

Sudan (2007) interviewed young Kashmiri students to explore their opinions on the causes and consequences of the conflict. A majority of the respondents pointed out that the long drawn-out conflict had not only created adverse economic and social conditions, but also left them feeling 'helpless and profoundly alienated'. One of the primary reasons for the dissatisfaction and helplessness among the youth is the overwhelming military presence in the region and the interference of the political and military systems in the everyday life of the people (Majumdar, 2015). Duschinski (2009) elaborates on the consistent environment of fear and threat in Kashmir resulting from legal impositions like the AFSPA (Armed Forces Special Powers Act), which provides unchecked impunity to armed forces, as well as practices such as asking for proof of identity, conducting interrogations at check points, and enforcing regular curfews and other acts of coercion and domination.

A survey carried out by doctors at the Government Psychiatric Diseases Hospital in Srinagar, Kashmir, revealed that a majority of children and adolescents have a low level of tolerance and get provoked on relatively minor issues. Kashmir's leading psychiatrist Dr. Mushtaq Ahmad Margoob told the Deccan Herald that emotional distress, psychological problems, and psychiatric disorders have definitely taken a toll on this most impressionable sub-group of the population. 'Compared to a child or an adolescent of 1980s, present age kids are short-tempered and get provoked on relatively minor issues. Most of the children have witnessed many events in the last two decades that would adversely affect the psyche of any human being in any part of the world', he said (Majid, 2013). Dr. Margoob said the present uncertain situation and conflict-related factors significantly contribute to the development of negative behavioural tendencies. 'Alarmingly high percentage of adolescents is falling prey to drug abuse and many other self-destructive tendencies', he revealed. Drug use increases in groups that have been displaced, especially among combatants and former combatants, which may be a way of coping with traumatic situations or memories (Bhui & Warfa, 2007).

Given the high incidence of traumatic events reported by Kashmiri samples across studies, the authors of the current paper wanted to explore further the salient incidents and aspects of violence that may be important to the youth in Kashmir. Hence, this paper follows an exploratory-qualitative approach towards the understanding of trauma exposure in Kashmir, in an attempt to find out those aspects of the experience that may be marginalised in current discourses. The idea was to get information from the participants regarding their experiences of violence in order to better understand the themes that emerged from this exercise and discover those aspects of the experience that may be less often reported in quantitative studies on trauma exposure.

The other objective was to get a broad idea about who the youth in Kashmir perceive as the main parties in conflict and who they hold responsible as perpetrators. This was done to contextualise the experiences of violence more in terms of the perceptions about the nature of violence (military or otherwise) and its impact on specific sections of the population.

Method

This study was done as part of a larger study on exposure to violence and its effect on emotional and behavioural outcomes among youth in Kashmir. The Exposure to Violence survey questionnaire was used to provide a quantitative measure of violence exposure; in addition, to address the main objective of this paper, it was decided to include a set of open-ended questions inquiring about the experiences of violence. The qualitative measure was self-report and participants had to write their responses in the questionnaire provided. The entire assessment took about 20–30 min for each respondent. Informed consent was taken and participants were made aware of the nature of the questions that could possibly cause some discomfort, given the theme of the study. Even though most of the reported experiences were asked as part of the quantitative survey on exposure to violence, many of the participants wrote a few lines under the open-ended sections, which we then analysed into broad themes and sub-themes. We also used two close-ended questions in order to ask youth about their perceptions of who had been the main perpetrators and victims of the conflict related violence in Kashmir.

Participants

96 (51 male and 45 female) participants in the age range of 18–30 years, from different regions in Kashmir, were recruited for the study. All participants were enrolled as students in Kashmir University, Srinagar. The participants were purposively recruited from across locations inside the Kashmir University campus. The researchers began by approaching university students with the help of a local student, who voluntarily agreed to assist in the recruitment process. This was done informally, by talking to and interacting with students on the campus. Thereafter, different departments were contacted and students were recruited at random from the various classrooms within a department. Participants were informed of the purpose and nature of the study, and only those who were willing to share their

opinions were included in the sample. Special attention was paid to explain about the possibly intrusive and distressing nature of some of the questions, and the participants were assured about the confidentiality of their opinions, considering the politically controversial topic.

Out of the 96, only 34 (20 male and 14 female) participants responded to the open-ended questions on experience of violence, while all 96 responded to the close-ended questions on perpetrator and victims. The low rate of response on the exposure to violence questions could be because many of the experiences were covered in the extensive survey tool used for the larger quantitative study. Secondly, from the experiences narrated by the respondents themselves, it becomes evident that most of the youth in Kashmir refer to a 'time in the past' (beaten as a child, harassed as a child) when talking about the conflict and related violence. Because most of the experiences of violence are retained in memory and not perceived to be part of the immediate present, it could deter participants from reporting the same. Thus, the low response rate might have been because the violent events were in the distant past and may not have been an immediate concern. Thirdly, Kashmir is perceived by some to be in a phase of transition from conflict to a post-conflict society. Though many would argue that the repeated incidents of violence that continue to happen in Kashmir make it a context of ongoing conflict, the engagement with peace and the conscious detachment from memories of the armed conflict may have led to the reduced interest in conversations about experiences of violence. Alternatively, considering the severe extent of violence exposure reported by the same sample based on the close-ended statements of exposure to violence in the quantitative questionnaire, the lack of responses to open enquiries could be an unconscious distancing by the youth in an attempt to cope with the trauma of violence. Palmberger (2010) talks about silencing of and distancing personal experiences from the collective memory of war as a 'discursive tactic' employed by members of the young generation to cope with the reality of the social context to which they are bound. This could be true for the youth in Kashmir as well, who continue to live, study, work, and spend their lives in a society that has been gravely damaged by conflict. The decision to express emotions and opinions about the experiences of violence or stay silent and distance themselves from the collective narrative of victimhood is usually a personal one and may depend on the individual and his or her immediate social groups.

Procedure for Analysis

The process of content analysis for the current sample was fairly simple and straightforward due to the nature of the responses, limitations in terms of number of questions asked, and the scope of the study. The responses were divided into broad themes that included the nature of events or kind of violence experienced by the participants. On re-examining and re-categorising the responses under each theme, a few sub-themes emerged that have been discussed in detail. There were indications of additional thematic strands of thought that need further exploration and have been presented as cases for enquiry and critical analysis in the future.

Summary of Themes

The analysis of responses to the questions revealed a few broad themes. These were:

1. Physical abuse (beaten up, physically tortured), with sub-themes like 'beaten up as a child', 'beaten up during crackdown' (crackdown is a local Kashmiri term used to refer to military raids on civilian homes during the insurgency, where local youth were interrogated, detained, and often physically tortured) and 'beaten up by military or CRPF' (Central Reserve Police Force—An Indian paramilitary agency).
2. The second major theme was 'witnessing violence or violent attacks' with sub-themes like 'witnessing violence on family members and neighbours for men', 'witnessing violence on boys or men' in the case of women, 'witnessing destruction of town', 'witnessing family members being detained or arrested', and 'witnessing people being humiliated or tortured'.
3. The third major theme was about 'mental torture or psychological torture' that was repeatedly used by the respondents, either as a single response or along with other forms of exposure to violence like 'witnessing violence on family members and others', 'being interrogated', 'being checked', and 'witnessing people being abducted (arrested or taken away) by the army'.
4. The fourth theme can be conceptualised as images and experiences of 'crackdown' where respondents spoke about 'home being broken into', 'forced to move out of home', 'army entering home', 'threatening and plundering', 'broken into home', and 'beaten up and interrogated during crackdown'.
5. A fifth category of experiences that have been reported can be thought of as 'harassment', with terms like 'ill treatment', 'searched and interrogated', 'proving identity' (Kashmiris were given identity cards to prove their identity to the military personnel), 'humiliated', 'harassed during examinations', 'road occupied by army and harassment of passersby', and other such accounts of difficulties faced as part of daily activities.
6. Lastly, an important theme that emerged was about the 'loss of freedom' with respondents talking about the absence of rights to speech and expression, movement and choice, which according to them are salient aspects of the experience of violence. Issues reported by participants included: 'No freedom to talk about truth', 'scared of moving out', and 'curfews' (when military rule is established civilian life comes to a standstill and movement is completely prohibited causing limitations on mobility and transport).

Discussion

Direct and Indirect Experiences of Violence

Being physically hurt was reported as a significant direct form of exposure to violence among men in Kashmir, with 60% of the participants (12/20) having experienced physical violence. While five of them mentioned that they had been beaten up as children, two of the male respondents specified paramilitary forces as the perpetrators of violence. Witnessing violence on others emerged as a salient experience of violence with 12 of the total 34 participants including five women reporting that they had witnessed various forms of violent attacks on other people. For the men, this included witnessing violence on neighbours and family members who were tortured, arrested, or detained by armed forces, witnessing the searching and occupation of their house, witnessing the destruction of town, and so on. Among the female participants, a common theme was the act of witnessing torture and physical violence directed at men, highlighting the gendered nature of exposure to violence. The significant role of witnessing violence is supported by findings from the quantitative part of the study, where witnessing violence was found to be more significantly associated with various socio-psychological aspects of cognitive and behavioural outcomes of youth when compared to direct experiences of violence (Majumdar, 2015). Though men seem to have more exposure to direct forms of violence than women, witnessing violence on friends and family was found to be a stronger predictor of emotional outcomes. The fact that a reasonable number of participants mentioned 'witnessing violence' as a salient incident of violence exposure is supported by findings from other contexts (Baker & Kanam, 2003; Qouta, Punamäki, Miller, & El-Sarraj, 2008; Schaal & Elbert, 2006) and re-emphasises the need to move beyond frameworks based on the understanding and evaluation of direct forms of violence and focus on how witnessing violence on others can affect the psychological and social adjustment of individuals living in a context of protracted conflict.

Gender and Exposure to Violence

Many studies have reported gender differences in exposure to trauma, highlighting the differences between men and women in the type and form of exposure and severity of response. Tolin and Foa (2006) did an extensive meta-analysis of studies on sex differences in trauma and PTSD that addresses many important questions about gender and the experience of violence. For instance, the authors found, across samples, that female participants were significantly at a higher risk of PTSD than their male counterparts, irrespective of the fact that in most populations, men were significantly more exposed to traumatic events (except adult sexual assault and childhood sexual abuse which was higher among women). This includes a category of 'exposure to combat, war and terrorism', which is of relevance for the present paper. One can infer from studies conducted in a variety of settings that exposure to violence and trauma, its meaning, experience, and impact may be different for men and women of a community. It is, however, more important to probe why these differences exist. Elklit and Petersen (2008) relate this difference in traumatisation to gender roles and socialisation patterns of men and women, where women are conditioned to be more sensitive to violence and stress. Memmi and Loû (2014) found that exposure to political violence legitimised domestic violence against women in Palestine. This has been supported by other research, where the association of intimate partner violence or sexual violence increased the likelihood of distress and PTSD among women and made women more vulnerable to trauma (Clark et al., 2010). Feminist theories have identified the domain of war and militarisation as a masculine space that systematically alienates women, through the lack of exposure and opportunity for contact with violence and consequently makes them second level participants and/ or victims of any political conflict (Majumdar & Khan, 2014). In a society like Kashmir, which largely adheres to patriarchal, traditional gender roles, there is a definite gap between men and women when it comes to direct exposure to traumatic events, like bombings, shootings, use of tear gas, etc. This is primarily because women continue to have less access to public spheres than men and are usually secondary participants in political activities. This is represented in the statements of respondents in the current study as well, where the majority of men reported having experienced physical beatings and other forms of direct violence, while the women spoke about witnessing violence on male counterparts. Twenty-nine percent of the women spoke about 'mental torture' as an important experience that was associated with witnessing violence, lack of freedom, restrictions on movement, and other related experiences of collective violence. Although the aspect of 'mental or psychological torture and harassment' was found to be common among men and women, men consistently reported their experiences with direct violence (being interrogated, checked, etc.) when compared to women who spoke about curtailment of movement and the 'fear of moving out'.

The Less Explored Nuances of Experiences with Violence

The loss of freedom is an interesting and important aspect of violence that emerged from this study. Around 10% of the sample talked about how living in a situation of ongoing conflict creates conditions where movement, speech, and other basic necessities are limited and often prohibited. The fact that the youth in Kashmir viewed loss of freedom as an essential element within the experience of violence points to the fact that experiences which are less related to the body or person and more intertwined with a socio-political sense of the self (in terms of freedom of choice and speech) may be significant memories of violence to certain individuals.

The curtailing of facilities can take many forms, such as the banning of movie theatres, periodic prohibition on phone services, loss of transportation when curfews are in effect, and generally the heavy presence of the military. Many of these conditions are disturbing for individuals living in these areas. The inability to move around freely may be more significant for certain age groups or for women who may have had less direct experiences with physical violence, but are constantly living with a fear of moving out of their safe places, fear of being sexually assaulted, and so on.

Most importantly, what can be gauged from the responses and the themes that have emerged from this study are that certain reported perceptions and experiences, like the repeated expression of 'mental torture' or the accounts of harassment, being forced to move out of home, to prove one's identity, being searched, and being interrogated, are extremely important forms of violence that need to be explored and understood as much as the experiences with physical violence, witnessing death and loss, and similar events. As many as 56% of the sample of respondents spoke about experiences of harassment and torture that were significant to them as events of violence and hence form a necessary part of the cycle of violence that needs to be considered for diagnostic as well as intervention purposes. The concept of trauma and what that entails will then include these additional personal variations.

Military Violence and Young Victims

Ninety percent of the respondents viewed the military and paramilitary forces as the main perpetrators of violence in Kashmir, while almost 22% also blamed the local police and Special Task Force that was formed to assist the military in the control of terrorism in the Valley. Interestingly, only four respondents (>5%) also mentioned that armed members of the local community (often termed as militants or insurgents) were responsible for the violence inflicted on the community. Most of the respondents (approximately 94%) believed that the local community members were the main victims of the violence that ensued, with less than 4% mentioning that local police and military personnel were also affected by the violence.

Half the sample of youth report that the elderly, women, and children have been victims of violence, though most of the youth report that young people have witnessed the maximum amount of violence followed by children, elderly, and then women. The negative perception about the role of the military and the militaristic nature of the violence that has ensued in the Valley has emerged out of a debate around the overwhelming presence of the Army in Kashmir and the various cases of human rights violations that have been reported over the last years. Duschinski (2009) points out that the highly militarised life in Kashmir is associated with civilians constantly living in fear of being reprimanded, detained, or arrested without just cause. The author emphasises that this produces a 'collective experience of being under siege', where they are reminded of their 'occupied' status everyday.

Since the outbreak of hostilities in 1989, Jammu and Kashmir has experienced a significant rise in cases of psychological disorders, including depression, recurrent, intrusive, and distressing recollection of events, irritability and outbursts of anger, difficulty in concentrating, insomnia, persistent sadness, poor mental health and coping, and disinterest in social activities (Jehangir, 2004; Khan & Ghilzai, 2002). Irrespective of group or class, many have been caught in the Kashmir conflict. The violence has precipitated a humanitarian crisis of tragic magnitude, causing untold

damage to young people's psychological, emotional, social, economic, and educational well-being. While the political complexities of the conflict are the subject of
high-level dialogue and discussion, the suffering and anguish of thousands of
victims of violence have been largely ignored.

Limitations and Future Directions

The present study had a few obvious methodological limitations pertaining to the
sample and the method used. The fact that very few of the sampled respondents
shared their experiences makes it difficult to assume or generalise the findings to the
population of Kashmiri youth and beyond. A more detailed and streamlined enquiry
that would engage the participants in a conversation about their experiences could
be more useful in drawing out the nuances of these experiences.

Secondly, while this study began to explore the possible usefulness of qualita-
tively engaging with the phenomenon of 'exposure to trauma or violence', only a
few statements were used for the study. Also, the sample was only male and female
college students and a larger sample of older Kashmiris could yield interesting
results in highlighting how violence may be experienced or remembered differently
across age groups, and how their present positioning in terms of the political and
ideological milieu in Kashmir influences the same.

Lastly, an in-depth narrative analysis of more substantial accounts and stories
from a Kashmiri sample (or a similar sample from another context of protracted
conflict) will be more representative of the diversities within this group and may
provide a basis to formulate a theoretical framework to guide the qualitative understanding of exposure to violence.

Conclusion

The paper brings forward a number of interesting insights into how populations who
are exposed to extreme violence make sense and remember the experience including which incidents and aspects of the experience seem more traumatic than others
and how these memories are explained in the context of conflict. This not only
opens up channels and frameworks that guide intervention in these societies by
pointing to experiences that are marginalised in the mainstream trauma or political
discourse such as the limitations to movement, the sense of harassment in having to
prove one's identity, the mental torture or psychological humiliation that is experienced when one is constantly living in a hostile environment, and the essential feeling of a lack of freedom, all of which could be significant drivers of emotions and
actions in these situations. Irrespective of the fact that the present enquiry yields
insightful knowledge about the experiences of violence and perceptions about
perpetrator and victims, it also brings to focus another aspect of the collective

experience of violence that is noteworthy; namely, the tendency of the participants to adhere to a dominant narrative of violence. This was also observed by the researcher while conducting interviews with the participants in Kashmir, who, in general, do not seem to deviate significantly from a master narrative that prescribes which aspects of the experience of violence is reiterated and who is perceived as perpetrators and victims.

Recchia and Wainryb (2011) describe this as the 'inflexibility in meaning making when youth are asked to narrate their experiences from different perspectives'. Hammack (2011) found a similar trend among Israeli and Palestinian youth who largely reproduced a 'polarised culturally exclusive dominant narrative' of a sense of existential insecurity for the Jewish participants and a collective sense of victimisation leading to the need for struggle and self-determination among the Palestinians (Recchia & Wainryb, 2011). This nature of collective identity is often responsible in carrying forward rigid ideas about the perpetration and victimisation in conflict and accentuating existing animosities. It is closely related to how groups maintain a self-fulfilling prophecy that can help in identification and even a sense of empowerment (Muldoon & Lowe, 2012). However, wherever a dominant narrative exists there is always the possibility for marginal identities to be sidelined and excluded from the debate. This is so because the boundaries of a victimised identity are often dictated by powerful elite which alienates minorities and other voices in a community.

Nonetheless, authors have time and again found that individuals are not passive receptors of experience; rather they are active agents who participate in the way events are perceived and represented in narratives (Daiute, 2010; Hammack, 2011; Muldoon & Lowe, 2012). Therefore, it is imperative to examine how power structures and collective identities shape the way individuals process their own experiences and how that is closely associated with the different attitudes toward violence and experiences of violence. A closer look at how a collective identity has been formed and maintained in Kashmir will not only help in deconstructing the narratives of the youth, but it will also allow for the people to reconsider and reconstruct their own experiences and perceptions.

References

American Psychiatric Association. (1994). *Diagnostic and statistical manual of mental disorders* (4th ed.). Washington, DC: Author.

Amin, S., & Khan, A. W. (2009). Life in conflict: Characteristics of depression in Kashmir. *International Journal of Health Sciences, 3*(2), 213–223.

Armstrong, M. I., & Boothroyd, R. A. (2008). Predictors of emotional wellbeing in at risk adolescent girls: Developing preventive intervention strategies. *Journal of Behavioral Health Services and Research, 35*(4), 435–453.

Baker, A. M., & Kanam, M. K. (2003). Psychological impact of military violence on children as a function of distance from traumatic event: The Palestinian case. *Intervention, 1*(3), 13–21. Retrieved from http://www.ourmediaourselves.com/archives/13pdf/13-21%20Ahmad%20Baker.pdf

Barber, B. K. (2009a). Glimpsing the complexity of youth and political violence. In B. K. Barber (Ed.), *Adolescents and war: How youth deal with political violence* (pp. 3–33). New York: Oxford University Press.

Barber, B. K. (2009b). Making sense and no sense of war: Issues of identity and meaning in adolescents' experience with war. In B. K. Barber (Ed.), *Adolescents and war: How youth deal with political violence* (pp. 281–313). New York: Oxford University Press.

Behera, N. C. (2006). *Demystifying Kashmir*. Washington, DC: Brookings Institution Press.

Bhat, B. (2014). *Mental health, anger expression and coping among male and female Kashmiri adolescents*. Unpublished doctoral dissertation, Jamia Millia Islamia, New Delhi, India.

Bhui, K., & Warfa, N. (2007). Drug consumption in conflict zones in Somalia. *PLoS Medicine, 4*, e354.

Bikmen, N. (2013). Collective memory as identity content after ethnic conflict: An exploratory study. *Peace and Conflict: Journal of Peace Psychology, 19*(1), 23–33. doi:10.1037/a0031472.

Clark, C. J., Everson-Rose, S. A., Suglia, S. F., Btoush, R., Alonso, A., & Haj-Yahia, M. M. (2010). Association between exposure to political violence and intimate-partner violence in the occupied Palestinian territory: A cross-sectional study. *The Lancet, 375*(9711), 310–316.

Dar, F. A. (2011). *Living in a pressure cooker situation: A needs assessment of youth in India-administered Kashmir*. Retrieved from Conciliation Resources website, http://www.c-r.org/downloads/IPK_youthreport_FayazAhmadDar_WEB.pdf.

Daiute, C. (2010). *Human development and political violence*. New York: Cambridge University Press.

De Jong, K., Kam, V. D. S., Ford, N., Lokuge, K., Fromm, S., Van Galen, R., et al. (2008). Conflict in the Indian Kashmir Valley II: Psychosocial impact. *Conflict Health, 2*, 11. Retrieved from http://www.biomedcentral.com/content/pdf/1752-1505-2-11.pdf

De Jong, K., Van der Kam, S., Swarthout, T., Ford, N., Mills, C., Yun, O., et al. (2011). Exposure to violence and PTSD symptoms among Somali woman. *Journal of Traumatic Stress, 26*(6), 628–634. Retrieved from http://www.mnchurches.org/refugee/healing/wp-content/uploads/Exposure-to violence-and-PTSD-symptoms-among-Somali-women-.pdf

Duschinski, H. (2009). Destiny effects: Militarization, state power, and punitive containment in Kashmir Valley. *Anthropological Quarterly, 82*(3), 691–717. Retrieved from www.academia.edu

Elklit, A., & Petersen, T. (2008). Exposure to traumatic events among adolescents in four nations. *Torture, 18*(1), 2–11.

Ganguly, S., & Bajpai, K. (1994). India and the crisis in Kashmir. *Asian Survey, 34*(5), 401–416.

Hammack, P. L. (2010). Identity as burden or benefit? Youth, historical narrative, and the legacy of political conflict. *Human Development, 53*(4), 173–201.

Hammack, P. L. (2011). Narrative and the politics of meaning. *Narrative Inquiry, 21*(2), 311–318.

Jehangir, R. (2004, August 18). Militancy increases psychological disorders in valley. *Kashmir Times*.

Jha, P. S. (1996). *Kashmir 1947: Rival versions of history*. Delhi: Oxford University Press.

Jones, L. (2002). Adolescent understandings of political violence and psychological well-being: A qualitative study from Bosnia Herzegovina. *Social Science & Medicine, 55*(8), 1351–1371.

Jones, L., & Kafetsios, K. (2005). Exposure to political violence and psychological well-being in Bosnian adolescents: A mixed method approach. *Clinical Child Psychology and Psychiatry, 10*(2), 157–176.

Kashmir: Conflict Profile, South Asia's Longest War. (2013). *Insight on conflict*. Retrieved from http://www.insightonconflict.org/conflicts/kashmir/conflict-profile/

Khan, W. (2009). Political violence and peacebuilding in Jammu and Kashmir. In C. J. Montiel & N. M. Noor (Eds.), *Peace psychology in Asia* (pp. 65–81). New York: Springer.

Khan, W. (2015, in press). Conflict in Kashmir: Psychological consequences on children. In S. Deb (Ed.), *Child safety, welfare and well-being* (Chapter 7). Delhi: Springer.

Khan, W., & Ghilzai, S. (2002). Impact of terrorism on mental health and coping mechanisms of adolescents and adults in Kashmir. *Journal of Personality and Clinical Studies, 18*, 33–41.

Majid, Z. (2013). Two decades of militancy spikes juvenile crime in Kashmir. *Deccan Herald*. Retrieved from :///C:/Users/Muslim/Desktop/Two Decades Of Militancy Spikes Juvenile Crime In Kashmir.html

Majumdar, S. (2015). *Moderating effect of mindset on aggression, emotion regulation, hope and optimism among youth exposed to violence in Kashmir*. Unpublished doctoral dissertation, Jamia Millia Islamia, New Delhi, India.

Majumdar, S., & Khan, W. (2014). Conflict and gendered representations of exposure to violence: The case of women in Kashmir. *International Journal of Education and Psychological Research, 3*(3), 69–73.

Margoob, M. A., Firdosi, M. M., Banal, R., Khan, A. Y., Malik, Y. A., Ahmad, S. A., et al. (2006). Community prevalence of trauma in South Asia: Experience from Kashmir. *JK Practitioner, 13*, S14–S17.

Margoob, M. A., Khan, A. Y., Mushtaq, H., & Shaukat, T. (2006). PTSD symptoms among children and adolescents as a result of mass trauma in South Asian region: Experience from Kashmir. *JK-Practitioner, 13*(1), S45–S48.

Memmi, S., & Loû, A. D. D. (2014). Choisir le sexe de son enfant? Nouvelles techniques de procréation assistée en Palestine. *Cahiers du Genre, 1*, 19–40.

Muldoon, O., Cassidy, C., & McCullough, N. (2009). Young people's perceptions of political violence: The case of Northern Ireland. In B. K. Barber (Ed.), *Adolescents and war: How youth deal with political violence* (pp. 125–143). New York: Oxford University Press.

Muldoon, O. T., & Lowe, R. D. (2012). Social identity, groups, and post-traumatic stress disorder. *Political Psychology, 33*(2), 259–273.

Palmberger, M. (2010). Distancing personal experiences from the collective. *L'Europe en Formation, 3*, 107–124.

Parlow, A. (2013). *Armed conflict and children's health: The case of Kashmir.* Unpublished doctoral dissertation, University of Wisconsin-Milwaukee, Wisconsin.

Paul, M. A., & Khan, W. (2014). *Prevalence of mental disorders among school children of Kashmir Valley.* Doctoral dissertation, Jamia Millia Islamia, New Delhi.

Qouta, S., Punamäki, R. L., Miller, T., & El-Sarraj, E. (2008). Does war beget child aggression? Military violence, gender, age and aggressive behavior in two Palestinian samples. *Aggressive Behavior, 34*(3), 231–244.

Rasmussen, D. J., Karsberg, S., Karstoft, K. I., & Elklit, A. (2013). Victimization and PTSD in an Indian youth sample from Pune City. *Open Journal of Epidemology, 3*(1), 12–19.

Rather, A. F. (2013). Armed conflicts in J&K and its impact on society: A case study of Kashmir Valley. *International Journal of Scientific and Research Publications, 3*(2), 1–3.

Recchia, H. E., & Wainryb, C. (2011). Youths making sense of political conflict: Considering protective and maladaptive possibilities. *Human Development, 54*(1), 49–59.

Schaal, S., & Elbert, T. (2006). Ten years after the genocide: Trauma confrontation and posttraumatic stress in Rwandan adolescents. *Journal of Traumatic Stress, 19*(1), 95–105.

Shoib, S., Dar, M. M., Bashir, H., Qayoom, G., & Arif, T. (2012). Psychiatric morbidity and the socio-demographic determinants of patients attempting suicide in Kashmir valley: A cross-sectional study. *International Journal of Health Sciences and Research, 2*(7), 45–53.

Stevens, G., Eagle, G., Kaminer, D., & Higson-Smith, C. (2013). Continuous traumatic stress: Conceptual conversations in contexts of global conflict, violence and trauma. *Peace and Conflict: Journal of Peace Psychology, 19*(2), 75–84.

Sudan, F. K. (2007). *Youth in violent conflict in Jammu and Kashmir: A comparative analysis of perceptions and attitudes of youth in Jammu University and Kashmir University and Migrants' Camp.* Retrieved from http://www.icyrnet.net/UserFiles/File/Publication%20Resources/Research%20Reports/Youth_Case_Study_Paper_FKSUDAN.pdf.

Tolin, D. F., & Foa, E. B. (2006). Sex differences in trauma and posttraumatic stress disorder: A quantitative review of 25 years of research. *Psychological Bulletin, 132*(6), 959.

Zatzick, D. F., Kang, S. M., Hinton, L., Kelly, R. H., Hilty, D. M., Franz, C. E., et al. (2001). Posttraumatic concerns: A patient centered approach to outcome assessment after traumatic physical injury. *Medical Care, 39*, 327–339.

Chapter 4
Implications of Coping Strategies and Perceived Community Cohesion for Mental Health in Colombia

Laura K. Taylor

Introduction

In the face of mass human rights violations and constant threats to security, there is growing recognition of the resiliency of people and communities (Kimhi & Shamai, 2004; Masten, 2014; Taylor et al., 2013). This paper builds on such work by investigating the effects of individual coping strategies, perceived community cohesion, and their interaction on mental health symptoms in Colombia. Previous research has indicated that a range of factors, such as exposure to past violence (Merrilees et al., 2011), current intergroup violence (Taylor et al., 2013), and post-conflict challenges, such as community acceptance (Betancourt et al., 2010), affect mental health. This in turn has implications for social outcomes, ranging from family well-being to civic engagement (Rodrigo, Martín, Máiquez, & Rodriguez, 2007; Taylor, 2016). However, when living in a stressful environment, individuals may respond in a number of ways; some coping responses may be constructive because they help people to face and overcome challenges, while other responses are destructive because they exacerbate the negative impact of stressors. Given this past research, the Caribbean coast of Colombia is an interesting setting to study factors related to individual resilience processes as ongoing violence related to paramilitary demobilisation and the emergence of new criminal groups continues to saturate the social ecology.

L.K. Taylor (✉)
School of Psychology, Queen's University, Belfast, UK
e-mail: l.taylor@qub.ac.uk

© Springer International Publishing AG 2017
M. Seedat et al. (eds.), *Enlarging the Scope of Peace Psychology*,
Peace Psychology Book Series, DOI 10.1007/978-3-319-45289-0_4

Resilience and Mental Health

There is growing consensus in theoretical and empirical literature to move away from pathologising individuals adversely affected by risk factors in their social environments (see Barber, 2013; Cummings, Goeke-Morey, Schermerhorn, Merrilees, & Cairns, 2009; Sousa, 2013a). This body of work converges around a broad conceptualisation of resilience as the capacity of a dynamic system to adapt successfully (Masten, 2014). This past research includes a number of studies across geographical contexts in Africa, Asia, Latin America, Europe, and the Middle East, which have found a link between experience with political conflict and negative mental health outcomes, specifically internalising problems such as depression, anxiety, and post-traumatic stress (Betancourt et al., 2010; Gelkopf, Berger, Bleich, & Silver, 2012; Merrilees et al., 2011; Murphy, 2007; Pedersen, Tremblay, Errázuriz, & Gamarra, 2008; Sousa, 2013b; Taylor et al., 2013; Tol et al., 2010). These studies represent a range of types of conflict (e.g. intergroup, political), intensities (e.g. missiles, threat), and varying in the timing of measurement (e.g. during ongoing conflict or in a post-accord period). Across the studies, the negative impact of experience with political conflict and greater internalising problems is consistent. However, not all individuals in these studies display negative mental health problems. That is, there are a number of factors and processes that are recognised as protecting those exposed to violence from negative mental health outcomes. An important goal, therefore, is to understand the conditions and factors that may decrease individual vulnerability to mental health problems in settings of political violence. Therefore, with the aim of improving overall mental health for those living amid ongoing conflict, research is needed to identify "modifiable moderators", or factors that can be changed, addressed, enhanced, or tempered in interventions (Luthar & Cichhetti, 2000). Both individual factors, such as coping, and community factors, such as cohesion, will be examined in this chapter.

Coping Strategies

In the stress and coping framework, a number of strategies have been identified as individual responses to adverse or stressful situations (Lazarus & Folkman, 1984). The literature examines how individuals both perceive a threat (primary appraisal) and then identify potential responses (secondary appraisal). "Coping is the process of executing that response" (Carver, Scheier, & Weintraub, 1989, p. 267). The efficacy of such coping responses, therefore, may vary based on the person, context, and type of stressor (Thoits, 1986). That is, for coping to be effective, and therefore buffer an individual from harm or perceived threat, it must provide the necessary resources (e.g. emotional, instrumental, financial) to help the individual deal with the given stressor. In other words, effective coping can be understood as promoting resilience through a "process by which social resources provided by informal and formal networks allow for instrumental and expressive personal needs to be met in everyday situations as well as under crisis" (Rodrigo et al., 2007, p. 330).

This definition emphasises a number of important dimensions about coping strategies. Firstly, individuals access these coping resources through both informal (e.g. friends and family) and formal (e.g. mental health services, seeking government assistance) ways. The strength of these social networks, as well as the quality of the advice and support they can provide, is important to understand how coping may affect an individual. Secondly, it calls for attention to the use of coping across a range of circumstances, including both higher and lower levels of threat, as well as episodic and chronic stress. As such, the growing literature on the topic can be traced as individuals cope with daily challenges as well as widespread crime and community violence and entrenched political conflict (Bryce, Walker, & Peterson, 1989; Ceballo & McLoyd, 2002; Norris & Kaniasty, 1992; Rodrigo et al., 2007).

Across these diverse settings and types of stressors, a number of consistent coping strategies have been identified (Carver et al., 1989). Originally, conceptualised as problem-focused and emotion-focused approaches to coping, there was also inclusion of strategies that may be less effective at buffering individuals from stress. Traditionally, a problem-focused coping approach includes planning, active suppression of competing activities, restraint, and instrumental social support. *Planning* involves "thinking about how to cope with a stressor" (p. 268), such as what strategy can best handle the situation, whereas *active* coping can be understood as steps taken to "remove or circumvent the stressor or to ameliorate its effects" (p. 268) and is often carried out in an effortful and stepwise manner. *Suppression of competing activities* involves constricting the range of inputs, or putting other things aside, to deal with the presenting stressor. This approach may be completed by *restraint* which also involves withholding, or a more passive response of not acting. Finally, *instrumental social support* "is seeking advice, assistance or information" that can help to deal with the stressor (p. 269). Together, this set of strategies has traditionally been combined as problem-focused as they are directed at the stressor that has threatened the individual.

Complementing the problem-focused coping approach, emotion-focused coping strategies include emotional social support, acceptance, positive reframe, denial, or turning to religion. Although often co-occurring with instrumental support, *emotional social support* is less about advice and more about getting "moral support, sympathy or understanding" (p. 269). When situations are chronic and unchangeable, *acceptance* may be an effective form of emotional coping that recognises the situation for what it is. *Positive reframing* is a strategy that focuses more on interpretation than dealing with the presenting issue; that is, more about managing distress rather than removing the stressor. Contrasting to acceptance and positive reframe, *denial* is another form of emotional coping in which the individual refuses to believe what is happening and to act as if it is not occurring. Finally, although *turning to religion* may serve more than one purpose, such as "a source of emotional support, as a vehicle for positive reinterpretation and growth, or as a tactic of active coping with a stressor" (p. 270), Carver et al. (1989) conceptualised it as a more general tendency of emotion-focused coping. This set of strategies focuses more on the appraisal of threat and the affective response, rather than directly on the stressor as in the problem-focused approach.

Finally, not all coping strategies may be effective, and at times perhaps, coping responses may even be harmful. Three additional coping strategies were recognised in this early conceptualising of the multidimensional ways in which individuals respond to stress. The *venting of emotions* includes focusing on the emotions, which in the long run may impede an individual from moving on to other coping strategies that could better manage stress. *Behavioural disengagement*, related to helplessness, is when an individual gives "up the attempt to attain goals with which the stressor is interfering" and may be more likely when "people expect poor coping outcomes" (p. 269). As a form of withdrawal, *mental disengagement* involves taking part in activities (e.g. daydreaming, sleep, watching TV) to take one's mind off a problem. These coping strategies demonstrate that not all responses will help to alleviate stress; in fact, some of these strategies may backfire and be related to greater distress in the long-run. Thus, there is a need for understanding how each of these coping strategies may affect different outcomes and across diverse contexts.

While the initial conceptualisation of these different coping strategies has been widely used, each approach is related yet distinct and may function in different combinations across distinct environments. And, even within a given context, similar coping strategies may function in different ways based on the type of stressor and outcome being studied (Taylor et al., 2013; Thoits, 1986). Individual factors, such as age, gender, ethnicity, and/or socio-economic status, may also influence use of coping strategies. However, Carver and colleagues have developed an overall scale, with the aforementioned coping strategies subscales, which has been widely used in cross-cultural settings. This scale has been translated and cross-validated in five languages, namely Spanish, French, German, Greek, and Korean. It has been adapted and used in other settings of political violence ranging from Northern Ireland (Taylor et al., 2013) to Sierra Leone (Sharma, Fine, Brenna, & Betancourt, in press) to Israel and Palestine (Dubow et al., 2012). In each of these contexts, as is the case in this study, the impact of demographic factors, such as ethnicity, gender, and/or age, is explored as relevant. Therefore, the current chapter will use Carver's coping scale and apply an exploratory quantitative technique to better understand how the various coping strategies affect mental health for adults living in the Caribbean coast of Colombia. To complement this focus on individual factors that may be related to resiliency, community-level factors will also be considered.

Perceived Community Cohesion

Community cohesion can be understood as the sources of support, solidarity, and resources available within a social environment (Thoits, 1995); it is a societal attribute, placing emphasis on trust, a sense of belonging, and willingness to participate (Chan, To, & Chan, 2006). This form of social support is essential for the maintenance of individual and collective well-being. Community cohesion considers both the amount of and the ability to mobilise social resources to achieve a given aim (Colic-Peisker & Robertson, 2015). Previous research has shown that these forms of perceived community support may have beneficial mental and physical health outcomes for individuals (Hurtado, Kawachi, & Sudarsky, 2011; Sousa, 2013a). Although some previous research has found communities are able to maintain perceived community cohesion even in the face of persistent violence (Taylor, 2012), others have suggested that ongoing threats and continued violence may erode some of these collective forms of social support. In either case, understanding how individuals potentially interact with the perceived community support and resources, especially with regard to mental health outcomes, remains an important area of research and will be explored in the Caribbean Coast of Colombia.

Colombia: A Context of Ongoing Threat

Colombia is a country that has been plagued by decades of internal armed conflict. From 1948 to 1957, Colombia was mired in a civil war known as *La Violencia* between two opposing political parties, the Conservatives and the Liberals. However, the conflict escalated with the emergence of leftist guerrilla movements during the 1960s and 1970s. The Revolutionary Armed Forces of Colombia (FARC) and the Army of National Liberation (ELN) were the two strongest rebel movements. Although many failed attempts at peace negotiations mark Colombia's history (Nasi, 2009), in 2012, after 8 years of a military solution pursued by then President Uribe, there is a renewed focus on peace negotiations currently underway between the FARC and President Santos' administration.

Paramilitarism, Demobilisation, Narcotrafficking, and Civil Society in the Caribbean Coast

In response to the violence between the guerrilla forces and the government, land owners recruited private defence forces to protect their holdings in the 1970s. The emergence of these paramilitary organisations was to a large extent condoned by the state and allowed to flourish through the 1990s (García-Godos & Lid, 2010). The expansion and increased power among paramilitaries were reinforced through their involvement in drug trafficking, particularly along the Caribbean coast. Despite being formally outlawed in 1989, these groups continued to consolidate power. In 1997, the United Self-Defence Forces of Colombia (AUC) was established as the national coordinating entity representing the majority of paramilitaries functioning in the region. Creating a representative body, however, also facilitated later negotiations with the central government.

Through a series of ceasefires and confidence-building mechanisms with President Uribe's administration, the AUC entered into a demobilisation process in 2005 through the Justice and Peace Law (Law 975, 2005). As a result, 32,000 AUC members put down their arms (Tate, 2009) and the Caribbean region became home to one third of the collective demobilised paramilitary groups (ICG, 2006). However, demobilisation did not lead to a decrease in threat across the coast. In fact, there has been a rise in illegal armed groups involved in narcotrafficking (INDEPAZ, 2010), and as such, an increase in drug-related violence related to these groups largely formed by reconstituted AUC members (ICG, 2008).

Despite the profile of violence and illegal activity, the Caribbean coast is also widely recognised for natural beauty, farming and agriculture, and diversity among inhabitants; large populations of Afro-Colombians, indigenous peoples, and *mestizos* [mixed-race] live in the region (Negrete, 2008). Civil society groups have formed to advocate on behalf of local communities, both within regional bodies and on national political levels (Esquivia Ballestas & Gerlach, 2009). The vibrant energy in Colombia has functioned as a buffer for communities from some of the harmful effects of political violence (Negrete & Garcés, 2010; Sánchez, 2013). The use of non-violence, as well as local community creativity, has worked to transform conflict in the Caribbean region, in particular (Esquivia Ballestas & Gerlach, 2009). The strong civil society movements often offer tremendous social resources within and across diverse stakeholders (CNRR, 2010); these groups are essential if movements toward peace are going to be sustainable (Bouvier, 2009). Thus, the Caribbean coast serves as an interesting region to study how mental health may be affected by individual coping strategies and community resources in a setting of threat and ongoing insecurity.

Current Study

Thus, the current study pursues three related research questions. The first question investigates the patterns of coping strategies employed by individuals in the Caribbean coast of Colombia when facing stressful situations in their lives. The second question examines the impact of these coping strategies on individual mental health, specifically depression. That is, to what degree do the different approaches to coping with stress increase or decrease symptoms of depression? The final research question integrates individuals' perceptions of the communities in which they live. This question addresses how perceived community cohesion directly relates to mental health outcomes and its interaction with coping approaches. The analyses will identify whether the perceived sense of support in the community enhances or mitigates the impact of individual coping strategies on depression.

Method

Participants and Procedures

The sample comes from a larger project that investigates the relations among political violence, transitional justice attitudes, mental health, and civic participation. The current analyses included 184 adults (49% male) who participated in data collection in 2010, 5 years after the demobilisation through the Justice and Peace Law. Participants were 42.5 years old ($SD=14.20$) and had 3.57 children ($SD=2.91$) on average; the majority were married or living as married (77%) and identified as being Catholic (67%) or Christian/Evangelical (20%). Fifty percent of participants did not complete high school, while the other half was evenly split between those with high school degrees and other with some form of higher education. Finally, 55% identified as *mestizo*, 14% as Afro-Colombian, and 10% as indigenous, while the remainder chose more than one category or did not select an ethnic/racial affiliation.

The survey was carried out by trained research assistants in partnership with two collaborating Colombian universities. After providing informed consent, all questionnaires were delivered through face-to-face interviews (approximately 45 min) in Spanish, the primary language of participants. The interviews were conducted in the location of the participants' choosing, most often their home or a neutral site in the community. Consistent with the practices in the region, no compensation was provided and research assistants travelled in teams of 3–4 people for security reasons. The study design and procedures were approved by the Human Subjects Review Board at the University of Notre Dame.

Participants were recruited with the assistance of multiple local contacts within each of the 14 municipalities visited, following an intentional sampling frame. That is, representation of diverse perspectives and experiences was sought to include important sectors of the Caribbean coast: Afro-Colombians, *campesinos* [peasants], churches, demobilised, displaced, indigenous, teachers, trade unionists, women, victims, and youth (Negrete, 2008).

Each of the municipalities was selected within the departments of Córdoba and Sucre along the Caribbean coast. A two-by-two matrix was constructed to generate variation in level of violence (e.g. fatalities, forced displacement) and civic participation (e.g. number of community-based organisations, unions). In addition, a balance of urban and rural areas was selected. The cells were populated based on consensus among experts at the two collaborating universities and confirmed through the triangulation with available data. The combination of the intentional sampling frame and municipality selection helped to generate within-case variation and increase the validity of a non-probability sample (White & McBurney, 2010).

Measures

All measures and demographic questions were administered in Spanish. When an existing version of the measure was not available in Spanish, the questions were translated by the author and then checked for accuracy by an external translator fluent in English and Spanish. The final wording of each question was refined through a brief pre-test and in consultation with faculties from the fields of psychology, social work, politics, law, and conflict studies at a collaborating university; this ensured that each scale had face validity and was appropriate to the context.

Coping strategies. The Spanish-language 24-item scale of the BriefCOPE (Carver, 1997; Moran, Landero, & Gonzalez, 2010), a scale that has been widely used in settings of varying degrees of political violence (Dubow et al., 2012; Sharma et al., in press; Taylor et al., 2013), was used to assess the degree to which individuals utilised the different approaches to confront and adapt to difficult situations. Participants were asked to think about a difficult situation they faced in the last year and how they actually responded. The 12 subscales included self-distraction, active, denial, substance use, emotional, venting, planning, humour, religion, acceptance, positive reframe, and behavioural disengagement. A Likert-scale included responses that could range from 1 = *I did not do this at all* to 4 = *I did this very often* for items, such as "I received emotional support from other people" (emotional), "I looked for something positive about what was happening" (positive reframe), "I tried to create a plan about what to do" (planning), "I used alcohol or other drugs to feel better" (substance use), and "I refused to believe what was happening" (denial). Higher scores indicated more frequent use of a particular strategy to cope with difficulties. Because each subscale only had two items, internal consistency was not calculated. The factor analysis below describes how the scale was used in the current study.

Perceived community cohesion. Participants were asked to "think about this community", that is, the town that they lived in. Participants were then asked to indicate the extent to which they agreed with the seven items (Backer, Kulkarni, & Weinstein, 2007). Responses ranged from 1 = *strongly disagree* to 5 = *strongly agree* on a Likert-scale for statements such as "despite our differences, we can work together on common goals" and "we can cooperate to achieve benefits for the community". This scale has been reported in other papers from the larger study and has shown to correlate with related constructs, such as social trust (Taylor, 2012), which suggests there is adequate convergent validity. Factor analyses, described below, also suggest high internal validity. Higher scores indicated greater perceived community cohesion with good internal consistency ($\alpha = .92$).

Depression. The Spanish-language translation of the Center for Epidemiologic Studies for Depression 20-item index was used in the current study (Radloff, 1977; Translation: Perczek, Carver, Price, & Pozo-Kaderman, 2000). This scale has also been widely used in other settings of political violence (Pat-Horenczyk et al., 2013; Taylor et al., 2013; Yakushko, 2008) and validated in Colombia with satisfactory psychometric properties (Galvis, 2010). Participants indicated how often in the past week they had felt fearful, depressed, or had difficulty concentrating. Responses ranged from 0 = *rarely or never* to 3 = *most of the time* on a four-point Likert scale, with higher scores representing more depression symptoms, with good internal consistency (Cronbach's alpha = .87). Depression was computed as a composite variable with a possible range from 0 to 60, with higher scores indicating more depression symptoms.

Results

Preliminary Analysis

The means, standard deviations, ranges, and bivariate correlations for the manifest scales for all study variables are displayed in Table 4.1. Subtotals for individual coping strategies subscales were included. Overall, compared to males, females reported more behavioural disengagement, less planning, lower levels of perceived community cohesion, and more depression symptoms. Behavioural disengagement was significantly and positively related to both denial and substance use. Moreover, active, emotional, planning, acceptance, and positive reframe all positively and significantly correlated with each other. More planning and acceptance, while less behavioural disengagement, was related to higher reported levels of perceived community cohesion. Finally, higher levels of depression were related to more denial and behavioural disengagement, and less reliance on active, emotional, planning, positive reframe and coping strategies, and to more perceived community cohesion.

In the current study, there were no *a priori* assumptions about the relations among the diverse coping strategies. Rather than imposing the problem- and emotion-focused groupings of the coping strategies, an exploratory factor analysis was conducted using the composite scores for each of the 12 coping subscales. Exploratory factor analyses (EFA) are useful to indicate the underlying structure or relation among manifest or measured variables. The EFA approach can be used to detect patterns among variables by identifying a common factor or latent construct that influences two or more of the manifest variables.

For these analyses, maximum likelihood estimation was used, which accurately estimates factor loadings under the assumption that data are missing at random. In addition, promax rotation was also used, which allows for the possibility of correlation among the underlying latent factors (not the manifest indicators). That is, varimax rotation assumes that each of the factors is orthogonal (i.e. not correlated), which is unlikely in any situation and especially in this case, given that each of the subscales assessed coping strategies.

Table 4.1 Means, standard deviations, ranges, and bivariate correlations for all study variables ($N = 184$)

		M	SD	Range	1	2	3	4	5	6	7	8	9	10
1	Female	51%			—									
2	Denial	4.18	1.77	2–8	.051	—								
3	Substance use	2.44	1.13	2–8	.004	.138	—							
4	Behavioural disengagement	3.18	1.47	2–8	.154*	.247**	.242**	—						
5	Active	6.26	1.56	2–8	-.058	.052	-.003	-.109	—					
6	Emotional	6.29	1.85	2–8	-.014	-.052	.012	-.098	.390**	—				
7	Planning	6.3	1.4	2–8	-.182*	-.112	-.002	-.065	.459**	.434**	—			
8	Acceptance	6.06	1.47	2–8	.014	.115	.028	-.039	.338**	.286**	.404**	—		
9	Positive reframe	6.17	1.68	2–8	-.057	-.041	.065	-.098	.539**	.431**	.494**	.302**	—	
10	Perceived community cohesion	34.68	6.92	9–45	-.178*	-.103	-.065	.016	-.061	.064	.178*	.158*	.047	—
11	Depression	16.57	10.45	0–44	.290**	.217**	.113	.288**	-.203**	-.303**	-.205**	-.049	-.189*	-.195*

Note: * $p < .05$; ** $p < .01$

Table 4.2 Factor loadings for constructive and destructive coping strategies

Coping subscale	Constructive	Destructive
Denial		0.46
Substance use		0.43
Behavioural disengagement		0.53
Active	0.71	
Emotional	0.59	
Planning	0.71	
Acceptance	0.52	
Positive reframe	0.76	

Using the scree plot, a two-factor solution was appropriate for the data. From this two-factor model, factor loadings over .40 were retained. The resulting pattern revealed in two distinct, yet related latent constructs, with no cross-loading of items between the two factors (Table 4.2). The first latent factor comprised of three manifest indicators for coping strategies: denial, substance use, and behavioural disengagement; this was labelled as a *destructive coping* approach. The second latent factor included five coping strategies: active, emotional, planning, acceptance, and positive reframing; this construct was labelled as a *constructive coping* approach.

In addition, although the perceived community cohesion scale has been used in other settings of political conflict and given this study was the first known use of this particular scale in Colombia, an exploratory factor analysis was conducted based on the logic outlined above. A single factor solution was identified with all seven items loading highly onto the single item (range .721–.835). This confirms what was indicated with the high internal consistency. Moreover, it further suggested that each item contributed to the meaning of this construct with relatively equal weight. That is, participants who responded to this set of questions tended to respond in a consistent way across all of the items. Based on these preliminary findings, the manifest scale of perceived community cohesion was used in all subsequent analyses.

Primary Analysis

The primary analyses included examining the direct relations or main effects of the two coping approaches and perceived community cohesion on depression symptoms, while controlling for gender. In addition, the interaction effects of coping approaches and perceived community cohesion were also estimated. To calculate the latent interaction, all manifest scales were centred. Each centred coping subscale was multiplied by the centred perceived community cohesion score for each individual and used as the indicators for the latent interaction. All of the main effects were allowed to correlate (Fig. 4.1).

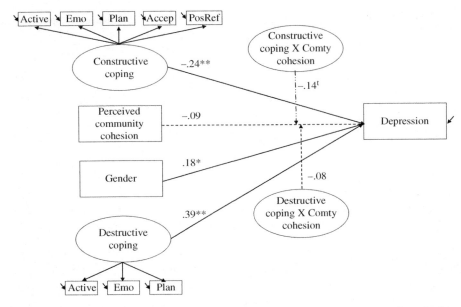

Fig. 4.1 Direct and moderation effects of the relations between perceived community cohesion, constructive, and destructive coping strategies on depression among adults in the Caribbean coast of Colombia. Standardised parameter estimates are presented with *dotted lines* representing non-significant paths for structural relations of interest. Coefficients for correlations among exogenous variables and error variances were omitted from the model for readability. $^t p < .10$, $^*p < .05$, $^{**}p < .01$. *Model fit*: ($\chi^2(137) = 321.49$, $p < .05$, $N = 186$; TLI $= .70$; CFI $= .79$; RMSEA $= .085$ (CI: .073, .097))

Overall model fit was assessed with the Tucker Lewis fit index (TLI), comparative fit index (CFI), and root mean square residual (RMSEA). Acceptable model fit indices are indicated by a TLI and CFI $\geq .90$ and a RMSEA $\leq .08$ (Hu & Bentler, 1999). The current model has adequate overall fit ($\chi^2(137) = 321.49$, $p < .05$, $N = 186$; TLI $= .70$; CFI $= .79$; RMSEA $= .085$ (CI: .073, .097)). Women reported more depression symptoms than men ($\beta = .18$, $p < .05$). There was a significant, direct effect of a constructive coping approach on depression outcomes ($\beta = -.24$, $p < .01$); greater use of constructive coping was related to lower levels of depression. At the same time, a destructive coping approach was significantly related to higher levels of depression symptoms ($\beta = .39$, $p < .01$). Although the direct effect of perceived community cohesion on depression was not significant, the interaction of perceived community cohesion and constructive coping was significant at the trend level ($\beta = -.14$, $p < .10$). That is, individuals who had a constructive coping approach and lived in settings with greater perceived community cohesion showed lower levels of depression. This may be interpreted that positive and proactive strategies to cope with stress are reinforced in environments of collective trust and efficacy.

Discussion

In a setting of continued violence and threat, individuals in the Caribbean coast of Colombia have utilised two general coping approaches; constructive and destructive, with positive and negative effects on depression, respectively. The constructive approach to coping included strategies such as active, emotional, planning, acceptance, and positive reframing and had beneficial effects for depression; moreover, these effects were enhanced when living in a cohesive community. On the other hand, participants who had a destructive coping approach, with strategies of denial, substance use, and behavioural disengagement, were more likely to report mental health problems. These individuals also did not derive any beneficial effects from living in supportive communities. Yet, a number of the coping strategies found in other areas of the world—religious, self-distraction, humour, and emotional venting—did not converge with either of the two coping approaches in this context (see Goeke-Morey, Taylor, Merrilees, Shirlow, & Cummings, 2014). Finally, females reported more depression symptoms compared to men overall.

Coping Approach Patterns and Community Cohesion

A *constructive coping* approach in a context of ongoing insecurity reveals a complementary mix of both traditional problem- and emotion-focused coping strategies. In contrast to some other areas of political conflict in which avoidance and distancing have been shown to be adaptive (Cairns & Wilson, 1989; Somer, Maguen, Or-Chen, & Litz, 2009), *planned* and *active* coping strategies still appear to be beneficial for the mental health of individuals in Colombia. That is, the ability to both think ahead and then enact those thoughtful plans seems to work together. Moreover, the combination of *acceptance*, given that individuals are living in largely intractable conflict situations, and the ability to *reframe* difficulties in a positive light is related to lower levels of depression. Finally, as to be expected, if individuals are able to find *emotional support* through talking about their feelings with loved ones, it alleviates the internalisation of problems. This constellation of coping strategies appears to work together as an overall constructive approach for dealing with stressors related to depression.

In addition, there appears to be an additive benefit for mental health outcomes when individuals use a constructive coping approach while living in cohesive communities. This *coherency* between coping strategies and social resources could be understood in a number of ways. For example, in denser social networks, individuals may have more opportunity to find sensitive peers or neighbours with whom they can talk about their feelings to bolster emotional support. In addition, there may be synergy between the types of thoughts and behaviours that facilitate planning and active coping strategies and the dimensions measured in perceived community cohesion. For example, this scale includes statements around cooperation and collaboration to work together toward shared goals; these collective actions require discussion, debate, and open communication in order to achieve societal benefits. Furthermore, the tendency for positive reframing may be reinforced by others in the community, as reflected in items such as "as a community, we can confront challenges without getting discouraged". Overall, the findings suggest that individuals who are able to successfully mobilise emotional social support through planning and active coping strategies, while at the same time accepting reality and inventing optimistic ways to view present challenges, are protected from deeper depression when they are surrounded by others who are able to work together for the greater good.

At the same time, some individuals used a more *destructive* coping approach that put them at greater risk for depression. For example, in contrast to other previous research that found distancing and denial to be adaptive when facing protracted conflict (Cairns & Wilson, 1989; Somer et al., 2009), in this study, the tendency to *deny* the reality they are facing may be harmful for mental health because they do not engage in the other positive coping strategies that could mobilise support. That is, if they ignore the stressors, they would be less likely to take part in planning and active coping strategies or seek emotional support from those around them. That is, by denying there are problems, the individuals may not be able to find the types of social support that may have benefits for mental health in this context. *Substance use*, such as turning to drugs or alcohol, and *behavioural disengagement* may also further social isolation. Using these coping strategies may lead to withdrawal and avoidance of the various networks, which could worsen depressive symptoms. It should also be noted that even when participants lived in more cohesive communities, it did not seem to lessen the negative impact of a destructive coping approach on mental health. For these individuals, living in a supportive community is not sufficient to protect them from deeper depression. Finally, analyses suggested that, compared to males, females reported more behavioural disengagement, less planning, lower levels of community cohesion, and more depressive symptoms.

Limitations and Future Research

The current findings should be interpreted in light of the study's limitations. Cross-sectional data should always be interpreted with caution. Longitudinal designs that could control earlier depression symptoms would improve the current analyses. Cross-lagged tests could also examine the sequence of events; that is, whether depression leads to a poor coping approach, a question not testable in the current dataset. In addition, although the exploratory quantitative approach is a strength of the current study, direct comparisons with other contexts might be simplified using the traditional problem- and emotional-focused categorisations. Moreover, the label of "destructive" coping approach was selected for the current factor analysis due to the negative implications for mental health and the lack of interaction with perceived community cohesion; future studies may examine how these coping strategies may work in protective ways for other outcomes. Alternatively, each subscale of coping strategies could also be analysed for cross-cultural comparisons; however, this fractured approach may not take into consideration underlying relations among different styles which can be measured and assessed in the current analyses.

The assessment of perceived community cohesion was developed in another context of political violence and showed good psychometric properties in the current sample, suggesting both external and internal validity. However, future research may further explore this construct with the use of other scales that may shed more light on related dimensions of community cohesion. Moreover, complementary approaches that use qualitative approaches to identify more localised understandings of community cohesion are warranted. Finally, individual conflict experience or traumatic past events may influence individual coping strategies that were not assessed in the present analyses. Future research may address some of these limitations and extend the impact of the current findings.

Intervention Implications

Given some of the macro-level political shifts in Colombia related to conflict transformation and security, the findings may have implications for mental health interventions. For example, in 2011, the Santos government passed the promising Law for Victims and Land Restitution (Law 1448, 2011). This law provides clear language for integrated psychosocial support for victims of the armed conflict. Articles 83.3 and 88(c) stipulate the need for collective attention and services to be provided for "individual and collective rehabilitation, [through the] creation of formative processes to strengthen the psychosocial environment, from a multidisciplinary perspective, for individuals, families and groups to support the mental health of the community" (p. 212). The current findings suggest that addressing coping strategies, and more specifically creating programmes that enhance constructive coping and build community cohesion, may help to advance the aims of this law.

Moreover, interventions should take into account not only past traumatic exposure, but also daily life stressors and everyday coping responses. Consistent with an approach that takes into account how individuals interact with different social ecological factors, such as perceptions about community-level dynamics (Miller & Rasmussen, 2010), interventions should help individuals seek and receive emotional support through informal and formal channels. Through this process, individuals should be encouraged to positively reframe their conceptualisation of the presenting stressors. Then, working collaboratively towards a plan for and taking action around the challenges they perceive in their lives, programmes will ideally include partnerships across the community with others who may share those issues and goals. For example, previous research has found opinions converging around the need for conflict transformation and community-input in designing reparations programmes and other victim-centred approaches (Taylor, 2015; Taylor, Nilsson, & Amezquita-Castro, 2015). To simultaneously deepen and strengthen community cohesion, these programmes should be designed and carried out in collaboration with community-based organisations. The goal is that engagement with local community partners, and interventions aimed at developing a constructive coping approach, will help bolster the mental health outcomes of a population hard hit by decades of war and ongoing insecurity.

Acknowledgements This research was funded by a Kellogg Institute Graduate Research Grant, Kroc Institute Graduate Research Summer Funding, and Institute for Scholarship in the Liberals Arts Graduate Student Research Award from the University of Notre Dame. I would like to thank the many individuals who have participated in the project, including the support of the Citizens Commission for Reconciliation in the Caribbean (CCRC), the research teams at the University of Sinú, Córdoba, and CECAR, Sucre, and David Backer for his consultation. I am grateful to John Paul Lederach and the members of the Peacebuilding Apprenticeship programmes for their guidance and support.

References

Backer, D., Kulkarni, A., & Weinstein, H. (2007). *West Africa transitional justice project—Liberia questionnaire (first wave)*. Unpublished manuscript, College of William and Mary, Williamsburg, VA.

Barber, B. K. (2013). Annual research review: The experience of youth with political conflict—Challenging notions of resilience and encouraging research refinement. *Journal of Child Psychology and Psychiatry, 54*, 461–473.

Betancourt, T. S., Borisova, I. I., Williams, T. P., Brennan, R. T., Whitfield, T. H., de la Soudiere, M., et al. (2010). Sierra Leone's former child soldiers: A follow-up study of psychosocial adjustment and community reintegration. *Child Development, 81*(4), 1077–1095.

Bouvier, V. (Ed.). (2009). *Colombia: Building peace in a time of war*. Washington, DC: United States Institute of Peace.

Bryce, J. W., Walker, N., & Peterson, C. (1989). Predicting symptoms of depression among women in Beirut: The importance of daily life. *International Journal of Mental Health, 18*, 57–70.

Cairns, E., & Wilson, R. (1989). Coping with political violence in Northern Ireland. *Social Science & Medicine, 28*, 621–624.

Carver, C. S. (1997). You want to measure coping but your protocol's too long: Consider the brief COPE. *International Journal of Behavioral Medicine, 4*, 92–100.

Carver, C. S., Scheier, M. F., & Weintraub, J. K. (1989). Assessing coping strategies: A theoretically based approach. *Journal of Personality and Social Psychology, 56*, 267–283.

Ceballo, R., & McLoyd, V. C. (2002). Social support and parenting in poor, dangerous neighborhoods. *Child Development, 73*, 1310–1321.

Chan, J., To, H., & Chan, E. (2006). Reconsidering social cohesion: Developing a definition and analytical framework for empirical research. *Social Indicators Research, 75*(2), 273–302.

Colic-Peisker, V., & Robertson, S. (2015). Social change and community cohesion: An ethnographic study of two Melbourne suburbs. *Ethnic and Racial Studies, 38*(1), 75–91.

Comisión Nacional de Reparaciones y Reconciliación (CNRR) [National Commission for Reparations and Reconciliation]. (2010). *La Tierra en Disputa: Memorias de Despojo y Resistencia Campesina en la Costa Caribe (1960–2010)* [Disputed land: Memories of displacement and peasant resistance in the Caribbean coast (1960–2010)]. Colombia: Colombo Andina de Impresos S.A.

Cummings, E. M., Goeke-Morey, M. C., Schermerhorn, A. C., Merrilees, C. E., & Cairns, E. (2009). Children and political violence from a social ecological perspective: Implications from research on children and families in Northern Ireland. *Clinical Child and Family Psychology Review, 12*, 16–38.

Dubow, E. F., Huesmann, L. R., Boxer, P., Landau, S., Dvir, S., Shikaki, K., et al. (2012). Exposure to political conflict and violence and posttraumatic stress in Middle East youth: Protective factors. *Journal of Clinical Child & Adolescent Psychology, 41*(4), 402–416.

Esquivia Ballestas, R., & Gerlach, B. (2009). The local community as a creative space for transformation: The view from Montes de María. In V. Bouvier (Ed.), *Colombia: Building peace in a time of war* (pp. 295–310). Washington, DC: United States Institute of Peace.

Galvis, F. H. (2010). Estructura factorial y propiedades psicométricas de una escala de depresión en universitarios de Colombia. [Factorial structure and psychometric properties of a scale for depression among university students in Colombia]. *Revista Panamericana de Salud Pública, 27*(2), 110–116.

García-Godos, J., & Lid, K. A. O. (2010). Transitional justice and victims' rights before the end of conflict: The unusual case of Colombia. *Journal of Latin American Studies, 42*(3), 492.

Gelkopf, M., Berger, R., Bleich, A., & Silver, R. C. (2012). Protective factors and predictors of vulnerability to chronic stress: A comparative study of 4 communities after 7 years of continuous rocket fire. *Social Science & Medicine, 74*, 757–766.

Goeke-Morey, M. C., Taylor, L. K., Merrilees, C. E., Shirlow, P., & Cummings, E. M. (2014). Adolescents' relationship with God and internalizing adjustment over time: The moderating role of maternal religious coping. *Journal of Family Psychology, 28*(6), 749–758.

Hu, L., & Bentler, P. M. (1999). Cutoff criteria for fit indexes in covariance structure analysis: Conventional criteria versus new alternatives. *Structural Equation Modeling, 61*, 1–55.

Hurtado, D., Kawachi, I., & Sudarsky, J. (2011). Social capital and self-rated health in Colombia: The good, the bad and the ugly. *Social Science & Medicine, 72*(4), 584–590.

Instituto de Estudios para el Desarrollo y la Paz (INDEPAZ). (2010). *V Informe sobre Narcoparamilitares en 2010*. Retrieved from http://www.semana.com/documents/Doc–2153_2011323.pdf

International Crisis Group (ICG). (2006, March 14). *Colombia: Towards peace and justice?* (Latin America Rep. No. 16). Retrieved from http://www.crisisgroup.org/~/media/Files/latinamerica/colombia/16_colombia_towards_peace_and_justice

International Crisis Group (ICG). (2008, October). *Correcting course: Victims and the justice and peace law in Colombia* (Latin America Rep. No. 29-30). Retrieved from http://www.crisisgroup.org/~/media/Files/latin-america/colombia/recting_course___victims_and_the_justice_and_peace_law_in_colombia.pdf

Kimhi, S., & Shamai, M. (2004). Community resilience and the impact of stress: Adult response to Israel's withdrawal from Lebanon. *Journal of Community Psychology, 32*, 439–451.

Law 975. (2005, June 25). *Ley de Justicia y Paz* passed by the Congress of Colombia. Retrieved from http://www.eclac.cl/oig/doc/col2005ley975.pdf

Law 1448. (2011, June 25). *Ley de Víctimas y Restitución de Tierras* passed by the Congress of Colombia. Retrieved from http://portalterritorial.gov.co/apc-aa-files/40743db9e8588852c19cb285e420affe/ley-de-victimas-1448-y-decretos.pdf

Lazarus, R. S., & Folkman, S. (1984). *Stress, appraisal, and coping*. New York: Springer.

Luthar, S. S., & Cichhetti, D. (2000). The construct of resilience: Implications for interventions and social policy. *Development and Psychopathology, 12*(4), 857–885.

Masten, A. S. (2014). Global perspectives on resilience in children and youth. *Child Development, 85*, 6–20.

Merrilees, C. E., Cairns, E., Goeke-Morey, M. C., Schermerhorn, A. C., Shirlow, P., & Cummings, E. M. (2011). Associations between mothers' experience with the troubles in Northern Ireland and mothers' and children's psychological functioning: The moderating role of social identity. *Journal of Community Psychology, 39*, 60–75.

Miller, K. E., & Rasmussen, A. (2010). War exposure, daily stressors, and mental health in conflict and post-conflict settings: Bridging the divide between trauma-focused and psychosocial frameworks. *Social Science & Medicine, 70*(1), 7–16.

Moran, C., Landero, R., & Gonzalez, M. T. (2010). COPE-28: A psychometric analysis of the Spanish version of the brief COPE. *Universitas Psychologica, 9*(2), 543–552.

Murphy, R. S. (2007). Mass violence and mental health—Recent epidemiological findings. *International Review of Psychiatry, 19*(3), 183–192.

Nasi, C. (2009). Colombia's peace processes, 1982–2002: Conditions, strategies, and outcomes. In V. Bouvier (Ed.), *Colombia: Building peace in a time of war* (pp. 39–64). Washington, DC: United States Institute of Peace.

Negrete, V. (2008). *Situación de conflicto y pobreza en el departamento de Córdoba y perspectivas de paz [The state of conflict and poverty in the department of Cordoba and perspectives on peace]*. Montería, Colombia: Louis Ángel Asocioado y Cia Ltda.

Negrete, V., & Garcés, M. (2010). *Análisis sociopolítico de Montería y propuestas sobre liderazgo, participación y compromiso ciudadano [Sociopolitical analysis of Monteria and proposals for citizen leadership, participation and commitment]*. Montería, Colombia: Universidad del Sinú.

Norris, F. H., & Kaniasty, K. (1992). A longitudinal study of the effects of various crime prevention strategies on criminal victimization, fear of crime, and psychological distress. *American Journal of Community Psychology, 20*, 625–648.

Pat-Horenczyk, R., Ziv, Y., Asulin-Peretz, L., Achituv, M., Cohen, S., & Brom, D. (2013). Relational trauma in times of political violence: Continuous versus past traumatic stress. *Peace and Conflict: Journal of Peace Psychology, 19*(2), 125–137.

Pedersen, D., Tremblay, J., Errázuriz, C., & Gamarra, J. (2008). The sequelae of political violence: Assessing trauma, suffering and dislocation in the Peruvian highlands. *Social Science & Medicine, 67*, 205–217.

Perczek, R., Carver, C. S., Price, A. A., & Pozo-Kaderman, C. (2000). Coping, mood, and aspects of personality in Spanish translation and evidence of convergence with English versions. *Journal of Personality Assessment, 74*, 63–87. Spanish version. Retrieved from http://www.psy.miami.edu/faculty/ccarver/sclspan.html

Radloff, L. S. (1977). The CES-D: A self-report depression for research in the general population. *Applied Psychological Measurement, 1*, 385–401.

Rodrigo, M. J., Martín, J. C., Máiquez, M. L., & Rodriguez, G. (2007). Informal and formal supports and maternal child-rearing practices in at-risk and non at-risk psychosocial contexts. *Children and Youth Services Review, 29*, 329–347.

Sánchez, G. (2013). Prólogo. In *¡Basta ya! Colombia: Memorias de guerra y dignidad* [Enough! Colombia: Memories of war and dignity] (pp. 13–16). Retrieved from http://www.elpais.com.co/elpais/archivos/bastaya.pdf

Sharma, M., Fine, S. L., Brennan, R. T., & Betancourt, T. S. (in press). *Coping and mental health outcomes among Sierra Leonean war-affected youth: Results from a longitudinal study. Development and Psychopathology.*

Somer, E., Maguen, S., Or-Chen, K., & Litz, B. T. (2009). Managing terror: Differences between Jews and Arabs in Israel. *International Journal of Psychology, 44*, 138–146.

Sousa, C. A. (2013a). Political violence, collective functioning and health: A review of the literature. *Medicine, Conflict, and Survival, 29*(3), 169–197.

Sousa, C. A. (2013b). Political violence, health, and coping among Palestinian women in the West Bank. *American Journal of Orthopsychiatry, 83*(4), 505.

Tate, W. (2009). From greed to grievance: The shifting political profile of the Colombian paramilitaries. In V. Bouvier (Ed.), *Colombia: Building peace in a time of war* (pp. 111–132). Washington, DC: United States Institute of Peace.

Taylor, L. K. (2012). *Relaciones entre la violencia, salud mental, participación ciudadana, y actitudes hacia la justicia transicional en la costa Caribe de Colombia.* [Relationships among political violence, mental health, and civic participation, and attitudes toward transitional justice in the Caribbean coast of Colombia]. *Palobra, 12*, 166–183.

Taylor, L. K. (2015). Transitional justice, demobilization, and peacebuilding amid political violence: Examining individual preferences in the Caribbean Coast of Colombia. *Peacebuilding, 3*(1), 90–108.

Taylor, L. K. (2016). Impact of political violence, social trust, and depression on civic participation in Colombia. *Peace and Conflict: Journal of Peace Psychology, 22*(2), 145–152.

Taylor, L. K., Merrilees, C. E., Cairns, E., Goeke-Morey, M. C., Shirlow, P., & Cummings, E. M. (2013). Risk and resilience: The moderating role of social coping for maternal mental health in a setting of political conflict. *International Journal of Psychology, 48*(4), 591–603.

Taylor, L. K., Nilsson, M., & Amezquita-Castro, B. (2015). Reconstructing the social fabric amid on-going violence: Attitudes toward reconciliation and structural transformation in Colombia. *Peacebuilding, 3*, 1–17.

Thoits, P. (1986). Social support as coping assistance. *Journal of Consulting and Clinical Psychology, 54*, 416–423.

Thoits, P. A. (1995). Stress, coping, and social support: Where are we? What next? *Journal of Health and Social Behavior*, 53–79.

Tol, W. A., Kohrt, B. A., Jordans, M. J., Thapa, S. B., Pettigrew, J., Upadhaya, N., et al. (2010). Political violence and mental health: A multi-disciplinary review of the literature on Nepal. *Social Science and Medicine, 70*, 35–44.

White, T. L., & McBurney, D. H. (2010). *Research methods* (9th ed.). Belmont, CA: Wadsworth, Cengage Learning.

Yakushko, O. (2008). The impact of social and political changes on survivors of political persecutions in rural Russia and Ukraine. *Political Psychology, 29*(1), 119–130.

Chapter 5
Integrated Education in Northern Ireland: Education for Peace?

Shelley McKeown

Introduction

Since the signing of the Good Friday/Belfast peace Agreement in Northern Ireland more than 15 years ago, tension between the two communities (Catholic and Protestant) continues to make the headlines almost on a daily basis (MacGinty, Muldoon, & Ferguson, 2007). While relations have substantially improved since the height of the conflict, the harsh reality is that segregation and negative attitudes remain a part of everyday life (Shirlow & Murtagh, 2006). With this in mind, there has been a push towards initiatives, both bottom up and top down, to improve intergroup relations. Many of these initiatives focus on educating young people.

With a focus on Northern Ireland, the aim of this chapter is to situate the movement towards integrated education and evaluate its effectiveness, in comparison to segregated education, using time series data from young people (16-year-olds) in the period from 2003 to 2013. The chapter concludes by presenting implications for education in Northern Ireland.

Intergroup Relations in Northern Ireland

Before presenting literature on the development of integrated education in Northern Ireland, a brief overview of the history of the conflict and how this is associated with current relations will be provided.

It has been well-documented that Ireland has witnessed conflict for centuries (Darby, 1995). The island was partitioned in 1921 after which events escalated cul-

S. McKeown (✉)
Graduate School of Education, University of Bristol, Bristol, UK
e-mail: s.mckeownjones@bristol.ac.uk

© Springer International Publishing AG 2017   75
M. Seedat et al. (eds.), *Enlarging the Scope of Peace Psychology*,
Peace Psychology Book Series, DOI 10.1007/978-3-319-45289-0_5

minating in the late 1960s and leading up to the recent conflict. At the most basic level, the recent conflict in Northern Ireland, known as the "troubles", began in 1968 following centuries of ongoing, but not always violent, conflict (Cairns, 1987; Darby, 1995). During this time, great inequality was experienced in the Northern Irish society. Unemployment was much higher among Catholics than Protestants; double the number of Catholics were on social security; Catholic children were more likely to finish school without qualifications and they were less likely to attend grammar schools than Protestant children (Cairns & Darby, 1998).

Often mistakenly viewed as a religious conflict, the troubles emerged due to a series of historical, religious, political, economic, and psychological factors (Cairns & Darby, 1998). It is commonly understood as a constitutional conflict between Protestants/Unionists/Loyalists and Catholics/Nationalists/ Republicans (Cairns & Darby, 1998). As is the case with any conflict, not everyone agrees on why the conflict began. The traditional Nationalist interpretation suggests that Ireland is one nation and Britain is at fault for keeping Ireland divided (Whyte, 1991). By contrast, the traditional Unionist interpretation claims that Unionists and Nationalists are distinct, and that the Nationalists' refusal to recognise this and to allow Unionists the same rights is the core of the problem (Whyte, 1991). One thing that is certain, however, is that competing political and national ideologies lie at the heart of the Northern Ireland conflict (Cairns & Darby, 1998).

The conflict has had devastating consequences on all aspects of Northern Irish society. It is estimated that approximately 3600 hundred people were killed and over 30,000 people were injured between 1968 and 1998 (Fitzduff & O'Hagan, 2009). Marking an "end" to the 30-year-period of sustained conflict, the road to peace started in 1998 with the signing of the Belfast/Good Friday Agreement. The Agreement aimed to ameliorate relations between the Protestant and Catholic communities, as well as between Northern Ireland and the Republic of Ireland, and between Northern Ireland and Britain. The Agreement proposed reforms to Northern Irish society and the promotion of equality for all. This included the formation of a power-sharing government, the reform of the police force (including the name change from the Royal Ulster Constabulary to the Police Service of Northern Ireland), the release of political prisoners, and the decommissioning of paramilitary weapons. The Agreement also aspired to achieve tolerance and mixing in education, by later introducing the policy framework "A Shared Future" to help achieve this. Subsequent policy documents have only referred to integrated education in passing, while others have not mentioned it at all (see Hansson, O'Connor Bones, & McCord, 2013).

Despite the promises of the Agreement, relations in Northern Ireland remain fraught (MacGinty et al., 2007). Talks to deal with contentious issues surrounding parades and flags have started and failed time and again. It is even argued that violence is still a daily occurrence in Northern Irish society (McGrellis, 2005). Moreover, the consequences of the conflict are clear to see in many aspects of everyday life. Segregation is rife, the majority of children attend religiously segregated schools and almost 40 % of neighbourhoods are religiously segregated, with an even higher percentage in low socio-economic areas. Visual markers of identity and a sense of belonging are painted on public streets and walls. Flags (British Union Jack and Irish

Tricolour) continue to fly and an increasing number of peace lines have been erected since the height of the conflict (Shirlow & Murtagh, 2006). At the same time, Northern Ireland's demographics are changing. Data from the 2011 census shows no group holds a majority of the 1.811 m population, in which 45% of the resident population self-identifies as Catholic and 48% self-identifies as Protestant.

This changing Northern Irish landscape and the de-escalation of violence leave Northern Ireland at a crucial stage to cement the road to peace. One way to help achieve this is through the education of Northern Ireland's youth.

Education in Northern Ireland

Northern Ireland has a long history of informal and formal education initiatives, aimed at improving intergroup relations (although often as a secondary goal). While there are many approaches to understanding the philosophy and rationale behind these interventions, such as through critical race theory (see Gillborn, 2006) and liberal multi-cultural education (see Jenks, Lee, & Kanpol, 2001), I situate my understanding and evaluation of these educational programmes in light of the principles of the contact hypothesis. At the most basic level, the contact hypothesis proposes that one way to reduce intergroup prejudice is by increasing intergroup contact between the groups (Allport, 1954). This works best when the contact occurs under favourable circumstances in which there is social or institutional support, there is equal status between the groups within the contact situation, and when there is co-operation in the pursuit of common goals. The contact hypothesis has been substantially empirically supported with decades of research in different countries and with different groups of people (Pettigrew & Tropp, 2006). The next section of this chapter will outline the development of informal education programmes and then move on to discuss the movement towards integrated education in Northern Ireland.

Informal education. During the height of the troubles, there was grave international concern for children and young people who were faced with the realities of living in highly conflicted areas, particularly during the marching season—a contentious time of the year. As a result of this concern, cross-community holiday schemes were developed (Robinson & Brown, 1991). The first scheme, arguably a form of informal peace education, took place in 1973 and since then there have been many schemes which vary greatly in their duration (from 5 days to 6 weeks) and their content (Trew, 1989). Typically, each scheme offers children the opportunity to travel to another country in Europe or the USA where they stay with local families.

Variations of these schemes still exist today, but their effectiveness in promoting community relations has come under fire (McKeown & Cairns, 2012). This is due to a number of key reasons. First, each scheme uses very different techniques (Trew, 1989). Second, many of the schemes do not directly address intergroup difference (McCartney, 1985; McWhirter & Trew, 1985; Robinson & Brown, 1991), and third, a lack of follow-up has meant that these holiday scheme experiences often do not transfer into the everyday lives of the children who partake in these initiatives (Robinson & Brown, 1991).

Despite these criticisms, time series survey data (among 16-year-olds living in Northern Ireland) lends support for cross-community programmes as a way to improve intergroup relations. Schubotz and Robinson (2006) reported that young people who attended cross-community programmes reacted more positively towards the outgroup than those who did not attend the programmes. Moreover, there is evidence that the majority of young people (82 % from the 2007–2008 data series) feel that relations would improve if more community programmes were available (Schubotz & McCarten, 2008). By providing further support for community programmes, research has shown that it can result in attitudinal and behavioural change. This was found when testing seating choice preference pre and post a cross-community programme (McKeown, Cairns, Stringer, & Rae, 2012).

Formal education. Recognising that children should be encouraged to interact with children from the "other" side more frequently than during the summer holidays, a series of initiatives (situated within the formal education system) have been developed over the past 40 years. These approaches have included the encouragement of contact between Protestant and Catholic schools through interschool programmes, the introduction of new curricula, and the emergence of integrated schools. Each of these will be discussed in turn, with a focus on the latter.

In the early mid-1980s, interschool contact initiatives were introduced into the Northern Ireland education system. These initiatives were originally funded by the Department for Education with the aim of increasing contact between Catholic and Protestant schools (Richardson, 1997). Smith and Dunn (1990) give a detailed account of an initiative in 1986, the Inter School Links Project, which involved eight schools (three elementary and five secondary). They reported the positive effects the scheme had on parents, pupils, and the teachers involved. Since the introduction of this specific project, additional funding was secured to develop further initiatives, but similar to the holiday schemes previously discussed, criticisms have been raised regarding their effectiveness in promoting positive relations. In addition to failing to discuss controversial issues surrounding the Northern Ireland conflict, the school contact initiatives were often viewed as a day off from school for the young people involved (Kilpatrick & Leitch, 2004; O'Connor, Hartop, & McCully, 2002).

The acknowledgement of the need for improved community relations in Northern Ireland also led to education curricula reform. In 1989, Education for Mutual Understanding (EMU) and Cultural Heritage (CH) were introduced into the school curricula (Richardson, 1997). In comparison to earlier initiatives, EMU and CH were not introduced to promote increased contact between Protestant and Catholic young people. Rather, the premise behind these initiatives was to promote acceptance of difference and to ensure fairness and respect (Richardson, 1997). While marking a change in the educational landscape, EMU and CH have been criticised for producing less than optimal outcomes (Gallagher, 2010).

At the same time when these informal and formal educational initiatives were introduced, Northern Ireland witnessed the emergence of a new type of school, which transformed the education system from one of religious division to one that now offered the opportunity for integration.

Integrated education. Today, the education system in Northern Ireland is divided into four types: controlled (mostly Protestant), grant-maintained (mostly Catholic), voluntary (grammar schools which are either predominantly Protestant or Catholic), and planned-integrated schools. The latter refers to schools which are driven to educate Catholics, Protestants, and young people regardless of faith or ethnicity, together (www.nicie.org.uk). In today's Northern Ireland, there are approximately 60 integrated schools (40 elementary and 30 secondary), with 5–7% of young people attending these schools.

Integrated education in Northern Ireland is the result of a bottom-up process whereby parents, from both sides of the divide, came together to campaign to educate "All Children Together". Known as ACT, the group engaged in campaigns for a number of years until 1981 when Lagan College, Northern Ireland's first planned-integrated secondary school, opened. The 1989 Education Reform Order (Northern Ireland) promised to aid and facilitate the development of integrated schools; up until that period, integrated schools were funded by parents and charities [see Hansson et al. (2013) for a review of policy changes relating to integrated education from 1999 to 2012].

Since the Education Reform Order, new schools have opened and others have transformed to integrated status (McGonigle, Smith, & Gallagher, 2003). In order to classify as an integrated school and to receive funding, a school must maintain at least 30% children of the smallest religious (Protestant/Catholic) community in the school's area, or have a ratio of 40:40 (Catholic:Protestant) and 20 children from other backgrounds. Commentators argue that integrated education in Northern Ireland is becoming increasingly popular, resulting in oversubscription (Hansson et al., 2013) [see Smith (2001) for further details on the emergence of integrated education in Northern Ireland].

With the underlying premise of integrated education to educate young people from all communities together, it is unsurprising that integrated schools have been viewed as an important way to improve relations between Protestant and Catholics living in Northern Ireland (Donnelly & Hughes, 2006). This is because integrated schools provide an opportunity for intergroup contact to occur, where it may not have been possible before, making integrated education an exciting opportunity for social change (Hayes & McAllister, 2009).

Research on the effectiveness of integrated education in promoting more positive group relations has produced mixed results. Early research found that young people attending integrated schools reported a significant increase in outgroup friendship over time (Irwin, 1991). Stringer et al. (2000) provided further support for this assertion, observing that young people attending integrated schools, compared to those attending religiously segregated schools, self-reported experiencing more intergroup contact and were more likely to support mixed religion marriage. In addition to increased friendship formation, research from a national survey (1996–2007) of Northern Irish adults also shows that compared to those who attended segregated schools, those who attended integrated schools were more optimistic about future intergroup relations in Northern Ireland (Hayes & McAllister, 2009).

Despite these positive outcomes, there have been some criticisms associated with integrated education. To begin with, each integrated school has a different philosophy with regard to its role in building peace; there is no single model of integrated education (McGlynn, Niens, Cairns, & Hewstone, 2004). Some teachers are of the opinion that the interaction of Catholics and Protestants in a school environment is sufficient, while others embrace additional activities to promote relations (Kilpatrick & Leitch, 2004). This has also been observed among the discourse of school principals (Montgomery, Fraser, McGlynn, Smith, & Gallagher, 2003). This is coupled with the fact that trainee teachers in Northern Ireland are not required to learn about community relations as part of their training (a voluntary module exists).

Given the wide range of ideas regarding what constitutes integrated education, it is not surprising that critics have commented (based on previous research) that many integrated schools do not facilitate the conditions outlined by the contact hypothesis (Niens & Cairns, 2008). The authors claim that this may be because many schools have transformed from segregated to integrated status, because schools often avoid discussing controversial issues, such as religion and politics, and because schools cannot merely rely on bringing young people together to promote relations. However, if the purpose of a school is understood to be primarily for learning, perhaps too much is expected from integrated education. This is particularly true when considering the following definition of peace education:

> Peace education is the process of teaching people about the threat of violence and strategies for peace. Peace educators strive to provide insights into how to transform a culture of violence into a peaceful culture. They have to build a consensus about what peace strategies can bring maximum benefit to the group (Harris, 2010, p. 11).

This may be part of the reason why there has been a movement towards a shared-education agenda.[1] Nevertheless, integrated education arguably has an important role to play in promoting intergroup relations. If we understand peacebuilding as a means to handle structural violence (i.e. the structural inequalities existing between Protestants and Catholics) and to promote social justice, then perhaps promoting intergroup contact through integrated education is a potential way to help achieve this in Northern Ireland (see Christie, Wagner, & Winter, 2001 for a review of peacebuilding). In support of the peacebuilding potential of integrated education, McGlynn (2004) argues that it is through integrated education that young people can learn about diversity and how to embrace identity. Other commentators have established frameworks for understanding how integrated education is related to peace and reconciliation across different contexts.[2]

Present Research

In addition to reviewing the role of education in helping to build peace in Northern Ireland, this chapter presents 11 years of cross-sectional national survey data collected among 16-year-olds during the period from 2003 to 2013. The aim is to address the following research questions:

---

[1] The purpose of this chapter is to relate findings to integrated education, so rather than review shared education here, I will return to this in the discussion section.

[2] For a review of the 3Rs of integrated education; respect, reconciliation and recognition, please see Ben-Nun (2013) who compares integrated education in Israel and Northern Ireland.

1. Do respondents attending integrated schools have more positive attitudes to mixing (school, neighbourhood, workplace) than those attending segregated schools?
2. Are respondents attending segregated schools more likely to think that religion will always make a difference in Northern Ireland, compared to those attending integrated schools?
3. Are any observed trends consistent over time?

It was predicted that respondents attending an integrated school would have stronger preferences for religious mixing and would be less likely to think that religion will always make a difference, when compared to respondents attending a segregated school.

Method

Sample

The sample was taken from data gathered for the Young Life and Times (YLT) survey (2003–2013). The survey monitors the attitudes and behaviour of young people in Northern Ireland. The respondents were children who turned 16 during February/March of the year in which the survey was conducted. Participants were given the opportunity to complete the survey either by post, online, or telephone, using their unique identification number indicated in the initial survey letter. During the period from 2003 to 2013, a total of 10,538 young people were involved in the survey. Table 5.1 presents the number of respondents for each annual survey.

Materials

All surveys contain demographics with additional questions relating to general health, community relations, attitudes to ageing, and others being added and removed over the years. For the purposes of the present research, questions of interest included: schools attended (e.g. What type of school do you attend? If you have left school, what type of school did you last attend?); preference for mixing in school (e.g. When deciding to which school you want to send your children, would you prefer a school with children of only your own religion, or a mixed-religion school?); the workplace (e.g. If you were looking for a job, would you prefer a workplace with people of only your own religion, or a mixed-religion workplace?); the neighbourhood (e.g. If you had a choice, would you prefer to live in a neighbourhood with people of only your own religion, or in a mixed-religion neighbourhood?); and attitudes towards religious difference (e.g. Do you think religion will always make a difference to the way people feel about each other in Northern Ireland?).

Table 5.1 Number of
respondents per year

Year	Number of respondents
2003	902
2004	824
2005	819
2006	772
2007	627
2008	941
2009	857
2010	786
2011	1433
2012	1210
2013	1367

Results

Analysis

Data sets from the 2003 to 2013 young life and times survey, made available through the ARK (archive research knowledge) website, were collated and re-coded in SPSS. A chi-square test of independence was performed to examine the relation between type of school attended (integrated or segregated) and responses to questions about preference for mixing (school, workplace, and school) and perceptions of religious difference. In addition to comparisons, which included all participants, separate tests were carried out for each year.

School attendance trends. For school attended, participants were asked to select between: planned-integrated, grammar, secondary, Irish language, special, or other schools. For the purposes of the present research, participants were categorised as attending either a planned-integrated school or a segregated school (encompassing all other answer options) (Table 5.2).

Trends show those attending integrated schools are the minority within our sample and this is reflective of the Northern Ireland education system. Moreover, for the majority of years (except for 2007 and 2012), our sample of those who attended an integrated school encompasses more Protestants than Catholics.

Preference for mixing. When asked which school they would send their children to, whether they would prefer to live in a mixed/segregated neighbourhood, and whether they would like to work in a mixed/segregated workplace, participants were asked to select between, "own religion only", "mixed religion", "other" or "don't know". For ease of analysis, respondents who chose "other" or "don't know" were recorded as missing data, leaving two categories of mixed religion or own religion only for analysis.

School. Combing respondents from all years, a chi-square test reveals that those who attended integrated schools were significantly more likely to report that they would send their child to an integrated school, compared to those who attended a

Table 5.2 Number of respondents (depending on religious identity) attending an integrated or segregated school by year

	Integrated		Segregated	
	Protestant	Catholic	Protestant	Catholic
2003	21	18	344	368
2004	15	13	298	337
2005	10	10	316	302
2006	15	9	266	274
2007	7	10	241	242
2008	20	12	331	359
2009	24	10	287	313
2010	18	13	252	297
2011	33	29	467	522
2012	25	27	402	431
2013	40	18	425	497

segregated school, $\chi^2(18,569) = 339.72$, $p < .001$. This finding was also consistent on a yearly basis from 2003 to 2013. Descriptive percentages are presented in Table 5.3 and chi-square tests, per year, are presented in Table 5.4.

Neighbourhood. For desires towards mixing in the neighbourhood, a chi-square test revealed that overall, respondents who attended an integrated school were more likely to support living in a mixed-religion neighbourhood, than those who attended a segregated school, $\chi^2(18,383) = 82.86$, $p < .001$. This observation was supported across the majority of years, except for 2007, 2009, and 2010, although the latter was close to significance ($p = .053$) (see Tables 5.3 and 5.4).

Workplace. In addition to having a stronger preference for mixing in the school and neighbourhood, it was observed that respondents attending integrated schools reported a significantly stronger desire for a mixed religion workplace, than those attending segregated schools, $\chi^2(18,406) = 35.65$, $p < .001$. This finding, however, was not supported across all years with data from 2005, 2007, and 2009 to 2012 finding no difference between the types of education on preference for workplace mixing (see Tables 5.3 and 5.4).

Religion will always make a difference. In addition to examining preferences for religious mixing, respondents were also asked whether they think that religion will always make a difference to the way people feel about each other in Northern Ireland. Respondents were given the option to select between "yes", "no", "other", or "don't know" as an answer. For ease of interpretation, responses in this research were categorised as "yes", "no", or "missing" ("other", or "don't know").

Combing respondents from all years, a chi-square test found no difference in responses comparing those who attended an integrated or segregated school, $\chi^2(19,082) = 1.68$, $p = .194$. When comparing by year, it was only in 2004 when significant differences were observed in which respondents who attended an integrated school were significantly less likely to say that religion will always make a difference in Northern Ireland than those who attended a segregated school (see Table 5.4).

Table 5.3 Percentage of respondents who chose a preference for mixed-religion workplace, neighbourhood, and to send their child to a mixed-religion school, and who state that religion will always make a difference in Northern Ireland

	School	2003	2004	2005	2006	2007	2008	2009	2010	2011	2012	2013
Mixing in school	Integrated	86.8	92.7	88.2	86.5	95.0	89.6	88.9	95.7	87.8	95.7	93.3
	Segregated	51.1	45.3	49.2	47.4	53.5	48.7	49.3	50.8	54.2	56.2	57.9
Mixing in neighbourhood	Integrated	80.8	78.6	84.4	88.2	80.0	85.7	81.1	83.0	90.7	92.8	84.4
	Segregated	59.2	57.6	64.7	63.1	73.0	66.6	71.0	69.6	73.1	66.3	73.3
Mixing in workplace	Integrated	92.0	92.9	91.2	97.1	85.0	97.8	92.5	93.5	93.8	94.6	98.9
	Segregated	80.4	78.5	81.9	84.0	85.3	84.0	87.1	84.2	89.7	89.1	90.3
Religion always	Integrated	94.0	82.5	78.8	89.2	90.5	90.9	87.5	87.2	78.9	84.3	89.7
	Segregated	91.0	92.1	89.6	88.8	87.9	86.1	89.6	85.8	84.5	87.3	87.9

Table 5.4 Chi-square test comparing school type and responses on preference for religious mixing (school, neighbourhood, and workplace) and whether religion will always make a difference in Northern Ireland

Year	Mixing in school	Mixing in neighbourhood	Mixing in workplace	Religion will always make a difference
2003	$\chi^2(1807)=25.407, p<.001$	$\chi^2(1775)=9.458, p=.002$	$\chi^2(1785)=4.112, p=.043$	$\chi^2(1839)=.452, p=.502$
2004	$\chi^2(1726)=34.866, p<.001$	$\chi^2(1705)=7.162, p=.007$	$\chi^2(1678)=4.985, p=.026$	$\chi^2(1750)=4.547, p=.033$
2005	$\chi^2(1693)=19.751, p<.001$	$\chi^2(1678)=5.230, p=.022$	$\chi^2(1680)=1.917, p=.166$	$\chi^2(1746)=3.824, p=.051$
2006	$\chi^2(1624)=21.315, p<.001$	$\chi^2(1597)=8.877, p=.003$	$\chi^2(1596)=4.235, p=.040$	$\chi^2(1644)=.005, p=.941$
2007	$\chi^2(1530)=13.378, p<.001$	$\chi^2(1509)=.408, p=.480$	$\chi^2(1509)=.001, p=.973$	$\chi^2(1549)=.129, p=.720$
2008	$\chi^2(1759)=30.134, p<.001$	$\chi^2(1720)=7.643, p=.006$	$\chi^2(1708)=6.420, p=.011$	$\chi^2(1797)=.829, p=.362$
2009	$\chi^2(1666)=31.117, p<.001$	$\chi^2(1671)=2.459, p=.117$	$\chi^2(1667)=1.267, p=.260$	$\chi^2(1740)=.247, p=.619$
2010	$\chi^2(1624)=35.393, p<.001$	$\chi^2(1636)=3.748, p=.053$	$\chi^2(1628)=2.863, p=.091$	$\chi^2(1679)=.078, p=.780$
2011	$\chi^2(11,162)=41.164, p<.001$	$\chi^2(11,122)=14.566, p<.001$	$\chi^2(11,131)=1.709, p=.191$	$\chi^2(11,207)=1.969, p=.161$
2012	$\chi^2(1906)=41.735, p<.001$	$\chi^2(1911)=20.650, p<.001$	$\chi^2(1938)=2.183, p=.140$	$\chi^2(1994)=.540, p=.462$
2013	$\chi^2(11,072)=42.857, p<.001$	$\chi^2(11,137)=.234, p=.629$	$\chi^2(11,086)=7.257, p=.007$	$\chi^2(11,137)=.234, p=.629$

It is worth noting here that the percentage of those thinking religion will always make a difference is particularly high (above 82%) among respondents regardless of year or school attended (see Table 5.3).

Discussion

Education is a powerful tool for promoting peace (Harris, 2010) and is used across the globe. The aim of this chapter was to review the effectiveness of integrated education as a tool for promoting peace in Northern Ireland. In addition to reviewing the literature, it presented data from the Young Life and Times Survey to compare preferences for mixing and attitudes towards religion in Northern Ireland depending on the type of school (integrated or segregated). In the remainder of this chapter, the results observed from the survey data will be discussed in relation to previous literature.The problems associated with conducting research in integrated schools will then be discussed, followed by a brief introduction to a new educational initiative, shared education, and implications on education for peace in Northern Ireland.

When responses from all survey years were combined, results consistently showed that participants who attended an integrated school were significantly more likely to prefer to work in a mixed-religion workplace, to send their child to a mixed-religion school and to live in a mixed-religion neighbourhood, compared to those who attended a segregated school. These observations were consistent, for the most part, across years for school and neighbourhood mixing. However, they were not consistent for mixing in the workplace. In addition, the percentages of preference for mixing in the workplace appear to be much higher than participants' responses to mixing in school or in the neighbourhood. This may be because the workplace is an abstract concept for the young respondents who are either still in school or have only recently left. As a result, they may be more likely to support mixing in the workplace than in school or the neighbourhood, both of which represent a reality for them.

These findings go some way to support previous research which has demonstrated behavioural effects of increased contact through integrated education. For example, Hayes and McAllister (2009) found that those who attended integrated schools were significantly more likely to have more intergroup contact through friendship and residency than those who didn't attend integrated schools. Moreover, research has repeatedly shown that attending an integrated school is associated with increased outgroup friendship formation (Hayes & McAllister, 2009; Irwin, 1991; Stringer et al., 2000). These positive attitudes and behaviours are important and may filter into further outcomes as there is evidence to suggest that pupils attending integrated schools are more liberal concerning "mixed marriage" (Stringer et al., 2000).

Research and Policy Implications

As integrated education appears to be slowly disappearing from the policy agenda (Hansson et al., 2013), this chapter serves as a way to highlight the importance of keeping integrated education at the forefront. Integrated education has the ability to improve intergroup attitudes and increase friendship formation, arguably a way to help build peace and move towards social justice. While it is recognised that integrated education is not the only means to promoting relations (see the later section on shared education), it should still be considered as a viable option. This is particularly important as integrated schools continue to be over-subscribed. Perhaps now is the time when Northern Ireland should move towards opening more integrated schools and put the rights of Northern Ireland's children, to live together in a peaceful society, above the demands of parents and others to maintain a segregated education system (see McGlynn, 2004).

The observed findings are particularly relevant in light of contact theory which claims that increased (positive) contact can improve intergroup relations (Allport, 1954; Pettigrew & Tropp, 2006). What cannot be assumed, however, is that preferences towards mixing will result in individuals engaging in intergroup contact with outgroup members. Therefore, it would be important to see how this translates in behaviour, for example, through exploring social networks and friendships and comparing these across types of schools, neighbourhoods, and religious identity.

While differences were observed in mixing preferences comparing school type, no such difference was found when considering perception of religious relations. Regardless of the type of school, percentages show that the overwhelming majority of respondents report that religion will always make a difference in Northern Ireland. This is a disappointing finding, not only for the effects of integrated education, but in general, especially given that Northern Ireland's youth perceive a future in which religion will always matter. It would be interesting to see how this compares to the older generations living in Northern Ireland to understand if young people are particularly pessimistic as they have not experienced the height of the conflict and, therefore, may think relations are worse than they are.

The results presented here offer some indication of the effects of integrated education on basic measures of intergroup relations, but are limited due to their cross-sectional nature and the reliance on self-report measures, arguably problematic when aiming to understand controversial issues. Moreover, the data is constrained due to the limited number of participants who attended an integrated school. In an ideal world, research would follow a triangulated approach and be longitudinal in nature, but aside from monetary and time constraints, conducting research in integrated schools can be difficult for a number of reasons.

The Problem of Conducting Research in Integrated Schools

Integrated schools have been criticised for their differing approach towards improving intergroup relations (Niens & Cairns, 2008). In particular, for having an avoidance culture (i.e. when assuming that physical co-presence is enough to promote relations) and for the rationale to obtain integrated status (i.e. some schools arguably transformed to integrated status to prevent closure or for financial reasons) (Niens & Cairns, 2008). In addition to these criticisms, commentators have argued that there have been problems with conducting research in integrated schools, making it difficult to assess their effectiveness (Stringer et al., 2009). According to Stringer et al. (2009), this is because of four key reasons. First, there is often strong resistance from gatekeepers, such as the school itself, teachers, parents, and administrators who do not want research to be conducted. Second, there may be concern with regard to the research findings. For example, if a school is found to be a poor example of integrated education, this could have serious consequences in terms of finance, recruitment, and general perceptions of the integrated education sector. Third, it can be difficult to understand what is meant by successful integrated education. For example, success can be defined in different ways, such as a focus on learning outcomes, simply bringing young people together, or the formation of intergroup friendships and the promotion of more peaceful relations. Fourth, there is a problem with the measures which are used. This is particularly salient when research focuses on cross-sectional, self-report measures, which arguably cannot tell us much about behavioural change over time (true of the present research). Similarly, self-report can be problematic when asking individuals to respond to sensitive issues, such as religion and intergroup relations. In these instances, respondents may be more likely to give socially accepted responses. This critique has been applied to contact research in a more general sense (Dixon, Durrheim, & Tredoux, 2005), sparking a movement towards the analysis of intergroup behaviour as it occurs in everyday life settings (e.g. Dixon & Durrheim, 2003; Koen & Durrheim, 2009). As an attempt to address this research problem in the Northern Ireland context, McKeown et al. (2012) examined the seating behaviour of young people in the classrooms of integrated schools. Despite this attempt to examine behaviours, it is still limited, since it is difficult to make conclusions from these behaviours. As such, we need to move towards a more comprehensive approach to understanding integrated education as a tool for promoting peace in Northern Ireland. It is only through doing so that we will be able to fully understand integrated education's potential.

Moving Beyond Integrated Education

Integrated education has existed in Northern Ireland since 1981 and produced some positive outcomes, but more than 20 years later, it still accounts for only approximately 5–7 % of the school population. As such, the movement towards integrated education has not developed as was hoped by earlier researchers (e.g. Fraser, 1973).

Recognising that it is unlikely that the majority of young people will attend integrated schools in the near future, an alternative has been put forward to help promote group relations for the majority of children who attend religiously segregated schools. This is particularly important, since although segregated schools are not the cause of the problems in Northern Ireland, they existed before the recent conflict, the majority of children in Northern Ireland attend these segregated schools. This alternative is known as shared education. According to the Ministerial Advisory Group (MAG) on shared education:

> Shared education involves two or more schools or other educational institutions from different sectors working in collaboration with the aim of delivering educational benefits to learners, promoting the efficient and effective use of resources, and promoting equality of opportunity, good relations, equality of identity, respect for diversity and community cohesion (Connolly, Purvis, & O'Grady, 2013, p. 17).

Unlike integrated education, shared education encompasses a broader goal, one which focuses on promoting relations (Hughes, 2011). At a basic level, shared education aims to facilitate collaboration between schools and encourage sharing in the pursuit of high quality education (www.schoolsworkingtogether.co.uk).

The focus on shared education has increased following the implementation of the Sharing Education Programme (SEP) in 2007, which uses psychological theories (including intergroup contact) to bring together young people from different schools and to promote the sharing of facilities, as well as general collaborations between schools. In an evaluation of the programme, Hughes, Lolliot, Hewstone, Schmid, and Carlisle (2012) report on its effectiveness at promoting intergroup relations, using data collected among young people who had taken part in the programme.

The momentum towards shared education continues today. In 2011, the Northern Ireland Executive set up its 2011–2015 strategic plan to establish a MAG to make recommendations on shared education, to enable all children to engage in a shared-education programme, and to increase the number of schools that share facilities. Subsequent to this plan, in 2013, the MAG published a 190-page report on shared education. It made 20 key recommendations for the government to consider, of which 17 related specifically to the advancement of shared education. As shared education moves forward, it is hoped that it will work alongside integrated education (arguably a form of shared education) and grow momentum to help create a more peaceful Northern Irish society. This is particularly important as Northern Ireland continues to become increasingly ethnically and religiously diverse.

Conclusion

Educating for peace remains as important as ever, as societies become increasingly diverse and as war continues to dominate the headlines. Peace education has the ability to profoundly change the lives of many and is enriched through its diversity in approach, in academic background, and in context. Without doubt, educational initiatives have helped Northern Ireland move towards a culture of peace.

In particular, by increasing the likelihood that individuals will encounter those from the "other side" and, therefore, reducing prejudice and widening friendship networks. The present research suggests that while shared education is an important step forward, we should not forget about the vital role integrated education can play in promoting peace in Northern Ireland. That said, we must hold caution because arguably the main aim of schooling is to promote learning, rather than peacebuilding, and as such, we should keep this in mind when evaluating integrated education's impact on improving intergroup relations. This is particularly relevant if we compare definitions of peace education, which often focus on teaching individuals how to address the cycle of violence. Despite this cautionary note, integrated education and associated programmes can be understood as education for peace. Moving forward, integrated education and shared education have great potential for continuing to transform Northern Ireland to a culture of peace.

References

Allport, G. A. (1954). *The nature of prejudice*. Reading, MA: Addison-Wesley.

ARK Young Life and Times Survey (1998–2013). Retrieved from http://www.ark.ac.uk/ylt/datasets/

Ben-Nun, M. (2013). The 3Rs of integration: Respect, recognition and reconciliation; Concepts and practices of integrated schools in Israel and Northern Ireland. *Journal of Peace Education, 10*(1), 1–20.

Cairns, E., & Darby, J. (1998). The conflict in Northern Ireland: Causes, consequences and controls. *American Psychologist, 53*, 754–760. doi:10.1037/0003-066X.53.7.754.

Cairns, E. (1987). Caught in crossfire: Children and the Northern Ireland conflict. Syracuse University Press.

Christie, D. J., Wagner, R. V., & Winter, D. A. (Eds.). (2001). *Peace, conflict, and violence: Peace psychology for the 21st century*. Englewood Cliffs, NJ: Prentice-Hall.

Connolly, P., Purvis, D., & O'Grady, P. J. (2013). *Advancing shared education*. Retrieved April 2013, from http://www.qub.ac.uk/schools/SchoolofEducation/MinisterialAdvisoryGroup/Filestore/Filetoupload,382123,en.pdf

Darby, J. (1995). Conflict in Northern Ireland: A background essay. In S. Dunn (Ed.), *Facets of the conflict in Northern Ireland*. England: Macmillan Press.

Dixon, J. A., & Durrheim, K. (2003). Contact and the ecology of racial division: Some varieties of informal segregation. *British Journal of Social Psychology, 42*, 1–23. doi:10.1348/014466603763276090.

Dixon, J. A., Durrheim, K., & Tredoux, C. (2005). Beyond the optimal contact strategy: A reality check for the contact hypothesis. *American Psychologist, 60*, 697–711. doi:10.1037/0003-066X.60.7.697.

Donnelly, C., & Hughes, J. (2006). Culture, contact and context: Integrated schools in Northern Ireland and Israel. *Comparative Education, 42*, 493–516. doi:10.1080/03050060600988395.

Fitzduff, M., & O'Hagan, L. (2009). *The Northern Ireland troubles: INCORE background paper*. Retrieved from http://cain.ulst.ac.uk

Fraser, M. (1973). *Children in conflict*. London: Secker and Warburg.

Gallagher, T. (2010). Building a shared future from a divided past: Promoting peace through education in Northern Ireland. In G. Solomon & E. Cairns (Eds.), *Handbook on peace education* (pp. 241–251). New York: Psychology Press.

Gillborn, D. (2006). Critical race theory and education: Racism and anti-racism in educational theory and praxis. *Discourse: Studies in the Cultural Politics of Education, 27*(1), 11–32.

Hansson, U., O'Connor Bones, U., & McCord, J. (2013). Whatever happened to integrated education? *Shared Space, 15*, 47–62.

Harris, I. (2010). History of peace education. In G. Salomon & E. Cairns (Eds.), *Handbook on peace education* (pp. 11–20). New York: Psychology Press.

Hayes, B., & McAllister, I. (2009). Education as a mechanism for conflict resolution in Northern Ireland. *Oxford Review of Education, 35*, 437–450. doi:10.1080/03054980902957796.

Hughes, J. (2011). Are separate schools divisive? A case study from Northern Ireland. *British Education Research Journal, 37*, 829–850. doi:10.1080/01411926.2010.506943.

Hughes, J., Lolliot, S., Hewstone, M., Schmid, K., & Carlisle, K. (2012). Sharing classes between separate schools: A mechanism for improving inter-group relations in Northern Ireland? *Policy Futures in Education, 10*, 528–539.

Irwin, C. (1991). *Education and the development of social integration in divided societies*. Belfast: Department of Social Anthropology, The Queen's University.

Jenks, C., Lee, J. O., & Kanpol, B. (2001). Approaches to multicultural education in preservice teacher education: Philosophical frameworks and models for teaching. *The Urban Review, 33*(2), 87–105.

Kilpatrick, R., & Leitch, R. (2004). Teachers' and pupils' educational experiences and school-based responses to the conflict in Northern Ireland. *Journal of Social Issues, 60*, 563–586. doi:10.1111/j.0022-4537.2004.00372.x.

Koen, J., & Durrheim, K. (2009). A naturalistic observational study of informal segregation: Seating patterns in lectures. *Environment and Behaviour, 42*, 448–468. doi:10.1177/0013916509336981.

MacGinty, R., Muldoon, O., & Ferguson, N. (2007). No war, no peace: Northern Ireland after the agreement. *Political Psychology, 28*, 1–12. doi:10.1111/j.1467-9221.2007.00548.x.

McCartney, R. L. (1985). *Liberty and authority in Ireland*. Derry: Field Day Theatre Company.

McGlynn, C. (2004). Education for peace in integrated schools: A priority for Northern Ireland? *Child Care in Practice, 10*(2), 85–94.

McGlynn, C., Niens, U., Cairns, E., & Hewstone, M. (2004). Moving out of conflict: The contribution of integrated schools in Northern Ireland to identity, attitudes, forgiveness and reconciliation. *Journal of Peace Education, 1*, 147–163. doi:10.1080/1740020042000253712.

McGonigle, J., Smith, A., & Gallagher, T. (2003). *Integrated education in Northern Ireland: The challenge of transformation*. UNESCO Centre, University of Ulster. Retrieved from www.arrts.gtcni.org.uk

McGrellis, S. (2005). Pure and bitter spaces: Gender, identity and territory in Northern Irish youth transitions. *Gender and Education, 17*, 515–529. doi:10.1080/09540250500192702.

McKeown, S., & Cairns, E. (2012). Peace-making youth programmes in Northern Ireland. *Journal of Conflict, Aggression and Peace Research, 4*, 69–75. doi:10.1108/17596591211208274.

McKeown, S., Cairns, E., Stringer, M., & Rae, G. (2012). Micro-ecological behavior and inter-group contact. *Journal of Social Psychology, 152*, 340–358. doi:10.1080/00224545.2011.614647.

McWhirter, L., & Trew, K. (1985). *Contact and conflict: Evaluating reconciliation projects*. Paper presented to the Annual Conference of the British Psychological Society, Swansea, UK.

Montgomery, A., Fraser, G., McGlynn, C., Smith, A., & Gallagher, A. (2003). *Integrated schools in Northern Ireland: Integration in practice*. UNESCO Centre, University of Ulster. Retrieved from www.arrts.gtcni.org.uk

Niens, U., & Cairns, E. (2008). Integrated education in Northern Ireland: A review. In D. C. Berliner & H. Kupermintz (Eds.), *Fostering change in institutions, environments, and people: A festschrift in honor of Gavriel Salomon*. London: Routledge.

O'Connor, U., Hartop, B., & McCully, A. (2002). *A review of the schools community relations programme 2002*. UNESCO centre, University of Ulster. Retrieved from www.deni.gov.uk

Pettigrew, T. F., & Tropp, L. R. (2006). A meta-analytic test of intergroup contact theory. *Journal of Personality and Social Psychology, 90*, 751–783. doi:10.1037/0022-3514.90.5.751.

Richardson, N. L. (1997). *Education for mutual understanding and cultural heritage*. Retrieved from http://cain.ulst.ac.uk/emu/emuback.htm

Robinson, A., & Brown, J. (1991). Northern Ireland children and cross-community holiday projects. *Children and Society, 5*, 347–356. doi:10.1111/j.1099-0860.1991.tb00500.x.

Schubotz, D., & McCarten, C. (2008). Cross-community schemes: Participation, motivation, mandate. *Ark Research Update 55*. Retrieved from www.ark.ac.uk

Schubotz, D., & Robinson, G. (2006). Cross community integration and mixing: Does it make a difference? *Ark Research Update 43*. Retrieved from www.ark.ac.uk

Shirlow, P., & Murtagh, B. (2006). *Belfast: Segregation, violence and the city*. London: Pluto press.

Smith, A. (2001). Religious segregation and the emergence of integrated schools in Northern Ireland. Oxford. *Review of Education, 27*, 559–575.

Smith, A., & Dunn, S. (1990). *Extending inter school links*. Coleraine: Centre for the Study of Conflict, University of Ulster.

Stringer, M., Irwing, P., Giles, M., McClenahan, C., Wilson, R., & Hunter, J. A. (2009). Intergroup contact, friendship quality and political attitudes in integrated and segregated schools in Northern Ireland. *British Journal of Educational Psychology, 79*, 239–257. doi:10.1348/97818 5408X368878.

Stringer, M., Wilson, R., Irwing, P., Giles, M., McClenahan, C., & Curtis, L. (2000). *The impact of schooling on the social attitudes of children*. Belfast: The Integrated Education Fund.

Trew, K. (1989). Evaluating the impact of contact schemes for Catholic and Protestant children. In J. Harbison (Ed.), *Growing up in Northern Ireland* (pp. 131–159). Belfast: Stranmillis University College.

Whyte, J. (1991). Interpreting Northern Ireland. Clarendon Press.

Chapter 6
If a Close Friend Is from Another Religion, Are You More Open to Other Faiths?

Reeshma Haji and Richard N. Lalonde

Interacting with someone from an outgroup is argued to decrease prejudice toward that outgroup (for a meta-analysis, see Pettigrew & Tropp, 2006). Furthermore, research on religion and prejudice suggests that some motivations toward religion are associated with heightened outgroup prejudice (for a review, see Hunsberger & Jackson, 2005). Thus, intergroup contact between people of different religious groups represents a complex situation in which beneficial effects of intergroup contact are likely to be mitigated by individual differences in approaches to religion. The present research was aimed at investigating how close relationships with religious outgroup members and religious orientations are related to interfaith attitudes in multicultural settings.

The approach taken to answer our research question may be described as one that uses a psychology of religion theoretical framework (dimensions of religiosity) to understand intergroup relations. It has been argued that spirituality is a unique motivation in its own right (Pargament, 2002, 2013), and we suggest here that it ought to be taken into account when investigating interfaith relations. Although intergroup relations research is often concerned with religious groups, variables pertaining specifically to religiosity are rarely examined. At least two related reasons compel the study of religiosity in the context of intergroup relations. First, research has documented links between certain religious orientations and prejudice toward outgroups (Allport & Ross, 1967; Batson, Schoenrade, & Ventis, 1993; Jackson & Hunsberger, 1999). Second, throughout world history, conflicts and wars have been carried out under the guise of religion. The present research focuses on the former of these reasons, but may very well have implications for the latter.

R. Haji (✉)
Laurentian University, Barrie, ON, Canada
e-mail: rhaji@laurentian.ca

R.N. Lalonde
Department of Psychology, York University, Toronto, ON, Canada
e-mail: lalonde@yorku.ca

© Springer International Publishing AG 2017
M. Seedat et al. (eds.), *Enlarging the Scope of Peace Psychology*,
Peace Psychology Book Series, DOI 10.1007/978-3-319-45289-0_6

Researchers have called attention to the importance of religion in cross-cultural psychology (Tarakeshwar, Stanton, & Pargament, 2003), and social psychologists have recently encouraged exploration of the role of religion in social contexts (Cohen & Neuberg, 2008; Shariff, 2008). An initial attempt at addressing the void in the area of religion and intergroup relations was provided by a social identity analysis of religion (Burris & Jackson, 2000) and by researchers who investigated religious beliefs and interfaith attitudes (Pargament, Trevino, Mahoney, & Silberman, 2007). The present research takes a different tack by applying past research on religion and prejudice to the study of intergroup attitudes of religious groups. Specifically, our focus is twofold. First, we assess relations between dimensions of religiosity and views of interfaith relationships. Second, we assess between-groups differences in interfaith attitudes of individuals with and without close interfaith friendships. We first consider the primary constructs contained within these two aims alongside relevant research findings, and then detail the studies on which this chapter reports.

Religious Orientations and Dimensions of Religiosity

Early conceptualisations of the relation between religion and prejudice suggested that such an association was not due to a problem with religion per se, but rather with an individual's approach to religion. Allport (1950) initially described immature and mature religion as developmental stages. Whereas immature religion was unreflective and guided by fear or utilitarian motives, mature religion was reflective and guided by higher order (rather than self-serving) goals. Mature religion was characterised by morality, purpose in life, and understanding that derived from reflection and doubt. In contrast, immature religion was unreflective in nature, and was consequently associated with prejudice and discrimination. Allport later refined these concepts into the intrinsic and extrinsic religious orientations, respectively. "The extrinsically motivated individual *uses* his religion, whereas the intrinsically motivated *lives* his" (Allport & Ross, 1967, p. 434).

Research on extrinsic and intrinsic religiosity and racial prejudice supported the notion that it was indeed extrinsic religious orientation and not intrinsic religious orientation that was related to prejudice (Allport & Ross, 1967). Subsequent researchers such as Daniel Batson (Batson et al., 1993), however, argued that the Allport and Ross (1967) measure of intrinsic orientation tapped into religious commitment, but not into a religious understanding that arose from reflection and doubt. The introduction of quest was an attempt to capture this aspect of religiosity (Batson & Schoenrade, 1991a, 1991b). Thus, Batson et al. (1993) proposed three dimensions of religiosity: extrinsic (religion as a means to an end), intrinsic (religion as an end in itself), and quest (a journey to religious understanding). They further argued that it was quest and not intrinsic religiosity that was consistently related to tolerance. It is of note that Batson et al. (1993) conceptualised religious orientations as dimensions, rather than as categories.

A review of 60 studies clearly indicated that the extrinsic dimension was more related to prejudice than the intrinsic dimension (Batson et al., 1993). In a similar vein, those highly involved in religious activities consistently showed less prejudice than those only moderately involved in religious activities. Batson et al. (1993) further uncovered that the target of prejudice matters. Some forms of prejudice (e.g. racism) were proscribed (or explicitly denounced) by contemporary Christianity. When non-proscribed forms of prejudice were assessed, however, such as prejudice toward gay men or lesbians, a positive association between the intrinsic religious dimension and prejudice was found (Batson et al., 1993). In contrast, the quest dimension was not correlated with and sometimes negatively correlated with both proscribed and non-proscribed forms of prejudice (see Hunsberger & Jackson, 2005).

There has been minimal research on the relations between the dimensions of religiosity and prejudice against religious groups. One exception to this trend is research conducted by Jackson and Hunsberger (1999). They explored the relations between religious dimensions and prejudice toward four target groups: Christians, believers, atheists, and non-believers. They found significant negative correlations between intrinsic religiosity and favourability ratings of atheists and non-believers and significant positive correlations between intrinsic religiosity and favourability ratings of Christians and believers (Study 2). Further, those high on the intrinsic dimension demonstrated in-group favouritism in their ratings of the four groups. A similar pattern of results was found for the extrinsic dimension. Interestingly, this research also found that among non-believers, attitudes toward atheists and non-believers were significantly more favourable than were attitudes toward Christians and believers. In sum, this research suggests that the extrinsic and intrinsic dimensions are related to non-proscribed religious outgroup prejudice among Christians, and that non-religious people also tend to show in-group favouritism along lines of faith.

Intergroup Contact and Intergroup Friendship

A large body of research supports the notion that contact between different groups can promote positive intergroup attitudes (Pettigrew, 1998; for meta-analysis, see Pettigrew & Tropp, 2006). The contact hypothesis, articulated by Allport (1954), claimed that physically bringing together members of different groups could promote positive intergroup attitudes, under favourable conditions. These favourable conditions were the equal status of the groups, common goals, absence of competition between the groups, and endorsement of the contact by authority and social norms. It should be noted that friendships typically develop in situations where the majority of these conditions are met. More recently, results from an extensive meta-analysis have suggested that even when the conditions are not optimal, intergroup contact can still promote positive attitudes (Pettigrew & Tropp, 2006).

Research has emphasised the role of intergroup friendship in promoting positive intergroup attitudes. These friendships are likely to have particularly potent prejudice-reducing effects because they meet many of Allport's conditions of optimal contact and they entail a high degree of intimacy (Pettigrew & Tropp, 2006). Consistent with this, research with seven national probability samples (Pettigrew, 1997) found that intergroup friendship was associated with greater reductions in prejudice than less intimate intergroup contact (i.e., neighbours and co-workers). Similarly, research with representative samples in the USA (Tropp, 2007) suggests that interracial friendship positively predicts feelings of closeness between Blacks and Whites, over and above variance predicted by contact alone.

There are many ways in which intergroup friendships may be beneficial for intergroup relations. Research with various Catholic and Protestant samples in Northern Ireland suggests that intergroup friendships between these groups are associated with decreased anxiety about future intergroup interactions (Paolini, Hewstone, Cairns, & Voci, 2004). Indeed, experimentally induced interracial friendships have been shown to reduce physiological indices of stress (i.e. cortisol) related to interracial interactions (Page-Gould, Mendoza-Denton, & Tropp, 2008). Furthermore, research on White and South Asian schoolchildren in the UK demonstrates that intergroup friendships promote positive outgroup attitudes via self-disclosure (Turner, Hewstone, & Voci, 2007). Participation in a social group with men of different ethnic backgrounds (Peterson, 2007) was associated with perceptions of similarities between people of different ethnic groups. Another potential mechanism for positive effects of intergroup friendships is a mere exposure effect on implicit attitudes (Turner et al., 2007). Indeed, even knowledge that an in-group member has a close friendship with an outgroup member can lead to reductions in prejudice (Paolini et al., 2004; Wright, Aron, McLaughlin-Volpe, & Ropp, 1997). Furthermore, meta-analytic findings support the generalisation of positive attitudes arising from intergroup contact to outgroups outside the contact situation (Pettigrew & Tropp, 2006), which was subsequently referred to as secondary transfer (Pettigrew, 2009). Thus, multiple indices support the prejudice-reducing potential of intergroup friendships.

Current Studies

The goal of the present research was to further explore generalisation effects of intergroup friendship in the specific context of interfaith friendships. We investigated how having a close friend from a religious outgroup was related to openness toward other religious groups on a variety of measures. Specifically, we compared the interfaith attitudes of individuals who had someone from a different religious group among their closest relationships and individuals who did not have close friends who were from a different religious group. We conducted our research in two geographical settings, one with a high degree of religious and ethnic diversity (Study 1) and one with a relatively low degree of religious and ethnic diversity (Study 2). This enabled us to determine whether generalisation effects were limited to a setting with frequent opportunities for interreligious contact or whether these generalisation effects could be replicated in a setting with limited opportunities for interreligious contact. We also assessed how dimensions of religiosity (extrinsic, intrinsic, quest) correlated with openness toward religious outgroups and whether those with and those without a close outgroup friend differed along these dimensions.

This research involved participants from a wide range of religious affiliations. In order to establish generalisability of the effects of close interfaith relationships, we assessed overall openness toward interfaith relationships (not only those pertaining to the group of the close friend).

Study 1

Method

Participants. Participants were 111 undergraduates from a psychology research participant pool at York University in Toronto. A criterion for participation was that participants have a religious affiliation. All research materials were presented online. The mean age of participants was 21.85 years. Most participants were women ($n=89$). The majority of participants were Christian ($n=71$), and the remaining participants were Muslim ($n=16$), Jewish ($n=9$), Hindu ($n=9$), and Buddhist ($n=4$). Two participants who did not report a specific religious affiliation were not included in the analyses.

Measures. The following variables were assessed and the measures are described in the sequence in which they were presented to participants.

Religious dimensions. Participants completed the revised Religious Life Inventory (Hills, Francis, & Robbins, 2005) in order to assess the extrinsic, intrinsic, and quest dimensions of religiosity. Because the original items were developed for use with Christians, they were reworded for applicability to a wider range of religious groups (Haji & Lalonde, 2009). For example, "church" was substituted with "place of worship" and examples were provided (e.g. temple, church, synagogue, mosque). Researchers belonging to diverse religious affiliations reviewed the items to ensure that the items and examples were appropriate for a variety of faith traditions. Participants rated their level of agreement on 7-point Likert scales (1 = *strongly disagree*, 7 = *strongly agree*) on items such as "a primary reason for my interest in religion is that my place of worship offers a friendly social atmosphere" (extrinsic), "my religious beliefs are what lie behind my whole approach to life" (intrinsic), and "questions are far more central to my religious experience than are answers" (quest). The means for the subscales were computed and the alpha reliabilities were .72, .91, and .80 for the extrinsic, intrinsic, and quest dimensions, respectively.

Friendship group assignment. Participants were divided into groups based on whether or not they were in a close relationship with someone from a different religious group. They were first asked to list the initials of the five people, outside of their family, whom they felt closest to. On the next screen, they were asked if any of these people were from a religious group that was different from their own. Those who responded "yes" (*Friend group*, $n=61$) were asked, on a separate screen, to select the person from their list who belonged to a different religious group and whom they were closest to; they were to think of this person as Person X, and to enter Person X's initials in a the space provided. Those who responded "no" (*Acquaintance group*, $n=48$) were asked, on a separate screen, to think of a person whom they knew (not necessarily someone they were close to) who belonged to a different religious group; they were to think of this person as Person X, and to enter Person X's initials in the space provided.

Characteristics of target person. Participants responded to a series of follow-up questions about Person X, including their relationship to Person X, the number of years they had known Person X ($1 = less\ than\ a\ year$, $7 = most\ of\ my\ life$), their closeness to Person X ($1 = not\ at\ all$, $5 = extremely$), and the religious affiliation of Person X. These items served as checks for the friendship group assignment procedure.

Similarity listing. Participants were given the opportunity to list up to ten similarities they perceived between their own religious group and the religious group of the target person.

Perceived interreligious similarity. Participants then rated the degree of similarity they perceived between their own religious group and the target person's religious group on a 5-point adapted version of the Inclusion of Other in Self Scale (Aron, Aron, & Smollan, 1992). They chose the pair of circles, out of 5 progressively overlapping pairs of circles, that best represented the degree of similarity they perceived between their own religious group and that of Person X.

Openness to relationships with religious outgroup members. Participants rated their preferred social distance (Bogardus, 1933) from a person from the same religious group as Person X. They indicated their willingness to engage in non-family (neighbour, boss, friend) and family (member of extended family, brother- or sister-in-law, boyfriend or girlfriend, spouse) relationships on 5-point scales ($1 = definitely$ $would\ not\ mind$, $5 = definitely\ would\ mind$). Scores were recoded in the direction of openness and means were computed separately for openness to non-family ($\alpha = .88$) and family relationships ($\alpha = .91$).

Interfaith dating opinions. Participants rated ten items on 7-point Likert scales ($1 = strongly\ disagree$, $7 = strongly\ agree$) that assessed their personal openness to an interfaith relationship (five items, e.g. *I am open to involvement in an interfaith relationship*) and their general attitude towards interfaith relationships (five items, e.g. *Interfaith relationships are doomed to fail*). The items were adapted from Lalonde, Giguère, Fontaine, and Smith (2007). Mean scores were computed in the direction of favourable views for the personal openness ($\alpha = .91$) and general attitudes ($\alpha = .91$).

Demographics. Participants completed a brief questionnaire that assessed religious affiliation, gender, age, and other background characteristics. This was followed by a brief questionnaire that probed reactions to the study materials.

Data analysis. The data analytic strategy involved two approaches. First, the interfaith friendship group was compared to the interfaith acquaintance group on all of the primary measures using independent samples t-tests. Next, correlations between dimensions of religiosity and all of the primary measures were examined.

Table 6.1 Study 1: Descriptive statistics of primary measures by friend and acquaintance relationships

Measure	Friend n=61		Acquaintance n=48	
	M	SD	M	SD
Time known target	3.67$_a$	1.47	2.69$_b$	1.55
Closeness to target	4.33$_a$	.63	2.92$_b$	1.13
Similarities listed	4.00	2.34	4.29	3.11
Extrinsic religiosity	4.40	.97	4.19	1.00
Intrinsic religiosity	4.70	1.29	4.70	1.42
Quest religiosity	4.20$_a$	.88	3.71$_b$	1.19
Perceived interreligious similarity	2.98$_a$	1.02	2.63$_b$	1.14
Openness to family	3.54$_a$	1.09	3.14$_b$	1.23
Openness to non-family	4.74$_a$	.48	4.44$_b$	.87
Openness to interfaith dating	4.41$_a$	1.67	3.82$_b$	1.89
Interfaith dating support	5.68	1.33	5.37	1.41

Note: Means with different subscripts within the same row are significantly different (See text for the corresponding p values)

Descriptive statistics for the primary measures are reported separately for the friendship and acquaintance groups in Table 6.1.

Results

Comparing interfaith friendship and acquaintance groups. There were a number of observed differences between the friendship and acquaintance groups. A summary of the means and standard deviations for all of the primary measures are reported in Table 6.1. In terms of group assignment checks, Table 6.1 shows that participants in the friendship group had known their target person for a longer period of time compared to those in the acquaintance group, $t(107)=3.40$, $p=.001$, $d=.66$, and felt closer to him or her, $t(107)=8.30$, $p<.001$, $d=1.60$. The frequencies of the types of relationships with the target person further corroborated the validity of the friendship versus acquaintance groups. Specifically, among the friendship group, approximately 97% of participants reported that the target person was a friend, boyfriend, girlfriend, or spouse, whereas among the acquaintance group, approximately 67% reported that the target person was a friend, boyfriend, or girlfriend (only 3 of these 32 relationships were boyfriends or girlfriends). There was also a significant between-group difference in the quest dimension of religiosity, $t(107)=2.46$, $p=.01$, $d=.48$. As shown in Table 6.1, the friendship group was higher in quest than was the acquaintance group.

There were a number of small to moderately sized differences between the friendship and acquaintance groups for the hypothesised outcome variables of interest in the predicted direction of difference. There was a significant difference in perceived interreligious similarity, $t(107)=1.72$, $p<.05$, $d=.33$, one-tailed. As

Table 6.2 Study 1: Correlations between religious orientations and primary measures

Measure	Dimension of religiosity		
	Extrinsic	Intrinsic	Quest
Perceived similarity	−.07	−.10	.15
Outgroup family	.07	−.33*	.26*
Outgroup non-family	−.03	−.09	−.12
Openness to interfaith dating	−.14	−.33*	.37*
Interfaith dating support	−.09	−.28*	.26*

*$p < .01$

shown in Table 6.1, individuals in the friendship group perceived somewhat more interreligious similarity than did individuals in the acquaintance group. There was also a between-group difference for openness to family relationships with someone from the religious group of the target person, $t(107) = 1.80$, $p < .05$, $d = .35$, one-tailed. As shown in Table 6.1, the individuals in the friendship group were somewhat more open than individuals from the acquaintance group. There was a similar significant between-group difference in openness to non-family relationships with someone from the target person's religious group, $t(107) = 2.25$, $p = .03$, $d = .44$. The friendship group was more open than was the acquaintance group. Finally, there was also a significant between-group difference for personal openness to interfaith relationships, $t(107) = 1.72$, $p < .05$, $d = .33$, one-tailed. The friendship group was more open to interfaith dating than was the acquaintance group.

Correlational analyses of dimensions of religiosity. Correlations between the dimensions of religiosity and the other measures are shown in Table 6.2. It can be seen that the intrinsic dimension was negatively correlated with openness to outgroup family, personal openness to interfaith dating, and interfaith dating support; the quest dimension was positively correlated with all of these measures. It should also be noted that extrinsic religiosity was unrelated to any of the attitude indices.

In sum, having a religious outgroup member as a close friend predicted more favourable responses to religious diversity. Specifically, those with close friendships with religious outgroup members perceived greater interreligious similarity and were more open to interfaith dating and family and non-family relationships with religious outgroup members. With respect to dimensions of religiosity, those with a close friendship with a religious outgroup member were higher in quest dimension of religiosity than those without a close friendship with a religious outgroup member.

The present findings should be considered within the context where the data were collected. This research was conducted in Toronto, a large city with extensive religious and ethnic diversity. Thus, intergroup friendships were probably more frequent and intergroup contact was probably more pervasive than in less religiously diverse geographical areas. Study 2 assessed the generalisability of our current results within a less religiously diverse context.

Study 2

Although Study 1 found some preliminary support for the more positive interreligious attitudes of those who have a close friend belonging to a religious outgroup, the research was conducted in one of the world's most multicultural cities, Toronto, where the visible minority population was 47% in 2011 (Statistics Canada, 2013). It is also Canada's largest city with an estimated population of 5,959,500 in its census metropolitan area in 2013 (Statistics Canada, 2014). In this large population, there is also religious diversity. Almost 79% of the population reported a religious affiliation in 2011 (Statistics Canada, 2013). The largest represented religious affiliations in the population were Roman Catholic (30.1%), Muslim (7.7%), and Hindu (5.9%). We were interested in whether the generalisation of interfaith attitudes observed in Toronto would replicate in a less diverse city where the frequency and degree of interreligious exposure would typically be lower. Additionally, we sought to determine if the correlational relationships with dimensions of religiosity would replicate in a setting with less religious diversity. Thus, Study 2 employed the same basic design as Study 1 but was conducted with university and college students in Barrie, Ontario.

Barrie is a moderately sized city with an approximate population of 197,800 in its census metropolitan area in 2013 (Statistics Canada, 2014). Almost 70% of the population reported a religious affiliation in 2011, with the majority of these belonging to Christian affiliations (Statistics Canada, 2013). The largest represented religious affiliations in the population were Roman Catholic (26.9%), United Church (10.7%), and Anglican (9.3%). The total visible minority population is substantially lower than Toronto and was 6.4% in 2011.

Method

Participants. Participants were 111 undergraduates from a psychology research participant pool at the Barrie Campus of Georgian College. A criterion for participation was that participants have a religious affiliation. All research materials were presented online. The mean age of participants was 22.11 years. Most participants were women ($n=67$). The majority of participants were Christian ($n=62$), and the remaining participants were Muslim ($n=2$), Buddhist ($n=2$) or Sikh ($n=1$) or provided their own labels that described their belief system. Participants who self-identified as Agnostic were excluded ($n=12$) and only participants who reported a religious affiliation were included in the analyses ($N=74$).

Materials and procedure. Materials and procedure were very similar to those from Study 1 although the data were collected at different points in time (3 years apart). The reliabilities for each of our measures were as follows: extrinsic religiosity ($\alpha=.78$), intrinsic religiosity ($\alpha=.93$), quest religiosity ($\alpha=.78$), openness to non-family ($\alpha=.74$), openness to family ($\alpha=.84$), personal openness to interfaith dating ($\alpha=.90$), and interfaith dating support ($\alpha=.84$).

Table 6.3 Study 2: Descriptive statistics of primary measures by friend and acquaintance relationships

Measure	Friend n=52		Acquaintance n=22	
	M	SD	M	SD
Time known target	3.84_a	2.02	2.77_b	1.95
Closeness to target	4.21_a	.85	3.05_b	1.36
Similarities listed	4.86	2.75	4.53	2.78
Extrinsic religiosity	4.23	1.26	4.18	1.26
Intrinsic religiosity	4.15_a	1.54	3.59_b	1.63
Quest religiosity	4.40_a	.93	3.64_b	1.60
Perceived interreligious similarity	3.582_a	1.23	2.52_b	1.03
Openness to family	4.44_a	.84	3.63_b	1.04
Openness to non-family	4.79_a	.50	4.43_b	.64
Openness to interfaith dating	5.32_a	1.63	4.42_b	1.60
Interfaith dating support	6.27	1.05	5.80	1.24

Note: Means with different subscripts within the same row are significantly different (see text)

Data analysis. The data analytic strategy was the same as in Study 1. Descriptive statistics can be found in Table 6.3.

Results

Group differences on individual difference variables. There were a number of differences between the friendship and the acquaintance groups. In terms of group assignment checks, Table 6.3 shows that participants in the friendship group had known the target person for a longer period of time compared to those in the acquaintance group, $t(71)=2.10$, $p=.04$, $d=.50$, and felt closer to him or her, $t(28)=3.72$, $p=.001$, $d=1.40$. The frequencies of the types of relationships with the target person further corroborated the validity of the friendship versus acquaintance groups. Specifically, among the friendship group, approximately 91% of participants reported that the target person was a friend, boyfriend, girlfriend, or spouse, whereas among the acquaintance group, approximately 55% reported that the target person was a friend and two people reported that the target was a girlfriend (but none reported that the target was a boyfriend or spouse). There was also a significant between-group difference for the quest dimension of religiosity, $t(27)=2.09$, $p=.05$, $d=.80$. As shown in Table 6.3, the friendship group had higher mean scores for both the intrinsic and quest dimensions than the acquaintance group.

Group differences on outcome variables. There were a number of moderate to large differences between the friendship and acquaintance groups on the outcome variables of interest. There was a significant difference in perceived interreligious similarity, $t(71)=3.47$, $p=.001$, $d=.82$. As shown in Table 6.3, the friendship group

Table 6.4 Study 2: Correlations between religious orientations and primary measures

Measure	Dimension of religiosity		
	Extrinsic	Intrinsic	Quest
Perceived similarity	−.10	−.11	.03
Outgroup family	−.04	−.15	.09
Outgroup non-family	−.03	−.17	.11
Openness to interfaith dating	−.09	−.35*	.07
Interfaith dating support	−.25**	−.36*	.01

*$p < .01$, **$p < .05$

perceived more interreligious similarity than did the acquaintance group. There was also a between-group difference for openness to family relationships with someone from the target person's religious group, $t(71) = 3.24$, $p = .002$, $d = .77$. As shown in Table 6.3, the friendship group was more open than was the acquaintance group. There was a similar significant between-group difference in openness to non-family relationships with someone from the religious group of the target person, $t(28) = 2.27$, $p = .03$, $d = .85$. The friendship group was more open than was the acquaintance group. Finally, there was also a significant between-group difference for personal openness to interfaith relationships, $t(71) = 2.16$, $p = .03$, $d = .51$. The friendship group was more open to interfaith dating than was the acquaintance group.

Correlational analyses of dimensions of religiosity. Correlations between the dimensions of religiosity and the other measures are shown in Table 6.4, where it can be seen that the intrinsic dimension was negatively correlated with personal openness to interfaith dating, and interfaith dating support. The extrinsic dimension was negatively correlated with interfaith dating support.

Results generally paralleled those of Study 1. Even in the less diverse context of Barrie, having a religious outgroup member as a close friend predicted more favourable responses to religious diversity. Specifically, those with close friendships with religious outgroup members perceived greater interreligious similarity and were more open to interfaith dating as well as family and non-family relationships with religious outgroup members.

As in Study 1, there were also individual differences between those with and without a close outgroup friend. Specifically, those with a close friendship with a religious outgroup member were higher in the intrinsic and quest dimensions of religiosity than those without a close friendship with a religious outgroup member.

Discussion

The main findings of this research relate to two primary themes. First, having a close relationship with someone of a religious outgroup is associated with favourable responses to religious outgroups. Second, dimensions of religiosity were related to attitudes toward religious outgroups, and intrinsic religiosity was consistently related to less openness toward interfaith relationships. These two themes will now be elaborated upon in turn.

The first major theme was individuals who had religious outgroup members among their closest relationships had more favourable responses to religious outgroups, compared to individuals who only had acquaintance relationships with religious outgroup members. Participants in the friendship group were more open to family and non-family relationships with a person from the religious outgroup of the target person. These results provide additional support for the finding that close interpersonal relationships with outgroup members are associated with more openness to close relationships with outgroup members (Van Laar, Levin, Sinclair, & Sidanius, 2005). Additionally, consistent with previous findings on contact and perceived similarity (Peterson, 2007), there was evidence that the friendship group perceived more interreligious similarity than the acquaintance group. Taken together, these results are consistent with the findings from contact research that suggest that intergroup contact is associated with positive outgroup attitudes (Hewstone, 1996; Pettigrew & Tropp, 2006) and provide evidence for the assumption that contact allows groups to recognise the similarities that they share (Hewstone, 1996). The present findings are also congruent with research that demonstrated that having interracial friendships (over and above interracial contact) predicts reports of interracial closeness (Tropp, 2007); for both our friendship and acquaintance groups, the target was someone with whom they were personally acquainted. Finally, the present findings suggest that interfaith close relationships predict positive outcomes analogous to those that have been found with other types of intergroup relationships.

Another important difference between the friendship and the acquaintance groups had to do with the generalisation of any positive attitudes associated with intergroup contact. One way of determining the extent of generalisation of attitudes from Person X to other outgroups was by assessing openness to interfaith dating. Indeed, participants in the friendship group were more open to interfaith dating than were participants in the acquaintance group. This is consistent with past research that has found generalisation of contact effects to outgroups not involved in the contact (Van Laar et al., 2005) and to general outgroup attitudes (Pettigrew, 1997). There was also evidence of generalisation of positive attitudes to the rest of Person X's outgroup among participants who had a close relationship with Person X. As mentioned above, participants in the friendship group were more open to family and non-family relationships with someone from Person X's religious group. Additionally, they saw more similarity between their own religion and that of Person X. Taken together, these findings suggest that close relationships with outgroup members are particularly likely to be associated with generalisation of contact effects to others in the outgroup of the close friend and to other outgroups as well.

Interestingly, there was a group difference in the friendship and acquaintance groups for the quest dimension of religiosity in both studies. Those in the friendship group were higher in quest than were those in the acquaintance group. This is consistent with past research that suggests that the quest dimension is associated with more open outgroup attitudes (Batson et al., 1993; Haji & Hall, 2014; Hunsberger & Jackson, 2005). Given the correlational nature of this result, multiple interpretations are possible. It could be that those who are high in quest are more likely to engage in close relationships with a person of another religion, or that those who are likely to engage in close relationships with a person of another religion become higher in quest. Regardless, the association between quest and openness to religious outgroups is consistent with past research on religious orientations and prejudice.

The second major theme was that dimensions of religiosity were related to openness toward interfaith relationships. In particular, intrinsic religiosity was consistently related to less favourable views of interfaith relationships. This appeared to be limited to close interfaith relationships, such as dating relationships and family relationships. Past research on religious dimensions suggests that intrinsic religiosity is associated with some forms of prejudice, particularly forms that are not outlawed or that are even endorsed by religious teachings (Batson et al., 1993; Hunsberger & Jackson, 2005). Results from the current research suggest that intrinsic religiosity may be associated with less open responses to intimate or family involvements with people of different religious groups. Whereas people high in intrinsic religiosity might be accepting of religious outgroup members when it comes to non-family relationships, this acceptance does not seem to extend to more intimate or family involvements. Family relationships and interfaith unions (and their offspring) may be perceived as particularly threatening to the future existence of the religious in-group, as past research on opinions about intimate interfaith relationships (Haji, Lalonde, Durbin, & Naveh-Benjamin, 2011) and interracial unions suggests (Lalonde et al., 2007).

The positive correlations between quest and favourable responses to close interfaith relationships appeared to be limited to the Toronto sample. Again, this may be related to different religious demographics in the two cities. The findings observed in Study 1 are consistent with past research that demonstrates a positive relationship between quest and favourable outgroup attitudes (Haji & Hall, 2014; Hunsberger & Jackson, 2005).

The present findings should be considered within the context of certain sample and design limitations. The younger adults that participated in the research are likely to differ from older adults in their religious motivations. Moreover, university students may have had particularly high levels of intergroup contact and more positive intergroup attitudes. Despite the ubiquity of intergroup contact in post-secondary settings, and in Toronto in particular, it is notable that there were still between-groups differences and that many of the findings were replicated with larger effect sizes in Barrie. The samples were predominantly Christian, and future research should assess the extent to which these results are replicated in other religious groups (e.g. Muslims, Jews, and Sikhs). Based on past research on intergroup contact, including meta-analytic evidence for the importance of cross-group friendship (Pettigrew & Tropp, 2006), one would expect similar results. An additional limitation is the cross-sectional and quasi-experimental design which does not allow for clear causal interpretations. However, past research (Pettigrew & Tropp, 2006) demonstrates that the causal sequence of contact on positive attitudes is substantially stronger than the reverse. Moreover, the strength of the present research design lies in its external validity and particularly in its usage of people's own real-world friendship experiences.

Conclusions and Implications

Having a close relationship with someone of a different religious group is related to positive reactions to religious diversity more generally. These positive reactions consisted of openness to relationships with religious outgroup members and greater perceptions of interreligious similarity. Intrinsic religiosity tends to be associated with less favourable views toward intimate and familial interfaith relationships, and subsequent research should examine more closely the relations between dimensions of religiosity and interfaith attitudes across a variety of settings.

The present results imply that one way to promote interfaith acceptance in diverse societies is through friendship. Even in societies with lower levels of diversity, and by extension fewer opportunities for interfaith contact, close interfaith friendship is associated with favourable views of interfaith relationships. To the extent that societal conditions facilitate interfaith friendships, peaceful relations between individuals may lead the way to more open interfaith attitudes in general.

Acknowledgment This research was partially supported by a Social Sciences and Humanities Research Council of Canada grant to the first author.

References

Allport, G. W. (1950). *The individual and his religion*. New York, NY: Macmillian.

Allport, G. W. (1954). *The nature of prejudice*. Cambridge, MA: Perseus Books.

Allport, G. W., & Ross, M. J. (1967). Personal religious orientation and prejudice. *Journal of Personality and Social Psychology, 5*, 432–443.

Aron, A., Aron, E. N., & Smollan, D. (1992). Inclusion of other in the self scale and the structure of interpersonal closeness. *Journal of Personality and Social Psychology, 63*(4), 596–612.

Batson, C. D., & Schoenrade, P. A. (1991a). Measuring religion as quest: 1) Validity concerns. *Journal for the Scientific Study of Religion, 30*, 416–429.

Batson, C. D., & Schoenrade, P. A. (1991b). Measuring religion as quest: 2) Reliability concerns. *Journal for the Scientific Study of Religion, 30*, 430–447.

Batson, C. D., Schoenrade, P., & Ventis, W. L. (1993). *Religion and the individual: A social-psychological perspective*. London, England: Oxford University Press.

Bogardus, E. (1933). A social distance scale. *Sociology & Social Research, 17*, 265–271.

Burris, C. T., & Jackson, L. M. (2000). Social identity and the true believer: Responses to threatened self-stereotypes among the intrinsically religious. *British Journal of Social Psychology, 39*, 257–278.

Cohen, A. B., & Neuberg, S. L. (2008, February). *The psychological omnipresence of religion*. Symposium presented at the Annual Meeting of the Society for Personality and Social Psychology, Albuquerque, NM.

Haji, R., & Hall, D. (2014). Quest religious orientation: Rising against fundamentalism. *Intellectual Discourse, 22*, 73–88.

Haji, R., & Lalonde, R. N. (2009, June). *Interreligious similarities: Predicting differences in religious outgroup bias*. Paper presented at the 11th International Symposium on the Contributions of Psychology to Peace, Coleraine, Northern Ireland.

Haji, R., Lalonde, R. N., Durbin, A., & Naveh-Benjamin, I. (2011). A multidimensional approach to identity: Religious and cultural identity in young Jewish Canadians. *Group Processes and Intergroup Relations, 14*, 3–18.

Hewstone, M. (1996). Contact and categorization: Social psychological interventions to change intergroup relations. In C. N. Macrae, C. Strangor, & M. Hewstone (Eds.), *Stereotypes and stereotyping* (pp. 323–368). New York, NY: Guilford Press.

Hills, P., Francis, L. J., & Robbins, M. (2005). The development of the revised religious life inventory (RLI-R) by exploratory and confirmatory factor analysis. *Personality and Individual Differences, 38*, 1389–1399.

Hunsberger, B., & Jackson, L. M. (2005). Religion, meaning, and prejudice. *Journal of Social Issues, 61*, 807–826.

Jackson, L. M., & Hunsberger, B. (1999). An intergroup perspective on religion and prejudice. *Journal for the Scientific Study of Religion, 38*, 509–523.

Lalonde, R. N., Giguère, B., Fontaine, M., & Smith, A. (2007). Social dominance orientation and ideological asymmetry in relation to interracial dating and transracial adoption in Canada. *Journal of Cross Cultural Psychology, 38*, 559–572.

Page-Gould, E., Mendoza-Denton, R., & Tropp, L. R. (2008). With a little help from my cross-group friend: Reducing anxiety in intergroup contexts through cross-group friendship. *Journal of Personality and Social Psychology, 95*, 1080–1094.

Paolini, S., Hewstone, M., Cairns, E., & Voci, A. (2004). Effects of direct and indirect cross-group friendships on the judgments of Catholics and Protestants in Northern Ireland: The mediating role of an anxiety-reduction mechanism. *Personality and Social Psychology Bulletin, 30*, 770–786.

Pargament, K. I. (2002). Is religion nothing but...? Explaining religion versus explaining religion away. *Psychological Inquiry, 13*, 239–244.

Pargament, K. I. (2013). Spirituality as an irreducible human motivation and process. *The International Journal for the Psychology of Religion, 23*, 271–281.

Pargament, K. I., Trevino, K., Mahoney, A., & Silberman, I. (2007). They killed our Lord: The perceptions of Jews as Descretators of Christianity as a predictor of antisemitism. *Journal for the Scientific Study of Religion, 46*, 143–158.

Peterson, T. J. (2007). Another level: Friendships transcending geography and race. *Journal of Men's Studies, 15*, 71–82.

Pettigrew, T. F. (1997). Generalized intergroup contact effects on prejudice. *Personality and Social Psychology Bulletin, 23*, 173–185.

Pettigrew, T. F. (1998). Intergroup contact theory. *Annual Review of Psychology, 49*, 65–85.

Pettigrew, T. F. (2009). Secondary transfer effect of contact: Do intergroup contact effects spread to noncontacted outgroups? *Social Psychology, 40*, 55–65.

Pettigrew, T. F., & Tropp, L. R. (2006). A meta-analytic test of intergroup contact theory. *Journal of Personality and Social Psychology, 90*, 751–783.

Shariff, A. F. (2008, February). *The social costs and benefits of religion*. Symposium presented at the Annual Meeting of the Society for Personality and Social Psychology, Albuquerque, NM.

Statistics Canada. (2013). *National household survey: Focus on geography series*. Retrieved from http://www12.statcan.gc.ca/nhs-enm/2011/as-sa/fogs-spg

Statistics Canada. (2014). Population of census metropolitan areas. *CANSIM table 051-0056*. Retrieved from http://www.statcan.gc.ca/tables-tableaux/sum-som/l01/cst01/demo05a-eng.htm

Tarakeshwar, N., Stanton, J., & Pargament, K. I. (2003). Religion: An overlooked dimension in cross-cultural psychology. *Journal of Cross-Cultural Psychology, 34*, 377–394.

Tropp, L. R. (2007). Perceived discrimination and interracial contact: Predicting interracial closeness among Black and White Americans. *Social Psychology Quarterly, 70*, 70–81.

Turner, R. N., Hewstone, M., & Voci, A. (2007). Reducing explicit and implicit prejudice via direct and extended contact: The mediating role of self-disclosure and intergroup anxiety. *Journal of Personality and Social Psychology, 93*, 369–388.

Van Laar, C., Levin, S., Sinclair, S., & Sidanius, J. (2005). The effect of university roommate contact on ethnic attitudes and behavior. *Journal of Experimental Social Psychology, 41*, 329–345.

Wright, S. C., Aron, A., McLaughlin-Volpe, T., & Ropp, S. A. (1997). The extended contact effect: Knowledge of cross-group friendships and prejudice. *Journal of Personality and Social Psychology, 73*, 73–90.

Chapter 7
Humanising and Dehumanising the Other: Ethnic Conflict in Malaysia

Daniel J. Christie and Noraini M. Noor

> *"Divide and rule, the politician cries; Unite and lead, is watchword of the wise".*
>
> ——Johann Wolfgang von Goethe

The origin of contemporary ethnic divisions in Malaysian society can be traced to Britain's imposition of a divide and rule policy that lasted until independence in 1957. Malaysians continue to grapple with inter-ethnic tensions and conflicts among ethnic groups and especially between Malays and Chinese Malaysians. While inter-ethnic divisions have structural roots that we will discuss, our emphasis is on the use of symbols in the form of statements by leaders of ethnic groups as a means of building political capital but at the cost of deepening ethnic divisions within the society. Specifically, we focus on the use of humanising and dehumanising rhetoric by political elite.

We begin by discussing the geohistorical context of Malaysia and government interventions and policies designed to prevent inter-ethnic violence. Then we turn to a consideration of the current state of inter-group relations and perceptions of the Other. The structural problem posed by the politicisation of education is raised and the prospect of improving relations through a reduction of politically motivated dehumanising rhetoric among political elite and the promotion of humanising rhetoric is proposed.

To these ends, in the current research we undertake four interrelated activities: We (1) develop and use a coding guide derived from previous conceptual and exploratory work on the twin processes of humanisation and dehumanisation; (2) delineate the semantic space occupied by humanisation and dehumanisation processes in the rhetoric of political elite; (3) test the degree to which the semantic

D.J. Christie (✉)
Institute for Social and Health Sciences, University of South Africa, Johannesburg, South Africa

Department of Psychology, The Ohio State University, Columbus, OH, USA
e-mail: christie.1@osu.edu

N.M. Noor
Department of Psychology, International Islamic University of Malaysia, Kuala Lumpur, Malaysia
e-mail: noraini@iium.edu.my

© Springer International Publishing AG 2017
M. Seedat et al. (eds.), *Enlarging the Scope of Peace Psychology*,
Peace Psychology Book Series, DOI 10.1007/978-3-319-45289-0_7

109

space we delineate on the basis of our coding system conforms to universal features of the constructs, humanisation and dehumanisation, as currently conceptualised in the scholarly literature as well as the extent to which the constructs are particularised, geohistorically situated, and do not conform to universalised features; and (4) identify specific ways in which rhetoric may be used more constructively in the Malaysian context to humanise the Other.

The Geohistorical Context of Malaysia

Throughout much of Southeast Asia, the preeminent concern is the pursuit of social justice through democratisation movements (Montiel & Noor, 2009) because historically many of these countries were under colonial rule, which was later replaced by authoritarian regimes that remain in power today (Noor, 2009). Colonial powers often consolidated their power through a "divide-and-rule" approach that created fault lines and conflict between ethnic groups, the remnants of which are evident in various contemporary identity-based conflicts (Rothman, 2012) around the world. In Malaysia, a country that was part of the British Empire, the dominant political party exploits ethnic divisions in order to remain in power.

Malaysia is a multicultural, multi-religious society comprised of three main ethnic groups: 61.4 % *Bumiputera* (50.4 % Malay and 11 % other indigenous groups), 23.7 % Chinese, 7.1 % Indian, and 7.8 % others. British colonialism, via its "divide-and-rule" policy effectively deepened the divisions between the ethnic groups by keeping them segregated geographically and treating them differently. The indigenous Malay peasantry lived in rural areas where they engaged in their traditional methods of agriculture and fishing, with little social mobility. The immigrant population of Chinese and Indian (known collectively as non-Malays), on the other hand, were involved with the British in large-scale commercial production in more urban areas. Ethnic division and conflict continue to be the focal concerns in Malaysia due to the legacy of colonialism.

Even before Independence in 1957, political parties in Malaysia were formed along ethnic lines with three main parties: United Malays National Organization (UMNO), Malaysian Chinese Association (MCA), and Malaysian Indian Congress (MIC). Malaysia's independence was made possible in large part through "the bargain", an informal agreement in which non-Malays received citizenship and were allowed unfettered economic activities in exchange for conceding political hegemony to Malays who controlled UMNO. Under "the bargain", the three political parties formed the Alliance coalition in which UMNO was the dominant partner and ruled the country until 1969.

"The bargain" was disturbed in the 1969 election when many Chinese voted for other Chinese opposition parties such as the Democratic Action Party and Gerakan Party, rather than the Alliance coalition. Malays perceived the loss of seats as a threat because according to "the bargain" their political dominance was supposed to counterbalance their disadvantaged economic position vis-à-vis Chinese. In the wake of Malay losses in the 1969 elections, inter-ethnic violence broke out in various parts of the country and although the official number of casualties was never made public, the memory of the inter-ethnic violence remains seared in the collective memories of Malaysians.

Policies to Prevent Inter-Ethnic Violence

According to popular consensus among the primary cause of violence was Malays' disadvantaged economic position. Therefore, in order to prevent further violence, the state vowed to take radical action to redress the economic disparity between Malays and Chinese Malaysians. The state aggressively implemented sweeping affirmative action policies designed to redistribute wealth to the Malays and reduce overall economic inequality in the society. The policies favoured Malays in politics and civil service, economics and business, education and language, as well as religion and culture (Haque, 2003).

Public education played a prominent role in affirmative action policies. The Malay language was aggressively promoted and English was gradually phased out of public education. Only private Chinese secondary schools were allowed to use English. Government funding to the vernacular primary schools (Mandarin and Tamil medium schools) was less than that given to Malay schools (Heng, 1997). At the tertiary level, quotas favouring Malays were introduced and government funding for scholarships was mostly limited to Malays. In the early years of the affirmative action programs, non-Malays generally accepted the view that these policies were needed to prevent a repetition of inter-ethnic violence and ensure long-term stability. The situation was also tolerable because the non-Malays did not perceive the increasing economic well-being of Malays in a zero-sum frame (Christie & Noor, 2012). The rapid economic growth between the early 70s to late 80s made it possible for non-Malays to continue to enjoy increases in their standard of living despite Malay centred-affirmative action policies (Lee, 2000).

Although over time the policies aimed at structural change did effectively redistribute resources, other policies introduced in the 1970s designed to assimilate non-Malays to the majority Malay ethnic culture (e.g. National Culture Policy) were contentious. Malay was declared the main language of the country and Islam, the religion of most Malays, became the state religion. Though this policy was replaced by *Bangsa Malaysia*, which emphasised an inclusive national identity under Prime Minister Mahathir Mohamed in the 1990s, politics remained ethnically based and the primacy of Malay culture eventually became non-negotiable. Anyone who raised questions about ethnic relations, affirmative action policies, or other matters could be prosecuted under the Sedition Act (Lee, 2000)—an Act that effectively increased state authoritarianism ostensibly to deter inter-ethnic conflict and promote "national unity". Although the consensus was that affirmative action policies were needed when they were enacted in order to correct for past structural injustices, the policies eventually became a source of contention between ethnic groups and exacerbated divisions.

Relations were further aggravated after the shock of the financial crisis in 1997. Malay elite reacted to the crisis by introducing Islamic discourse into mainstream politics thereby promoting a sense of in-group cohesion among Muslims to combat and suppress rising Malay dissent directed against the Malay elite—the main beneficiaries of the affirmative action programs.

Perceptions of the Other

The ethnic conflict remains manifest in perceptions of the "Other". For Malays, the other is "Chinese"—Chinese economic prowess and dominance in the corporate sector. From the non-Malay perspective, the "other" is "Malay"—Malay political dominance, their monopoly of the public and government sector, and preferential treatment. Malay is equated with being Muslim and hence, for the non-Malay the "Other" is not only the beneficiary of preferential government policies but also Muslim.

The Politicisation of Education as an Obstacle to Harmonious Relations

Under the British, education for the majority of the Malays was only at the primary level, except for children of aristocrats who were educated in English to prepare them for future positions in the colonial administration (Tilman, 1969). Education for Indians was also provided at the elementary level. The British, however, did not provide education for the Chinese; instead they were allowed to establish their own schools with their own curricula, teachers, and texts from China (Abdullah, 2004). Thus, during British colonial rule, there were four separate education systems: Malay, Chinese, Tamil, and English which differed in the medium of instruction and course contents. The main communication link between the ethnic groups was through their political leaders (Shastri, 1993).

Even before independence, it was recognised that the four separate education systems created by the British were deepening the division between groups. The main source of tension between the groups was the language of the education system. The Barnes Report (1951) proposed establishing a national public school with bilingual education favouring English over Malay, while the Fenn-Wu Report (Fenn & Wuu, 1951) advocated the continuation of the vernacular schools with Malay and English being taught together. The Razak Report of 1956, however, recommended continuing the vernacular schools but adopting a common curriculum. This was later modified to make Malay the official language of instruction at the secondary school level, an act that was seen as a move from a fragmented colonial education system to one that was more integrated along national lines. Malay was chosen over

English as the national language because of the latter's association with colonial rule. The use of Malay was also "a patriotic nationalist sentiment that was instrumental in resisting imperial hegemony and restoring the consciousness of the 'disadvantaged people'" (Quayum, 2003, p. 184).

Although the current government endorses national unity, the education curriculum continues to have a political agenda that emphasises loyalty and obedience to the current administration—UMNO. The politicisation of education has its roots in the colonial period, when the British sought to appease the Malay Sultans by claiming "Malaya as the ancestral land of the Malays", which was later reinforced during the Japanese occupation of Malaya, thereby fanning the flames of nationalistic sentiments in the Malays (Hwang, 2003). In recent years, the state has engaged in a form of historical revisionism by asserting *ketuanan Melayu*, which translates to Malay supremacy, Malay sovereignty, or Malay primacy. Radical Malay nationalists use *Ketuanan Melayu* to justify a nationalistic discourse (Ting, 2009; Vickers, 2002) that has found its way into the education curriculum. As evidence, Ting (2009) analysed the narratives of the latest editions of secondary history textbooks published by *Dewan Bahasa dan Pustaka*, the official body for coordinating the Malay language in the country. These new textbooks, published in 2002–2003, have been fiercely contested. Ting's (2009) research demonstrated how the reappearance of this term in early 2000s has gradually shifted the discourse on affirmative action from political and economic necessity to one of indigenisation and historical entitlement. The seeping of *ketuanan Melayu* discourse into history textbooks indicates the acceptance of an exclusive Malay nationalism within the state. These recent textbooks frame Malays and non-Malays as native and immigrant, respectively, and emphasise the foreignness of the non-Malays while stressing the indigenous status of the Malays. This historical revisionism is tantamount to a form of cultural violence in which Malay is privileged as the dominant national identity and positioned as the original people of the land (*Bumiputera*—sons of the soil), thereby justifying Malay dominance. Brown (2005) also came to a similar conclusion when analysing the curricula used in Moral Education and History (known as Local Studies at the primary level)—that Malaysians are defined first by their ethnicity, and second, indoctrinated to support the existing state. Hence, education has been politicised with the present curriculum promoting ethnic divisions rather than transcending ethnic loyalties. Today, *ketuanan Melayu* represents an ideology deeply embedded in UMNO to garner political and cultural dominance while, at the same time, deepen the ethnic divide.

In the context of Malay dominance, the Chinese have struggled to maintain their vernacular schools at the primary level and independent schools at secondary level. At present, there are two parallel education systems, the government system for the majority of Malays and the private system for the Chinese numerical minority. These separate systems reinforce the image of the "Other", threatening inter-ethnic harmony and national unity. The wider sociopolitical context has shaped the structure of the education system, maintaining and reinforcing separation between the ethnic groups, rather than enabling each group to reach out to the other to deal with the past and move forward to address the future.

A Case for Delineating Dehumanising and Humanising Rhetoric

Remnants of the British' "divide-and-rule" policy continue to be reproduced in Malaysian society in a number of ways including the segregated educational system (Hirschman, 1986). Theoretically inter-ethnic relations could be improved through the application of "contact theory" in which the polarised groups would be brought together to work cooperatively toward common goals, not unlike the way in which reconciliation continues to be promoted in Northern Ireland and elsewhere (cf. Hewstone, Cairns, Voci, Hamberger, & Niens, 2006). There have been calls for the state to implement psychologically informed policies that employ contact theory to improve intergroup relations (Christie & Noor, 2012) and recent research indicates that such an approach is feasible and has the potential to produce improvements in intergroup attitudes (Al Ramiah, Hewstone, Little, & Lang, 2014).

Indeed, since 2004, the Malaysian government has been implementing a large nation-building effort through the National Service Program, a multifaceted program that is in part designed to improve inter-ethnic relations. Every year, the program brings together about 100,000 17- to 18-year-old youth (out of approximately 400,000), selected carefully so that the composition represents the proportion of the three major ethnic groups in the society: Malay, Chinese, and Indian. Al Ramiah et al. (2014) examined the effects of the contact provided by this 3-month program with 859 participants from nine National Service camps that took place in Peninsular Malaysia. Controlling for intergroup contact prior to the program, the results indicated that intergroup contact during the program was associated with positive outgroup attitudes along with a reduction in the perception of realistic and symbolic threat and anxiety for most ethnic groups. These results are encouraging but as Al Ramiah and Hewstone (2012) concluded it is "a challenge to achieve the various factors promoting positive intergroup contact experiences in a climate that is fraught with longstanding inter-ethnic tensions and structural inequalities between groups (p. 253)". Another concern is that after the program, Malaysian youth return to their segregated schools, communities, and workplaces and continue to live within a deeply divided political system.

Notwithstanding the structural impediments to direct intergroup contact in Malaysian society, research on the potential impact of contact on intergroup relations as a result of National Service camps seems like an extraordinary opportunity to advance theory and practice. In addition, the Malaysian context seems well suited for efforts to improve relations through indirect means such as: (a) extended contact which occurs when one learns that an in-group member has an outgroup friend; (b) imagined contact in which a member of one ethnic group imagines interacting with a member of another group; and (c) vicarious contact, when a member of one ethnic group observes another member of the group interact with an outgroup member (Dovidio, Eller, & Hewstone, 2011).

Our approach complements previous efforts to promote intergroup harmony. Our work is based on the notion that when opportunities for direct and indirect contact between groups are minimal, a symbolic approach to improving relations is sometimes a viable option. Inspired by the work of Freire (1970), in the current research we sought to heighten awareness of the use of dehumanising and humanising language in Malaysian society. From Freire's (1970) perspective, conflict transformation is essentially a process in which the "Other" is made more fully human and humanisation is accomplished through three integral processes: critical reflection, dialogue, and action. Given the political realities of Malaysia and the segregated educational system, there are few opportunities for dialogue and action. However, the promotion of a "critical reflection" is possible and therefore, our approach is aimed at beginning the process of mapping the semantic space occupied by humanising and dehumanising rhetoric based on the statements of politicians. The use of political statements by political elite seems most appropriate as a starting point to increase awareness in Malaysian society because Malaysia's political system has authoritarian elements and Malaysians tend to accept hierarchical order in which everybody has their place. Deference to seniority, elders, and those in positions of authority is highly valued (see Hofstede, 1991). We suggest that shedding light on the way in which political leaders dehumanise the Other could heighten awareness among the populace.

However, the constructs of humanisation and dehumanisation lack clarity and consensus with respect to how and when such constructs are manifest in individual and collective statements and narratives. Therefore, we began our research with an exploratory study to evaluate the feasibility of the coding system we developed to identify humanising and dehumanising statements in the rhetoric of politicians. In the current research, we seek to further refine the coding system by using two different politically leaning newspapers and systematically sampling political statements from these newspapers. Our intention is to develop a coding guide that will allow researchers and practitioners to reliably identify instances of the twin constructs of "humanisation" and "dehumanisation" in Malaysia and potentially in other geohistorical contexts.

Methods

Development of a Coding Guide

Although an integrative model of dehumanisation does not exist, Haslam (2006) has provided a thoroughgoing review of the literature and a useful conceptualisation of dehumanisation processes. We drew on the research of Haslam, and Leyens et al. (2001) for both the exploratory study and current research. Specifically, Haslam

(2006) proposed a model of the dehumanisation process that consisted of two distinct types: *Uniquely Human (UH)* and *Human Nature (HN)*. *UH* distinguishes humans from animals and therefore, whenever "Others" are denied characteristics that distinguish them from animals, dehumanisation of the *UH* kind has occurred. *UH* dehumanisation often engenders a vertical comparison implying that the "Other" is below "Us". In contrast to *UH*, the *HN* type of dehumanisation refers to characteristics humans possess that are typical or central to their nature, such as warmth and personality as contrasted with cold, machine-like characteristics. Instead of the vertical comparisons associated with *UH* characteristics, *HN* often engenders horizontal comparisons that imply distance from human characteristics; the "Other" is not subhuman as in the case of *UH* comparisons; instead, the "Other" is nonhuman, distant, alien, foreign, automaton-like. *UH* and *HN* are not exclusive and individuals may be dehumanised in both ways.

Leyens et al. (2001) prefer the term "infrahumanisation" which refers to the common everyday experience of viewing outgroup members as less human than in-group members. Infrahumanisation does not deny the humanness of the Other and regards the Other as capable of experiencing basic emotions that are shared with animals (e.g. fear). However, the Other is not viewed as capable of complex, secondary emotions in which there is an emotional reaction to basic, primary emotions (e.g. being ashamed of experiencing fear). Hence, the Other is not fully human.

Recognising there is very little literature available to inform our efforts to develop a guide to identify if and when political elite use "humanising" statements, in the current study we assumed that humanising statements would be on the same semantic continua as dehumanising statements, albeit at the opposite ends. For instance, if dehumanisation is manifest when someone refers to the Other as "uncivil" (an animal-like referent), then humanisation occurs when the Other is referred to as "civil". A similar approach drawing on Haslam's (2006) conception of *UH* and *HN* traits has been used by Costello and Hodson (2010); however, their work asked participants to judge the degree to which the Other possessed the dehumanising trait (e.g. uncivil).

The left column of Table 7.1 presents a coding guide for characteristics that fall under the general category of dehumanisation of the *UH* type; their semantic opposites that characterise humanisation are found in the right column. Subscripts in Table 7.1 indicate whether the characteristics listed are taken from Haslam's (2006) model and review of the literature, or the research of Leyens et al. (2001).

Table 7.2 presents a coding guide for characteristics that fall under the general category of dehumanisation of the *HN* type along with their semantic opposites. Subscripts indicate whether the characteristics are taken from Haslam's (2006) review, model, or represent extrapolations from the model.

Finally, because some statements were selected that could not be coded using the system we developed, we placed these statements into thematic categories (e.g. statements of solidarity, equity) and later tested the degree to which statements could be reliably classified.

Table 7.1 Coding guide for characteristics of dehumanising and humanising, Uniquely Human (*UH*) or "animal-like" type

Dehumanisation	Humanisation
How they are seen: They are...	How they are seen: They are...
• Below us[a]	• Equal to us
• Uncivil (lack or have inferior culture)[a]	• Civil (have a respectable culture)
• Coarse or crude[a]	• Refined
• Immoral[a]	• Moral
• Childlike[a] (includes lazy/laid-back; ungrateful; greedy; irresponsible)	• Mature (includes hardworking; grateful; generous; responsible)
• Dominating[b]	• Accommodating
• Predatory/dangerous[b]	• Safe/innocuous
• Dependent[b]	• Independent
What they lack that is human. They...	What they have that is human. They...
• Are unintelligent or cognitively unsophisticated[b]	• Are intelligent or cognitively sophisticated
• Are irrational or illogical[b]	• Are rational or logical
• Lack language capabilities[b]	• Have language capabilities
• Have only primary emotions: anger, fear, surprise, joy, sadness, disgust.[c]	• Have secondary emotions: such as sorrow, fondness, contempt, conceit, admiration, disillusion
• Lack religious beliefs[b]	• Have a religion
Emotions and treatment they elicit. They elicit...	Emotions and treatment they elicit. They elicit...
• Contempt[b]	• Admiration
• Disgust or revulsion[b]	• Attraction
• Humiliation and degrading treatment[b]	• Dignity and respectful treatment

[a]Based on Haslam's (2006) model
[b]Based on Haslam's (2006) review of the literature
[c]Based on Leyens et al. (2001)

Sources of Data

Students of social psychology under the supervision of the second author examined newspapers for statements by politicians as part of a course assignment on stereotypes and prejudice, taught during the second year of the undergraduate psychology program at the International Islamic University Malaysia. The students were doing the same course but in two different sections. In one section, there were 46 students and 42 students in the other. Within each section, students were asked to work together in groups of 5–6 people, resulting in 8 groups per section. The majority of students were Malays and about 10–15% were international students (e.g. Sri Lanka, Indonesia, Sudan). Each group was assigned one of two newspapers, either *Utusan Malaysia* or *The Star*. The former is a Malay newspaper catering mostly to Malay readers and owned by UMNO; the latter is an English newspaper that has the largest circulation of all Malaysian newspapers with sales between 290,000 and

Table 7.2 Coding guide for characteristics of dehumanising and humanising, Human Nature (*HN*) or "machine-like" type

How they are seen: They…	How they are seen: They…
• Are distant from us (nonhuman, not subhuman)[a]	• Are close to us
• Do not have human qualities (machine-like)[a]	• Have human qualities
• Are passive and ineffectual[a]	• Are active and efficacious (have agency)
• Are cognitively closed or rigid[a]	• Are cognitively open or flexible
• Are superficial[a]	• Are deep
• Are objectified[b]	• Are personalised
• Lack personality traits[b]	• Have an agreeable personality
• Have an identity that is alien to our identity[b]	• Have a common or identity inclusive of us
• Are emotionally unresponsive[a]	• Are emotionally responsive
Emotions and treatment they elicit. They elicit	Emotions and treatment they elicit. They elicit
• Indifference toward them[c]	• Positive regard toward them

[a]Based on Haslam's (2006) model
[b]Extrapolated from Haslam's (2006) model
[c]Based on Haslam's (2006) review

300,000 copies daily. MCA is its biggest shareholder. As much as possible, the English newspaper was assigned to the group that had international students.

Students were not informed about the real purpose of the study but were asked to examine their assigned newspapers, which covered a 3-month period. Their task was to select statements from politicians that reflected the characteristics found in the scoring guides depicted in Tables 7.1 and 7.2. In order to aid students in how to select and code statements, they were provided examples from newspapers based on a previously conducted exploratory study. For the current study, newspapers covered a 2-year period, from January 2011 to December 2012. Table 7.3 indicates the newspapers and time periods covered by each group of students.

After the students collected and categorised statements, two Research Assistants (one for each section) and one of the authors (NMN) examined each statement and through consensus decided which statements best fit the characteristics in the coding guide depicted in Tables 7.1 and 7.2. Only at this stage were students informed of the purpose of the study.

Results

Table 7.4 provides the final tally of dehumanising and humanising statements by newspaper and year.

In Table 7.4, the number of "generated statements" refers to the number of statements students originally identified in the newspapers. The number of "selected statements" denotes the number of generated statements that were retained after the

Table 7.3 Time periods examined by eight groups of students from two sections of the social psychology course

Group	Section 1 Newspaper and time period	Section 2 Newspaper and time period
1	*The Star*: Jan–Mac 2011	*The Star*: Jan–Mac 2012
2	*The Star*: Apr–Jun 2011	*The Star*: Apr–Jun 2012
3	*The Star*: Jul–Sep 2011	*The Star*: Jul–Sep 2012
4	*The Star*: Oct–Dec 2011	*The Star* : Oct–Dec 2012
5	*Utusan M'sia*: Jan–Mac 2011	*Utusan M'sia*: Jan–Mac 2012
6	*Utusan M'sia*: Apr–Jun 2011	*Utusan M'sia*: Apr–Jun 2012
7	*Utusan M'sia*: Jul–Sep 2011	*Utusan M'sia*: Jul–Sep 2012
8	*Utusan M'sia*: Oct–Dec 2011	*Utusan M'sia*: Oct–Dec 2012

Table 7.4 Final tally of dehumanising and humanising statements

		Dehumanising statements				Humanising statements	
Year	Newspaper	No. of generated statements	No. of selected statements	Newspaper	No. of generated statements	No. of selected statements
2011	*The Star*	47	26	*The Star*	38	21
	Utusan M'sia	82	26	*Utusan M'sia*	13	16
2012	*The Star*	18	3	*The Star*	22	1
	Utusan M'sia	64	19	*Utusan M'sia*	45	6
	Total	201	74		118	45

researcher and research assistants discarded statements that did not fit the coding scheme. The researcher and assistants agreed that all of the retained statements fit the categories of the coding guide.

For both newspapers, every time period examined yielded more dehumanising than humanising statements. Overall, the number of humanising and dehumanising statements in reference to the Other decreased from 2011 to 2012 suggesting that both Malays and non-Malays toned down the rhetoric of humanisation and dehumanisation during the time period examined. During the time period, an election was expected to be held at the end of 2012. However, the election was postponed to May 5, 2013, which could account for the decline in rhetoric. No consistent differences in the newspapers were found.

Table 7.5 categorises dehumanising and humanising statements of the uniquely human (*UH*) type (animal-like or not like). *UH* themes include seeing the other group as below one's identity group, uncivil, coarse or crude, immoral, childlike in various ways (e.g. ungrateful, irresponsible, dependent), dominating, dangerous, incompetent, irrational, and lacking language abilities and religious beliefs. Emotions elicited include contempt and disgust. Finally, the dehumanised Other is treated in a humiliating and degrading way. In contrast, humanising processes that are seen as opposite of animal-like qualities included views of the Other as civil, refined, moral, mature, accommodating, independent, competent, rational, religious, admirable, and competent in language.

There were fewer instances of dehumanising and humanising statements that were coded as lacking the qualities associated with human nature *(HN);* that is, machine-like or its opposite. As indicated in Table 7.6, when *HN* statements were identified, they included references such as cognitively closed or rigid, passive and ineffectual, superficial, emotionally unresponsive, and having an alien identity. The Other was treated with indifference. When the features of human nature were identified (i.e. *HN*), statements conformed the following categories: warmth, friendly, loyal, obedient, tolerant, efficacious, cognitively open or flexible, emotionally responsive, and they are treated with positive regard.

Because the selection and classification of statements occurred in the Malaysian context, it seemed useful to elaborate on the context of the statements. Appendices 1 and 2 provide some context for the statements that were selected and classified in Tables 7.5 and 7.6. Appendix 1 offers some context for dehumanising statements and Appendix 2 for humanising statements. Superscripts denote the sources and dates of the statements.

The Semantic Structure of Humanising Statements

Statements by politicians (as recorded in newspapers) were readily coded using the categories depicted in the dehumanisation guide. In contrast, humanising statements were more difficult to code. A total of 22 humanising statements did not fit the coding categories. Apparently the process of humanising the Other is not simply the opposite of "dehumanisation" (e.g. civil versus uncivil). Rather, humanisation processes seem to have a semantic structure that is different from the well-documented structure of dehumanisation processes (Haslam, 2006).

Accordingly, we decided to take a more grounded approach and used the 22 humanising statements as data from which we inferred emergent categories, thus forming a more inclusive semantic structure of humanisation than the a priori structure based on categories that were the opposite of dehumanisation. The 22 statements were sorted and organised into the minimum number of categories that seemed to subsume all of the statements. The result was six additional humanising categories. The categories and defining features of each are given in Table 7.7.

Two judges independently placed the 22 statements into the six categories. They agreed on the placement of 18 of 22 statements and with further discussion appreciated each other's rationale for placement. Table 7.8 presents the consensus on statements that are subsumed by each category.

Table 7.5 Examples of dehumanising and humanising statements, Uniquely Human (UH) or "animal-like" type

Dehumanisation			Humanisation		
Categories and subcategories	Statements	Statements	Categories and subcategories	Statements	Statements
How they are seen: They are…	**How Chinese are seen: They are…**	**How Malays are seen: They are…**	**How they are seen: They are…**	**How Chinese are seen: They are…**	**How Malays are seen: They are…**
Below us	• Immigrants or *pendatang* vs. host or *tuan* (temporary vs. permanent) • Not allowed to buy land, rent, or live there because land is reserved for those with indigenous status	• Descended from *Sakai* (aborigines), thus, uncivilised	• Equal to us	• Chinese also sacrificed their lives (Japanese occupation and Communist insurgency) and this must not be disputed and should be remembered • Chinese language is an important asset of cultural diversity in Malaysia • Not all Chinese are rich; they should be helped on the principles of justice	
Uncivil (lack or have inferior culture)	• Causing discomfort to locals and inviting many adverse effects • Gathering turned into a show of anger unbecoming of Confucian values	• Practicing politics of hate rather than civil discourse	Civil (Have a Respectable Culture)	• Culture promotes and expects them to care for their descendants • Taking good care of the welfare of their people	

(continued)

Table 7.5 (continued)

Dehumanisation				Humanisation			
Categories and subcategories	Statements	Statements		Categories and subcategories	Statements	Statements	
Coarse or crude	• arrogant statements insulting Mahathir as senile and irrelevant • say disparaging things because they believe that not everyone understands their language			Refined			
Immoral	• Use various means to garner Malay votes by hiding the truth	• Misuse quotas and allocations • Majority frequent gambling centres • Many graft recipients		Moral	• Extends assistance to all races • Continues to serve the community despite losing seats in last election • Continuously strived to contribute to students despite their different political beliefs	• Channels aid transparently, regardless of race, religion and political background of victims • As-Siddiq Association offered aid to poor Chinese	

Childlike	• MCCA will strike back if bullies attack the party	• Keep asking for things, complacent, and tend to remain in their comfort zone • Squandering opportunities under the NEP • Continuous infighting among themselves • Still living in the past and highlighting things of the past	Mature	• Poem by Lim Swee Tin, titled "United Malays" has fired participants' passion • Cannot say the Muslim call to prayer (*azan*) as harassing the non-Muslims because religious festivals of the other races also are equally noise	• Highlighting shared values instead of racial or religious differences • Even the PM has publicly apologised to the people and promised to make changes
Lazy, laid-back		• Want to live well but are lazy and don't work hard • Lazy work attitudes and daydreaming	Hardworking		

(continued)

Table 7.5 (continued)

Dehumanisation			Humanisation		
Categories and subcategories	Statements	Statements	Categories and subcategories	Statements	Statements
Ungrateful	• Question Malay rights, Malay as national language, Islam as state religion • Push for Chinese primary and secondary education—makes Malay feel they are not inclined toward integration to acknowledge the identity of the land • Incessant attitude of asking seen as extreme and offensive. They take advantage because they know the government needs their support		Grateful		

			Generous
Greedy (wanting more than what is given, squandering opportunities, expecting something in return for some work)	• Want more than what they are given • Want to establish a Chinese township with Chinese uni., industries, etc., on the ground of bringing in Chinese investors, as if other races do not exist • No future in being a teacher because pay is too little	• Abused their special position to advance their own interests • Will not contribute willingly	
Irresponsible	• Building a Chinese cemetery near a Malay village	• Blame other races	Responsible

(continued)

Table 7.5 (continued)

Dehumanisation			Humanisation		
Categories and subcategories	Statements	Statements	Categories and subcategories	Statements	Statements
Dominating	• Dominate Penang government • Malay besieged by Chinese economies • If Kampung Baru is developed, only non-Malays can afford it • Did not give way to any Malay candidates	• Affirmative action instituted in recognition of their superiority • Will remain in power • Majority of employees in public sector are Malay	Accommodating		• Willing to vote for candidates who are not from the same ethnic group • All welcomed into the mosques, but must be respectful

Predatory/dangerous		Safe/innocuous
• Targets Malay youth who are ignorant of their history. • Opposed Malay hegemony. • Playing with issues relating to Islam—insensitive and dangerous • Chinese newspapers free to criticise the government, distort facts, manipulate situation, unethical, and do not care about other people's sensitivity.	• Mistrust the Chinese education system	

(continued)

Table 7.5 (continued)

Dehumanisation			Humanisation		
Categories and subcategories	Statements	Statements	Categories and subcategories	Statements	Statements
Dependent	• MCA must stand up for the Chinese • Dependent on Chinese organisations to fight for their rights and issues	• UMNO must stand up for the Malays. • Dependent on government for welfare aid	Independent	• Get into business to avoid working under other people	• Twenty-first century Malays no longer dependent on government handouts, and are able to compete with other races
What they lack that is human. They…	**What Chinese lack that is human. They…**	**What Malays lack that is human. They…**	**What they have that is human. They…**	**What Chinese have that is human. They…**	**What Malays have that is human. They…**
Are Unintelligent, Cognitively Unsophisticated, or Incompetent		• 67% of the population but control only 19% of country's economy • Fail to be entrepreneurs government assistance	Are Intelligent or Cognitively Sophisticated (e.g. can be engaged, cultivated to accommodate the "Other")	• Besides sciences and mathematics, also known for their business and entrepreneurial knowledge	

Are Irrational or Illogical	• Highly superstitious • The two numbers (4 and 7) are considered "bad"	• Islamic guidelines to be applied even to non-Muslims	Are Rational (e.g. able to discuss differences of views, dissenting opinions openly)	• Fresh approaches in responding to the demands of a changing political landscape…. • Gathering may get out of control, so better to seek a peaceful solution	
Lack language capabilities	• Young Chinese becoming monolingual • Chinese journalists not fluent in Malay language face difficulty in analysing issues in Malay papers • Chinese in villages unable to communicate in the national language	• Low graduate employability due to lack of English proficiency • Malays do not understand Chinese language	Have Language Capabilities	• Chinese-speaking populace gives the country an advantage • Foreign language proficiency is dominated by the Chinese • 24 % (seven million) ethnic Chinese can speak Mandarin, Hokien, Cantonese, Hakka, Teochew, Fuchow, and other Chinese dialects.	• More Malays speak Mandarin than ever before
Have only primary emotions: anger, fear, surprise, joy, sadness, disgust			Have secondary emotions: such as sorrow, fondness, contempt, conceit, admiration, disillusion		

(continued)

Table 7.5 (continued)

Dehumanisation		Humanisation		
Categories and subcategories	Statements	Categories and subcategories	Statements	Statements
Lack religious beliefs		Have a religion	• Festival promoted Buddhist core values • Celebrated the Nine Emperor Gods festival where Taoists and others pay respect to the gods	• Promoting *hudud* laws in Opposition-led states • Reminded Muslim and non-Muslim to maintain religious harmony in the country • Urged Malays to be united based on their Islamic faith • Make Islam the country's foundation using the *wasatiyyah* (moderation) approach • No compromise when it comes to the issue of their faith and practice

Emotions and treatment they elicit. They elicit	Emotions and treatment they elicit. Chinese elicit	Emotions and treatment they elicit. Malays elicit	Emotions and treatment they elicit. They elicit...	Emotions and treatment they elicit. Chinese elicit...	Emotions and treatment they elicit. Malays elicit...
Contempt (disrespect or intense dislike)	• Economically powerful though they are immigrants • Asking for flexibility in hiring quota for non-Malays	• Special privileges because they are Malays	Admiration (Good Example to Follow)	• Excel in basketball • Contributed to education • Known for their diligence, hard work, thrifty • Emulate the Chinese way of politicking	• Confident, public service-oriented young Malays who aren't bound by the legacies of the past
Disgust or revulsion	• Separate areas for sale of pigs and non-*halal* produce in markets and supermarkets		Attraction		
Humiliation and degrading treatment		• Give scant attention to the contributions of non-Malay communities, when they had played key roles in country's development	Dignity and Respectful Treatment		

Table 7.6 Examples of dehumanising and humanising statements, Human Nature (*HN*) or "machine-like" type

Dehumanisation			Humanisation		
How they are seen: They are	How Chinese are seen: They are	How Malays are seen: They are	How they are seen: They are	How Chinese are seen: They are	How Malays are seen: They are
Are distant from us (nonhuman, not subhuman)			Are close to us	• Develop their own language	
Do not have human qualities (machine-like includes materialistic; calculating; greedy)	• Insincere (DAP not sincere in accepting Malay members and do not trust them with important party roles)		Have human qualities	• Opportunists	• Warm • Friendly, conforming, loyal, obedient • Easygoing and tolerant • Malay's value system is one of tolerance and willingness to help, regardless of race
Are passive and ineffectual		• Depending on others considered normal	Are active and efficacious (have agency)	• Contributed to the country's economy	
Are cognitively closed or rigid	• Misunderstands Malay cultural symbols, equating them to religious beliefs • Never saw anything good in Malays and Islam • Issues reported in Chinese newspapers are biased	• Lack open-mindedness—cannot question their rights • Term "Allah" should only be used exclusively by them—suspicious that the word could be a ploy to convert Muslims	Are cognitively open or flexible	• Forum to educate MCA members on *hudud* • Ability is what counts, not a person's colour or race	

Are superficial	• History never showed that DAP fought for Malay rights	• Helping the Chinese community to fish for votes	Are deep	
Are objectified	• Exploit Malays for their votes	• Malays in DAP are puppets to be used	Are personalised	
Have an identity that is alien to our identity	• Chinese • Youth do not mix with other races • Go to Chinese schools, watch Chinese television shows, and socialise only with each other • Racist in demanding that non-Chinese speaking teachers be removed from vernacular schools • Language used as a race card because many things are politicised	• *Bumiputra* • "Malayness" determined by ethnic nationalists and religious fundamentalists • Race and other communal issues priorities among the Malays • Language used as a race card because many things are politicised	Have a common or identity inclusive of us	
Are emotionally unresponsive			Are emotionally responsive	• Young Chinese feel strongly about being treated differently, esp. in race-based policies

(continued)

Table 7.6 (continued)

Dehumanisation			Humanisation		
Emotions and treatment they elicit. They elicit	Emotions and treatment they elicit. Chinese elicit	Emotions and treatment they elicit. Malays elicit	Emotions and treatment they elicit. They elicit	Emotions and treatment they elicit. Chinese elicit	Emotions and treatment they elicit. Malays elicit
Indifference toward them	• "Chauvinistic"—concerned only with the Chinese, not thinking of the larger national agenda for all		Recognition of them	• Najib praises the Chinese community contributing to education in Malaysia • Organisers of the Selangor Taoism Unity dinner made sure the food was *halal*—Taoists respecting Muslim guests	• Do not question the rights of other races. We gave them citizenship rights, and we respect their rights

Table 7.7 Six categories or types of humanisation and their defining features

(1) Emphasising similarity
This is reflected in statements that point out that all groups are similar in some way or at some level. Typical statements emphasise similar, shared or common beliefs, values, interests, or social identities
(2) Honouring differences
This is reflected in statements that speak to the importance of allowing identity groups to be different from one another, endorsing tolerance and respect for everyone. Emphasis is placed on the importance of a multicultural society, the endorsement of tolerance and respect for everyone, preserving cultural differences, learning about other cultures, the value of pluralism or inter-ethnic harmony
(3) Espousing equal rights and treatment for all
This is reflected in statements that promote equality, fairness, and rights for everyone, an inclusive society in which power is shared and the interests and needs of all groups are taken into account; a society in which all people have representation and voice in matters that affect their well-being
(4) Solidarity
This is reflected in statements that underscore unity and standing together, uniting across societal divisions and power to all people
(5) Prosocial attributions
This is reflected in statements when members from one group refer to members of the other group as helpful, caring, cooperative, or serving others and society. Also reflected in statements that suggest members of the other group contribute in some way to the society or country
(6) Compound humanising statements
This is reflected in statements that include two or more of the five categories referred to earlier. Typically compound statements acknowledge or honour differences between the groups and then underscore the importance of solidarity, equality, or unity. Other combinations are also possible (e.g. equality and unity)

Discussion

Drawing on the substantial body of work on the concept of dehumanisation (cf. Haslam, 2006), we have developed a coding guide designed to begin mapping the semantic space occupied by the rhetoric of political elite when they dehumanise and humanise the Other. The geohistorical context in which the current study took place was Malaysia, a society that on the surface seems to be a stellar example of a place that tolerates and celebrates multiculturalism, but below the surface there are deep divisions between ethnic groups, especially Malays and Chinese Malaysians.

When there are intergroup divisions and conflicts in a society, psychologists often recommend interventions that reduce prejudice (Paluck & Green, 2009). Arguably, the preeminent method used to improve intergroup relations is derived from contact theory, which specifies and prescribes certain conditions under which group members are likely to form more favourable attitudes toward one another (Fisher, 1997; Johnson & Johnson, 1999; Pettigrew & Tropp, 2006). The Malaysian government has initiated a program in nation building that increases intergroup contact among youth; however, the short duration (i.e. 3 months) and extent (25% of

Table 7.8 Examples of humanising statements that were selected but outside the rubric of the guide

(1)   **Emphasising similarity**
Statement of similarity appears in (6) later

(2)   **Honouring differences**
An approach adopted by certain non-government organisations when championing Malay interests was "neither ensible nor necessary". They should take into account the sensitivities of the various races in our plural society. The parties should not be carried away by their emotions
"The country's founding fathers agreed on this multi-education approach so that the different races of the nation could continue to use their mother tongue as well as practise their traditions and cultures. Our founding fathers had opted for integration—rather than assimilation—among the different races". said Najib
The spirit of the Constitution was one of accommodation, compassion, and tolerance for all. Malay privileges were offset by safeguards for the interests of other communities
Most importantly, we all respect one another and we also know the limits of Islam such as they cannot take non-halal food, liquor
"Malaysia and its people have come very far since independence and are respected by many other countries for its achievements as well as multiracial harmony"

(3)   **Espousing equal rights and treatment for all**
Every race must be represented in the government
Funds were distributed regardless of Malays, Indians, and Chinese
What we want is a two-party system where all Malaysians could be taken care of, not UMNO takes care of the interests of the Malays, the MCA takes care of the Chinese, and the MIC takes care of the Indians (Also coded in category 4)
People regardless of race are invited to attend the ceremony
PM reminded the Cabinet ministers to recognise the rights of the people regardless of race and religion
We must pay attention to the needs of all races and demonstrate our intentions through action. We have to be fair to everyone
All citizens have the same rights under the Constitution, regardless of their ethnic background
Disagree with the idea of Malay supremacy; the power must lie in the hands of the *rakyat* (people)

(4)   **Solidarity**
The unity between the three races shaped our nation and the Malaysian race
Open houses during festive season are being held to strengthen the unity
Unfairness faced by the Chinese was also faced by the non-Chinese. We should stand together to ensure our children's future

(5)   **Prosocial attributions**
Although they are Chinese, it did not stop them from joining the parade together with the Malays

(6)   **Compound humanising statements**
It was important to promote togetherness, the Prime Minister said. "We all may be different in our (religious) beliefs but there are values we have in common that can strengthen unity and promote peace and harmony (1, 2)
Following others' cultures will not change us. We are still Malaysians (2, 4)
"We in Malaysia are rich in culture; that is why we need to respect all the festivals and invite our friends from other communities to celebrate them together through open houses" (2, 4)
Malaysians have to accept the political reality that the country is multiracial and everyone must work together to make it a peaceful and developed place (2, 4)
The use of different mother tongue was not a hindrance to national unity as 60,000 Malays had sent their children to Chinese schools (2, 4)

17–18 year olds) of the program combined with the difficulty of meeting optimal conditions prescribed by contact theory (Al Ramiah & Hewstone, 2012) pose serious obstacles. Hence, the remnants of a "divide-and-rule" policy instituted by the British continue to be reproduced throughout the society. Inter-ethnic contact between children is minimal because of segregated schooling, differences in medium of instruction, and different religious affiliations. Moreover, intergroup cooperation is undermined and inter-ethnic competition is sustained through the identity politics in which parties are organised by ethnicity.

Given the structural impediments that make intergroup contact difficult, we sought to offer an additional approach to improve relations by borrowing from some of the tenets of liberation psychology and in particular Freire's (1970) contention that the key to conflict transformation is through a humanisation process in which the "Other" is made more fully human. Our approach sought to document instances in which the political elite in Malaysia engaged in dehumanisation and humanisation of the "Other".

Evidence from the current research demonstrated the usefulness of Haslam's (2006) and Leyens et al. (2001) conceptions of dehumanisation as a guide for developing a coding system to classify the statements of political leaders. There was ample evidence that political elite often viewed the "Other" as animal-like and below them, using descriptions of the Other as uncivil, coarse, immoral, childlike, dependent, dominating, and dangerous. The Other was also depicted as machine-like with references such as superficial, lacking personality, and emotionally unresponsive.

Our analysis of articles from two newspapers over a period of time yielded more dehumanising than humanising statements. These findings could be an artefact of a negative selection bias in which students were more attuned to dehumanising statements or perhaps our coding system did not encompass all of the semantic space occupied by the construct of humanisation. At the same time, the emphasis on dehumanising the Other is consistent with the colonial legacy of Malaysia and the political mobilisation of ethnicity in which politicians are inclined to dehumanise rather than humanise the Other in order to garner support from their identity-based constituents. As Ratnam (1965) argued, ethnically structured parties would lose their influence and prominence if they acted to promote inter-communal partnerships, endorsed mutual concessions, and sought intergroup consensus on policies. In an ethnically structured society such as Malaysia, political party support and patronage are based on ethnic sentiments.

Humanising: A Prescription for Making the Other "More Fully Human"

Our analysis has produced evidence of humanisation. In the rare instances of humanisation, the Other was described as civil, moral, and mature. The particular cluster of dehumanising statements varied depending on whether the target was Malay or Chinese Malaysian. Malays, for example, viewed Chinese Malaysians as being below Malays. In contrast with the term *tuan* which signifies belonging or permanency, Malays refer to Chinese Malaysians as immigrants or *pendatang*, suggesting that they are temporary residents who do not belong to the land of Malaysia. Malays also viewed Chinese Malaysians as coarse (using profanities to describe the other), uncivil (disrespectful of others, ill-mannered, and uncouth), and childlike (ungrateful for questioning Malay rights, and greedy for wanting more than they are given). In the context of their business acumen and disproportionate influence on economic development, Malays viewed Chinese as dangerous (targeting Malay youth ignorant of Malay history, questioning Malay hegemony, and criticising the government in the Chinese media) and as dominating the economy. Malays also viewed Chinese as irrational, highly superstitious, and poorly proficient in the Malay language. Although the Chinese are often associated with Buddhism and Taoism, the Malays considered them to be lacking religious commitments. Malay contempt and disgust for the economic power of Chinese were sometimes expressed through sentiments like "Chinese Malaysians eat practically anything".

Through our coding analysis we noted that the Malays also see the Chinese as possessing *machine-like* characteristics: they are seen as highly materialistic, expedient, calculating, greedy, insincere, untrustworthy, cognitively closed to understanding Malay cultural symbols and religious beliefs.

In our coding analysis, Chinese Malaysians in turn view Malays as inferior by virtue of their aboriginal origins. From the Chinese perspective Malays are immoral, misuse privileges, and engage in corrupt practices like gambling and bribery. Chinese newspaper reports project Malays as childlike; they are said to relentlessly ask for things, squander opportunities, constantly fight among themselves, are overly dependent on others, lazy, and irresponsible. While Chinese Malaysians are viewed by Malays as lacking religious commitments, the news reports construct Malays as incompetent, passive, and ineffectual and lacking in business and entrepreneurial skills as, well as proficiency in English which is the preferred language of the private sector and commerce. Chinese Malaysians view Malays as irrational with respect to their adherence to Islamic teachings. In the news reports Malays as beneficiaries of government affirmative action policies are subject to Chinese ridicule, especially when the Chinese feel that their contributions have not been sufficiently recognised.

In summary, our coding analysis shows that members of each ethnic group view the Other as not fully human; however, the specific clusters of deficits vary depending on the source and target. Since it is possible to identity precisely the particular cluster of deficits each group possesses from the perspective of the Other, the current research points to a number of very practical and specific ways in which political elite could render the Other more fully human. For instance, Malay politicians could emphasise the contributions of Chinese Malaysians, exhibit admiration for their business acumen, and underscore the richness of a multicultural society with distinct ethnic groups united by a sense of belonging to the wider society. Chinese Malaysians could acknowledge the ways in which Malays exhibit responsible behaviour toward their families and society, engage in entrepreneurial ventures, and how many leaders are proficient in English and open to cultural and religious variations in society. Similar implications apply to journalists who may wish to engage in peace journalism and focus on instances in which inter-ethnic interactions are humanising rather than dehumanising (Galtung & Fischer, 2013).

Dehumanisation and Humanisation as a Function of Geohistorical Context

Our initial coding of dehumanising statements was based on a deductive approach whereby existing conceptual models of the dehumanisation process were used to arrive at categories to classify and code the dehumanising statements of Malaysia's political elite that appeared in newspapers. Statements were coded as humanising when they were the opposite of dehumanising statements (e.g. civil versus uncivil). However, after classifying as many statements as possible, there were additional statements that were selected in newspapers that were judged to be humanising but did not fit the classification scheme.

We used these additional statements and inductively arrived at six categories of humanisation: (1) comparisons that allude to intergroup similarity, (2) the honouring of intergroup differences, (3) espousal of equal rights and treatment for all, (4) the promotion of intergroup solidarity, (5) prosocial attributions, and (6) compound humanising statements that typically began with an acknowledgment of intergroup differences followed by one or more of the remaining aforementioned categories of humanisation (e.g. we are different but our values are similar). These six categories substantially enlarge the meaning of humanising the Other in the Malaysian context and underscore the importance of considering geohistorical context when attempting to map the semantic space occupied by the construct of humanisation. More broadly, the findings underscore the dangers of relying on binary conceptions of humanisation as simply the opposite of dehumanisation.

Although the Malaysian context is marked by deep ethnic polarisation, the dominant norms explicitly endorse multiculturalism rather than assimilation (Goh & Holden, 2009; Noor & Leong, 2013). An assimilation approach to intergroup relations would seek to diminish differences between groups, discourage distinct social identities, and emphasise a common identity based on hegemonic norms. There have been efforts to demonstrate how a common identity can be encouraged as a means of improving intergroup relations in some societies. For instance, research that employs the Common In-group Identity Model (Gaertner & Dovidio, 2000) is designed to re-categorise distinct identity groups into a single, superordinate group.

In the context of Malaysia, such an approach would encourage members of the ethnic groups to see themselves as Malaysians—an inclusive, superordinate group—not as Malays or Chinese.

However, in light of how firmly Malaysians have embraced a multicultural model, the notion of a single social identity that diminishes the importance of ethnic differences is not tenable. Instead, a Dual Identity Model (Dovidio, Gaertner, & Saguy, 2007) that honours differences while endorsing intergroup harmony and mutual well-being would seem most appropriate and desirable for improving intergroup relations. In Malaysia, the kinds of statements we observed that fit this general formula for improving relations were the "compound humanising statements" (e.g. "Yes, we have different beliefs but the values are universal like politeness, respect for elders, trust and diligence"). Hence, it seems likely that the semantic referents that define what it means to humanise the Other will vary depending on the larger geohistorical context in which the society is embedded.

Conclusions

The results of the current study suggest that the social fabric of Malaysia continues to be divided by political elite who use dehumanisation as a tool to shore up support among members of their own party. In order to move toward some kind of reconciliation, it would seem important to raise awareness of dehumanising and humanising processes that divide and unite people. In this respect, politicians have an important role to play. They can act as models and use the media as a means of humanising the Other thereby promoting constructive rhetoric that lays the foundation for dialogue, intergroup contact, collaborative relationships, and joint problem-solving. An important question to be explored is how constituencies react to efforts by politicians to humanise the Other? The question of reactions to humanising initiatives, particularly when the Other is viewed as an adversary or enemy, seems like a fruitful question to pursue in further research as we seek to more acutely comprehend the nature, function, and consequences of humanising and dehumanising processes.

Finally, our results also compel us to exercise caution about a priori notions of what constitutes humanising statements in a particular society. It is clear that the process of humanising the "Other" is complex and occupies a semantic space that is not simply the opposite of dehumanisation. Moreover, we would expect humanising processes to be socially constructed and nuanced by geohistorical context. In Malaysia, for instance, given the value placed on multiculturalism, an approach to humanising the Other that emphasises only intergroup similarities and ignores the salience of distinct social identities seems unlikely to improve intergroup relations. Instead, for the Malaysian context, an affirmation of different social identities combined with some sort of recognition of common purpose or similarity seems most likely to create conditions that favour intergroup harmony and equity. Accordingly, we suspect future investigators will find it most useful to use a grounded approach and inductive procedures in order to arrive at categories of humanisation that are sufficiently nuanced and appropriate for other geohistorical contexts.

Appendix 1: Some Context for Selected Dehumanising Statements

Dehumanisation		
[*UH*] How they are seen: They are…	[*UH*] How Chinese are seen: They are…	[*UH*] How Malays are seen: They are…
Below us	• Words like *pendatang* and *penumpang* directed at fellow non-Malay citizens[a] • Kampung Baru is located on Malay reserved land, thus non-Malays are not allowed to buy land, rent or live there[b]	• Assume Malays are descended from Sakai (aborigines), thus, uncivilised[c] (trans.)
Uncivil (lack or have inferior culture)	• Penang DAP government, sponsored by a beer company, organised a massive concert in Batu Feringgi causing discomfort to locals and inviting many adverse effects[d] (trans.) • What was touted as a peaceful gathering to highlight the serious shortage of Chinese vernacular school teachers turned into a show of anger, hardly reflective of the community's cherished Confucian values[e]	• The Malay community has made a mistake by practicing the politics of hate while containment measures are not taken[f] (trans.)
Coarse or crude (profanities used to describe the other)	• Pua's arrogant statement insulting Mahathir as senile and irrelevant. This is due to the statesman saying that voting for the opposition is like voting for George Soros, the rogue currency speculator (DAP, Tony Pua)[g] (trans.) • Chinese newspapers seen as daring to say anything they like because they believe that not all Malaysians understand their language[h]	
Immoral (misuse quotas, gambling, and receiving grafts)	• DAP leaders use various means to garner Malay votes by hiding the truth[i]	• Misuse quotas and allocations[j] • 90 % of those who frequent gambling centres are Malay Muslim[k] (trans.) • Many graft recipients are Muslim[l] (trans.)

(continued)

(continued)

Dehumanisation		
Childlike	• MCA will strike back if "bullies" attack the party again. We cannot allow people to spit on us anymore[m]	• …people who keep asking for things, complacent and remain in one's comfort zone[n] (trans.) • Greedy of squandering opportunities under the NEP • Malays continuous infighting among themselves will result in their decreased dominance and power and eventually, destroy themselves[o] (trans.) • UMNO still living in the past, they keep highlighting things of the past, like the shepherd boy intimidating people. This scenario is often mentioned and repeated with the assumption that voters will vote for them[p] (trans.)
Lazy, laid-back		• These *Bumiputra* want to live well but are lazy to work[q] (trans.) • Lazy work attitudes and daydreaming among indigenous entrepreneurs hinder government efforts to make them successful businessmen[r] (trans.)

(continued)

(continued)

Dehumanisation		
Ungrateful (questioning rights of Malays, and not wanting to integrate)	• Ungrateful because they <u>question Malay rights, Malay as national language, Islam as state religion</u> • <u>Push for Chinese primary and secondary education</u> by the Chinese community has caused the Malays to feel they are <u>not inclined toward integration that acknowledges the identity of the land</u>^s • The <u>Chinese community</u> in the country <u>should be grateful</u> to <u>government for recognising Chinese education</u>. Datuk Seri Muhd Hilmi said, "This <u>incessant attitude of asking</u> by the Chinese community is now <u>seen to be extreme and offensive</u> by the other races especially Malays. They seem to <u>take advantage</u> because they know the government needs the support and they ask all sorts of things^t (trans.)	
Greedy (wanting more than what is given, squandering opportunities, expecting something in return for some work)	• Ungrateful for <u>wanting more than what they are given</u>. • To <u>establish a Chinese township with Chinese university, industries, etc.</u> on the ground of bringing in Chinese investors, as if other races do not exist^u (trans.) • In the past Chinese considered a <u>teacher's pay is too little</u> and thus, there is <u>no future in being a teacher</u>^v (trans.)	• *Bumiputras* <u>abused their special position</u> (as in the Malaysian Constitution and certain public policies) <u>to advance their own interests</u>^w • Dr. Mahathir: "Now, if we ask (UMNO) members to continue to contribute, <u>they will ask for something in return</u>"^x
Irresponsible	• <u>Building a Chinese cemetery</u>, 76.4 hectares, <u>near a Malay village</u>. Villagers protested because the number of non-Malays around the area is only 2000 compared to 17,000 Malays^y (trans.)	• Often <u>blame other races</u>, accusing them of grabbing our opportunities^z (trans.)

(continued)

(continued)

Dehumanisation		
Domination	<ul><li>Chinese dominate Penang government[aa]</li><li>Malay besieged by Chinese economies[ab] (trans.)</li><li>Kampung Baru will disappear as an area for Malays if it is developed because only non-Malays can afford it[ac]</li><li>The Chinese dominated party did not give way to any Malay candidates including Zairil Khir Johari who served as political secretary to DAP's secretary-general, Guan Eng[ad] (trans.)</li></ul>	<ul><li>Malays think that the affirmative action instituted by the government is recognition of their superiority[ae]</li><li>Kampung Baru is located on Malay reserved land, thus non-Malays are not allowed to buy land, rent, or live there[af]</li><li>Malays will remain in power in the country if UMNO continues to be a strong party[ag] (trans.)</li><li>Chinese find it difficult to interact within the public sector because majority of its employees are Malay[ah] (trans.)</li></ul>
Predatory/dangerous	<ul><li>DAP targets Malay youth who are ignorant of their history by creating a perception of materialism, freedom, etc. to weaken them[ai] (trans.)</li><li>DAP's platform at that time was the Setapak Declaration of Principles, which in principle opposed Malay hegemony[aj] (trans.)</li><li>Lately, DAP has been playing with issues relating to Islam, which is deemed insensitive and dangerous[ak] (trans.)</li><li>Chinese newspapers are free to criticise the government, distort facts, manipulate situation, unethical, and do not care about other people's sensitivity[al] (trans.)</li></ul>	<ul><li>Malay mistrust the Chinese education system[am] (trans.)</li></ul>
Dependent	<ul><li>"MCA must stand up for the Chinese and similarly, UMNO for the Malays and MIC, the Indian community". Political parties still racially divided[an]</li><li>Dependent on a number of Chinese organisations (Hua Zong) to fight for their rights and issues[ao] (trans.)</li></ul>	<ul><li>"MCA must stand up for the Chinese and similarly, UMNO for the Malays and MIC, the Indian community". Political parties still racially divided[ap]</li><li>Malay community too dependent on the government for welfare aid[aq]</li></ul>

(continued)

(continued)

Dehumanisation		
[*UH*] What they lack that is essentially human. They…	**What Chinese lack that is essentially human. They…**	**What Malays lack that is essentially human. They…**
Are unintelligent, cognitively unsophisticated, or incompetent		• *Bumiputra* make up 67 % of the Malaysian population but they control only 19 % of country's economy[ar] (trans.) • Failure of Malay entrepreneurs despite the many government assistance given[as] (trans.)
Are irrational or illogical	• Chinese couples avoid suspicious months and choose more favourable times to fix their wedding days. Chinese community highly superstitious[at] • The two numbers (4 and 7) are considered "bad" as 4 sounds like death in Chinese while the Hungry Ghost Festival falls on the 7th month of the lunar calendar[au]	• PAS wanted Islamic guidelines to be applied more strictly, even among non-Muslims[av]
Lack language capabilities	• Young Chinese seem to have become almost monolingual. If approached in Mandarin or Cantonese, when you reply in English, they will struggle to converse with you, said Dr Ghauth[aw] • Because Chinese newspaper journalists are not fluent in both Malay (and English), they face difficulty in analysing issues in the Malay papers[ax] (trans.) • Most Chinese living in Chinese villages are unable to communicate in the national language[ay] (trans.)	• He (Ghauth Jasmon) mentioned that (Malay) students had the lowest graduate employability rate due to lack of English proficiency[az] • Because Chinese have been in this country for a long time, they understand Bahasa Melayu but Malays do not understand Chinese language[ba] (trans.)
Have only primary emotions: anger, fear, surprise, joy, sadness, disgust		
Lack religious beliefs		
[*UH*] Emotions and treatment they elicit. They elicit	**Emotions and treatment they elicit. Chinese elicit**	**Emotions and treatment they elicit. Malays elicit**
Contempt (disrespect or intense dislike)	• Economically powerful though they are immigrants • Asking for flexibility in hiring quota for non-Malays in the public sector[bb] (trans.)	• Special privileges because they are Malays

(continued)

(continued)

Dehumanisation		
Disgust or revulsion	• Eat pigs, blood—separate areas for the sale of these products in markets and supermarkets	
Humiliation and degrading treatment		• History textbooks do not highlight and give scant attention to the contributions of the non-Malay communities, when they had key roles in the development of the country[bc]
[HN] How they are seen: They	**[HN] How Chinese are seen: They are**	**[HN] How Malays are seen: They are**
Are distant from us (nonhuman, not subhuman)		
Do not have human qualities (machine-like): includes materialistic; calculating; greedy; cold; insincere)		
	• Kit Siang and Guan Eng (DAP) are not sincere in accepting Malay members and at the same time do not trust them in giving important roles in the party[bd] (trans.)	
Are passive and ineffectual		• *Bumiputra* consider depending on others as normal[be] (trans.)
Are cognitively closed or rigid	• Misunderstand Malay cultural symbols as part of religious beliefs, e.g. Chinese wearing a baju kurung is like betraying one's faith[bf] • Muhyiddin said DAP never saw anything good in Malays and Islam[bg] • Many issues reported in Chinese newspapers are biased[bh] (trans.)	• Lack open-mindedness, e.g. cannot question their rights • Malay Muslims feel that the term "Allah" should only be used exclusively by them. They are suspicious that the word, so closely associated with Islam, could be a ploy to convert Muslims[bi]
Are superficial	• DPM Muhiyuddin warned Malay voters not to fall for the tricks of the DAP, saying it might field Malay candidates in the next general election. Also said history never showed that DAP fought for Malay rights[bj]	• Chua Soi Lek said Nik Abdul Aziz (PAS) is suddenly interested in helping the Chinese community, as a means of fishing for votes[bk]

(continued)

(continued)

Dehumanisation		
Are objectified	• DAP just want to exploit Malays for their votes[bl] (trans.)	• The few Malays in DAP are seen as puppets to be used as was done by Lee Kuan Yew years ago[bm] (trans.)
Lack personality traits		
Have an identity that is alien to our identity	• Chinese	• *Bumiputra* • Notion of "Malayness" is increasingly being determined by these two forces—Perkasa fronting ethnic nationalists and PAS *ulama* leading the religious fundamentalists[bn]
Are closed, clique together	• Chinese youth do not mix with those from other races[bo] (trans.) • DAP, though a socialist party is only concern with fighting for the Chinese[bp] (trans.) • Currently, Chinese children go to Chinese schools, watch Chinese television shows, and socialise only with each other[bq] (trans.) • Dong Zong (United Chinese School Committees Association of Malaysia) was criticised for being racist in demanding that non-Chinese speaking teachers be removed from vernacular schools[br] • Because many things are politicised, even language is used as a race card rather than a national vision to unite the groups[bs] (trans.)	• Race and other communal issues figured prominently as priorities among the Malays. 47 % said race and ethnicity issues would affect the way they vote[bt] • Because many things are politicised, even language is used as a race card rather than a national vision to unite the groups[bu] (trans.)
Are emotionally unresponsive		
[*HN*] Emotions and treatment they elicit. They elicit	**Emotions and treatment they elicit. Chinese elicit**	**Emotions and treatment they elicit. Malays elicit**
Indifference toward them	• Dong Zong's actions could be considered "chauvinistic" because they are only concerned with the Chinese without thinking of the larger national agenda for all races in Malaysia[bv] (trans.)	

[a]"1 Malaysia-20 months on", *The Star*, Thursday, January 6, 2011
[b]"Kampung Baru redevelopment—an ambitious project", *The Star*, Saturday, July 30, 2011
[c]"Kisah seorang budak Cina", *Utusan Malaysia*, October 2, 2011

(continued)

(continued)

[d]"Penduduk kesal konsert anjuran kerajaan DAP Pulau Pinang", Jamaluddin Hashim, *Utusan Malaysia*, November 13, 2012

[e]"Be civil even when angry", *The Star*, March 29, 2012

[f]"Kerjasama Politik Elak Perpecahan", *Utusan Malaysia*, Jun 25, 2012

[g]"Penghinaan Tony Pua perbuatan biadab", *Utusan Malaysia*, October 10, 2012

[h]"Ketidakadilan kebebasan akhbar di Malaysia—Zainuddin Maidin". *Utusan Malaysia*, August 4, 2012

[i]"Keluar pakatan jika tentang *hudud*", *Utusan Malaysia*, September 18, 2012

[j]"Malaysia's 'Ali Baba' entente under strain", *The Star*, March 22, 2011

[k]"90 % pelanggan pusat judi Melayu" *Utusan Malaysia*, April 11, 2011

[l]"Hanya orang tidak beriman terlibat rasuah", *Utusan Malaysia*, April 17, 2011

[m]"Party to strike back at the 'bullies'," *The Star*, Monday, October 3, 2011

[n]Datuk Seri Najib Tun Razak on, "Saham bumiputera tinggal RM 2 billion" *Utusan Malaysia*, Mar 25, 2011,

[o]"UMNO 65 tahun dan perjuangan Melayu", *Utusan Malaysia*, May 13, 2011

[p]"Isu-isu akhbar Cina", *Utusan Malaysia*, December 13, 2012

[q]"Isu-isu akhbar Cina", *Utusan Malaysia*, October 6, 2011

[r]"Sikap malas, suka berangan kekang usahawan bumiputera", *Utusan Malaysia*, February 27, 2011

[s]"1Malaysia-20 months on", *The Star*, Thursday, January 6, 2011

[t]Masyarakat Cina jangan terlalu meminta-minta, *Utusan Malaysia*, Oktober 19, 2012

[u]Dr. Mohd Ridhuan Tee, "Dimana agenda nasional?" *Utusan Malaysia*, Mei 1, 2011 http://blis2.bernama.com/getArticle.do?id=44289&tid=97&cid=3

[v]"Isu-isu Akhbar Cina", *Utusan Malaysia*, February 23, 2011

[w]"1Malaysia-20 months on", *The Star*, Thursday, January 6, 2011

[x]"Dr. M: UMNO not ready for polls", *The Star*, Monday, October 3, 2011

[y]"Penduduk bantah bina jirat Cina", *Utusan Malaysia*, October 9, 2011

[z]"Jangan salahkan bangsa lain", *Utusan Malaysia*, Mac 24, 2011

[aa]"Starts of Lim's Malay dilemma", *The Star*, Sunday, August 14, 2011

[ab]"Perjuangan A. Samad Said" *Utusan Malaysia* Mei 28, 2011, http://blis2.bernama.com/getArticle.do?id=54221&tid=97&cid=3

[ac]"Kampung Baru one of my failures, admits Dr Mahathir", *The Star*, Tuesday, January 11, 2011

[ad]"Tiada calon Melayu dipilih", *Utusan Malaysia*, December 16, 2012

[ae]"Dr M and the new dilemma", *The Star*, Friday, March 11, 2011

[af]"Kampung Baru redevelopment—an ambitious project", *The Star*, Saturday, July 30, 2011

[ag]"Melayu dominan jika UMNO kuat", *Utusan Malaysia*, September 22, 2012

[ah]"Isu-isu akhbar Cina", *Utusan Malaysia*, Ogos 9, 2012

[ai]"Waspada Serangan Psikologi DAP lemahkan Melayu" *Utusan Malaysia*, Mei 23, 2011

[aj]"Digniti Melayu Abad Ke-21", *Utusan Malaysia*, February 16, 2011

[ak]"Kenyataan Guan Eng terus dikecam", *Utusan Malaysia*, December 26, 2012

[al]"Ketidakadilan kebebasan akhbar di Malaysia-Zainuddin Maidin". *Utusan Malaysia*, August 4, 2012

[am]"Penting persepsi Melayu kepada pendidikan Cina", *Utusan Malaysia*, April 5, 2012

(continued)

(continued)

[an]"MCA needs your support, Adnan tells Chinese", *The Star,* Thursday, January 13, 2011

[ao]"Isu-isu akhbar Cina". *Utusan Malaysia*, Ogos 9, 2012

[ap]"MCA needs your support, Adnan tells Chinese", *The Star,* Thursday, January 13, 2011

[aq]"Malays must change their freebie mindset, says Dr M", *The Star*, October 13, 2011

[ar]"Bumiputera perlu bangkit kuasai ekonomi", *Utusan Malaysia*, Februari 27, 2011,

[as]"Bertindak susun semula ekonomi Melayu" *Utusan Malaysia*, Mac 31, 2011

[at]"11.11.11—The hottest date to wed", *The Star*, Monday, October 3, 2011

[au]"Johor Sultan is owner of number plate WWW 1", *The Star*, Tuesday, May 29, 2012

[av]"Cinema ban unfair to Bangi folk, says MCA", *The Star*, Friday, October 21, 2011

[aw]"A handicap we must overcome", *The Star*, Sunday, March 13, 2011

[ax]"Akhbar-akhbar Cina tiup sentimen perkauman", *Utusan Malaysia,* April 26, 2011

[ay]"Isu-isu akhbar Cina", *Utusan Malaysia*, Oktober 6, 2011

[az]"A handicap we must overcome", *The Star*, Sunday, March 13, 2011

[ba]"Isu-isu akhbar Cina", *Utusan Malaysia*, Disember 29, 2011

[bb]"Isu-isu akhbar Cina", *Utusan Malaysia*, Ogos 9, 2011

[bc]"Factual gaps and biases", *The Star*, Sunday, September 25, 2011

[bd]"Rasis dan kroni", *Utusan Malaysia*, Januari 29, 2012

[be]"Isu-isu akhbar Cina", *Utusan Malaysia*, Oktober 6, 2011

[bf]"Blurring race and religion", *The Star*, Sunday, February 27, 2011

[bg]"DPM: All we need is UMNO", *The Star*, Wednesday, November 30, 2011

[bh]"Jangan pandang mudah akhbar Cina", *Utusan Malaysia*, Jun 20, 2012

[bi]"Find a way out of this deadlock", *The Star*, Sunday, March 20, 2011

[bj]"DAP fielded Malays in all 10 GEs, says Kit Siang", *The Star*, May 26, 2011

[bk]"Chua: No need to meet Nik Aziz", *The Star*, April 11, 2011

[bl]"Melayu muak penghinaan DAP", *Utusan Malaysia*, Oktober 23, 2012

[bm]"DAP, rasis, Kuan Yew dan Anwar", *Utusan Malaysia*, Disember 19, 2010

[bn]"For sure public advocacy is here to stay", *The Star*, Tuesday, November 8, 2011

[bo]"Perpaduan antara jalan penyelesaian", *Utusan Malaysia*, Oktober 29, 2011

[bp]"Realiti Perkauman Politik DAP" *Utusan Malaysia,* Mei 3, 2011

[bq]"Perpaduan antara jalan penyelesaian", *Utusan Malaysia*, Oktober 29, 2011

[br]"Puad Zarkashi blasts 'racist' Dong Zong", *The Star*, April 2, 2012

[bs]"Pasar bahasa dan sikap bangsa", *Utusan Malaysia*, Oktober 6, 2011

[bt]"Penang Malays want recognition", *The Star*, Friday, November 18, 2011

[bu]"Pasar bahasa dan sikap bangsa", *Utusan Malaysia*, Oktober 6, 2011

[bv]"Cubaan timbulkan kebencian", *Utusan Malaysia*, November 27, 2012

Appendix 2: Some Context for Selected Humanising Statements

Humanisation		
[*UH*] How they are seen: They are…	[*UH*] How Chinese are seen: They are…	[*UH*] How Malays are seen: They are…
Equal to us	• "Chinese also sacrificed their lives during the Japanese occupation and Communist insurgency", said Najib, adding that this must not be disputed and should be remembered[a] • Ismail Sabri believed that the Chinese language is an important asset in the cultural diversity heritage of Malaysia besides Bahasa Melayu. He also added that only when we understand the cultures of other races, can the bond of unity be fostered[b] (trans.) • Not all Chinese are rich; some are poor with low income. They should also be helped on the principles of justice[c]	
Civil (have a respectable culture)	• Chinese culture promotes and expects them to care for their descendents by engaging in economic activities[d] (trans.) • Taking good care of the welfare of their people[e] (trans.)	
Refined		
Moral	• We may be a Chinese-based party, but when it comes to helping others, we extend assistance to all races[f] • "MCA is always relevant. We continue to serve the community despite losing many seats in the last election"[g] • has continuously strived to contribute to students despite their different political beliefs[h] (trans.)	• Aid is channelled transparently, regardless of race, religion, and political background of the victims[i] • As-Siddiq Association (Muslim charitable organisation) offered aid to poor Chinese (trans.)[j]

(continued)

(continued)

Humanisation		
Mature	• A poem titled "United Malays" by Lim Swee Tin has fired participants' passion at the Convention on New Economic Empowerment Models in Shah Alam[k] (trans.) • Not proper to charge that the Muslim call to prayer (azan) is harassing the non-Muslims as the religious festivals of the other races also are equally noisy[l] (trans.)	• Shared values should be highlighted instead of racial or religious differences. PM: "All religions teach us good. Yes, we have different beliefs but the values are universal like politeness, respect for elders, trust and diligence"[m] • Even the PM has publicly apologised to the people and promised to make changes[n] (trans.)
Open		• Willingness of Malays to vote for candidates who are not from their ethnic group[o] (trans.) • Non-Muslims, including politicians are welcomed into mosques, but they must have proper respect such as the dress code[p] (trans.)
Independent	• Chinese go into business because they do not have a choice and are compelled to do so to avoid from working under other people[q] (trans.)	• The current Malays in the twenty-first century are no longer dependent on government handouts, but are able to compete with the other races[r] (trans.)
[UH] What they have that is essentially human. They…	**[UH] What Chinese have that is essentially human. They…**	**[UH] What Malays have that is essentially human. They…**
Are intelligent or cognitively sophisticated (e.g. can be engaged, cultivated to accommodate the "other")	• Besides academic knowledge in such fields as the sciences and mathematics, the community is also known for their quest of business and entrepreneurial knowledge[s]	
Are rational (e.g. able to discuss differences of views, dissenting opinions openly)	• Fresh approaches in responding to the demands of a changing political landscape… likely to be the call of the MCA leadership today[t] • Dr Koh Tsu Koon said that the gathering may get out of control, it was better to seek a peaceful solution via discourse with the panel[u]	

(continued)

(continued)

Humanisation		
Have language capabilities	• "Malaysia's <u>Chinese-speaking populace gives the country an advantage over other countries</u> and we should leverage on this uniqueness"[v] • <u>Foreign language proficiency is dominated by the Chinese</u>. The school emerged as champion in the English debate[w] (trans.) • Malaysia is very fortunate because 24 % or seven million are <u>ethnic Chinese who can speak Mandarin, Hokien, Cantonese, Hakka, Teochew, Fuchow, and various other Chinese dialects. Malaysia</u>, he said, is the only country outside China with a Mandarin education system[x] (trans.)	• "Today, <u>more Malays speak Mandarin than ever before</u>—part of transforming Malaysia to help give us the vital business edge in years to come"[y]
Have a religion	• The <u>festival</u> aimed to <u>promote Buddhist core values</u> through visual medium and to create greater awareness among the general public about the teachings of Buddhism[z] • The Leng Eng Tian Temple in Sungai Way, PJ celebrated the Nine Emperor Gods festival, an annual event where hundreds of Taoists and visitors alike thronged the quaint temple to pay respect to the gods[aa]	• PAS has been <u>promoting *hudud* laws</u> quietly in Opposition-led states like banning alcoholic drinks for Muslims, preventing non-Muslims from selling alcohol, banning Western concerts, forcing non-Muslim businessmen in Kedah to stop operations during Ramadan[ab] • The Sultan also reminded <u>Muslims and non-Muslims to maintain religious harmony</u> in the country[ac] • Mahathir urged the <u>Malay community to be united based on their Islamic faith</u>[ad] • Making <u>Islam as the foundation of the country using the *wasatiyyah* (moderation) approach</u>[ae] (trans.) • But there is <u>no compromise</u> when it comes to the issue of their <u>faith and practice</u>[af]

(continued)

(continued)

Humanisation		
[*UH*] Emotions and treatment they elicit. They elicit...	**[*UH*] Emotions and treatment they elicit. Chinese elicit...**	**[*UH*] Emotions and treatment they elicit. Malays elicit...**
Admiration (good example to follow)	• Chinese in the country are the ones who <u>excel</u> in basketball. Even in the US, where African Americans dominate, a Chinese stole the show (Yao Ming)[ag] • <u>Chinese schools make immense contribution to the education</u> in Malaysia[ah] • Najib said that the Malaysian <u>Chinese community is well known for its diligence, hard work, thrifty,</u> and today we need to add the values of selflessness[ai] (trans.) • Emulate the Chinese way of politicking. Despite the different names of the parties, their goals are still the similar[aj]	• Nik Nazmi is a product of the NEP's success in creating a viable Malay middle-class. These are <u>confident, public service-oriented young Malays who aren't bound by the legacies of the past</u>[ak]
[*HN*] How they are seen: They...	**[*HN*] How Chinese are seen: They ...**	**[*HN*] How Malays are seen: They...**
Are close to us	• Chinese helped build the country, so they should be. <u>allowed to develop their own language</u>[al] (trans.)	
Have human qualities: including warm; friendly; conforming, loyal; obedient; tolerant		• By nature, the Malay's value system is one of tolerance and willingness to help, regardless of race[am] (trans.)
Are active and efficacious (have agency)	• The <u>contribution of the Chinese community in the economic sphere is very imp</u>ortant to the overall development of the country[an] (trans.)	

(continued)

(continued)

Humanisation		
Are cognitively open or flexible	• Dr Chua: "There's nothing wrong in educating my own members. We don't believe *hudud* will not affect the non-Muslims and we are holding this (forum) to educate them"[ao] • "You don't look at the person's colour or race but at his ability, which is what DAP has always believed in. The fact that a person is non-Chinese or Chinese or half-Chinese doesn't matter"[ap]	
Are emotionally responsive	• Large number of young Chinese feel strongly about being treated differently, especially in terms of race-based policies[aq]	
[HN] Emotions and treatment they elicit. They elicit…	**[HN] Emotions and treatment they elicit. Chinese elicit…**	**[HN] Emotions and treatment they elicit. Malays elicit…**
Positive regard toward them	• Najib praises the community, thanking Chinese schools for contributing to education in Malaysia[ar]	• Malays do not question the rights of other races. We gave them citizenship rights, and we respect their rights[as] (trans.)

[a]"Najib: Every race contributed to a successful Malaysia", *The Star*, Sunday, January 23, 2011
[b]"Pentingnya penguasaan bahasa kedua", *Utusan Malaysia*, September 14, 2011
[c]"UMNO terus bela semua kaum", *Utusan Malaysia*, April 23, 2012
[d]"Berani Melangkau sempadan", *Utusan Malaysia*, Mac 14, 2011
[e]"Isu-isu akhbar Cina", *Utusan Malaysia*, Ogos 9, 2012
[f]"Prosthetic arm gives fisherman renewed hope", *The Star*, Friday, June 3, 2011
[g]"Liow slams Opposition", *The Star*, Sunday, October 2, 2011
[h]"Bantuan tanpa mengira idealogy politik", *Utusan Malaysia*, Januari 2, 2012
[i]"RM1.27mil paid to east coast flood victims", *The Star*, Friday, December 16, 2011
[j]"As-Siddiq bantu keluarga nelayan miskin Cina" *Utusan Malaysia,* June 3, 2011
[k]"Puisi Bersatulah Melayu bakar semangat peserta", *Utusan Malaysia,* Ogos 19, 2011
[l]"Festival agama lain pun bising—Soi Lek", *Utusan Malaysia,* Januari 18, 2011
[m]"Observe mutual respect", *The Star*, Thursday, December 15, 2011
[n]"UMNO dinamik dan tetap relevan", *Utusan Malaysia*, Mei 13, 2012
[o]"UMNO mendakap demokrasi, bukan rasis", *Utusan Malaysia*, Disember 2, 2011
[p]"Ahli politik perlu peka adab dan susila agama lain—Jamil Khir", *Utusan Malaysia*, Januari 2, 2011
[q]"Isu-isu akhbar Cina", *Utusan Malaysia*, Disember 29, 2011
[r]"Melayu abad ke-21", *Utusan Malaysia*, Oktober 1, 2011
[s]"PM: Only Malaysia has national-type school system", *The Star*, Saturday, March 26, 2011
[t]"MCA to adopt fresh approaches to meet new demands", *The Star*, Sunday, October 2, 2011
[u]"Maintain racial and religious harmony, says Soi Lek", *The Star*, October 18, 2011
[v]"Chua: Multi-lingualism can further boost economic growth", *The Star*, Friday, November 4, 2011
[w]"SMK Damansara Jaya johan debat bahasa Inggeris", *Utusan Malaysia,* Mei 30, 2011
[x]"Malaysia pilihan ahli perniagaan Cina", *Utusan Malaysia*, November 13, 2012

[y]"Najib praises Chinese community's role in improving education in Malaysia", *The Star*, Sunday, September 25, 2011

[z]"Free screenings: Buddhist societies present third Wesak International Film Festival", *The Star*, Friday, June 3, 2011

[aa]"Where the stars shine", *The Star*, Thursday, Oktober 6, 2011

[ab]"Make your stand clear, Tee Yong tells DAP", *The Star*, Tuesday, October 11, 2011

[ac]"Sultan orders Jais to counsel Muslims involved", *The Star*, Tuesday, October 11, 2011

[ad]"Malays must change freebie mindset, says Dr M", *The Star*, Thursday, October 13, 2011

[ae]"Wasatiyyah pendekatan terbaik", *Utusan Malaysia*, June 30, 2011

[af]"Tweet and die", *The Star*, September 30, 2012

[ag]"MPs, the ball is really in your court now", *The Star*, Friday, November 18, 2011

[ah]"15 Chinese schools get RM15mil", *The Star*, Sunday, September 25, 2011

[ai]Datuk Seri Najib, in, "Kaum Cina sumbang untuk kebaikan pendidikan negara", *Utusan Malaysia*, September 25, 2011

[aj]"Jana transformasi minda, jiwa Melayu hadapi lautan perubahan zaman", *Utusan Malaysia*, Disember 5, 2012

[ak]"For sure public advocacy is here to stay", *The Star*, Tuesday, November 8, 2011

[al]"Isu-isu akhbar Cina", *Utusan Malaysia*, November 3, 2011

[am]Karim Chan, in, "Sin Chew Daily, Ting Hien 'super rasis'" *Utusan Malaysia*, April 28, 2011

[an]"Sumbangan kaum Cina penting", *Utusan Malaysia*, Jun 26, 2011

[ao]"Chua: Make mandarin a compulsory exam subject", *The Star*, November 28, 2011

[ap]"Chong: Choose SUPP chief on ability, not race", *The Star*, Wednesday, September 7, 2011

[aq]"Reading the Chinese mindset", *The Star*, Sunday, June 5, 2011

[ar]"15 Chinese schools get RM15mil", *The Star*, Sunday, September 25, 2011

[as]"Orang Melayu perlu berani pertahan hak", *Utusan Malaysia*, Mac 28, 2011

References

Abdullah, H. (2004). *One hundred years of language planning in Malaysia: Looking ahead to the future*. Retrieved January 10, 2011, from http://languageinindia.com/nov2004/abdulla1.html

Al Ramiah, A., & Hewstone, M. (2012). "Rallying around the flag": Can intergroup contact intervention promote national unity? *British Journal of Social Psychology, 51*, 239–256.

Al Ramiah, A., Hewstone, M., Little, T. D., & Lang, K. (2014). The influence of status on the relationship between intergroup contact, threat, and prejudice in the context of a nation-building intervention in Malaysia. *Journal of Conflict Resolution, 85*, 1202–1229.

Barnes Report on Malay education and Fenn-Wu report on Chinese education. (1951). Retrieved March 20, 2012, from http://www.digitalibrary.my/dmdocuments/malaysiakini/02_report%20on%20barnes%20report%20on%20malay%20education%20and%20fennwu%20report%20on%20chinese%20education%201951.pdf

Brown, G. (2005). *Making ethnic citizens: The politics and practice of education in Malaysia*. Retrieved February 8, 2012, from http://www.crise.ox.ac.uk/pubs/workingpaper23.pdf

Christie, D. J., & Noor, N. M. (2012). Sustaining peace through psychologically informed policies: The geohistorical context of Malaysia. In P. T. Coleman & M. Deutsch (Eds.), *Psychological components of sustainable peace* (pp. 153–175). New York, NY: Springer.

Costello, K., & Hodson, G. (2010). Exploring the roots of dehumanization: The role of animal—Human similarity in promoting immigrant humanization. *Group Processes & Intergroup Relations, 13*(1), 3–22.

Dovidio, J. F., Eller, A., & Hewstone, M. (2011). Improving intergroup relations through direct, extended and other forms of indirect contact. *Group Processes & Intergroup Relations, 14*, 147–160.

Dovidio, J. F., Gaertner, S. L., & Saguy, T. (2007). Another view of "we": Majority and minority group perspectives on a common ingroup identity. *European Review of Social Psychology, 18*, 296–330.

Fenn, W. P., & Wuu, T. Y. (1951). *Chinese schools and the education of Chinese Malayans*. Kuala Lumpur: Kuala Lumpur Government Press.

Fisher, R. J. (1997). *Interactive conflict resolution*. Syracuse, NY: Syracuse University Press.

Freire, P. (1970). *Pedagogy of the oppressed*. London, England: Penguin.

Gaertner, S. L., & Dovidio, J. F. (2000). *Reducing intergroup bias: The common ingroup identity model*. Philadelphia, PA: The Psychology Press.

Galtung, J., & Fischer, D. (2013). High road, low road: Charting the course for peace journalism. In J. Galtung & D. Fischer (Eds.), *Johan Galtung: Pioneer of peace research* (pp. 95–102). Berlin: Springer.

Goh, D. P. S., & Holden, P. (2009). Introduction: Postcoloniality, race and multiculturalism. In D. P. S. Goh, M. Gabrielpillai, P. Holden, & G. C. Khoo (Eds.), *Race and multiculturalism in Malaysia and Singapore* (pp. 1–16). Oxon, UK: Routledge.

Haque, M. S. (2003). The role of the state in managing ethnic tensions in Malaysia: A critical discourse. *American Behavioral Scientist, 47*, 240–266.

Haslam, N. (2006). Dehumanisation: An integrative review. *Personality and Social Psychology Review, 10*, 252–264.

Heng, P. K. (1997). The new economic policy and the Chinese community in Peninsular Malaysia. *The Developing Economies, 35*, 262–292.

Hewstone, M., Cairns, E., Voci, A., Hamberger, J., & Niens, U. (2006). Intergroup contact, forgiveness, and experience of "The Troubles" in Northern Ireland. *Journal of Social Issues, 62*, 99–120.

Hirschman, C. (1986). The making of race in colonial Malaya: Political economy and racial ideology. *Sociological Forum, 1*, 330–361.

Hofstede, G. (1991). *Cultures and organizations: Software of the mind*. Maidenhead, UK: McGraw-Hill.

Hwang, I. W. (2003). *Personalized politics: The Malaysian state under Mahathir*. Singapore: Institute of Southeast Asian Studies.

Johnson, D. W., & Johnson, R. T. (1999). Making cooperative learning work. *Theory Into Practice, 38*(2), 67–73.

Lee, H. G. (2000). *Ethnic relations in Peninsular Malaysia: The cultural and economic dimensions*. Singapore: Institute of Southeast Asian Studies.

Leyens, J. P., Rodriguez-Perez, A., Rodriguez-Torres, R., Gaunt, R., Paladino, P. M., Vaes, J., et al. (2001). Psychological essentialism and the attribution of uniquely human emotions to ingroups and outgroups. *European Journal of Social Psychology, 31*, 395–411.

Montiel, C. J., & Noor, N. M. (Eds.). (2009). *Peace psychology in Asia*. New York: Springer.

Noor, N. M. (2009). The future of peace psychology in Asia. In C. J. Montiel & N. M. Noor (Eds.), *Peace psychology in Asia* (pp. 307–322). New York: Springer.

Noor, N. M., & Leong, C. H. (2013). Multiculturalism in Malaysia and Singapore: Contesting models. *International Journal of Intercultural Relations, 37*, 714–726.

Paluck, E. L., & Green, D. P. (2009). Prejudice reduction: What works? A review and assessment of research and practice. *Annual Review of Psychology, 60*, 339–367.

Pettigrew, T. F., & Tropp, L. R. (2006). A meta-analytic test of intergroup contact theory. *Journal of Personality and Social Psychology, 90*(5), 751–783.

Quayum, M. A. (2003). Malaysian literature in English: Challenges and prospects in the new millennium. In D. Zaman & M. A. Quayum (Eds.), *Silverfish new writing 3: An anthology of stories from Malaysia, Singapore and beyond*. Kuala Lumpur: Silverfish Books.

Ratnam, K. J. (1965). *Communalism and the political process in Malaya*. Kuala Lumpur: Oxford University Press.

Rothman, J. (2012). *From identity-based conflict to identity-based cooperation*. New York: Springer.

Shastri, A. (1993). *Preferential policies in Malaysia* (Pew Case Studies in International Affairs, Case No. 458). Washington, DC: Institute for the Study of Diplomacy, School of Foreign Service, Georgetown University.

Tilman, R. O. (1969). Education and political development in Malaysia. In R. O. Tilman (Ed.), *Man, state, and society in contemporary Southeast Asia*. New York: Praeger.

Ting, H. (2009). Malaysian history textbooks and the discourse of Ketuanan Melayu. In D. P. S. Goh, M. Gabrielpillai, P. Holde, & G. C. Khoo (Eds.), *Race and multiculturalism in Malaysia and Singapore* (pp. 36–52). Oxon, UK: Routledge.

Vickers, E. (2002). Conclusion: Deformed relationships—Identity politics and history education in East Asia. *International Journal of Educational Research, 37*, 643–651.

Part III
Toward a Socially Transformative Peace Psychology

Chapter 8
Identifying and Mobilising Factors That Promote Community Peace

Sandy Lazarus, James R. Cochrane, Naiema Taliep, Candice Simmons, and Mohamed Seedat

This chapter deals with a South African case study that brings together academic and community-embedded views on peace to identify key factors that could contribute to peacebuilding at a community level. The discussion focuses on how these conceptions were integrated into an intervention in the local community through SCRATCHMAPS (Spiritual Capacity and Religious Assets for Transforming Community Health through Mobilising Males for Peace and Safety), a community-based violence prevention and peace promotion project aimed at mobilising religious assets and enabling spiritual capacity to promote peace. Although process and outcome evaluations of this project have been conducted (Isobell et al., 2015; Van Gesselleen et al., 2015), this is not the focus of this chapter which looks primarily at the factors identified through a participatory research process.

The SCRATCHMAPS project, housed in the Violence, Injury and Peace Research Unit of the South African Medical Research Council and University of South Africa, arose from a recognition of the high levels of violence in South Africa and the overrepresentation of males as both perpetrators and victims of violence in South Africa and globally (Krug, Dahlberg, Mercy, Zwi, & Lozano, 2002; Lazarus,

S. Lazarus (✉) • N. Taliep • C. Simmons • M. Seedat
Institute for Social and Health Sciences, University of South Africa,
Johannesburg, South Africa

South African Medical Research Council-University of South Africa Violence,
Injury and Peace Research Unit, Cape Town, South Africa
e-mail: sandylazarus1@gmail.com; Naiema.Taliep@mrc.ac.za;
Candicesimmons19@gmail.com; Seedama@unisa.ac.za

J.R. Cochrane
International Religious Health Assets Programme (IRHAP), University of Cape Town,
Cape Town, South Africa
e-mail: jrcochrane@gmail.com

© Springer International Publishing AG 2017
M. Seedat et al. (eds.), *Enlarging the Scope of Peace Psychology*,
Peace Psychology Book Series, DOI 10.1007/978-3-319-45289-0_8

Tonsing, Ratele, & van Niekerk, 2011), and the relatively unexplored area of religious assets and spiritual capacity for addressing violence and promoting peace (ARHAP, 2006). Violence is understood to include both direct violence (referring to conflict that harms individuals) and structural violence (resulting from social, political, and economic structures and processes, including various disparities linked to social, economic, and spatial inequalities) (Britto et al., 2014; Christie et al., 2014; Dawes & van der Merwe, 2014).

Religion and spirituality, though often associated with violence, also represents a potential resource for peace promotion, our focus. A literature review (Amos, 2010) on religion and violence prevention revealed that religion and spirituality can act as positive resources by promoting beneficent human values and norms and cultivating a sense of hope and purpose through religious and community activities, including rituals and ceremonies, provision of safe spaces, pastoral counselling, and the facilitation of dialogue. Similarly, the potential of religions, faith, spirituality, and service to transform people in promoting peace is highlighted by Britto et al. (2014); Hunsberger and Jackson (2005) have established links between some aspects of religion and positive intergroup attitudes, an important factor for peace-building; the Lille Declaration on a Culture of Peace views religion as a fundamental resource for fostering a culture of peace (European Council of Religious Leaders—Religions for Peace, 2009); and Little (2006) speaks of the 'constructive side' of religion that can contribute to addressing violent conflict. Religious practitioners and leaders like Martin Luther King Jr., Mahatma Gandhi, or Thich Nath Hahn have, of course, long had an interest in conflict resolution, mediation, arbitration, reconciliation, and other non-violent techniques, while others have played a key role in truth and reconciliation commissions aimed at effective and peaceful change through restorative justice (see Little, 2006). More generally, deep threads exist within many faith traditions that emphasise mutual respect, loving-kindness, and compassion, all of which can contribute to peace promotion by helping people develop a sense of responsibility for their actions; a positive perception of and empathy for others; and non-harming, compassionate, and altruistic action (DerlanYeh, 2006; Mandour, 2010).

Responses to violence encompass a range of disciplinary and intellectual traditions representing the spectrum of the social and health sciences. Yet there seems to be limited recognition of the generative potential of religious assets and spiritual capacities in the prevention of violence and peacebuilding. In SCRATCHMAPS the concept of *religious assets* has been defined as locally embedded religious images, values, practices, people, and organisations that are both tangible (e.g. a mosque/church) and intangible (e.g. compassion) (Cochrane et al., 2015). These assets are leveraged through local and translocal agency that might issue in action to heal and promote peace.

Conceptually, the SCRATCHMAPS research began by exploring the relevance of the concepts of religious assets for peace. Some research participants, however, reacted to the idea of 'religion', suggesting instead that the research focus on 'spirituality', which seemed more generalisable. The idea of spiritual capital

(Berger & Hefner, 2003; Finke, 2003; Iannaccone & Klick, 2003) was also mooted but was not perceived to be particularly helpful for this research project. After much discussion and further work by the research team, the new notion of spiritual capacity was adopted. Linked to but not equal to the sum or some subset of 'intangible' religious assets, it underpins them all, and, we believe, can be made precise and generalisable enough to cover the wide diversity of phenomena of interest to the study. It should be noted at this point that the authors have decided to use the terms 'tangible' and 'intangible' when referring to religious assets in this chapter, even though some, particularly in psychological circles, may believe that these terms may be better understood as 'objective' and 'subjective'. Whichever way we go, the terms could be viewed as problematic, but, in our view, the concepts of 'tangible/intangible' work best for the research reported in this chapter. It should be noted that 'intangible' has two important meanings (from the Oxford Dictionary) which are relevant for this discussion: 'not having physical presence', and, in relation to an asset or benefit, it is seen as 'not a physical object, yet of a value not precisely measurable'. Religious assets, including 'spiritual capacity', cannot be reduced to something 'subjective' without undermining both those meanings.

The concept of *spiritual capacity*, introduced in the SCRATCHMAPS Conceptual Position Paper (Cochrane et al., 2015), refers to specific human capacity that animates action, compassion, and solidarity in the fullness of life. It describes the extraordinary and universal human capacity of 'creative freedom' which allows us, to a degree not true of any other creature, to add to phenomena that which does not reside in them and thereby imagine something that does not exist and bring it into being. The 'possible' in this sense transcends the 'actual,' even if always constrained by physical realities and our relation to others and our environment. This capacity can be turned to destructive possibilities (to the point of destroying humanity and the earth itself) or to generative ones. It thus also contains within it the moral question of how we *ought* to act or live and to what ends. The various *specific forms of spirituality* that mark human experience, whatever their ambiguity otherwise, express our awareness of this power, of the responsibility that comes with it, of need for a coherent grasp of the whole that grounds it, and of the embodiment of practices and attitudes that help shape it.

Spiritual capacity, as proposed by Cochrane and fully articulated with the help of McGaughey (n.d.) is not some content or substance, but the non-material ground of our experience of creative freedom, the effects of which we see everywhere around us: in buildings we make, machines we construct, ways we alter our environment, living arrangements and social institutions we invent, art we create, music we perform, and symbols we invent to describe and order the world. We cannot prove it but we must assume it if we are to account for our experience. Moreover, every human person, irrespective of all other differences and as long as they retain the core of their humanity (which can be destroyed), possesses this capacity. It is not dependent upon biology or culture and is not infrequently expressed even under severe constraints (such as torture or extreme deprivation). It is a condition of what it means to be/become human.

Even if this capacity of creative freedom is taken as intrinsically good, it can be turned to either good or evil actions, and therefore it is our basic choice about how we orient ourselves in the world and toward others, about how we think and act. This inherent capacity thus unavoidably faces us in every non-trivial act with a profound *moral responsibility* for what we do. Whether or not we intend the good or ill is thus our primary choice (though, because we never control the consequences of our actions, choosing to act out of the good does not guarantee a good result). At the same time, how we orient ourselves in the world and toward others is not a merely individual matter, for we need a community of others that can enhance and encourage us in our personal choice about how we use our capacity of creative freedom. This is the key point in relation to the potential role of religious or faith traditions and spiritual insights and practices in the promotion of peace.

It is clear from the earlier discussion that religious assets constitute an important resource for peace promotion, and that the concept of 'spiritual capacity' highlights key aspects relevant to peace. The focus on peace promotion in the SCRATCHMAPS project includes the mitigation of direct and structural violence (Christie et al., 2014), but also a proactive, positive approach aimed at building peace, including embracing and promoting values, attitudes and behaviours that reject violence and actively promote peace) (Britto, Gordon, et al., 2014). The SCRATCHMAPS project has included all aspects of peace promotion: peacemaking (enhancing positive communication, usually associated with conflict resolution), peacekeeping (associated with third-party intervention) and peacebuilding (addressing root causes of violence and developing infrastructure) to promote social transformation and justice, capacity building, and reconciliation (Britto, Gordon, et al., 2014; Boutros-Ghali, 1995; Maiese, 2003; United Nations, 1995). Strategies employed in the project have included, to a lesser and greater extent, the priority action areas identified by the UN Programme for Action (UN Resolution A/RES/53/243, 1999): Fostering a culture of peace through education; advancing understanding, tolerance, and solidarity; promoting sustainable economic and social development; promoting respect for all human rights; ensuring equality between men and women; and fostering democratic participation.

The SCRATCHMAPS project has placed a particular emphasis on building a culture of peace through education (discussed in more detail later), fostering democratic participation (particularly through the participatory methodology pursued in the project), and promoting equality between men and women (with an emphasis on promoting positive forms of masculinity). Although not a focus for this chapter, it is important to note that hegemonic masculinity (a dominant set of beliefs and expectations about what men should and should not do, in relation to the construction of manhood) has been identified as a major risk area for violence (Lazarus et al., 2011). We were thus specifically interested in exploring and identifying positive forms of masculinity, noting that egalitarian, non-violent, non-patriarchal, generative, or positive aspects of masculinities are recognised as a potentially powerful protective factor to address violence and promote peace (Barker & Ricardo, 2005; Seedat, van Niekerk, Jewkes, Suffla, & Ratele, 2009).

The concept of 'culture of peace' (Chowdhury, 2014, p. xvi) is defined as 'a set of values, attitudes traditions, and modes of behaviour and ways of life', based on prosocial behaviour, respect for various rights and human needs, fairness, trust, empathy and compassion, and the principles of freedom, justice, equality, democracy, tolerance, solidarity, cooperation, pluralism, cultural diversity, dialogue—fostered by enabling environments (see Britto, Gordon, et al., 2014; Christie et al., 2014; Goodman, 2012; Leckman, Panter-Brick, & Salah, 2014b; Reber-Rider, 2008). An enabling environment includes the elimination of poverty and inequalities, non-discrimination, and access to economic development and participation. The focus on values, attitudes, and behaviour, emphasised in this concept, links directly to the concepts of spiritual capacity, and the mobilisation of religious assets, discussed in some detail earlier.

Given the aforementioned commitments, the need for a holistic and comprehensive approach to peace promotion is clear, and so a systems approach to peace work is supported by various peace activists and researchers. For example, Britto, Gordon, et al. (2014) talk about the 'ecology of peace' framework, and a dialectic ecosystemic approach is outlined by Hinde and Stevenson-Hinde (2014). A systems approach emphasises the need to intervene at various levels of the system within a dynamic view of interconnections between the different levels and the multidirectional influences that contribute to the development of peace. Christie et al. (2014) argue for an 'agentic' perspective which sees individuals as producers and products of social environments, with effective interventions depending on aligning actions at the different systems levels. They also note that successful programmes usually employ a participatory approach, central to the SCRATCHMAPS strategy.

How then can one mobilise community assets, with a focus on spiritual capacity and religious assets, to promote community peace? To answer this question, the objectives of the SCRATCHMAPS project were to develop an appropriate theoretical and conceptual framework; understand the processes whereby religious assets, and spiritual capacity in particular, might promote peace; develop, implement, and evaluate an intervention to mobilise religious assets and enhance spiritual capacity to create peace; and draw out lessons on the participatory community-engaged research process itself. The next section outlines the process we used to pursue some of these objectives, followed by a presentation of the key findings emerging from this study. This is succeeded by a discussion on key issues emerging, with a particular focus on our growing understanding of the concept of 'spiritual capacity', and recommendations for further peace research and action.

Research Methodology

In this section, we provide an overview of our research approach, followed by a summary description of the community context and participants, and design and procedures pursued during the research process.

Research Aims

Within the context of the broader aims of the project (refer earlier), this chapter focuses specifically on the identification of factors that promote peace and how they were integrated into the planned peace intervention.

Research Approach

The SCRATCHMAPS project was informed by a critical perspective, which is characterised by the adoption of a human rights perspective; focusing on actively transforming society, with social justice as a central goal; utilising a historical and contextual approach to understand 'persons-in-context'; focusing on various issues of power and oppression; and engaging with and mainstreaming marginalised voices, including indigenous and community-embedded knowledge (Ratele, Suffla, Lazarus, & Van Niekerk, 2010). An ecosystems approach also informed the way we understood and pursued our study, including identifying risks and protective factors at individual, relationship, community, and social levels, with a recognition that understanding violence includes a recognition that factors often cut across system levels, and that a comprehensive approach to violence is required (Lazarus et al., 2011).

Within the context of the above meta-theoretical framing, the SCRATCHMAPS research has been guided by the values and principles of a Community-Based Participatory Research (CBPR) approach (Israel, Eng, Schulz, & Parker, 2005; Wallerstein & Duran, 2008). This (a) treats the 'community' as the unit of focus; (b) works with a partnership approach; (c) engages the community at all levels of the research process; (d) promotes colearning and coconstruction of knowledge; (e) ensures that the research is relevant to the community; (f) builds on the strengths and resources of the community; (g) embodies a commitment to action research, with a dynamic relationship between theory and practice; and (h) accepts that it is a long-term process with commitment to ownership and sustainability.

The SCRATCHMAPS project utilised a grounded-theory approach in its theory-building and knowledge construction processes.

> Grounded theory is an approach that allows us to study a relatively unknown social phenomenon around which no specified theory may exist yet. In the process we will literally build a theory from the ground up, brick by brick … Our bricks in this case are the concepts we ground as we proceed through the analysis process (Babbie & Mouton, 2009, p. 499).

The grounded-theory approach was pursued in various ways in this project. This included: (a) The inclusion of local community members in all steps of the research process itself; (b) collectively identifying and pursuing creative methodologies to elicit the views of community members on the key concepts; (c) involving the local research team in the analysis of the emerging data; and (d) creating opportunities, including through an academic-community colloquium, to debate and clarify the concepts developed. This process was informed by the principles of colearning and coproduction of knowledge, central to a CBPR approach.

Research Context and Participants

The local community for research and action is situated in the Helderberg Basin in the Western Cape province of South Africa, a low-income community of roughly 164 houses and twice as many backyard dwellings. The residents, mostly Afrikaans speaking, were previously categorised as 'coloured'[1] by the Apartheid regime, and many of the current realities of this community reflect the legacy of the structural violence of Apartheid. Most of the residents have low educational levels, and almost half earn an income below the poverty line. There have been housing and other forms of social service initiatives in this community, but they have been fragmented, and currently the community is struggling to survive in the face of seriously high levels of national economic disparity.

The SCRATCHMAPS project team comprises about 15 psychology, public health, and religious studies scholars (with particular expertise in health and peace promotion research) and 10 local community members. Two local community structures were established to manage and conduct the research in the local community: an advisory committee (comprising local community leaders/members and service providers), and a community research team (including 10 unemployed or underemployed local residents, of both genders, half of whom are considered to be 'youth').

Research Design and Procedure

A description of the research process pursued to identify and mobilise factors that promote peace is outlined in Table 8.1. This story tells of how we moved from an initial academic framing of the project to an integration of theory and practice through engagement with the grounded-theory development pursued in the SCRATCHMAPS project. This process was guided by the objective of deepening our understanding of whether and how religious assets and spiritual capacity, as community assets, can promote peace, for the purposes of integrating these understandings into a peacebuilding intervention.

Theory building. Beginning with a number of relevant literature reviews and a theory colloquium in 2010, SCRATCHMAPS produced a Conceptual Position Paper in 2013 (Cochrane et al., revised in 2015) that included inputs from 15 academic researchers (from IRHAP and VIPRU). Necessarily tentative in nature, given our grounded-theory approach, this helped frame the research and action pursued within the local community. The initial Conceptual Position Paper captures the main concepts that define the project and provides short working definitions of them. The Paper includes a major section on religious

---

[1] While Apartheid racial categories are used in this analysis, the use of these terms does not indicate endorsement of these classifications.

Table 8.1 Design and procedures

	Theory-building
	• Literature reviews, academic seminars, writing a Conceptual Position Paper
	• Grounded theory: focus group discussions
	• Academic-community colloquium
	Developing community safety and peace indicators
	• Document analyses
	• Community asset mapping
	• Data collection: interviews, focus group discussions, community conversations, learner essays, building a House of Safety and Peace
	Identification of factors that promote peace
	• Triangulation of findings
	• Identification of factors at relationship, community, and social levels
	Developing values, principles, and capacities: Building Bridges Mentoring Programme
	•Prioritising values, principles, and capacities
	•Inclusion as 'thrust' in Building Bridges Mentoring Programme Manual

assets and spiritual capacity, linked to the idea of 'Leading Causes of Life' (LCL), healthworlds, and health, safety and peace promotion; and an exploration of the concept of masculinities (specifically, positive forms of masculinity). The concept of 'spiritual capacity' emerged from attempts to accommodate the different views on religion and spirituality in the research team and in the broader academic community, to engage with the different faith communities represented in the team and community, and to capture what appeared to be central capacities that link to theoretical understandings and action goals of peace promotion. The development of this concept has remained fluid throughout the project, allowing for genuine engagement with the grounded-theoretical findings from the community research.

In line with the grounded-theory approach, in 2013 the SCRATCHMAPS research team conducted 14 focus group discussions with 57 participants, including community members, service providers, and local religious leaders. These discussions, guided by semistructured Focus Group Discussion schedules, focused on the exploration of key concepts. They were facilitated and content analysed by the 10 community researchers and then triangulated by four VIPRU researchers.

At a 3-day colloquium in August 2013, which included 14 academic researchers (primarily from VIPRU and IRHAP), 10 local community researchers, and the two community advisory committee chairpersons, the Conceptual Position Paper was brought into relationship with the grounded-theory research from the community (for a full report, see Simmons, Isobell, & Lazarus, 2014).

Developing community peace indicators. Central to the goals of SCRATCHMAPS was a process of developing peace indicators for the purposes of enabling the community to judge their own development toward becoming a peaceful community. The process, pursued in the local community from 2012 to 2015, included: (a) document analyses (including various global 'peace indicator' documents); (b) data collection through, (1) a number of community conversations conducted by the local researchers—which resulted in the inclusion of participants' views on 'bricks' ($n = 175$) for the community 'House of Safety and Peace' developed during a public event at the end of 2012; and (2) 14 focus group discussions with religious leaders, youth, adults, and service providers ($n = 57$); (c) the collection of 117 learner essays from the local school; and (d) an analysis of the community asset mapping research report (Lazarus, Taliep, & Olivier et al., 2014). All of these methods included a focus on the question of 'what factors promote safety and peace in this local community'.

Given the 'strengths-orientation' of the CBPR approach (Kramer, Amos, Lazarus, & Seedat, 2012), community asset mapping was used as an appropriate strategy in the preparation phase of SCRATCHMAPS as a tool to uncover and understand existing assets for violence prevention, peace promotion, and community building in general. Three community workshops (including 74 community participants), a service providers workshop (involving 18 service providers), and a general community action planning workshop (including 41 community members and service providers), were facilitated by the SCRATCHMAPS research team, guided by Facilitator Manuals (drawing primarily from IRHAP's existing community asset mapping toolsets; see de Gruchy, Cochrane, Olivier, & Matimelo, 2011). This generated both qualitative and quantitative data, the former analysed using simple statistical computations, the latter using thematic content analysis methods.

The data sets from all of the earlier methods were analysed by the research team, with the community researchers playing a central role in the process after undergoing relevant research training (for further details, see Lazarus, Taliep, & Olivier, 2014). The findings were then presented and validated at the public community event in December 2012.

Identifying of factors that promote peace. The project lent itself to comprehensive triangulation (Hussein, 2009), which can be defined as the use of various methods, and/or theories, and/or observers, and/or data sources to enhance the validity of a study (see Babbie & Mouton, 2009; Creswell, 2007). In this project, triangulation was used by (a) drawing on different sources (groups of people) to answer the same questions; (b) using multiple methods to collect data; (c) using the same analysis framework across methods, to facilitate triangulation of findings; and then (d) checking the findings across methods to identify key themes or factors emerging from the different results. The main aim of this process was to get the best possible understanding of factors that could potentially promote peace and to incorporate priority values, principles, and capacities into the SCRATCHMAPS intervention. This process meant examining all data sets to identify key themes and categories relevant to 'peace' and peace promotion, placing this information into tables, comparing the findings across all methods and data sets, and then identifying common or core factors.

It should be noted that the process of identifying 'indicators' linked to the factors identified through the above-mentioned process is still underway, located within a broader Community Safety Index Project of the Violence, Injury and Peace Research Unit (VIPRU). The process of refining and operationalising the findings from the SCRATCHMAPS project, together with the findings from three other VIPRU community projects, will result in a Community Safety Index instrument which will be able to be used by local communities.

Developing values, principles, and capacities: The Building Bridges Mentoring Programme. In the next step (refer Table 8.1), the SCRATCHMAPS team prioritised core values, principles, and capacities that they believed should be incorporated into the intervention (which itself was developed by the team). The team then conducted a public community workshop in 2014, which included 35 community members, where the values, principles, and capacities prioritised by the team were presented and validated. The prioritised list was then infused into the Building Bridges Mentoring Manual, discussed in the findings section later.

Ethical Considerations. The values and principles of CBPR embody the key ethical principles guiding this project. Specific ethics approvals required by law were obtained, and an ethics agreement was signed by the academic and community partners. Consent forms were used for all data collection purposes, with voluntary participation and confidentiality upheld. Research translation has been taken seriously: all reports and publications have been shared with key community stakeholders, with 'action' aimed at building a safe and peaceful community being a central commitment in the project.

Findings

The analyses of the data from the above-mentioned data collection methods were extensive and are captured in various reports and articles (see Isobell et al., 2015; Isobell & Lazarus, 2014; Lazarus et al., 2014). In this chapter, where the focus is specifically on the identification of factors that are believed to promote community peace, only the triangulated summary findings are outlined. It should be noted that the analysis framework developed by the research team categorised the findings into the four levels of the ecological framework, and further divided these into 'tangible' and 'intangible' factors (as per the ARHAP Religious Health Assets framework) (see Isobell & Lazarus, 2014 for a full presentation of the findings). In this chapter, we do not use the systems framing in our presentation of the key findings because further analysis of the triangulated data clearly revealed that many of the factors identified cut across system levels. The findings are thus presented as they were categorised under (1) tangible factors that promote peace, and (2) intangible factors that promote peace.

Tangible Factors That Promote Peace

Table 8.2 provides a snapshot of the main themes, which emerged as key patterns across the data, relating to tangible factors that promote peace. Where appropriate, the factors that were identified across system levels are noted.

It is interesting to note that most of these factors were located at different levels of the system during the collective analysis process. Also, given the interest in religious assets and spiritual capacity in this study, it is interesting to note that participants identified prayer or meditation, as well as churches and other religious institutions as key community assets that should be mobilised for peace, with an emphasis on their role in promoting personal and collective growth and healing. Thus, factors relating to 'religious assets' were clearly identified, including the

Table 8.2 Tangible factors that promote peace

Tangible factors that promote peace
Prayer, meditation, and mindfulness practices (*individual level*)
Working and standing together, including police and neighbourhood watch working together with the community (*relationship and community levels*)
Adult and peer guidance and supervision (*relationship and community levels*)
Drug-free environment, and provision of drug habilitation and other health services (*individual, relationship, community, and social levels*)
Crime and violence-free environment (particularly absence of women and child abuse, and the absence of gambling spots) (*relationship and community levels*)
Employment opportunities/job creation (*community and social levels*)
Access to formal and non-formal education (*community and social levels*)
Safe and clean environment (including safe places for child-play, and the provision of lights, and trees) (*community level*)
Community facilities and amenities, especially churches and other religious institutions, and non-profit organisations (*community level*)
Recreational facilities (especially sport and cultural activities, and especially for youth) (*community level*)
Improved housing (*community and social levels*)
Poverty alleviation (*individual, community, and social levels*)
Development and availability of effective community leaders (*individual and community levels*)
No corruption (*individual, community, and social levels*)
Role models for positive forms of masculinity (*individual, relationship, community levels*)

important role of religious leaders in promoting peace through their leadership in communities. Activities organised by faith-based organisations, for example, youth programmes, were also recognised as important assets as they bring people together and help to promote belonging, agency, and responsibility. Religious education was also seen as important to peace promotion in promoting positive values and principles. Finally, the role of helpful faith-based rituals and practices, including prayer and meditation, were considered to be peace promoting.

Intangible Factors That Promote Peace

The findings of the fieldwork revealed a major emphasis on 'intangible' factors that the local community believes play a central role in promoting peace. Factors that emerged as key patterns or trends in the triangulation analysis are included in Table 8.3. Once again, where the factors were located at more than one level of the system, these levels are noted. It should also be noted that many of these 'intangible' factors can be 'seen' in certain behaviours, which are usually linked to specific 'indicators' in measurement terms. As mentioned earlier, the 'indicator' operationalisation of these factors is still underway. However, definitions of the key terms used in the SCRATCHMAPS intervention will be provided later.

Once again it is interesting to note that most of the factors are related to more than one level of the system, including concepts such as cohesion, connectedness, healing, trust, empowerment, hope, and positive morals and values. It is particularly noteworthy that a number of values, principles, and behaviours identified could be

Table 8.3 Intangible factors that promote peace

Intangible factors that promote peace
Respect (for self, and others), including a positive sense of identity (*individual and relationship levels*)
Love and care of self, others, animals, and the environment (*individual, relationship, community, and social levels*)
Empathy and compassion (*individual and relationship levels*)
Open, honest communication (*individual and relationship levels*)
Cohesion and unity—with family and community cohesion being particularly noted (*relationship and community levels*)
Connectedness (to God, to oneself, to others, to family, to school, to the community) (*individual, relationship, and community levels*)
Healing, including forgiveness, with an emphasis on family and community healing (*individual, relationship, and community levels*)
Trust (*individual, relationship, and community levels*)
Empowerment—including experiencing 'power within', taking responsibility, and exercising agency (*individual, relationship, and community levels*)
Hope, and a positive mindset (*individual and community levels*)
Positive morals/values (*individual, relationship, community, and social levels*)

linked to the need for *relationship*. This includes the concept of connectedness, which could be seen as a sense of oneness with oneself and/or one's 'God', as well as a sense of oneness with others which includes a view of life flowing through links and ties to others. The need for belonging is important here. This refers to a recognised basic human need, including a safe and secure relationship with a particular body or group of people, and/or beyond this, to include the community and the world at large. Cohesion includes the notion of working together for a common purpose, perhaps a crucial prerequisite for bringing about change in communities. And, lastly, communication, verbal and non-verbal, in a one-way or two-way direction, between two or more people, can be seen as a means of nourishing the spirit and fostering unity.

When considering what 'action' should be considered in relation to some of the factors noted earlier, the following suggestions were made by research participants: Utilise religious and other community leaders to promote values and morals that build peace; promote love, respect, sharing, positivity, and personal responsibility; and provide opportunities for community building (with an emphasis on healing, cohesion and unity, and responsibility). It is important to note that many of the factors identified were related to the concepts of empowerment and agency, which is picked up in more detail in the discussion later.

Values, Principles, and Capacities: The Building Bridges Mentoring Programme

In line with initiatives that combine research and action in efforts to promote peace, the findings discussed earlier were used to direct a community intervention aimed at mobilising religious assets and enabling spiritual capacity to promote peace. The SCRATCHMAPS team, including the community researchers and advisory committee, developed an intervention based on research findings and lessons from 'best practices' identified by the doctoral student who was a central researcher in the project. Figure 8.1 provides a snapshot of the intervention developed within the SCRATCHMAPS project. The diagram identifies specific foci or strategies pursued at each level of the system.

The training and implementation guidelines for this intervention were included in a Manual which provided information, instructions, interactive exercises, and handouts for those facilitating the 6-month programme. Relevant experts evaluated a first draft of the Manual using a Delphi-method evaluation technique and made revisions accordingly. The Manual then guided the pilot implementation of the programme in 2014 and was then revised based on the process and outcomes evaluation of its implementation (Taliep, Simmons, van Niekerk, & Phillips, 2015; refer to Table of Contents in Table 8.4 below).

Peace education, which has been the key peacebuilding strategy pursued in the project, lays an emphasis on changing mindsets, instilling fundamental principles, changing behaviour, and developing necessary skills and knowledge (Chowdhury, 2014). The peace education curriculum developed in SCRATCHMAPS is in line

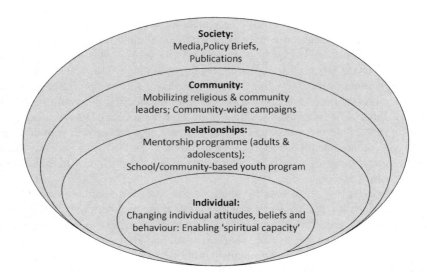

Fig. 8.1 SCRATCHMAPS' Building Bridges Mentoring intervention

with others which typically include understanding key concepts and causal factors relating to violence and peace, developing communication skills, conflict resolution, healing programmes, peer mediation, and values education (Bacani, 2004; Bretherton, Weston, & Zbar, 2005). The Building Bridges Mentoring Programme used multiple methods, including drama, role plays, reflection on attitudes and behaviours, and community meetings and actions, all of which have been found to be effective (Barker, Ricardo, & Nascimento, 2007). Barker, Ricardo, Nascimento, Olukoya, and Santos (2010) also argue that integrated programmes combining community outreach strategies, mobilisation, and mass media campaigns appear to be more effective in producing behaviour change than group education on its own.

As mentioned earlier, the values, principles, and capacities included as a thrust in the Manual were initially prioritised and chosen by the research team on the basis of analysis of all research findings, and then confirmed through the public community workshop held in 2014. The key values or principles that were prioritised for inclusion were as follows: Empowerment (including experiencing 'power within', taking responsibility, and exercising agency), hope and a positive mindset, respect (for oneself and others), empathy and compassion (including mindfulness practices), and trust. The Manual includes a strong emphasis on various aspects of building positive relationships, particularly between genders, and an emphasis on healing, focusing on personal, interpersonal, as well as broader community healing. The latter aspect was constantly linked to the need for healing from the damaging legacy of South Africa's Apartheid heritage.

Once identified, the key concepts were defined in the Manual. This process included the full research team, and the Delphi evaluation process which included a number of

Table 8.4 Table of contents of SCRATCHMAPS Building Bridges Mentoring Programme

Modules	Sessions
Recruitment, selection, and orientation	
Module 1: Manual Overview	1. Project Overview
	2. Getting Started: Laying the Foundation
	3. Procedural Requirements and Forms for Mentors
	4. Procedural Requirements and Forms for Mentees
	5. Mentor/Mentee Matching Procedural Requirements and forms
Mentor training	
Module 2: Mobilising Spiritual Capacity & Religious Assets	1. Values
	2. Leadership
Module 3: Violence and Safety & Peace Promotion	1. Understanding Violence
	2. Gender and Violence
	3. Violence Prevention and Safety and Peace Promotion
Module 4: Across Gender Boundaries—Masculinities and Femininities	1. Perceptions of Masculinities and Femininities
	2. Reflecting on, and Healing my Past
	3. Redefining Masculinity and Femininity
	4. Building Connections with Others
	5. Generative Parenthood
	6. Finding Healing in the Wilderness
Mentee training—mentoring phase	
Module 5: Mentoring in Action	1. Mentoring Skills
	2. Needs and Goal Setting
	3. Values
	4. Resolving Conflict Peacefully
	5. Across Gender Boundaries—Masculinities and Femininities
Community building	
Module 6: Community Building: Giving Back Together	1. Mobilising to take Action to Change
	2. Unemployment Campaign
	3. Substance Abuse Campaign
Community certificate ceremony	

experts in the various areas of expertise covered by the programme. Although specific measurable 'indicators' were not developed at this point in time, the concepts or factors were operationalised through workshop interactive processes in the programme. The next section provides a snapshot of how these concepts were unpacked. It should be noted that linkages between related concepts were made where considered appropriate.

Agency is viewed as the power to do or to act in the world in ways that alter it and ourselves. This is linked to: (a) the intrinsic *creative freedom* that allows us to act while placing before us the responsibility of how we act; and (b) *empowerment*, which is seen as including personal power (*in-powerment* or a sense of authority within oneself) and collective power, which includes working with others to take control of one's life—all of which helps individuals and groups to express and responsibly use their creative freedom.

Hope was seen as a deep expectation of a comprehensively fulfilled and flourishing life. It includes a positive anticipation of change (linked to the concept of personal empowerment), and a willingness to risk the new, a forward-looking imagination of the possible in the midst of the actual. It involves positive steps toward achieving something better (such as peace in the community) and a certain measure of faith (in the possible). The development of hope is linked to the idea of developing a *positive mindset* identified by research participants as an important capacity for peace.

Directly linked to the concepts discussed earlier, *responsibility* means being answerable for one's own actions, which may include commitments to others. Linked to 'agency', it can be exercised through appropriate leadership (the ability to guide and direct others to achieve goals within a common set of values), role modelling ('doing what you say' so that your behaviour acts as an example that can be emulated by others, especially youth), and consistent action-taking (the ability to persist appropriately in a course of action or belief).

Respect, which was emphasised in this research, includes the unbiased regard for the rights, values, and beliefs of all. This includes: (a) self-respect, knowing one is worthy of regard; and (b) respect for others, acknowledging the worth and value of every individual. Respect is linked to notions of dignity—the recognition that every person, simply because they are human, has inherent value and worth—and equality of rights, opportunities, and status.

Empathy and compassion refers to being deeply aware of and understanding the suffering of others, and, on the basis of that understanding, acting to ease suffering and bring comfort. 'Empathetic compassion' (Goleman, 2007) is thus the ability to understand a person's situation and to spontaneously move to help them.

Mindfulness as a practice was identified as being a useful strategy for developing and enacting compassion. Mindfulness has been defined as awareness that arises through intentionally attending, in an accepting way, to whatever is arising in the present moment (Shapiro & Carlson, 2009). Black (2011) sees it is an inherent quality of human consciousness, and therefore, from our point of view, a 'spiritual capacity'. This links to concepts such as prayer and meditation. Prayer is viewed as being an exhortation that can be a source of strength and security, offering a sense of wholeness and hope, while meditation is seen as a practice and expression of focusing one's mind, becoming calm, and seeking insight.

Trust is the belief that someone is reliable (trustworthy). It includes attestation (giving witness to who and what one is), and dependability (being consistently reliable), and is encouraged by healing (restoration and reparation, often needed if trust is broken) and forgiveness (a willingness to stop blaming or being angry with someone).

Although not the focus for this chapter, evidence from the process and outcomes evaluations of the above-mentioned Building Bridges Mentoring Programme (Isobell et al., 2015; Van Gesselleen et al., 2015) suggests that the values education infused into the mentorship programme has had a major impact on the personal lives of the mentors and mentees, and on their ability to contribute to healing family life and to building a more peaceful community. Thus, the emphasis on intangible aspects linked to the concept of spiritual capacity seems to have contributed to peacebuilding in this context.

Discussion

In this discussion we focus primarily on the 'intangible' factors that have emerged from this research, and the importance of mobilising and enabling values, beliefs, principles, capacities, and behaviour in peacebuilding initiatives. Peace experts and activists have emphasised the importance of values, attitudes, modes of behaviour, and ways of life, linked to the concept of a culture of peace (Britto, Salah, et al., 2014; Chowdhury, 2014; Christie et al., 2014; Goodman, 2012; Leckman et al., 2014b; Reber-Rider, 2008). This includes values that promote harmony, social justice (including respect for human rights and needs), freedom, equality, and democracy, with a particular focus on promoting a propensity toward prosocial behaviour (including solidarity and cooperation), and the capacity for empathy and compassion, respect for others, fairness, trust in others, tolerance and inclusion of others, and open dialogue. It is interesting to note that the Building Bridges Mentoring intervention developed within the SCRATCHMAPS project reflects global trends in various ways. It clearly reveals a 'capabilities-based' approach (Britto, Salah, et al., 2014), using a peace education strategy as a major focus. In short, our findings are congruent with those of leading peace scholars.

It is important to note that the SCRATCHMAPS project did not ignore the need to address structural violence (Christie et al., 2014; Dawes & van der Merwe, 2014), including poverty and inequalities, the painful trauma of our Apartheid past, ongoing forms of prejudice and discrimination, access to employment, economic development and participation, and substance abuse. SCRATCHMAPS was guided by an ecosystemic approach (Britto, Salah, et al., 2014; Christie et al., 2014; Hinde & Stevenson-Hinde, 2014), and within that frame, attempted to address both direct and structural violence. The Building Bridges Mentoring intervention that was developed therefore reflected a commitment to a comprehensive approach to peacebuilding, with a strong emphasis on enacting an 'agentic' approach (Christie et al., 2014). Although most of the activities focused on personal and interpersonal development (individual and relationship levels), there was a strong emphasis on facilitating opportunities for the mentors and mentees, together with other community members, to participate in various community building activities aimed at promoting peace.

The idea of spiritual capacity, emphasised in this chapter, is intrinsically present in the peace literature, for example, in the statement that peace critically depends upon ways to 'foster a capacity to act, predicated on a fundamental recognition of freedom and dignity of all people' (Leckman et al., 2014b, p. 6). The creative freedom that marks the human being and which defines the concept of spiritual capacity, including the moral responsibility it evokes and the orientation to others and to the world it implies, can, as we noted earlier, be influenced by conditions that allow and enhance it or that inhibit, damage, or destroy it (e.g. through torture). These are both material conditions (such as poverty or the use of drugs) and relational conditions (primary relationships and group memberships, or their absence, for example). Analysing such conditions and their impact on the human spirit, that is, on the capacity of persons to exercise their creative freedom, is what makes the concept useful for the SCRATCHMAPS research.

As indicated, human spirit capacity is embodied not just materially—which is why basic needs are relevant—but also relationally (presupposing an emerging sense of self)—which is why attachment, affirmation, nurture, and sociality matter. Basic needs, a sine qua non, are not our concern here. What has been our concern is to articulate specific patterns of human becoming or flourishing that are efficacious at all levels of human relationships and that stimulate and enhance our spiritual capacity (creative freedom and its moral imperative) or, by virtue of their negation, subdue or diminish it. To be useful they would need to be regular, identifiable, and elegant (simple enough to grasp, yet discrete enough to express a complex range of relevant experiences and phenomena).

For this purpose, we turned to another notion from the work of IRHAP, that of the 'leading causes of life' (Gunderson & Cochrane, 2012; Gunderson & Pray, 2006). A clear play on the public health concept of the 'leading causes of death', it is intended to raise our awareness of the importance of generative sources for health alongside the dominant focus on degenerative or pathological sources of illness and disease. It is also, however, a specific conceptual framework that identifies five 'leading causes' of life as most central and relevant to flourishing human life: coherence, connection, agency, intergenerativity (or 'blessing', affirmation), and hope. Spiritual capacity is understood as a meta-dimension of all five 'causes' in a double-sense: all five 'causes' express the way in which our creative freedom is embodied in our emergence as persons in a world of other persons; and all five 'causes' feed back into our ability to exercise our creative freedom and to take up the moral responsibility it implies.

This offers us a perspective that helps us assess the empirical data from the SCRATCHMAPS work in the field, and place the central dynamics, virtues, and values regarded by the community within a framework that makes new sense of them. For example, one element seen by participants in the fieldwork as of critical importance to peace promotion was personal *agency* and its extension into group and communal agency. Similarly, questions of coherence, expressed in convictions about the importance of mindfulness and self-love in particular, frequently arose; so too did connectedness or connection, most strongly expressed in values and virtues linked to relationships with others. Also evident was a hint of intergenerational affirmation or 'blessing', present in the idea of role modelling; while hope, the last of the five 'causes of life', is specifically named and frequently invoked in the

research, seen as an anticipatory expectation of a transformed future to whose actualisation one contributes through one's own actions.

Conclusion

The specific emphasis of the SCRATCHMAPS project was on mobilising religious
assets and enabling spiritual capacity to promote peace. The chapter provides a
snapshot of the project, presents pertinent findings, focusing on identifying factors
that promote peace, and makes an argument for the recognition of the importance
of enhancing spiritual capacity, a new concept that is briefly defined, in peacebuilding interventions.

The notion of spiritual capacity emerges as being highly relevant to what one
observes from the grounded-theory produced from research in the field. That it links
so well to what the community itself thinks is critical to peacebuilding in its context.
This suggests two things: first, material and environmental factors, unquestionably
vital, are matched in their importance by non-material or human, that is, spiritual,
factors. Second, paying attention to enhancing the capabilities, virtues, and values
that express human spiritual capacity in all its dimensions offers much to any intervention for peace. It may indeed be critical to the motivational and emotional drives
that enable people to take on greater responsibility for transforming themselves and
the conditions within which they live.

This points to the importance of agency and responsibility, highlighted in this
research, and noted as being a central element of 'leading causes of life', and fundamental to the concept of spiritual capacity. Particularly interesting in the research
data is the theme of moral responsibility for one's actions. Autonomy (taking
responsibility for oneself) rather than heteronomy (handing one's moral responsibility over to some external authority) appears crucial to the way in which community members have expressed themselves about what makes for peace. Here
responsibility is linked to respect, empathy, care, and compassion, all essential to
living out the moral imperative that our creative freedom places before us in ways
that promote the good rather than ill or evil.

This striking finding on agency and taking responsibility for oneself in relationship with others and the community in general has major implications for our practice as peace activists and psychologists. Linked to notions of empowerment, it
reinforces the importance of enhancing the agency in ways that enable new actions
to be undertaken with some possibility of breaking through a distorted, painful actu-
ality marked by violence and insecurity. Equally significant, the suggestion by
community members of the idea of *in*-powerment is a clear indication of awareness
that one's orientation to the world is as important as one's capabilities. This finding
links with other research that emphasises the importance of facilitating personal and
collective empowerment, and the need to mobilise moral responsibility at individual
and community levels (Bettez, 2011). The challenge of enhancing spiritual capacity
is central to this.

In conclusion, while this research provides a useful contribution to understanding factors that promote peace, and some ideas on how 'intangible' factors can be mobilised and enabled within peacebuilding initiatives, it remains limited to one community in South Africa. Thus, a systematic review of similar initiatives would add to the global relevance of the points made here. A further limitation, and motivation for further research, links to the conceptual aspect of this project. The ongoing participatory development of the conceptual framework has meant a cyclic process of 'learning as we go', resulting in possible incongruencies within the process and outcomes. We have travelled quite far on the road to understanding the notions of religious assets and spiritual capacity in relation to peace promotion, but further research and theoretical engagement with these concepts is needed.

In sum, while structural factors are considered to be centrally important in attempts to promote peace, the authors argue that more attention should be focused on understanding and mobilising factors that link to the concept of spiritual capacity. This includes understanding how to instill and enhance these capacities for peace to effect change at all levels of the system. This raises a number of challenges to those involved in peace psychology.

Acknowledgements We dedicate this chapter to Cathy Hendricks, one of the local community researchers who participated in the research from 2011 to 2015, who has sadly passed on. Her contribution to her community is recognised by us all.

This research would not have been possible without the financial support of the South African National Research Foundation (Grant No. 103705 is recognised in particular), and the University of South Africa's Community Engagement grants. We are also extremely grateful to our VIPRU and IRHAP partners, and the local research team and wider community of Erijaville, for their invaluable contributions to the knowledge and actions emerging from this research. Finally, special thanks are due to Douglas McGaughey of Willamette University, Oregon, also Corresponding Member of the Research Institute on Political Philosophy, University of Tübingen, Germany, for his critical contributions to the notion of spiritual capacity.

References

African Religious Health Assets Programme (ARHAP). (2006). *Appreciating assets: The contribution of religion to universal access in Africa.* Report for the World Health Organization. Cape Town: ARHAP.

Amos, T. (2010). *Literature review on mobilizing assets to promote safety and peace.* Tygerberg: Medical Research Council-UNISA. Unpublished manuscript.

Babbie, E., & Mouton, J. (2009). *The practice of social research.* South Africa: Oxford University Press.

Bacani, B. (2004). Bridging theory and practice in peace education: The Notre Dame University peace education experience. *Conflict Resolution Quarterly, 21*(4), 503–511.

Barker, G., & Ricardo, C. (2005). Young men and the construction of masculinity in sub-Saharan Africa: Implications for HIV/AIDS, conflict, and violence. *Social development papers: Conflict prevention & reconstruction,* Paper No. 26. Washington, DC: The World Bank.

Barker, G., Ricardo, C., Nascimento, M., Olukoya, A., & Santos, C. (2010). Questioning gender norms with men to improve health outcomes: Evidence of impact. *Global Public Health, 5*(5), 539–553.

Barker, G., Ricardo, C., & Nascimento, M. (2007). *Engaging men and boys in changing gender-based inequity in health: Evidence from programme interventions.* Geneva: World Health Organisation.

Berger, P. L., & Hefner, R. W. (2003). *Spiritual capital in comparative perspective.* Retrieved July 24, from www.metanexus.net/archive/spiritualcapitalresearchprogram/pdf/Berger.pdf.

Bettez, S. C. (2011). Critical community building: Beyond belonging. *Educational Foundations, 25*(3–4), 3–19.

Black, D. S. (2011). A brief definition of mindfulness. *Mindfulness Research Guide.* Retrieved from http://www.mindfulexperience.org.

Boutros-Ghali, B. (1995). *An agenda for peace.* New York: United Nations Department of Public Information.

Bretherton, D., Weston, J., & Zbar, V. (2005). School-based peace building in Sierra Leone. *Theory Into Practice, 44*(4), 355–362.

Britto, P. R., Gordon, I., Hodges, W., Sunar, D., Kagitcibasi, C., & Leckman, J. F. (2014). Ecology of peace. In L. F. Leckman, C. Panter-Brick, & R. Salah (Eds.), *Pathways to peace: The transformative power of children and families* (pp. 27–39). Cambridge, MA: MIT.

Britto, P. R., Salah, R., Abu-Nimer, M., Bhabha, J., Chowdhury, A. K., Gunderson, G. R., et al. (2014). Creating effective programs and policies to reduce violence and promote peace. In L. F. Leckman, C. Panter-Brick, & R. Salah (Eds.), *Pathways to peace: The transformative power of children and families* (pp. 361–384). Cambridge, MA: MIT.

Chowdhury, A. K. (2014). Foreword: The culture of peace. In L. F. Leckman, C. Panter-Brick, & R. Salah (Eds.), *Pathways to peace: The transformative power of children and families* (pp. xiii–xx). Cambridge, MA: MIT.

Christie, D. J., Panter-Brick, C., Behrman, J., Cochrane, J. R., Dawes, A., Goth, K., et al. (2014). Healthy human development as a path to peace. In L. F. Leckman, C. Panter-Brick, & R. Salah (Eds.), *Pathways to peace: The transformative power of children and families* (pp. 273–302). Cambridge: MIT.

Cochrane, J. R., Seedat, M., Lazarus, S., Ratele, K., Suffla, S., & Taliep, N. (2015). *Spiritual capacity and religious assets for transforming community health by mobilising males for peace and safety (SCRATCHMAPS): Position paper on the concepts of religious assets and spiritual capacities, resilience and connectedness, and masculinity and violence prevention, in the context of peace and safety promotion.* Tygerberg: MRC/UNISA.

Creswell, J. W. (2007). *Qualitative inquiry and research design: Choosing among five traditions* (2nd ed.). Thousand Oaks, CA: Sage.

Dawes, A., & van der Merwe, A. (2014). Structural violence and early childhood development. In L. F. Leckman, C. Panter-Brick, & R. Salah (Eds.), *Pathways to peace: The transformative power of children and families* (pp. 233–250). Cambridge, MA: MIT.

de Gruchy, S., Cochrane, J. R., Olivier, J., & Matimelo, S. (2011). Participatory inquiry on the interface between religion and public health: What does it achieve and what not? In J. R. Cochrane, B. Schmid, & T. Cutts (Eds.), *When religion and health align: Mobilizing religious health assets for transformation* (pp. 43–61). Pietermaritzburg: Cluster Publications.

Der-lanYeh, T. (2006). The way to peace: A Buddhist perspective. *International Journal of Peace Studies, 11*(1), 91–112.

European Council of Religious Leaders—Religions for Peace. (2009). *Lille declaration on a culture of peace.* Retrieved from http://www.rfp-europe.eu/index.cfm?id=241899.

Finke, R. (2003). *Spiritual capital: Definitions, applications, and new frontiers.* Retrieved July 24, from www.metanexus.net/archive/spiritualcapitalresearchprogram/research_articles.asp.html.

Goleman, D. (2007). *Three kinds of empathy: Cognitive, emotional, compassionate.* Retrieved June 12, from http://www.danielgoleman.info/three-kinds-of-empathy-cognitive-emotional-compassionate/.

Goodman, A. (2012). Human ecology as peacebuilding. In L. Williams, R. A. Roberts, & A. McIntosh (Eds.), *Radical human ecology: Intercultural and indigenous approaches* (pp. 257–274). Surrey, England: Ashgate.

Gunderson, G. R., & Cochrane, J. R. (2012). *Religion and the health of the public: Shifting the paradigm.* New York: Palgrave MacMillan.

Gunderson, G. R., & Pray, L. (2006). *Leading causes of life*. Memphis, TN: The Center of Excellence in Faith and Health, Methodist Le Bonheur Healthcare.

Hinde, R. A., & Stevenson-Hinde, J. (2014). Framing our analysis: A dialectical perspective. In L. F. Leckman, C. Panter-Brick, & R. Salah (Eds.), *Pathways to peace: The transformative power of children and families* (pp. 19–26). Cambridge, MA: MIT.

Hunsberger, B., & Jackson, L. M. (2005). Religion, meaning, and prejudice. *Journal of Social Issues, 61*, 807–826.

Hussein, A. (2009). The use of triangulation in social sciences research: Can qualitative and quantitative methods be combined? *Journal of Comparative Social Work, 1*, 1–12.

Iannaccone, L. R., & Klick, J. (2003). *Spiritual capital: An introduction and literature review*. Retrieved July 24, from www.metanexus.net/archive/spiritualcapitalresearchprogram/pdf/review.pdf.

Isobell, I., & Lazarus, S. (2014). *SCRATCHMAPS Development of Safety and Peace Indicators Research Report: Report on process and findings of the process of developing safety and peace indicators in Erijaville during 2012-2013*. Tygerberg: SAPPRU (Medical Research Council/ University of South Africa).

Isobell, I., Lazarus, S., Taliep, N., Simmons, C., James, E., Jonas, M., et al. (2015). *SCRATCHMAPS outcomes evaluation research report*. Tygerberg: VIPRU (MRC/UNISA).

Israel, B. A., Eng, E., Schulz, A. J., & Parker, E. A. (2005). *Methods in community-based participatory research for health*. San Francisco: Jossey-Bass.

Kramer, S., Amos, T., Lazarus, S., & Seedat, M. (2012). The philosophical assumptions, utility and challenges of asset mapping approaches to community engagement. *Journal of Psychology in Africa, 22*(4), 539–546.

Krug, E., Dahlberg, L. L., Mercy, J. A., Zwi, A. B., & Lozano, R. (2002). *World report on violence and health*. Geneva: World Health Organization.

Lazarus, S., Taliep, N., Olivier, J., Cochrane, J., Seedat, M., Cutts, T., et al. (2014). *SCRATCHMAPS Community asset mapping research report: Report on community asset mapping conducted in Erijaville during 2012*. Tygerberg: VIPRU (Medical Research Council/University of South Africa).

Lazarus, S., Tonsing, S., Ratele, K., & van Niekerk, A. (2011). Masculinity as a key risk and protective factor to male interpersonal violence: An exploratory and critical review. *African Safety Promotion, 9*(1), 23–50.

Leckman, J. F., Panter-Brick, C., & Salah, R. (2014b). Peace is a lifelong process: The importance of partnerships. In L. F. Leckman, C. Panter-Brick, & R. Salah (Eds.), *Pathways to peace: The transformative power of children and families* (pp. 3–18). Cambridge, MA: MIT.

Little, D. (2006). Religion, conflict and peace. In *Proceedings from symposium: Rebuilding Nation Building*. Cleveland, OH: Case Western Reserve University School of Law.

Maiese, M. (2003). Peacebuilding. In G. Burgess & H. Burgess (Eds.), *Conflict information: Beyond intractability*. Consortium, University of Colorado Boulder. Retrieved from http:// www.beyondintractability.org/essay/peacebuilding.

Mandour, T. M. (2010). Islam and religious freedom: Role of interfaith dialogue in promoting global peace. *Brigham Young University Law Review*, 885–893. Retrieved from www.aensi-web.com/old/jasr/jasr/2012/2920-2924.pdf.

McGaughey, D. (n.d.). *Freedom on this and the other side of Kant*. Retrieved from http://criticalidealism.org/wp-content/uploads/2014/10/Freedom-on-This-and-the-Other-Side-of-Kant.pdf.

Ratele, K., Suffla, S., Lazarus, S., & Van Niekerk, A. (2010). Towards the development of a responsive, social science-informed, critical public health framework on male interpersonal violence. *Social Change, 40*(4), 415–438.

Reber-Rider, L. (2008). Building cultures of peace in the world: One peace center at a time. *International Journal of World Peace, 25*(1), 73–88.

Seedat, M., van Niekerk, A., Jewkes, R., Suffla, S., & Ratele, K. (2009). Violence and injuries in South Africa: Prioritising an agenda for prevention. *Lancet, Health in South Africa Series, 5*, 1–12.

Shapiro, S. L., & Carlson, L. E. (2009). The art and science of mindfulness: Integrating mindfulness into psychology and the helping professions. *American Psychological Association, 194*, 3–14.

Simmons, C., Isobell, I., & Lazarus, S. (2014). *Report on SCRATCHMAPS Colloquium. Report on process and findings of three-day colloquium including academic and community researchers.* Tygerberg: SAPPRU (Medical Research Council/University of South Africa).

Taliep, N., Simmons, C., van Niekerk, D., & Phillips, S. (2015). *Building Bridges Mentorship Programme manual.* Tygerberg: Medical Research Council.

United Nations. (1995). *UN agenda for peace: Supplement.* Retrieved from http://www.cfr.org/world/un-agenda-peace-supplement/p24231.

Van Gesselleen, M., Lazarus, S., Taliep, N., Isobell, D., Carelse, H., & Phillips, S. (2015). *Process evaluation of the implementation of a community-based violence prevention intervention using participatory methodologies. Research Report presented to academic and community partners.* Tygerberg: VIPRU (MRC/UNISA).

Wallerstein, N., & Duran, B. (2008). The theoretical, historical, and practice roots of CBPR. In M. Minkler & N. Wallerstein (Eds.), *Community based participatory research for health* (2nd ed., pp. 25–46). San Francisco: Wiley.

Chapter 9
Interrogatory Destabilisation and an Insurgent Politics for Peacebuilding: The Case of the Apartheid Archive Project

Garth Stevens, Norman Duncan, and Hugo Canham

> *In exploring and producing archives, be they alternative, interrogative, or fictional, [they] are not simply questioning the authenticity, authority or authorship of the archive; rather, they are unlocking its regenerative, radical potential.*

> (Downey, 2015)

Peace, Destabilisation and Insurgency: Inimical?

The latter half of the twentieth century witnessed the ascendancy of a specific mode of managing conflict and its attendant forms of direct and structural violence at national, regional and global levels. This mode of conflict management essentially became captured by the hegemonic discourse of peace, in which the cessation of forms of direct violence, political settlements and the establishment of systems of social stability dominated. In essence, this discourse acted as a bulwark that helped to shore up a range of political imperatives associated with this period of history—not the least of which included an avoidance of a repetition of the genocidal atrocities associated with WWII; an awareness of the technological accoutrements related to waging war that could wreak global havoc; legitimising international bodies such as the United Nations as well as the dominance of western forms of liberal democracy; maintaining conditions during the Cold War that minimised the opportunities for further conflict escalation between the superpowers; and intervening in conflict

G. Stevens (✉) • H. Canham
Department of Psychology, University of the Witwatersrand, Johannesburg, South Africa
e-mail: Garth.Stevens@wits.ac.za; Hugo.Canham@wits.ac.za

N. Duncan
Department of Psychology, University of Pretoria, Pretoria, South Africa
e-mail: Norman.Duncan@up.ac.za

© Springer International Publishing AG 2017
M. Seedat et al. (eds.), *Enlarging the Scope of Peace Psychology*,
Peace Psychology Book Series, DOI 10.1007/978-3-319-45289-0_9

zones that had the potential to threaten global stability during a period of increased transnationalism and globalisation (Christie, Wagner, & Winter, 2001). In this context, peace involved the active reduction of political and social instability and a curtailing of a politics of insurgency.

However, while this specific approach to peace made important contributions to the reduction of direct forms of violence globally, and resonated with of much of the work in peace psychology pertaining to peacekeeping and peacemaking (Christie, Tint, Wagner, & Winter, 2008), it is the more difficult and arduous process of peacebuilding that we are concerned with in this chapter. Drawing on writers such as Christie et al. (2001) in the terrain of peace psychology, who argue that peacebuilding is centrally connected to social justice imperatives and the eradication of structural violence (that is also frequently implicated in forms of direct violence) in transitional and post-conflict societies, this chapter endorses the idea that peacebuilding may of necessity incorporate elements that run counter to the status quo. To this end, we argue that peacebuilding can indeed, and perhaps always should, encompass forms of interrogatory destabilisation and a politics of insurgency.

By interrogatory destabilisation, we refer to forms of consciousness raising that critique the continuing ideological and material bases for structural forms of violence, inequality, privilege and power within a given social formation, especially those social formations transitioning away from violent conflict and authoritarianism (Freire, 2000; Martín-Baró, 1994). Of necessity, interrogatory destabilisation involves a repetitive critical deconstruction of the taken-for-granted assumptions and regimes of truth that suggest that power differentials and structural inequalities are normative in such societies, thereby unsettling the stable nature of status quos. As such, the process is deeply subjective and personally transformative on the one hand, but because it is directed towards an illumination and critique of the operation of ideology and is based in the embodied and material experiences of populations, is also a collective process of conscientisation that may potentially be socially transformative, on the other.

In addition, we argue that this process of interrogatory destabilisation can often find fertile ground on which to settle within organic and deliberate social movements that embrace a political project that encourages an insurgent citizenship and politics (Holston, 2009). This type of insurgency that Holston (2009) refers to incorporates a politics of resistance amongst those who are precariously positioned in societies and deprived of even their most basic human rights in many social formations today. Instead of perpetuating their positions on the periphery of society, these social movements attempt to reclaim elements of their rightful citizenship by resisting hegemonic constructions of who is included and excluded as valued citizens. This may involve active forms of social protest and conscientisation, but may also include everyday forms of social relating that are characterised by "in-your-face-incivilities and aggressive aesthetics" (Holston, 2009, p. 275) that run counter to what is hegemonically considered an acceptable form of dissent. As such, an insurgent citizenship and politics is a disruptive mode of engaging and living in the social world, but is also fundamentally premised on a politics of antagonism (Hook, 2014).

Thus, rather than considering peace as a process in which docile subjects are generated, we hold Foucault's view of many contemporary democracies that suggests that:

> In the smallest of its cogs, peace [...] is waging a secret war. To put it in another way, we have to interpret the war that is going on beneath peace; peace is itself a coded war. [...] a battlefront runs through the whole of society, continuously and permanently, and it is this battlefront that puts us all on one side or the other. There is no such thing as a neutral subject. We are all inevitably someone's adversary (Foucault, 2003, p. 53).

As an illustrative exemplar of interrogatory destabilisation and the possibilities for a politics of insurgency, we examine the productive and critical use of archives within a South African initiative, called the Apartheid Archive Project (Stevens, Duncan, & Hook, 2013). The chapter essentially argues for the importance of understanding and addressing the phenomenon of racism still confronting South African society, in order to avert the potential for both ongoing psychological and social disruption. We reflect on the ways in which archives and the Apartheid Archive Project in particular, may be sites of struggle and contestation that allow for a reclamation, refiguring and democratisation of history. In addition, we argue that expanding this archive allows us to examine apartheid's historical and continued effects into the present; to move beyond a mere recognition of woundedness and entanglements; and to raise questions about the mechanisms that sustain ongoing disparities in access, power and privilege at a political, social, cultural, psychological and material level. We argue that archives open up spaces for an interrogatory destabilisation that is fundamental to an insurgent citizenship and politics, which is central to our conceptualisation of peacebuilding. Here, we deliberately uncouple peace from processes seeking to produce compliant subjects and instead suggest that it is a process that rests on a repetitive dialectic of critically engaging strategic relations of power within the status quo, to seek more equitable social arrangements that address both direct and structural violence.

Apartheid: A History Still in the Making

It is exactly 22 years since the installation of the first post-apartheid government in South Africa; an event that announced the transition from a system of vicious racial oppression to a non-racial and democratic order. The current conjuncture arguably represents an opportune moment to reflect on the extent to which South Africa has been able to deal with its ruinous past, and to question the extent to which apartheid can be relegated to the status of historical artefact, or whether it continues to echo recalcitrantly in the present.

Denials, Elisions and the Imperative to Re-engage the Past

A peculiarity of South African society is that during the period that immediately followed the first non-racial, democratic general elections in 1994, many South Africans displayed a marked disinclination to engage or deal with the racism of the old apartheid order. Indeed, during this period there appeared to be a growing number of South Africans who, when referring to pre-1994 South Africa, seemed to dismiss (as no longer relevant) or negate the profoundly devastating effects of apartheid on the lives of millions of South Africans.[1] The establishment of the Apartheid Archive Project in 2009 was in part a reaction to this tendency.

Moreover, the establishment of the project was also driven by the assumption that it is largely because of the consistent elision or denial of the racism of the past, as well as the belief that it is no longer a feature of South African society, that we are currently witnessing some of the vilest manifestations of racism and race-related violence that were so frequently associated with the old order. As such, a further premise of the project is that the unremitting nature of racism may indeed be related to the weakening of the moral imperative to address racism both historically and in contemporary South Africa, partly as a result of the salient tropes of forgiveness and nation-building that were so central to the reconciliation project that accompanied the dismantling of the apartheid regime. To deny our past transgressions, we believe, is to deny the humanity of those against whom we have transgressed, and to diminish the humanity of the *other* is to make future transgressions against the latter all the easier.

As authors, our own experience of clearly benefiting from the liberating effects of democracy while also experiencing the continuities of a racialised order have made this project deeply personal. All three of us are black, South African, middle-class men whose life opportunities and trajectories have been radically altered from a likely path of struggle, experiences of overt racism and foreclosed possibilities. We are academics at institutions that were previously almost exclusively accessible to white South Africans. Notwithstanding the possibilities enabled by the end of apartheid, we remember that period in ways that inform how we experience the present. We also continue to experience both direct and subtle 'everyday racisms'. Our positionality as South Africans that have lived in both apartheid and democratic South Africa has enabled us to utilise the archive as both contributors and researchers. Our experiences are both personal and publicly shared through the archive. However, our current class positions mean that we are somewhat sheltered against more overt forms of racism that appear to continue unabated, as is evidenced as follows:

A Snapshot of Events

Disconcerting incidents such as the following, which have been reported with increasing regularity in the media in recent years and which serve as intractable reminders and *ex post facto* evidence of the perverse legacy of the apartheid order provide compelling support for this assumption. All of the following incidents reported in South African media occurred during the 2014–2015 period:

06 August 2014: In addition to painting their faces black, two University of Pretoria students stuffed their bodies with materials to exaggerate their buttocks and breasts and dressed as domestic workers, in apparent disparagement

---

[1] Rüsen (in Villa-Vicencio, 2004) comments on similar processes of denial amongst large sections of the German public during the period immediately following the Holocaust.

of black women's bodies, features and social class. In response to this incident, Bateman of ENCA (2014, n. p.) reported that, "The University of Pretoria has moved swiftly to institute disciplinary steps against two female students after pictures emerged showing the women dressed up as black domestic workers". While the university acted speedily to suspend the students, it can be argued that the subsequent reconciliatory actions allowing the students to return to the university in 2015 could be interpreted as an indication of a soft approach to racism. The SA Human Rights Commission spokesperson, Isaac Mangena, noted that "As a result of the [mediation process] the students are entitled to return to the residence in 2015" (ENCA, 6 August 2014, n. p).

23 September 2014: Barely a month after the University of Pretoria incident, at a party at one of the student residences of the University of Stellenbosch, young students blackened their faces and dressed up as the African American tennis champions Venus and Serena Williams. Like the preceding incident, this should be interpreted against the context of the long history of mocking black people through blackening and exaggeration of features. In response, the university issued the following statement on its website: "The pursuance of critical debate and conciliatory conversations is of much greater value to Stellenbosch University's student community than action against the students that caused the buzz on social media last week after a birthday party at Amazink in Kayamandi" (Times Live, 30 September 2014, n. p.). Arguably, the lack of punitive measures might be read as a negation of the pain that is inflicted and the stereotypes perpetuated in such a racist incident.

October 2014: Five young white men, three of whom were arrested and charged for attacking a black 52-year-old mother of six outside a nightclub in Cape Town (Daily Maverick, 27 November 2014).

11 November 2014: In Cape Town's Waterkant, while waiting to use an electronic cash machine, a violent brawl ensued after a white man called a black man a 'kaffir'[2] (Eye Witness News, 11 November 2014).

11 March 2015: Affluent suburbs in Worcester in the Western Cape were recently exposed for requiring gardeners and domestic workers to carry identification cards reminiscent of the apartheid era's 'dompas'.[3] News24 (11 March 2015, n. p) reported that it "emerged … that the Worcester SAPS [South African Police Service] and Community Policing Forum (CPF) introduced the cards bearing the photographs and personal details of the workers back in 2012 after a proposal by the neighbourhood watches of certain suburbs. The cards have to be carried when workers, including gardeners and builders, enter affluent parts of the town. Workers who do not carry the cards are reportedly treated with suspicion by the CPF". The racialised and classed nature of this surveillance can be seen as constructing people of colour as interlopers when the latter enter spaces of (white) affluence.

---

[2] 'Kaffir' is a derogatory term used in South Africa to dehumanise black people in ways that are similar to the use of the word 'nigger' in the USA.

[3] A 'dompas' served as an identity document used to track the movement of Africans within the country and was a means of advancing the apartheid ideology and practise of segregation, and the control of the movement of blacks into and in urban 'white areas'.

March 2015: A black female student at the University of the Witwatersrand was allegedly assaulted and called an "unnecessary (sic) black bitch" when she confronted
two white female students for laughing at the accent of their black lecturer in a law
class (Vuvuzela, 4 March 2015).

The frequency and intensity of these racial skirmishes or hostilities have become
increasingly commonplace and marked. Various commentators (see, for example, Faul, 2008) have observed that rather than progressively becoming less pro-
nounced (as could have been expected, given the length of the period following
the 1994 elections and the increasing maturation of post-1994 democratic structures and processes in South Africa), racism remains as unremitting as ever in
contemporary South Africa and indeed at times appears to be disconcertingly
overt. This is not to suggest that racism has become more commonplace, but
perhaps largely reflects increased media interest and incredulity at continuing
racism two decades after the birth of democracy.

Continuities and Discontinuities

Of course, there are the much more 'ordinary' and everyday racist processes that
insistently remind us of the apartheid days, but which do not grab the imagination
of the media in quite the same manner as the more dramatically 'sensational' events
previously described. Elsewhere, Essed (1991) has called this 'everyday racism'—
relational moments of apparent banal differentiation, slights and insults that include
racialised micro-aggressions and everyday incivilities (Sonn, 2013). But beyond
these there are also the ongoing 'everyday' struggles of hundreds of thousands of
impoverished black people still trying to access a life better than the one that they
had been relegated to by the apartheid order. In this context, 'everyday racism' sig-
nals the structural violence of racism which is fuelled by raced inequality. In this
regard, we note that social change has had limited benefits for those on the margins
of the economy who are overwhelmingly black and poor. The effects of racism are
thus both personal and structural.

An example of the structural inequalities is evident in research published by
Statistics South Africa (2014) which shows that currently the unemployment rates
for Blacks, Coloureds, Indians and Whites are 40%, 28%, 18% and 8%, respectively. Furthermore, government statistics reveal that only 10% of black households
fall within the top income bracket in South Africa compared to 65% of white
households (Faul, 2008). According to Statistics South Africa (2014), 54% of Blacks
are currently living in poverty. These statistics very forcefully illustrate the sharply
racialised nature of poverty and the persistent continuities of apartheid era patterns of
inequality.

While the 1990s saw South Africa's rapid reintegration into the regional and
global economies, current levels of (largely racialised) disparity and inequality
remain alarmingly stark. For example, according to Statistics South Africa (2014),
the Gini-Coefficient for South Africa currently stands at 0.65, with race remaining
the strongest indicator of inequality.

Whereas the persistent trends in inequality in South Africa are undoubtedly fuelled in part by the effects of globalisation and the influence of various multinational corpocracies that have reinvested in South Africa's economy, they are arguably also due to a growing culture of selfish individualism, a frenzied quest for self-enrichment, cut-throat corporate competition and a drive for individual economic and social mobility at the expense of the broader populace (Bond, 2000; Desai, 2002; Terre Blanche, 2006).

Gqubule (2006) notes that the transformation of the South African economy has not been in step with political change. This has resulted, inter alia, in ongoing labour unrest and the violent and highly racialised service delivery protests seen in so many black, working-class communities in the past several years. Within this context, any meaningful attempts at addressing the sedimented effects of apartheid racism are increasingly being marginalised.

Villa-Vicencio (2008, p. 24) provides a rather poignant illustration of how the inability or unwillingness to deal with the racism of the apartheid order is perpetuating the consequences of the said order during the post-1994 era:

> A … visit to Vryburg … presented me with a picture of excessive opulence cheek by jowl with poverty and exclusion—divided largely along racial lines. Young white males swagger in the streets with holstered guns on display. Black learners are relegated to schools that barely function, in order to allow white learners to pursue the privileges their parents demand. The main high school … an "Afrikaans school" … is essentially white, and an "English school" … is black.

Within the context of ever-deepening socio-economic inequalities we have however of late also witnessed various robust contestations over the symbolic remnants and portrayals of colonial and apartheid era white supremacy. For example, the grandiose statue of Cecil John Rhodes on the upper campus of the University of Cape Town has recently been the focus of much debate and protest, with the university often described as holding onto colonial tropes of excellence and continuing to centre the white experience (Mamdani, 1997). Similar to many corporate spaces, university campuses are increasingly being seen as elite spaces where government has little influence to effect change. Canham (2014) has illustrated that corporate spaces have only permitted access to certain kinds of easily assimilable bodies, while repelling certain discordant bodies that challenge values that symbolise whiteness. Likewise, many historically white universities tend to produce tolerable white and black bodies that corporations readily absorb in contemporary South Africa. Within a context in which the state is attempting to influence the way in which the past is remembered through the erection of statues and other memorials of anti-apartheid icons and events in public spaces, such as at airports and parliament, the uneven ways in which space is occupied at historically white universities both by people and memorials are becoming increasingly conspicuous and contested.

Of course, we have also witnessed one of the more frightening consequences of apartheid era racism in the form of xenophobic violence. Aimed at 'foreigners' from the rest of Africa and Asia, it first emerged in the mid-1990s and reached a crescendo in 2008 and 2015. Here, issues of relative poverty, access to the public space, unemployment, endemic poverty, a history of colonial and apartheid *othering*, the racialised politics of statecraft, a weakened state and the breach of the social contract between government and its citizens to ensure the even distribution of rights and obligations have all been cited as some of the contributing factors for the xenophobic violence (Duncan, 2012; Hassim, Kupe, & Worby, 2008; Landau, 2011). Clearly many of these emanate from deep historical forms of alienation and inequality that persist in contemporary South Africa, with much of the resulting hostility being misdirected against those who are frequently as marginalised as poor black South Africans, but from other parts of Africa and Asia.

What is apparent is that the political discontinuities that have marked the transition from apartheid to democracy in South Africa are deeply contrasted with the psychosocial, socio-cultural and economic continuities that persist across the historical watershed of the political transition. Indeed, despite the democratisation of South Africa and the widespread reconciliation project that was undertaken, disruptions to these continuities and the fundamental transformation of human relations in many material and non-material ways have not occurred as anticipated.

Archives, Interrogatory Destabilisation and Peacebuilding

Given South Africa's apparent self-imposed, and often carefully managed, amnesia about the apartheid era (cf. Villa-Vicencio, 2004), as well as its blindness to the ongoing impact of the institutionalised apartheid racism of the past on extant intergroup and inter-personal relationships (as evidenced by the reports and statistics previously presented in this chapter), we believe that it is important for South African society to review its past, so as to acknowledge and address it. Here, the orchestrated amnesia refers to the material, political and psychological investment in not acknowledging the exploitation and oppression of blacks enabled by apartheid, in order to not engage with the current need for fundamental structural change, including the redistribution of resources to address past dispossession. Key within our approach to the archive of apartheid, are three elements that we believe to be central to critically interrogating the relationship between history and the present, facilitating consciousness-raising, and destabilising the unequal nature of the status quo in the service of peacebuilding. First, we aim to uncover a more comprehensive and complex history of apartheid. Second, we rely on the everyday accounts of ordinary people to disrupt, augment, supplement and contest the dominant historical accounts of apartheid. Third, we utilise these narrational resources as analytic tools to critically interrogate and subvert the dominant discourse that suggests that post-apartheid South Africa is distinct and discontinuous from apartheid South Africa, and to contest the common trope that ongoing forms of structural inequality are natural or merely normative features of all transitional societies.

Of course, the Truth and Reconciliation Commission (TRC) has already made a critical contribution to the process of remembering the excesses of the apartheid order (Cassan, Cayla, & Salazar, 2004; Villa-Vicencio, 2004). However, given the TRC's tendency to focus on the more 'dramatic' or salient narratives of apartheid atrocities and the fact that it thereby effectively (albeit unintentionally) foreclosed the possibility of a systematic exploration of the more quotidian, but no less significant, manifestations of apartheid abuse, means that much of the details of apartheid racism have not been publicly acknowledged or assessed. Our reference to the 'grand' or 'dramatic' narrative here points to the prevalence of the recognisable testimony of various anti-apartheid struggle stalwarts as well as an assortment of apartheid apparatchiks presented at the TRC hearings.

It is largely for the preceding reason that the Apartheid Archive Project has, since its inception, endeavoured to foreground stories and narratives of the everyday experiences of 'ordinary' South Africans during the apartheid era, rather than simply focusing on the 'grand',[4] highly mediatised narratives of the past or the privileged narratives of academic, political and social elites. In effect, the project attempts to fill the gaps interspersed between the 'grand' narratives recorded by the TRC and the carefully orchestrated amnesia about the past. 'Ordinary' narratives refer particularly to the narratives of the 'non-elites' that ordinarily do not or would not be captured by the public or mainstream record. As such, they represent an analytic borderland in which the enactments of everyday incivilities, micro-aggressions and resistances potentially reveal the complex ways in which ordinary people were implicated in the maintenance and contestation of apartheid. In addition, they highlight ways in which social inequalities may be maintained and agentically resisted in the present.

This project is conceptualised as an initiative aimed at facilitating the reclamation of the humanity of those whose dignity, well-being and indeed, personhood, had been systematically eroded by the apartheid order. As such, it is more than an initiative that simply seeks to expose apartheid's excesses. It is a project of affirmation and peacebuilding that emphasises the complex positionality of those victimised by the violence of South Africa's colonial and apartheid pasts.

Of course, the Apartheid Archive Project is not merely oriented towards this past, but also to the present and the future. The past two decades have seen the emergence of a new generation that has been relatively 'untainted' by the more brutal expressions of the institutionalised racism that epitomised apartheid. This cohort, in some way, represents a generational rupture in the continuity of the historical archive. We are also deeply interested in understanding how young South Africans engage *with* this legacy and live *through* it in generative ways. The questions that consequently arise are as follows: how do young South Africans who have been part of the 'born free'[5] generation relate to their freedom and subjectivity in a country that has been systematically defined by its racialised past and history? How do they 'do' or perform the idea of freedom and non-racialism in a context that is ostensibly free from apartheid, but yet inexorably connected to South Africa's recent racialised and racist past?

---

[4] In this context 'grand narratives' refer to the totalising or homogenising political narratives and narrative schemes of apartheid and anti-apartheid struggle elites (cf. Lyotard, 1979).

[5] The generation born after the first non-racial elections in 1994 is frequently referred to as the 'born free' generation.

This project therefore hopes to contribute to the development of a historical archive which the post-1994 generation and future generations may draw upon to understand the present. The project also seeks to gather an expansive body of silenced life stories and narratives to be recorded before they are lost to history. Moreover, it is also a project of solidarity with the formerly oppressed as it enables a process of public witnessing where younger generations are able to learn about the past, understand their own ongoing experiences of everyday racism as related to the foregoing narratives of earlier generations and build a future based on more equitable material and social relations.

In essence, the Apartheid Archive Project aims to examine the nature of the experiences of racism of (particularly 'ordinary') South Africans under the old apartheid order and their continuing effects on individual and group functioning in contemporary South Africa. Thus, the project gathers stories and narratives of both black and white South Africans, of representatives from elites[6] and marginalised social categories, of racist perpetration and victimisation, and of complicity, trauma and resilience. Important to note is that for us, the role of psychology as a disciplinary lens has the critical potential to offer certain insights into how a transformative psychosocial praxis may be realised in relation to the violence of race, racism and related social asymmetries, thereby contributing to a peacebuilding project.

In particular, this disciplinary lens allows us to revisit and refigure the archive as a site of liberation, democratisation and peacebuilding, as individual stories and narratives have the potential to challenge the 'grand' narratives of official histories that tend to occlude the voices and experiences of 'ordinary' South Africans whose identities and subjectivities continue to be shaped by their memories and experiences of the apartheid order (Stevens, Duncan, & Sonn, 2013).

The Importance of Memory

In the context of the Apartheid Archive Project, stories and narratives have a liminal quality, allowing for a reflection of the past, but through the narrational context of the present. The Apartheid Archive Project therefore encourages the study of a *critical psychosocial mnemonics*—a terrain in which memory is invoked and utilised to craft stories of the past, but in which the story itself is constantly transformed as a function of the narrational context of the present; where stories can tell us more about our past, but simultaneously also about our present and a future that is yet to emerge.

The Apartheid Archive Project is also a space where memories and stories can tell us as much about personal experiences as about the social world in which they are situated (Stevens, Duncan & Hook, 2013). Given the over-determined nature of racism and racialisation processes in South Africa, such a framing also gives us the

---

[6] In this context, elite refers to those who occupy positions of social, political and/or economic privilege who also have an 'ordinary' story to tell. This is important as we are also interested in the nuanced story of simultaneous complicity and victimhood.

opportunity to examine the material, social, cultural and libidinal or affective components that sustain, reproduce and contest such racialisation processes (Stevens, Duncan & Hook, 2013). From a methodological perspective, much of the work of the Apartheid Archive Project could be characterised as falling within the domain of a decolonising praxis, focusing on the recalcitrant socio-cultural and psychosocial resonances of race within the postcolonial context, and foregrounding the subaltern voice as a means of avoiding the silences that often relegate the experiences of the marginalised to the shadows of consent in matrices of social inequality (Sonn, Stevens, & Duncan, 2013).

Furthermore, the very nature of the project occupies the symbolic and applied psychoanalytic function of a potential space, a transitional space and a containing space in which unprocessed experiences of the past that may be imbued with traumatic libidinal content, can in fact be processed both personally and socially, allowing for the forging of alternative subjectivities and collective memories (Long, 2013). This function in turn has the potential for creating public dialogue, citizen participation and intercommunal spaces in which a 'knowing' of the self and the other can be realised in processes of social transformation (Stevens, Duncan & Sonn, 2013). This is important as public dialogue and citizen participation take the work beyond the academic realm and into the lived experience of people. However, while mutual recognition of the manner in which black and white lives have historically been and continue to be imbricated is important, public dialogue also creates opportunities to determine the extent of these continuities as well as the manner in which new axes of power and privilege manifest to undermine the emergence of a transformed and egalitarian society. Even as narratives are comprised of individual accounts, the analysis by researchers places them in social conversation with each other. Further to this, different presentations including the project's web-based portal, the electronic repository of stories, public presentations, various books and academic articles have allowed for the narratives to be engaged with by a range of publics.

Stories as Archival Material

Most of the research emanating from the Apartheid Archive Project has been conducted within a qualitative framework, largely in recognition of the value of the qualitative tradition in giving voice to the marginalised as well as to capture the nuances, complexities and contradictions that form part of the human experience. Furthermore, this framework is given preference because it places social subjects' actions and experiences at the centre of processes of knowledge production and generation within the research endeavour.

While apartheid has frequently been personified by the likes of DF (Daniel François) Malan, Hendrik Verwoerd, John Vorster, Adriaan Vlok, Eugene De Kock and Wouter Basson, it was 'ordinary' enfranchised white citizens that repeatedly renewed their mandate implicitly or explicitly (TRC Report, 2008). Moreover, the daily 'work' of apartheid was carried out in 'routine', 'everyday' racist interactions with the subjugated. Therefore, such stories and narratives represent a critical component of the historical archive through which South Africans may come to terms with their past, as a means of engaging more constructively with their present. The project attempts to provide a space that affords 'ordinary' South Africans the opportunity to place their stories in unmediated form at the centre of public record, scrutiny, commentary and analysis. This matters because the stories are not collected with the sole purpose of research analysis but for their ability to speak for themselves as living texts. In this manner, this project aims to insert the experiences of 'ordinary' South Africans into the written history of South Africa. The work is thus political as it recognises the importance of the lives reflected in 'marginal' stories as seminal to our history and personhood.

Specifically, the analysis of stories and narratives is a central feature of much of the research conducted within the project. To paraphrase Sonn et al. (2013), stories do matter, because of their pivotal functions in the construction of identities, subjectivities and collective narratives. Hatch and Cunliffe (2006) note that narratives are never pure reflections of deeds, behaviours and events. They are always sites within which the personal investments of speakers, listeners, the invisible interlocutors who may apprehend such stories and the influence of the social context on our interpretations of the world converge to give rise to a constructed version of the event (Sands, 2004). Squire (2013, p. 1) further reminds narrative researchers that talk is significant for the narrator's story of 'who they are' and "stories are about representation itself in that the uncertain, changeable nature of written, spoken and visual symbol systems means that stories are distanced from the happenings they described, have many meanings, and are never the same when told twice". In this regard, while the narratives are captured in the archive in an unmediated form, we recognise that narratives are nonetheless fundamentally always mediated, as narrators choose what to say and how to say it. They also remember the past in different ways. Moreover, the awareness of the audience that might read the story and the guidelines that we provide to frame the story suggests that narratives are products of co-construction. For us then, the transformative or reconstitutive nature of the narrative form is significant as it gives space for people to express their view of how society was, is and should be (Fraser, 2004).

Ross (2000, p. 41) states that "among the most characteristic approaches in the Critical Race Theory genre are storytelling, counter-storytelling, and analysis of narrative". In addition to the fact that black history has often been passed on through the art of storytelling, narrative accounts have also been found to be powerful in that they allow the protagonists an agency to tell their story in their own words (Sonn et al., 2013). In the context of reflecting on racism, the value of this agency in re-humanising marginalised groups cannot be overstated.

Narratives and storytelling have elsewhere (Lieblich, Tuval-Mashiach, & Zilber, 1998) been likened to therapy and their effects as cathartic. While the Apartheid Archive Project does not seek to make claims of the therapeutic effects that storytelling has on the participants, it does claim to provide a space for the emergence of multiple voices, and the inscription of these voices into the recorded history of South Africa. The project not only solicits stories and narratives from the direct victims of apartheid racism, but as indicated earlier also actively encourages racially privileged groups to recount personal narratives that allow for reflections on the effects of apartheid racism on themselves as bystanders, complicit perpetrators and indirect victims. An acknowledgement of one's role in perpetuating the racist ideology of the state, even indirectly, is possible and desirable for social transformation. Moreover, this approach allows for the application of nuanced understandings of complicity in ways that complicate the binaries of the 'grand' narrative of apartheid. This is in line with Dlamini's (2009, 2014) attempts to illustrate that life under apartheid was multidimensional and involved moments of agency and alienation for both black and white South Africans, albeit to vastly differing degrees. Similarly, personal accounts may reveal the complex nature of both black and white subjectivities in contemporary South Africa, by exposing new elites that may recentre white supremacy, power and privilege in both spectacular and insidious ways, as well as the continuities and discontinuities between old and new formations of resistance associated with decolonising moments in the current period.

Some Findings and Implications

Our interest in the narratives collected for the Apartheid Archive Project lies predominantly in participants' stories and narratives of their experiences of racism from the pre-democratic period of South Africa's history. In this sense, the focus of the project is located in the 'pre-history' that the apartheid era appears to have become. As indicated earlier in the chapter, we have problematised this notion of a 'pre-history' and argue instead that the apartheid past lives on in the present in both amplified and insidious ways. However, a substantial number of writings from within the Humanities and the Social Sciences in South Africa today avoid a robust engagement with this 'pre-history', while others frequently and implicitly encourage ignorance, elisions and an uncritical acceptance of apartheid history as a sanitised and a priori form of knowledge. The consequent silence has prompted a hegemonic discourse that minimises the historical and continued effects of apartheid racism within contemporary South Africa and has served to systematically deprive an entire generation of people of the opportunity and space to recount their stories and to understand their present life circumstances within South Africa's recent history—a situation that certainly is antithetical to peacebuilding.

Complexifying the Raced Subject

To date, the project has focused significantly on the complex nature of raced subjectivities in apartheid and post-apartheid South Africa. Using Nuttall's (2009) concept of entanglement, Straker (2013) highlights how the histories of blacks and whites, together with their associated subject positions, are intertwined and entangled in ways that both reproduce and contest the oppressor-oppressed binary in subtle and complicated ways in both apartheid and post-apartheid South Africa. Consequently, our work has focused on these complexities in subject positions and the possibilities that they may yield for dialogue, understanding, critique and psychosocial transformation in contemporary South Africa. More specifically, various researchers have highlighted the gendered nature of racialisation processes (Shefer, 2013; Sullivan & Stevens, 2013), the sexualisation of race (Ratele & Shefer, 2013), memory and witnessing as a vehicle for psychosocial transformation (Laubscher, 2013), the precariousness of blackness and whiteness (Straker, 2013), racialised subjectivities and diasporic communities (Sonn, 2013), the affective or libidinal dimensions of racialisation processes (Hook, 2013; Long, 2013), methodological tensions in the use of stories and narratives (Eagle & Bowman, 2013), the intersections of race and space, and the emergence of nostalgic formulations of the past in differential styles of remembering across the stories and narratives (Duncan, Stevens, & Sonn, 2012), to mention but a few.

Towards a Performative Social Science and an Insurgent Politics

In the main, this project envisages a reconstruction of aspects of the racism of the apartheid order (as narrated by a range of social actors), as a means not merely of understanding the functioning and mutation of this phenomenon over time, but also as an attempt to understand and address the problems of racism still confronting South Africa. This is conceived of as fundamental to peacebuilding efforts as it recognises that when racism is ignored, it has potential for both psychological and social disruption. However, a central feature of the project is a commitment to ensuring that stories that are 'gifted' to the project do not simply remain in the deconstructive realm of the academy, but are reinserted into the public domain to promote critical dialogue. In this regard the embracing of a *performative social science* (Gergen & Gergen, 2010) is a cornerstone of the project, with much of the academic analyses being translated and complemented by other modalities of representation, such as poetry, drama, photography and a publicly accessible archive (see www.apartheidarchive.org) containing all the stories and products of the project (Sonn et al., 2013).

Furthermore, given the decolonial moment in contemporary South Africa in which there are renewed calls to examine the past and its continued effects on the present realities of many South Africans, we envisage that many of the analyses from within the project will be inserted into an actional and insurgent form of citizenship and politics that contests the current inequalities that remain highly racialised. Sweeping waves of service delivery protests, calls for the transformation of higher education and demands for wealth and land redistribution are all exemplars of this decolonial moment. While it is impossible to determine the extent to which the project's analyses are embedded within these movements, there are clearly significant resonances and synergies between the analytic positions espoused in the project and those often articulated by these movements. Holston (2009) argues that in contexts where the precariat experience their marginalisation despite formalised political democracy, new forms of social mobilisation towards social justice emerge organically. However, such an actional insurgent politics must of necessity encompass modes of interrogatory destabilisation—a move beyond the mutual recognition of our entanglements towards a repetitive critique of the status quo along cleavages and axes of power that sustain inequality and systemised domination.

For Hook (2014), this process can also be likened to a politics of antagonism— a process beyond dialogue that is much more challenging of the prevailing strategic relations of power, and that may even allude to fantasies of violence as a rhetorical register. Hook (2014, p. 32) suggests that "if we indulge in illusions of inter-racial harmony and dialogue […], we will fail to move beyond them. By proving unwilling to confront such conditions and the fantasies that they give rise to, by prohibiting expressions of social antagonism and associated violent reveries, we thus preserve prevailing conditions of social pathology". While not advocating for violence, the point that should be made is that violent reverie that may be inserted into a politics of antagonism or an insurgent politics may very well feel uncomfortably destabilising, but may also minimise the actual enactment of direct violence if it is mobilised politically in the service of social justice and equality. Such an insurgent politics that is premised on persistent critique and deconstruction may open up the possibilities for engaging with new configurations of power that highlight the intersectionalities of race, class, gender, citizenship, etc. in the maintenance of inequality—a focus on the role of white liberalism and colour blindness, white conservatism and supremacy, black elitism and narrow black chauvinism; but also on the revival of old forms of resistance that may be accompanied by new forms of radicalisation and opposition that we are yet to fully comprehend. This uncomfortable outcome may yet offer us an important trajectory in the peacebuilding project.

Conclusion

For reasons discussed in this chapter, including the constitutive license of recalling, memory and the interpretative biases inherent in qualitative work, it is important to emphasise that the stories and narratives that are being collected cannot constitute a reflection of 'what really happened' during the apartheid period, nor can it provide a picture of *the* reality of apartheid or post-apartheid South Africa. Nonetheless, we believe that this project and the stories and narratives that it is currently generating will serve the important function of not allowing one of the most horrendous systems of institutionalised racism to be suppressed, elided and denied. Importantly too, this project offers those who participate in it, directly or vicariously, an opportunity to work through aspects of their apartheid era lives, and to robustly critique the contemporary social formation, so as to take greater control of their past, present and future. Indeed, as Krog (in Villa-Vicencio, 2004) observes, allowing people the opportunity to tell their personal stories of past trauma allows them to take control not simply of their past, but also of their futures.

References

"I will fuckin' kill you, you black bitch" (2015, March 04), *Vuvuzela*. Retrieved March 15, 2015, from http://witsvuvuzela.com/2015/03/04/i-will-fuckin-kill-you-you-black-bitch/.

Black face students face disciplinary action (2014, August 6), *Eye Witness News*. Retrieved March 15, 2015, from http://ewn.co.za/2014/08/06/Tuks-blackface-students-face-disciplinary-action.

Bond, P. (2000). *Elite transition*. London: Pluto Press.

Canham, H. (2014). Outsiders within: Non-Conformity among four contemporary black female managers in Johannesburg, South Africa. *Gender in Management: An International Journal., 29*(3), 148–170.

Cape Quarter bans two men involved in racist brawl. (2014, November 11), *Eye Witness News*. Retrieved March 15, 2015, from http://ewn.co.za/2014/11/11/Cape-Quarter-management -bans-two-men-in-racist-brawl.

Cape Town racist club assault: The tragedy and danger of an ahistorical upbringing. (2014, November 27), *Daily Maverick*. Retrieved March 15, 2015, from http://www.dailymaverick. co.za/opinionista/2014-11-27-cape-town-racist-club-assault-the-tragedy-and-danger-of-an-ahistorical-upbringing/#.VQbpFvKNOSo.

Cassan, B., Cayla, O., & Salazar, P. (2004). Dire la vérité, faire la réconciliation, manquer la réparation (Speaking the truth, reconciling and failing to offer reparation). In B. Cassan, O. Cayla, & P. Salazar (Eds.), *Vérité, réconciliation, reparation (Truth, reconciliation and reparation)* (pp. 13–26). Paris: Seuil.

Christie, D.J., Tint, B.S., Wagner, R.V., & Winter, D. (Eds.). (2008). Peace psychology for a peaceful world. *American Psychologist, 63*(6), 540-552.

Christie, D. J., Wagner, R. V., & Winter, D. A. (Eds.). (2001). *Peace, conflict, and violence: Peace psychology for the 21st century*. Englewood Cliffs, NJ: Prentice-Hall.

Desai, A. (2002). *We are the poors'. Community struggles in post-apartheid South Africa*. New York: Monthly Review Press.

Dlamini, J. (2009). *Native nostalgia*. Auckland Park: Jacana.

Dlamini, J. (2014). *Askari*. Auckland Park: Jacana.

Downey, A. (Ed.). (2015). *Dissonant archives: Contemporary visual culture and contested narratives in the Middle East*. New York: I. B. Tauris.

Duncan, N. (2012). Reaping the whirlwind: Xenophobic violence in South Africa. *Global Journal of Community Psychology Practice, 3*(1), 104–112.

Duncan, N., Stevens, G., & Sonn, C. (2012). Of narratives and nostalgia. Peace and conflict. *Journal of Peace Psychology, 18*(3), 205–213.

Eagle, G., & Bowman, B. (2013). Self-consciousness and impression management in the authoring of apartheid related narratives. In G. Stevens, N. Duncan, & D. Hook (Eds.), *Race, memory and the apartheid archive: Towards a transformative psychosocial praxis* (pp. 275–294). London/ Johannesburg: Palgrave Macmillan/Wits University Press.

Essed, P. (1991). *Understanding everyday racism*. Newbury Park: Sage.

Faul, M. (2008, February 29). *Apartheid dead, but racism endures*. Retrieved March 10, 2015, from http://seattlepi.nwsource.com/national/1105ap_south_africa_racism_endures.html.

Foucault, M. (2003). *Society must be defended. Lectures at the Collège de France 1975-76* (M. Bertani & A. Fontana (Eds.), Trans.). London: Allen Lane.

Fraser, H. (2004). Doing narrative research analysing personal stories line by line. *Qualitative Social Work, 3*(2), 179–201.

Freire, P. (2000). *Pedagogy of the oppressed.* New York: Continuum.

Gergen, M. M., & Gergen, K. J. (2010). Performative social science and psychology. *Forum: Qualitative Social Research, 12*(1). Retrieved March 5, 2015, from http://www.qualitative-research.net/index.php/fqs/article/view/1595.

Gqubule, D. (Ed.). (2006). *Making mistakes, righting wrongs: Insights into black economic empowerment.* Johannesburg: Jonathan Ball.

Hassim, S., Kupe, T., & Worby, E. (Eds.). (2008). *Go home or die here: Violence, xenophobia and the reinvention of difference in South Africa.* Johannesburg: Wits University Press.

Hatch, M. J., & Cunliffe, A. L. (2006). *Organisation theory: Modern, symbolic, and postmodern perspectives.* New York: Oxford University Press.

Holston, J. (2009). *Insurgent citizenship: Disjunctions of democracy and modernity in Brazil.* Princeton, NJ: Princeton University Press.

Hook, D. (2013). On animal mediators and psychoanalytic reading practice. In G. Stevens, N. Duncan, & D. Hook (Eds.), *Race, memory and the apartheid archive: Towards a transformative psychosocial praxis* (pp. 146–162). London/Johannesburg: Palgrave Macmillan/Wits University Press.

Hook, D. (2014). Antagonism, social critique and the "violent reverie". *Psychology in Society, 46,* 21–34.

Landau, L. (Ed.). (2011). *Exorcising the demons within.* Johannesburg: Wits University Press.

Laubscher, L. (2013). Working with the Apartheid Archive: Or, of witness, testimony, and ghosts. In G. Stevens, N. Duncan, & D. Hook (Eds.), *Race, memory and the apartheid archive: Towards a transformative psychosocial praxis* (pp. 45–60). London/Johannesburg: Palgrave Macmillan/Wits University Press.

Lieblich, A., Tuval-Mashiach, R., & Zilber, T. (1998). Narrative research. Reading, analysis, and interpretation. *Applied Social Research Methods Series, 47.* Thousand Oaks: Sage.

Long, C. (2013). Transitioning racialised spaces. In G. Stevens, N. Duncan, & D. Hook (Eds.), *Race, memory and the apartheid archive: Towards a transformative psychosocial praxis* (pp. 61–80). London/Johannesburg: Palgrave Macmillan/Wits University Press.

Lyotard, J. F. (1979). *La condition postmoderne: rapport sur le savoir.* Paris: Editions Minuit.

Mamdani, M. (1997). *Citizen and subject.* Princeton, NJ: Princeton University Press.

Martín-Baró, I. (1994). Towards a liberation psychology (A. Aron, Trans.). In A. Aron & S. Corne (Eds.), *Writings for a liberation psychology: Ignacio Martín-Baró* (pp. 17–32). Cambridge: Harvard University Press.

No action against 'blackface' student, says Stellenbosch University, (2014, September 30), *Times Live.* Retrieved March 15, 2015, from http://www.timeslive.co.za/local/2014/09/30/no-action-against-blackface-student-says-stellenbosch-university.

Nuttall, S. (2009). *Entanglement: Literary and cultural reflections on post-apartheid.* Johannesburg: Wits University Press.

Politicians slam Western Cape Town's 'dompas' system. (2015, March 11). *News 24.* Retrieved March 15, 2015, from http://www.news24.com/SouthAfrica/News/Storm-over-Western-Cape-towns-dompas-system-20150311.

Ratele, K., & Shefer, T. (2013). Desire, fear and entitlement: Sexualising race and racialising sexuality in (re)membering apartheid. In G. Stevens, N. Duncan, & D. Hook (Eds.), *Race, memory and the apartheid archive: Towards a transformative psychosocial praxis* (pp. 188–207). London/Johannesburg: Palgrave Macmillan/Wits University Press.

Ross, T. (2000). The Richmond narratives. In R. Delgado & J. Stefancic (Eds.), *Critical race theory* (2nd ed., pp. 42–51). Philadelphia: Temple University Press.

Sands, R. G. (2004). Narrative analysis: A feminist approach. In D. K. Padgett (Ed.), *The qualitative research experience* (pp. 48–75). New York: Thomson Brooks/Cole.

Shefer, T. (2013). Intersections of 'race', sex and gender in narratives on apartheid. In G. Stevens, N. Duncan, & D. Hook (Eds.), *Race, memory and the apartheid archive: Towards a transfor-*

mative psychosocial praxis (pp. 169–187). London/Johannesburg: Palgrave Macmillan/Wits University Press.

Sonn, C. C. (2013). Engaging with the Apartheid Archive Project: Voices from the South African diaspora in Australia. In G. Stevens, N. Duncan, & D. Hook (Eds.), *Race, memory and the apartheid archive: Towards a transformative psychosocial praxis* (pp. 128–145). London/Johannesburg: Palgrave Macmillan/Wits University Press.

Sonn, C. C., Stevens, G., & Duncan, N. (2013). Decolonisation, critical methodologies, and why stories matter. In G. Stevens, N. Duncan, & D. Hook (Eds.), *Race, memory and the apartheid archive: Towards a transformative psychosocial praxis* (pp. 295–314). London/Johannesburg: Palgrave Macmillan/Wits University Press.

Squire, C. (2013). *Doing narrative research*. London: Sage.

Statistics South Africa. (2014). *Poverty trends in South Africa: An examination of absolute poverty between 2006 and 2011*. Pretoria: Author. Retrieved from http://beta2.statssa.gov.za/publications/Report-03-10-06/Report-03-10-06March2014.pdf.

Stevens, G., Duncan, N., & Hook, D. (2013). The Apartheid Archive Project, the psychosocial and political Praxis. In G. Stevens, N. Duncan, & D. Hook (Eds.), *Race, memory and the apartheid archive: Towards a transformative psychosocial praxis* (pp. 1–17). London/Johannesburg: Palgrave Macmillan/Wits University Press.

Stevens, G., Duncan, N., & Sonn, C. C. (2013). Memory, narrative and voice as liberatory praxis in the apartheid archive. In G. Stevens, N. Duncan, & D. Hook (Eds.), *Race, memory and the apartheid archive: Towards a transformative psychosocial praxis* (pp. 25–44). London/Johannesburg: Palgrave Macmillan/Wits University Press.

Straker, G. (2013). Unsettling whiteness. In G. Stevens, N. Duncan, & D. Hook (Eds.), *Race, memory and the apartheid archive: Towards a transformative psychosocial praxis* (pp. 91–108). London/Johannesburg: Palgrave Macmillan/Wits University Press.

Sullivan, L. G., & Stevens, G. (2013). Gendered subjectivities and relational references in black women's narratives of apartheid racism. In G. Stevens, N. Duncan, & D. Hook (Eds.), *Race, memory and the apartheid archive: Towards a transformative psychosocial praxis* (pp. 208–227). London/Johannesburg: Palgrave Macmillan/Wits University Press.

Terre Blanche, M. (2006). Two nations: Race and poverty in post-apartheid South Africa. In G. Stevens, V. Franchi, & T. Swart (Eds.), *A 'race' against time* (pp. 73–90). Pretoria: UNISA Press.

Villa-Vicencio, C. (2004). Oublie, mémoire et vigilance (Failure to remember, memory and vigilance). In B. Cassan, O. Cayla, & P. Salazar (Eds.), *Vérité, réconciliation, reparation (Truth, reconciliation and reparation)* (pp. 319–338). Paris: Seuil.

Villa-Vicencio, C. (2008, March 14–19). A neglected moral vision. *Mail & Guardian*, p. 24.

Chapter 10
Structural Violence and the Struggle for Recognition: Examining Community Narratives in a Post-apartheid Democracy

Ursula Lau and Mohamed Seedat

The burgeoning of a post-apartheid democracy saw the deracialisation of local government, a developmental local government ethos and intergovernmental channelling of increased resources to the municipal tier (Atkinson, 2007). Despite these transformations, democratic South Africa continues to be rocked by mass protests, violent demonstrations and petitions, as the poorer citizens of state grow increasingly frustrated with the very same daily struggles (inadequate housing, poor sanitation, lack of water and ablution facilities) that characterised their existence under the apartheid (Leibbrandt, Woolard, & Woolard, 2009). The casualties of protest violence are often the protesters themselves at the hands of the police, but also increasingly the ward councillors who are perceived as unresponsive and callous bureaucrats to the communities they represent (Buccus, as cited in Mngxitama, Alexander, & Gibson, 2008).

The protests highlight the experiences of the poor, Black[1] majority citizens in post-apartheid South Africa who, despite having acquired constitutionally enshrined

---

[1] We do not denote an essentialised 'race' but racial categories are used here as a social constructs to locate participants within a sociopolitical, cultural, and historical context in South Africa, which shapes the narratives produced.

U. Lau (✉)
Institute for Social and Health Sciences, University of South Africa, Johannesburg, South Africa

South African Medical Research Council-University of South Africa Violence, Injury and Peace Research Unit, Cape Town, South Africa

Institute for Dispute Resolution in Africa, University of South Africa, Pretoria, South Africa
e-mail: Lauu@unisa.ac.za

M. Seedat
Institute for Social and Health Sciences, University of South Africa, Johannesburg, South Africa

South African Medical Research Council-University of South Africa Violence, Injury and Peace Research Unit, Cape Town, South Africa
e-mail: Seedama@unisa.ac.za

© Springer International Publishing AG 2017
M. Seedat et al. (eds.), *Enlarging the Scope of Peace Psychology*,
Peace Psychology Book Series, DOI 10.1007/978-3-319-45289-0_10

203

civil and political liberties, cannot access their basic social rights (Friedmann, as cited in Miraftab & Wills, 2005). Surges in protest violence may be attributed to a vibrant democracy in which citizens have power to exercise voice and choice, but they also point to the continuation rather than a disruption of the apartheid narrative; that despite a much celebrated end to apartheid, the circumstances associated with its legacy have in essence remained unaltered (Mngxitama et al., 2008).

In this chapter, we analyse our opening conversations with community leaders of the peri-urban township of Thembelihle, which revealed two dominant narratives of structural violence in a post-apartheid context: *poverty and need*, and *struggle for recognition*. We attempt to locate the two narratives, in relation to a conceptual framework of peace psychology and critical psychology, and to highlight their implications for a critical community psychology within a twenty-first century democratic South Africa. In our analysis, we locate our representation within an academic and scholarly space as an enactment of academic citizenship and activism guided by the principles of social justice and peace. The chapter accordingly encourages peace scholars (including ourselves) to assume a reflexive stance about the influence of scholarship as manifestations of academic citizenship and activism.

This chapter emerges from *Community Storylines*, a collaborative project between the Institute for Social & Health Sciences and the Institute for Dispute Resolution in Africa. It is focused on eliciting community narratives of peace and violence and local knowledge in dispute resolution through various modalities of storytelling. The project seeks to privilege local voices to mobilise community meanings to create community-generated solutions to challenges. It draws upon three interrelated conceptual elements, which we refer to as "the community story", "relationality" and "process" to bridge "indigenous" and "Western" epistemologies as a means to elicit community-centred meanings (see Lau & Seedat, 2014). In a nutshell, these elements are envisioned as avenues to elicit bottom-up, subjective worldviews of participants as active meaning-makers, which are privileged alongside processual insights to reveal relational, interactive and community-specific ways of knowing. We do not prescribe specific forms of knowledge but allow these to emerge in the spaces of interaction between individuals and within the community itself. To date the project has resulted in an evolving nexus of data collection and intervention modalities, such as group oral storytelling, forum theatre and digital storytelling. Given our positioning as critical community and peace psychologists, we are mindful of how Rappaport (1995, p. 796) contextualises the importance of storytelling and narrative in furthering community and by extension peace psychology enactments:

> For … those who lack social, political or economic power, the community, neighbourhood or cultural narratives that are available are either negative, narrow, 'written' by others for them, or all of the above … The goals of empowerment are enhanced when people discover, or create and give voice to, a collective narrative that sustains their own personal life story in positive ways. This process is reciprocal, such that many individuals, in turn, create, change and sustain the group narrative.

Violence as Structural and Symbolic

The observation that racial, structural and social inequalities of apartheid have persisted and re-emerged across the South African post-apartheid landscape has been the subject of inquiry by social psychologists, sociologists, social movement theorists and political scientists (see for example, Durrheim, Mtose, & Brown, 2011; Leibbrandt et al., 2009; Seekings, 2008). In the present chapter, we highlight the psychological implications of persistent structural and social disparities from a peace psychology and critical psychology perspective. Whilst adopting a "psychological" lens, our focus centres on the collective dimension, as opposed to an individualist or interpersonal focus. Specifically, we are interested in exploring the implications of a persistence of structural violence and how it plays out in protest violence as *both* a demand for economic justice and struggle for recognition—where both are viewed as integral to the quest for peace.

In peace psychology, a social structure is deemed violent by virtue of a vertical arrangement of power and inequality, where the privileged elite mobilise the control of resources that are disproportionately balanced against the deprivations of the masses who struggle to meet their basic needs (Christie, 1997; Galtung, 1990; Montiel, 2001). This vertical arrangement determines who has or lacks access to social and economic resources. Though related to the concrete and physical enactments of direct violence, structural violence is more gradual and normalised (Opotow, 2001) and, to draw on Montiel's (2001) summary of Galtung (1975) lacks intent, subject, object and interpersonal action. As such, agency and responsibility are vague; there may be no identifiable person who directly harms another (Opotow, 2001).

Earlier scholarship on peace psychology tends to emphasise the socio-economic injustices of structural violence and less explicitly the injustices of recognition (see for example, Christie, 1997). To foreground injustices of recognition as a form of colonising violence on its own, we turn to the notion of injustice as cultural/symbolic. Galtung (1990) views "cultural violence" as the symbolic aspects of culture (religion, ideology, art, science) that legitimate structural violence and allows it to be accepted in a society. For Fraser (1998, p. 71), cultural or symbolic injustice is "rooted in social patterns of representation, interpretation and communication". This includes cultural domination, non-recognition or *mis*recognition and disrespect through disparaging public representations. The injuries of mis/non-recognition have been conceptualised by social and political theorists in related ways: as a form of oppression that distorts the sense of self to a reduced mode of being and even a crippling self-hatred (Taylor, 1994), as a dialectic struggle for identity between self and other (Hegel, as cited in Oliver, 2001) and an impaired view of self that constrains self-realisation, freedom of action and expression of positive worth in a community (Honneth, 1992). For Taylor (1994), the consequence is real damage and oppression suffered by a people when society "mirrors back" to them a disparaging picture of themselves. Influenced by Hegel and Mead, Honneth (1992) conceives of the consequences of social ostracism and the denial of human integrity as akin to a "social death". In every social order, rights and privileges are unequally allotted. In an oppressive social order, this inequality is exacerbated in how it aligns its beliefs, values and institutional powers and "how it dispenses life and death to its citizens" (Bulhan, 1985, p. 176). A consideration of cultural/symbolic injustice alongside the socio-economic is important, for as Fraser (1998) highlights, the struggle for recognition plays out reciprocally in contexts of stark material inequalities. In other words, the disproportionate disadvantage of some groups over others rests in the mutually reinforcing processes and practices of both structural and cultural violence forms.

Violence as a Challenge to Oppression

Injustice, conceived in both its structural and cultural/symbolic forms, has the effect of restricting full access to resources, impeding equal participation in the cultural and public realms of everyday life, contributing to a vicious cycle of cultural and economic domination (Fraser, 1998). However, the injuries of violence extend beyond being stripped of labour power, material resources and access to civil society. Ontologically, they speak to violence that imposes a suffering directed against one's being/existence as human; that is, it imposes "an absence of presence", a non-recognition of another's humanness (Wilderson, 2008). The polarities of economic and cultural/symbolic injustice have some parallels with a Fanonian view of violence and oppression. In Bulhan's (1985) elaboration of Fanon, a dialectic between violence and oppression is distilled. In simplified terms, the oppressed is colonised on two fronts: *of land* (its material dispossession, manifesting in a loss of control/ownership of space, economics, health, quality of life) and *of psyche* in its individual and collective forms (manifesting in an inferiority complex, self-destruction, loss of identity, self-determination and social bonding capacity).

Given that structural violence is infused into the social fabric, entrenched in prevailing norms and masked in everyday practices and cultural and material arrangements of society (e.g. media, law, education, labour relations), Fanon (1963, p. 94) proposes that challenging its logic and force entails a confrontation with both fronts—the oppressor both *within* and *without*. For Fanon, revolutionary violence (distinguished from wanton violence) is a "cleansing force" that "disintoxifies" the oppressed; that is, by confronting the source of his humiliation, revolutionary violence reinstates agency, reconstitutes bonding, reclaims identity, individuality, freedom and control over destiny (Bulhan, 1985; Fanon, 1963; Howard, 2011). Acts of defiance as articulated within the resistance philosophy of Black Consciousness movement have been referred to as practices of self-actualisation (Mngxitama et al., 2008). However, this is not simply an act of catharsis as often misconstrued, but a "rehabilitation" or "cleansing" of the self—an emotionally complex state or coming into being of moments of self-recognition, of seeing oneself not as an object of another, but a subject in his own right with a will to action (Bulhan, 1985; Fanon, 1963). Wilderson (2008, p. 100) expressed this as "the recognition of ourselves as beings void of the inertia of objects; endowed at last with the force of subjects".

According to the Fanonian formulation, failure to confront both the oppressor *within* and *without* risks transforming the vertically imposed structural violence into horizontal violence. For Fanon (1963), through a psychological process of "identifying with the aggressor", repressed counter-violence is enacted against one's own. These theorisations provide a critical lens through which we attempt to grapple with meanings of violence extracted from community leaders' layered stories of Thembelihle that reflect a conflicted social context, one mired in the chaos of protest violence over unmet basic needs amidst the simultaneous quest for recognition on various fronts—geospatial recognition, participatory citizenship and belonging, human dignity and voice. In the following section, we examine how features of structural violence and the struggle for recognition play out in their stories.

Method

Drawing from the dual lens of criticality and peace psychology (Swart & Bowman, 2007), we subject the emerging conversations with community leaders to a formal analysis (Carr, 2010). These conversations were part of the community entry/trust-building phase of the *Community Storylines* project. Our initial meeting served to recognise the community leadership, introduce, discuss and elicit their approval for the project. We regarded the community entry conversations as stories in their own right, contributing to evolving community narratives of violence and peace. Carr (2010) notes that stories are more than just anecdotes or epigraphs. As "experiential sources of information" (p. 220), they communicate important insights into process as well as articulations of specific phenomena; the reflections thereof revealing "the developing" position of themselves and the place of researchers and participants in research. In the processes of the analysis conducted herein, we draw attention to dominant narratives that may be read as stories of structural and cultural/symbolic violence.

We employed a narrative analysis to "produce stories as the outcome of research" (Polkinghorne, 1995, p. 15). The outcome is not an objective account of reality, but a finding that emerges out of a series of constructions. The narrative is achieved through stories to reveal a particular worldview or ideology that gives legitimacy to values and goals (Polkinghorne, 1995). Thus, it is a discourse composition that draws together various events, happenings and actions as a whole. *Emplotment* is the process by which events, happenings and actions are brought together to produce the narrative, providing both its coherence and direction in an unfolding movement that build up towards an outcome. The *plot* (or thematic thread) provides narrative meaning to events (Polkinghorne, 1995).

In attending to these elements, it is important that we recognise the social aspect of stories, the *context* (interactional, historical, political, discursive, etc.), which emerges in storytelling. These contextual features give meaning to storied events and support the plot (Polkinghorne, 1995). Thus, we situate our approach to narrative interpretation within an integrated approach, which presupposes that told stories consist of three analytical levels: the (intra)personal, interpersonal and public narrative (Stephens & Breheny, 2013). Rather than focusing analysis on a single level, an integrated approach considers that the (intra)personal (the individual story told from lived experience), interpersonal (the story that is told with an audience in mind, co-created between teller and listener), positional (the social location and social characteristics of the teller has effects on the stories told) and ideological levels (the ideologies and assumptions held by society that constructs people's everyday experiences). Situating our analysis as such is significant on two counts. First, unveiling the oft-disguised structural forces that perpetuate oppression of marginalised peoples necessitates that we show how the ideological connects to the intrapersonal level of lived reality. Second, it lends itself to ways of thinking about challenging oppressive structures from a "bottom-up" individual level to "imagine where the spaces for resistance, agency and possibility lie" (Weis & Fine, 2004, p. xviii). Thus, we attempt to go beyond the dominant personal level to consider the influence of social processes, whilst never losing sight of the humanist elements that are embedded in the told story (Murray, 2000). Moreover, in a community setting, group stories comprise spontaneous reenactments of defining events in the life of the group and do not possess the distinct beginning, middle and end demarcations of individual interviews. The exchanges are treated as a collaborative story produced dialogically by the group of community leaders in a spirited exchange with the academic research team (Riessman, 2008).

Participants

The targeted research community is Thembelihle, a low-income informal settlement located on the peri-urban fringes of southwest Johannesburg, South Africa. Our work in this community began in the early 1980s and included violence prevention interventions, addressing the social, economic and psychological dimensions. This was undertaken in partnership with a cohort of residents with whom RL, the community engagement facilitator in our team, developed interpersonal relationships within community engagement as praxis. This work was interrupted from late 2001 when this cohort of social actors was relocated to another area set aside by the government's formal housing programme, the Reconstruction and Development Programme. Consequently, our intervention work also relocated. From mid-2001 to present, RL maintained intermittent contact with other informal leaders in Thembelihle but more active engagement moved to other low-income communities where we enjoyed long-standing engagement.

The participants comprised seven "Black" male community leaders[2] of Thembelihle. We opted for a snowball approach in connecting with "informal" leaders, relying on one community member with whom the Institute had a long-standing contact as the point of entry. The community leaders were invited to an interactive stakeholders meeting with the academic researchers. The project proposal was pre-

---

[2] The gender imbalance is noticeable despite having opened up the invitation for participation to all leaders in the community.

sented to elicit buy-in, followed by a "question-and-answer" session that invited discussion about the project. With their permission, the discussions were audio-recorded to document the process dimensions of the research. To reiterate, these discussions were initially not treated as data in themselves, but their potential for rich analytical insights from a narrative frame emerged in hindsight. With this in mind, we sought additional consent to use and transcribe the conversations for analysis purposes (see Appendix for transcription guidelines). The transcripts were analysed to identify: (1) the overarching narrative and their supporting plots and (2) speakers' self-positionings and their supporting plot elements (events, actions, outcomes).

Analysis

In this section, we direct focus to two separate but interrelated stories presented by the community leaders. Whilst all community leaders contributed to these dominant narratives through the collective conversation, two excerpts were selected specifically because they stood out as oral narratives in the traditional sense. With discernable story structures (abstract, orientation, complicating action, etc.) (Labov, 1972), the processes of emplotment could be explored to highlight the emerging narratives. Whilst question and answer exchanges characterised our engagement, we draw attention to the storytelling mode that participants used to frame and precede their questions. These stories were spontaneously volunteered despite the imposed structure of the question-and-analysis session. In the analysis later, we follow the logic of narrative reasoning, moving from storied episode to episode to show how these contribute to emplotment, rather than moving from identifying particulars as instances of general concepts or "common themes" (as in paradigmatic reasoning). In this context, the narrative is a form of discourse, which operates by configuring incidents and events into a temporal unity achieved through the plot (Polkinghorne, 1995).

Poverty and Need

"Poverty and need" emerged as the overarching narrative. As a narrative discourse, "poverty and need" highlights a relationship of stark inequality and contextualises an exchange wherein one party is in want/need and the other is in a "privileged" provider position (see, for example Durrheim et al., 2011). To appreciate the complexities of this narrative, we begin with an account of P_1 who positions himself as the community leader/activist. P_1 describes Thembelihle as a "squatter camp", a scene of geospatial deprivation where the failure to meet basic human needs play out. The "squatter camp" refers to the informal township, a dominant place type during apartheid that bears scars of poverty, inequality and neglect that persist in the post-apartheid context. Themes of neglect and decay, exclusion and disease as thematic threads are intricately woven into the chaos storyline with a dramatic end.*Transcript 1A: P_1*

86.	My name is P_1
87.	Eh (.) what we are experiencing here in Thembelihle, you find that because it's a squatter camp …
88.	So me what I have experienced, because I am originally from Soweto.
89.	Since I came here from 1988 until now.
90.	So I also experience most of the things because I'm working on the [name of] organisation.
91.	So we are solving the cases, and all that in Thembelihle (.)
92.	We have found out that because most of the people they are not educated (.)
93.	Some of them they don't know where to go.
94.	You also find that, eh because eh some of them they not eh educated (.) and when they, when they get a problem, like the IDs [identity documents], they can't even eh to eh apply for a [social] grant.
95.	Sometimes when someone is sick—most of people they die in front of me because they don't get the grant.
96.	They don't know.
97.	They need someone to educate them.
98.	We need to open the workshops.
99.	Most of people they don't understand.
100.	Sometimes I saw most of people eh they living for you know the (???) and all that.
101.	But most of people here, here in Thembelihle once they not working they got to drink LIQUOR.
102.	You know they destroy their lives (.)
103.	For them like eh another lady she died last year.
104.	Eh she had the HIV positive.
105.	That's because the treatment wasn't all right, because she didn't have the ID so there was no one to help him [sic].
106.	Even me also, as a person on the [name of organisation] I didn't know where to go to help him [sic], eh this lady.
107.	This lady you know she didn't even have something to eat, because she didn't have the ID book
108.	So what happened to this lady, you know she gets suffered and one day she came to me.
109.	The the she was very very sick now and no one was supposed to help him [sic].
110.	After that, eh two months she died that lady, because she didn't have that help!

P_1's active strategy of telling buttresses his story as a credible one, told from a position of authority. P_1 devotes some time (86–91) to positioning himself as having authority to deal with the concerns of Thembelihle. Although he acknowledges his initial "outsider" status (line 88), his more than two-decade presence in the community not only as resident (line 89) but also as a leader and member of a civil society organisation (line 90). This self-positioning as "knower" persuades the listener to accept his account as a legitimate one based on his experiential knowledge and work on the ground (90, 91). Despite P_1's influence as an authority figure in the community, this is offset against his positionality as helpless, ineffective, uncertain—not due to fault of his own—but owing to the hopeless context of marginalisation.

P_1's account reveals a *chaos plot*, characterised by lack/deficiency ("not educated" [92], "not working" [101], having no food [107]), (in)action ("no one to help" [105]) and consequence (suffering, progressive illness and death [108–110]). As the organising templates for an overarching narrative of poverty and need, the chaos plot is characteristically one that leads to no resolve (Frank, 2012). A chain of negative events brings life into collapse. Efforts to thwart collapse are seen as futile with each attempt and potential solution blocked.

Foregrounded in his story is an account of "another lady" who was left to die of HIV/AIDS (103–110), emphasising the regularity of such events and their intersections of the poverty story with class and gender (and implicitly "race"). Government institutions of power (welfare, health, education) are rendered almost invisible, having no name, presence or reach into this community, and citizens in this neglected township having little means or know-how ("they are not educated/they don't know where to go" [92, 93], "they don't get the grant/they don't know") [95, 96]) to access the appropriate channels to secure their rights to a basic quality of life. Institutional violence,[3] conceptualised as mediating personal and structural forms of violence, in this respect takes on disguised forms, as opposed to blatantly enshrined policies and practices of the apartheid era (Bulhan, 1985). Though obscured by post-apartheid transformational policies undergirded by democratic principles of "equal access" to welfare, education, health and citizenship, institutional violence as revealed in P_1's story, nevertheless surreptitiously and insidiously seeps into the lived realities of these Thembelihle residents.

P_1 points to the destructive effects, socially, physically and psychologically, on those who do not have employment ("… once they are not working they got to drink LIQUOR/You know they destroy their lives" [101, 102]). Alcohol and drug abuse are not considered isolated occurrences, for as P_1 points out, this is a method for coping for "most of the people here" (101).

Bulhan (1985) makes the link between structural violence and premature death, which is typically masked as "the natural order of things" in societies steeped in structural violence. In P_1's cause-and-consequence recounting of events, the links between obvious social neglect and premature death are explicit, yet the cause for the tragic outcome is unidentifiable, unknowable and unnameable ("no one was supposed to help" [109], "I didn't know where to go to help [her]" [106], "there was no

---

[3] For Bulhan (1985), microsocial systems (e.g. prisons, health institutions, educational institutions, the family) on closer inspection reveal elements of institutional violence. Structural violence is "a feature of social structures" (Bulhan, 1985, p. 136), presents as having a more abstract nature and cannot be associated with a particular institution. Its general formula is "inequality, mainly in the distribution of power" (Galtung, 1975, p. 173). Both institutional and structural violence supersede personal violence. Although conceptually distinguished here, in practice the three are interrelated rather than distinct.

one to help him" [105]). Not only are the government institutions of support rendered unknowable by its citizens, the ordinary resident in a marginalised township community (represented by "the lady") remains unknowable, unrecognised and unnamed by the State. For P_1, not having a name and identity effectively excludes her from accessing the necessities for survival ("she didn't even have something to eat, because she didn't have the ID book" [107]). Agency and accountability are blurred, and roles and responsibility are not easily discerned but dissolved in a system of oppression that routinises violence as an everyday part of social reality.

P_1's story is not an isolated one. Other community leaders reiterated similar themes, producing accounts that were knitted together in a collective narrative of poverty and need. For example, P_2's story (not reproduced here) reiterates themes of decay and deterioration in an enumeration of adverse events signalling social breakdown and impending collapse: "street is dirty" (217), "some children they get sickness in our place" (219), "they take crime, break house and take someone's things" (222). The chaos plot underpinning the collective narrative of poverty and need presents the community as helpless and hopeless victims of circumstance, acted upon by forces beyond their control, as victims of exploitation, robbed for their space, time, energy, mobility and social bonding—all vital needs for physical, psychological and social well-being (Bulhan, 1985). Community leaders themselves do not escape these constructions. P_1 positions himself dually as an impassioned but powerless leader confronted with the challenges of a needy and exploited community.

Struggle for Recognition

P_3 offers a contrasting story, one that centres on a *plot of struggle for recognition*. For Martineau, Meer, and Thompson (2012, p. 6), recognition is not merely a courtesy nod we give to others but is a "seeing others as like ourselves". Its counterpoint, *mis*recognition, is the withdrawal of this social recognition. In the context of marginalised groups, it amounts to epistemic injustice, where their knowledge claims go unheard, silenced or misinterpreted.*Transcript 1B: P_3*

142.	You know there is one thing that happened in 2011.
143.	(.) I was phoned by a journalist.
144.	She said to me, 'P_3 I heard that you will be barricading the streets?'
145.	Right, 'No no, we will not barricade'.
146.	The story that [s]he had heard was wrong.
147.	I said, 'no we are not –
148.	We are just picketing the (.) the miners who were killed in Marikana for their anniversary'.[4]

---

[4]P_3 refers to a supportive march to demonstrate solidarity for the Marikana miners who in 2012 were engaging in a 'wildcat' strike in protest against unfair labour conditions. The deaths of 44 miners and injury of 78 at the hands of the police who used brutal force to quell the protest has been referred to in the media as 'Marikana massacre' (BBC, 2012).

149.	But she wasn't interested in us.
150.	She never came!
151.	They never even send their newspaper, because what they were looking for, it was something that we were burning tyres.
152.	'Are you going to burn tyres. Are you going to burn tyres?
153.	You know, they want bad things.
154.	So like we are saying
155.	If we are giving both sides of the story –
156.	Yes there are.
157.	We've got criminal elements in Thembelihle, in fact everywhere in South Africa.
158.	But there are stories where it needs to be told so that when one sees, you will have your own opinion.
159.	So for us the MEDIA, especially in areas like Thembelihle they are not playing any role!
160.	Uhm you will have a protest by workers (.) right (.) here in Lenasia because of certain Indian community are mistreating our black workers.
161.	The, the journalist or reporter will come to that protest of the workers.
162.	Come next week the story is no more the same in the newspaper.
163.	You understand how it hurts, because now all the protests by the workers against a certain group of race is not being publicised.
164.	So stories like these, if we can have something a copy that we can even give to the community and sell it to them.
165.	Then that's where maybe a library, like the comrade was saying, we can organise through the story that has been said by comm— what you call the people from the community.
166.	So for me, honestly I want these things to be publicised.
167.	You know as a person I have been perceived like somebody who will go to a camp and say, 'People must go and BURN', you know, things
168.	And if you get the side of my story, and get who's P_3, where he comes from, you will get a different story.
169.	But now where ever I go, even to the police station when I go to police station to speak to station commander.
170.	The first thing if my name is being mentioned, the station commander will say, 'Oh is this …?' you know.
171.	But if I give my story and somebody gives their story, then there will be a balance of the stories.
172.	For instance I was here and the director came and said: 'P_3 I know', you can even ask Mr Royal [community liaison officer].
173.	I asked him, 'Am I really being known by bad things or good things?'

174.   He answered me in a very good way.
175.   He said, 'There are those who will see you as a good person and
              there are those who will see you as a bad person'.
176.   But if no story is being told, how am I going judged?
177.   I will only be judged by being a bad person.
178.   So I one hundred percent support it, the initiative [i.e., the research
              project].

In P_3's account, the community story (142–167) converges with the personal story (167–177). In each case, the storyline centres on marginalised voices. He points to the perceptions of deviance and criminality held by colonising agents of police (170) and media (143, 151, 159) (and by extension the general public) towards Thembelihle. P_3's narrative points towards the violence of *mis*recognition that affirms a Manichean worldview in a society that structures both the material arrangements and psyches of people to vilify one group as "bad" and another as "good" (Bulhan, 1985). A *plot of struggle* structures his story, with its main opponents, powerful vocal institutions offset against a powerless voiceless community. His use of a series of juxtapositions offers contrasting versions of "truth" and positioning that represent contesting voices. This typically takes the form of direct speech: "... heard that you will be barricading the streets?" (144)/"...no, we will not barricade" (145); "bad things"/"good things" (173); "bad person"/"good person" (175). This device not only lends veracity to his account of events, but simultaneously sketches "both sides of the story" (155, 157, 171). He therefore positions himself as a reasonable man, given into the logic of measured understanding. This stance is strengthened further in his appropriation of "Mr Royal['s]" "balanced" perspective of things (171–177) which he draws upon as a voice of authority and consensus.

The struggle plot, however, does not find positive resolve. In contrast to the government institutional structures that are depicted as absent and neglectful, the media in P_3's narrative has a powerful presence, making direct and deliberate contact with residents on the ground, but choosing to exert a benign influence only insofar as it is able to extract information that meets its insular interests and perspective on reality. Against the residents' struggles for humane representation, the media emerges as the victor in all instances (159, 161, 162), in subtle ways reinforcing the arrangements of a structurally violent society. Different from P_1, P_3 constructs himself (and his community) not so much as victims of resource deprivation, but as victims exploited of voice. The narrative of oppression, writes Tigar (2009, p. 34) is "not only a narrative about what is done to people, but also about what is taken from them". The media's colonising power as portrayed in P_3's story has the effect of plundering a community for purposes of self-interest (142–150, 161, 162). The media's persistent representation of Thembelihle as "violent protestors" and concomitantly the failure to recognise their oppression both racially and economically ("certain Indian community are mistreating our black workers [160]; all the protests by the workers against a certain group of race is not being publicized" [163]) for P_3 constitutes a loss of voice and the pain of being overlooked ("you understand how it hurts" [163]). Like P_1 who describes his story as a "sad story", P_3's story contains raw emotional power. P_3's account is a plea for recognition of personhood (168), a request that the balance of power be tipped in their favour by publicising *their* story (171).

In this respect, P_3's narrative may also be read as a struggle for identity (personal and collective), human dignity, respect and well-being, the social–psychological pillars of social bonding and peace (Fraser, 1998; Honneth, 1992; Taylor, 1994). In other words, the underside of protest action is the resistance against the commonly shared experiences of disrespect, social shame and degradation that provide the moral incentive for a collective struggle for recognition (Honneth, 1992). This speaks to Fanon's (1963) view of revolutionary violence as "disintoxifying" at both the collective and individual level. Violence for Fanon (1963) is a process through which the nation and the individual find liberation and freedom from the oppressor. The process of violence has liberatory potential for the reason that it reinstates agency to the colonised, restoring self-determination, individuality, identity, self-respect, and moral and social worth (Honneth, 1992; Howard, 2011). Both narratives of *poverty and need* and *struggle for recognition* highlight the dialectic influence of economic injustice on cultural/symbolic injustice and vice versa (Fraser, 1998).

Whilst these narratives point overwhelmingly to portrayals and self-positionings of passive victimisation, these community leaders also positioned themselves, albeit in less certain terms, as active change agents in their spheres of influence. Moreover, as active protestors who often resort to tactics of violence (e.g. burning tyres, damage to property, interpersonal violence) to buttress their voices for change, they straddle the lines between "criminality" and "political activism".

Discussion

The narrative of *poverty and need*, which points to structural violence, leads us to ask critical questions about the move from apartheid to neoliberalism, where the "material legacies of racial capitalism are ultimately reduced to the liberal problem of equal access" (Mngxitama et al., 2008, p. 9). Thus, the post-apartheid era seems to reflect a "partial freedom" as Mngxitama et al. (2008) suggest. The lived experiences of structural violence painted in this narrative highlight a continuing struggle to satisfy basic human needs. In this democratic era, however, the quest/struggle for access is against a bureaucratic ruling class whose arrangement of institutions, systems, dominant ideas (ideals) and values, rather than reflect a reform of the apartheid structure, reinforce the relations which Bulhan (1985) refers to as "master" and "slave", "elite" and "non-elite". These ideals and values reflect claims of entitlement to white wealth, and practices of unsavoury competition for place and position in a white world—all of this done under the banner of transformation that falls short of dismantling the structures of "accumulation, production and redistribution created by colonialism and apartheid" (Mngxitama et al., 2008, p. 16). The effects of this economic system is rendered visible, tangible and experiential/visceral in the community leaders' stories of community chaos experienced through the witnessing and encountering residents embattling exploitation, hunger, disease and death in marginal spaces of township life.

The narrative of *oppression and struggle* and the quest for recognition and peace towards which it refers appears to echo or converge with Biko's radical humanism, conceived as "a true humanity", the call for "a more human face" of South Africa, characterised by intimacy, trust, communalism, right to equal treatment and human value (Mngxitama et al., 2008, p. 214; Oliphant, 2008). The plea, struggle, quest, search, hope or dream of P_3 and his fellow protesters as summarised in his narrative is one of cultural/symbolic recognition (Fraser, 1998). If anti-colonial struggles and liberation movements are "acts of culture" as Cabral (1979, p. 141) conceives, persistent ruptures of violent protests in Thembelihle may paradoxically symbolise the call for peace, a recognition of worth, dignity, personhood in a more inclusive and caring post-apartheid society where the wealthy elite do not thrive on the exploitations of the poor. This seeming paradox contained in the struggle for peace through violence (see Lau & Seedat, 2013) is an inherited practice of the apartheid liberation struggle. Violence as an enacted demand for equality and freedom symbolised a "removal of the barrier to their humanity" (Bulhan, 1985, p. 144) outside of the alternative methods of challenging the oppressor (pleas for justice, negotiation, avoidance behaviour, etc.) that go unheard but also intensify the dehumanisation. The persistence and resurgence of system of exclusion provide both the context and triggers that reignite the script of "liberation through violence", and in the process, keeps alive the demand, desire and quest for recognition. In the post-apartheid context, state actors point to the destructive power of protests, while marginalised communities hold onto its constructive power, eliciting ideals of the liberation struggle.

The stories provide ways of understanding more deeply the complex psychological meanings of oppression, poverty and violence in South Africa. The community leaders' stories as exemplified in these narratives foreground the everyday lived realities of individuals engaged in daily struggles for survival. Yet the analysis also raises questions for the authors. There appears to be a ritualised patterning in protest violence in Thembelihle but also in other contexts of deprivation in South Africa. The act of destroying (burning tyres, defacing property and community structures) commonplace in protest violence seems to carry with it a complex emotional ambivalence. On the surface, the destruction of community structures appears as a self-defeating act of eroding the very resources on which the community is dependent. Furthermore, not uncommon is the horizontal enactment of violence, the wilful injuring or killing of fellow compatriots yoked under the same oppressive burdens, who are perceived less loyal to the protest cause. Perhaps these occurrences may be theorised in terms of a dual identification with both the oppressive "other" and the oppressed "victim" (see Lau, Seedat & Suffla, 2010). To apply the Fanonian formulation, perhaps these acts symbolise a confrontation with the oppressor *without* (externally), without the simultaneous confrontation with the oppressor *within*, resulting in the forms of horizontal violence observed (Fanon, 1963). Yet, there is something wanting in these explanations.

These seemingly illogical acts reflect a tension between "desiring" and "othering". Aside from horizontal forms of violence noted earlier, the targets of destruction (burning councillors' homes, community structures) in most cases represent the symbols of top-down, exclusionary elitist bureaucracy from which they have been alienated. Community councillors, designated as representative "community voice" in marginalised townships, are paradoxically viewed by such communities as callous, self-absorbed and gluttonous; as corrupt officials who reap the benefits of wealth, status, and power acquired through the privileges of government position, who are able to extract a means of extravagant existence from which the poor on the ground are increasingly removed (Harber, 2011). They point us back to the tensions emanating from our analysis—the uneasily resolved tension between economic justice and recognition and the dichotomy between peace and violence (see Lau & Seedat, 2013).

As we have noted elsewhere (see Lau & Seedat, 2013), viewing peace as the absence of violence is problematic for it produces an "either-or" binary of agency, whereby subjects are called into positions as either "victims" or "perpetrators". In spaces of "insurgent citizenship", the distinction between "criminal" and "revolutionary", or "violence" and "democracy" are not only blurred but are in shifting relationship (See Miraftab & Wills, 2005; von Holdt, 2012, 2014). The two narratives, whilst delineated separately for the purposes of analysis, are nevertheless read as a gestalt. They function synergistically as part of the quest for social justice and freedom within the South African democratic aspirations. The narrative of "struggle for recognition" is as much about social justice as is the narrative of "poverty and need". Both synergistically construct a marginalised community's quest for social justice in a democratically evolving society. In tandem, both narratives point to the interconnection between symbolic and physical forms of violence in making of the social order (von Holdt, 2012), but also point to possibilities for their subversion (Weis & Fine, 2004).

As critical and peace psychologists engaged in applied research, how we position our analyses of narrative data is important if we are to contribute to a social justice project to unmask the webs that connect social structures with individual lives. To confine our analysis solely to the personal dimension without unveiling the webs of power that link individual lives to social contexts is to be complicit in masking the socio-political structures that perpetuate social inequities (Weis & Fine, 2004). By choosing to frame our analysis within an integrated approach (Stephens & Breheny, 2013), we have attempted to render visible the structural forms of violence that are often disguised, hidden and routinised as an everyday natural occurrence (Bulhan, 1985; Opotow, 2001) yet without silencing the intimate articulations of lived experience.

More broadly, the analysis also raises questions about our engagements as community, peace and liberation psychologists in South Africa in the twenty-first century. More specifically related to *Community Storylines*, how do we speak to these tensions in the project that seems to encourage spaces of community dialogue? If we accept that violence "disintoxifies" the oppressed to restore agency and identity, how do we creatively utilise our spaces of community engagement to bring forth noble ideals of inclusion, economic justice and recognition? How do we navigate these tensions and paradoxes conceptually and in praxis? How do we utilise community stories as a peacemaking intervention that moves the community actors *away* from choosing violence (despite its ambiguous relationship to peace)? How do we lift the stories to bring these polarities to a dialogue?

In reaching this conceptual impasse, we acknowledge that while more questions are raised than answered, the sense-making and potential solutions might emerge not through the application of outcomes-based models of community intervention, but in navigating the spaces of uncertainty, of "not knowing" and being guided by processes of engagement (Lau & Seedat, 2013, 2014). It is in these unfolding processes of community engagement with the Thembelihle community that we witness potentially rich possibilities for peacemaking. These spaces, which have included stakeholder meetings, digital storytelling workshops, youth community and forum theatre, and symposia bring together differentially located organised and non-organised social actors who seek to contest representations and obtain community legitimation. When sensitively facilitated, contesting voices are brought to the fore in expressions of anger and frustration, yet without attendant expressions of physical violence. The storytelling processes in such spaces may help contain the tensions and anger constructively, and provide avenues for redirection and promote collective conversations about how to engage the state in the quest for social justice. In turn, they may stimulate conversations about how to strengthen citizen participation in development within young democracies. Likewise, stories in safe spaces may stimulate conversations about how to organise "violent-free" public protests and modes of meaningful engagement between contesting groups in marginalised contexts. In short stories in safe spaces can help communities articulate repressed rage that may be misdirected at loved ones or culminated in the symbolic burnings of state property, at the same time, affording liberatory potential by fostering individual and collective self-awareness and insight. They offer avenues to cultivate modes of internal engagement and exercise collective citizenship in "invited" and "invented spaces" (see Miraftab & Wills, 2005), as part of the larger ongoing quest for social justice in a society marked by political democracy and socio-economic inequalities.

Appendix

Transcript Notation
[]   Explanation of term/utterance
/.../   Omitted text
CAPS   Speaker's emphasis
???   Indecipherable text
[sic]   Speech quoted verbatim

References

Atkinson, D. (2007). Taking to the streets: Has developmental local government failed in South Africa. In S. Buhlungu, J. Daniel, R. Southall, & J. Lutchman (Eds.), *State of the nation: South Africa* (pp. 53–77). Cape Town: Human Sciences Research Council.

Bulhan, H. A. (1985). *The psychology of oppression*. New York: Plenum Press.

Cabral, A. (1979). *Unity and struggle: Speeches and writings*. New York: Monthly Review Press.

Carr, E. R. (2010). The place of stories in development: Creating spaces for participation through narrative analysis. *Development in Practice, 20*(2), 219–226. doi:10.1080/09614520903564165.

Christie, D. (1997). Reducing direct and structural violence: The human needs theory. *Peace and Conflict: Journal of Peace Psychology, 3*, 315–332.

Durrheim, K., Mtose, X., & Brown, L. (2011). *Race trouble: Race, identity and inequality in post-apartheid South Africa*. KwaZulu Natal, SA: UKZN Press.

Fanon, F. (1963). *The wretched of the earth*. New York, NY: Grove.

Frank, A. W. (2012). Practicing dialogical narrative analysis. In J. A. Holstein & J. F. Gubrium (Eds.), *Varieties of narrative analysis* (pp. 88–93). California, CA: Thousand Oaks.

Fraser, N. (1998). From redistribution to recognition? Dilemmas of justice in a "post-socialist" age. In A. Phillips (Ed.), *Feminism and politics* (pp. 430–460). Oxford, UK: Oxford University Press.

Galtung, J. (1975). Violence, peace, and peace research. In J. Galtung (Ed.), *Essays in peace research: Peace: research, education, action* (Vol. 1, pp. 109–134). Copenhagen: Christian Ejlers.

Galtung, J. (1990). Cultural violence. *Journal of Peace Research, 27*(3), 291–305. doi:10.1177/00 22343390027003005.

Harber, A. (2011). *Diepsloot*. Johannesburg: Jonathan Ball.

Honneth, A. (1992). Integrity and disrespect: Principles of a conception of morality based on the theory of recognition. *Political Theory, 20*(2), 187–201.

Howard, N. (2011). Freedom and development in historical context: A comparison of Ghandi and Fanon's approaches to liberation. *Journal of Pan African Studies, 4*(7), 94–108.

Labov, W. (1972). *Language in the inner city: Studies in the Black English vernacular*. Philadelphia: University of Pennsylvania Press.

Leibbrandt, M., Woolard, C., & Woolard, I. (2009). *Poverty and inequality dynamics in South Africa: Post-apartheid developments in the light of the long-run legacy*. Paper presented at the IPC-DRCLAS Workshop, Brazil.

Martineau, W., Meer, N., & Thompson, S. (2012). Theory and practice in the politics of recognition and misrecognition. *Res Publica, 18*, 1–9.

Miraftab, F., & Wills, S. (2005). Insurgency and spaces of active citizenship: The story of Western Cape anti-eviction campaign in South Africa. *Journal of Planning Education and Research, 25*(2), 200–217. doi:10.1177/0739456X05282182.

Mngxitama, A., Alexander, A., & Gibson, N. C. (2008). Biko lives! In A. Mngxitama, A. Alexander, & N. C. Gibson (Eds.), *Biko lives! Contesting the legacies of Steve Biko* (pp. 1–20). New York: Palgrave Macmillan.

Montiel, C. J. (2001). Toward a psychology of structural peacebuilding. In D. J. Christie, R. V. Wagner, & D. D. Winter (Eds.), *Peace, conflict, and violence: Peace psychology for the 21st century* (pp. 282–294). Upper Saddle River, NJ: Prentice Hall.

Murray, M. (2000). Levels of narrative analysis in health psychology. *Journal of Health Psychology, 5*(3), 337–347.

Oliver, K. (2001). *Witnessing: Beyond recognition*. Minneapolis: University of Minnesota Press.

Opotow, S. (2001). Social injustice. In D. J. Christie, R. V. Wagner, & D. D. Winter (Eds.), *Peace, conflict, and violence: Peace psychology for the 21st century* (pp. 102–109). Upper Saddle River, NJ: Prentice Hall.

Polkinghorne, D. E. (1995). Narrative configuration in qualitative analysis. *International Journal of Qualitative Studies in Education, 8*(1), 5–23. doi:10.1080/0951839950080103.

Rappaport, J. (1995). Empowerment meets narrative: Listening to stories and creating settings. *American Journal of Community Psychology, 23*(5), 795–807.

Riessman, C. K. (2008). *Narrative methods for the human sciences*. California, CA: Sage.

Seekings, J. (2008). The continuing salience of race: Discrimination and diversity in South Africa. *Journal of Contemporary African Studies, 26*(1), 1–25. doi:10.1080/02589000701782612.

South Africa's ANC to discuss mine shootings row. (2012, August 27). *BBC News*. Retrieved from http://www.bbc.co.uk/news/world-africa-19388584

Stephens, C., & Breheny, M. (2013). Narrative analysis in psychological research: An integrated approach to interpreting stories. *Qualitative Research in Psychology, 10*(1), 14–27. doi:10.108 0/14780887.2011.586103.

Swart, T. M., & Bowman, B. (2007). Activating action: Aims, methods and imperatives of research in community psychology. In N. Duncan, A. Naidoo, J. Pillay, & V. Roos (Eds.), *Community psychology: Analysis, context and action* (pp. 432–449). Cape Town, SA: UCT Press.

Taylor, C. (1994). The politics of recognition. In K. A. Appiah, J. Habermas, S. C. Rockefeller, M. Walzer, & S. Wolf (Eds.), *Multiculturalism: Examining the politics of recognition* (pp. 25–73). Princeton, NJ: Princeton University Press.

Tigar, M. (2009). Narratives of oppression. *Human Rights Brief, 17*(1), 6.

von Holdt, K. (2012). The violence of order, orders of violence: Between Fanon and Bourdieu. *Current Sociology, 61*(2), 112–131. doi:10.1177/0011392112456492.

von Holdt, K. (2014). On violent democracy. *The Sociological Review, 62*(S2), 129–151. doi:10.1111/1467-954X.12196.

Weis, L., & Fine, M. (2004). *Working method: Research and social justice*. New York: Routledge.

Wilderson, F. B., III. (2008). Biko and the problematic of presence. In A. Mngxitama, A. Alexander, & N. C. Gibson (Eds.), *Biko lives* (pp. 95–114). New York: Palgrave Macmillan.

Chapter 11
Gender Justice: "Gender" in the Bangsamoro Development Plan

Teresa Lorena Jopson

"The peace negotiations and ceasefire [between the Government of the Philippines (GPH) and the Moro Islamic Liberation Front (MILF)] allowed communities in Mindanao to dream of peace and development", observed Haneefa Macapado, a young woman speaking for Muslim youth at a forum at the University of the Philippines (Macapado, 2015). Before the peace talks and since the 1970s, more than 120,000 people were killed in the separatist war (Wadi in Lontoc, 2006). The ceasefire has been in place since 1997 and the latest peace process commenced in 2001 to address one of Asia's longest conflicts. As the GPH races to conclude the peace process during the term of the Aquino administration, remarkable progress has been made in the last 3 years compared to the preceding decade of negotiations. The Bangsamoro Basic Law (BBL) was drafted and published in 2013. If enacted, a Bangsamoro government will rise where the Autonomous Region for Muslim Mindanao (ARMM)[1] stood. The Bangsamoro ministerial government will prioritise development in the resource-rich but poorest region of the Philippines. To this end, the Bangsamoro Development Plan (BDP) was an initiative drafted by the MILF's Bangsamoro Development Agency (BDA) in anticipation of the passage of the BBL and was published online in May 2015. As the peace talks and the BBL hang in the balance, the contents of the BDP identify what is at stake for women and men in building the Bangsamoro Government.

This chapter reviews gender roles in Moro history, women's participation in peace processes, and gender equity as an agenda in peace negotiations. My purpose is to illustrate that critical attention to gender contributes to an effective peace and

---

[1] ARMM is limited in its scope and strength and thus, in developmental impact. The BBL sets up a Bangsamoro government with more economic and political powers that are expected to lead to societal development.

T.L. Jopson (✉)
Coral Bell School of Asia Pacific Affairs, Australian National University,
Canberra, ACT, Australia
e-mail: teresa.jopson@anu.edu.au

© Springer International Publishing AG 2017
M. Seedat et al. (eds.), *Enlarging the Scope of Peace Psychology*,
Peace Psychology Book Series, DOI 10.1007/978-3-319-45289-0_11

221

development policy. I refer to gender as the social construction of the sexes, as it is commonly understood (Baden & Goetz, 1998; Sardenberg, 2007), but with awareness that my approach to gender is as a relational category, opting for "dynamic and historically situated notions of masculinity and femininity and an emphasis on power relations" (Costa, 1994 in Sardenberg, 2007, p. 55). I therefore foreground the conflict in Southern Philippines by considering the sources of conflict and gender constructs reflected in the history of the Bangsamoro people from the twelfth century to present. I then review women's participation and incorporation of gender as an agenda in peace negotiations in Southeast Asia to situate the BDP within peace efforts in the region. Moving to consider the current peace process between the MILF and GPH, I examine how gender is framed in the language and content of the BDP.

The main method used in chapter is a critical discourse analysis that traces the logic of text. After reviewing the entirety of the BDP, I studied the way the word "gender" is used each time it appears in the body (Vision, Chapters 1–15) of the 216-page document available from the Bangsamoro Development Agency website. I perform a critical frame analysis, following Ron Schmidt Sr., to visibilise how gender has been framed in the text. In my discussion, I look at BDP's "gender" discourse in the "(re)production and challenge of dominance" (Van Dijk, 1993, p. 249) in the properties of the text and its local meanings. I underscore the power of words in producing meanings and action and highlight underlying conflicts that should be addressed for long-term peace. Discourse analysis affords a qualitative exploration of gender in this particular piece of policy and allows for a thoughtful review of the language of the plan in relation to wider contexts; in fact, the meanings emerge only in relation to them (Fairclough, 1995).

Historical Injustices Against the Bangsamoro

The conflict in Mindanao is long and complex. In this section, I present a concise narrative focusing on the roles played by men and women in the making of the Bangsamoro nation. I do this to draw out the gender order in the Bangsamoro history and illustrate how gendered social relations construct the conflict. I revisit these roles later in my analysis.

Male merchant Arabs and migrant settlers shared Islam to indigenous people in Mindanao since the twelfth century (Abubakar, 1983). The Sultanates of Mindanao were led by men portrayed as charismatic heroes who were able to unite Muslim indigenous people under their rule since the fifteenth century (Majul, 1999). The different sultanates and ethnic organisations made "a constellation of royal houses which had unreconciled claims to legitimacy and historicity" (Tan, 1987, p. 44) the root of *ridos* or clan wars. In this situation, a larger clan would be deemed more formidable in force, and thus women's fertility is highly valued. Patriarchs protect their families by launching offensives and counter-offensives against rival clans. The clans who are successful in doing so are deemed stronger and thus deter rival attacks, headed by clan heroes that provide and protect.

When the Spanish colonised the islands in the sixteenth century, they found the Muslim men resistant to the occupation, referred to them as Moros,[2] and depicted them as an enemy. As they were losing the war against Filipino revolutionaries, Spain sold the Philippine Islands, including Mindanao, to the United States by way of the Treaty of Paris in 1898. After the Philippine-American War, Moro men were systematically marginalised by land and power dispossession[3]. For instance, the U.S. claimed indigenous lands in Mindanao for settlement by non-Moro inhabitants, drastically shifting the demographic population in the Philippine's second largest island. By the late 1960s, the political influence of the Sultans weakened and social unrest had intensified (Dwyer & Cagoco-Guiam, 2012).

The human rights violations committed by the Philippine government, such as the Jabidah massacre[4] in 1968, fired the establishment of the Moro National Liberation Front (MNLF) in 1969. The MNLF declared an aspiration for an egalitarian Bangsamoro Republic, separate from the Republic of the Philippines. In the assertion of self-determination of Muslims in Mindanao, the pejorative Moro became a distinction and a positive source of pride. The disempowered Moro men who lost lands and positions of power in the public sphere found a new purpose in armed social movements.

To control civilian unrest, then President Ferdinand Marcos formed in the 1970s the Civilian Home Defense Force (CHDF) and supported the Christian militia ILAGA (Ilonggo Land Grabbers' Association), which claimed to defend Christians from attacks perpetrated by Muslims, but in reality grabbed land by force and killings (Macasalong, 2013). Terror was built by attacks on mosques, such as the Malisbong massacre[5] in 1974. However, the people's resistance against Martial Law only grew. By 1976, the GPH and the all-male MNLF panel signed the Tripoli Agreement, signaling peace talks under the framework of autonomy. Following the peace deal, the Moro Islamic Liberation Front (MILF) fighters broke away to pursue the separatism that was abandoned by the MNLF.

By way of the Visiting Forces Agreement and the Joint Military Training signed in 1999, the United States military forces were involved in the Philippine government's all-out war policy in Mindanao in 2000. After 9/11, the MILF was linked to Jemaah Islamiyah and Al-Qaeda groups, allegedly the rationale for the continuing U.S. presence in Mindanao. In the war waged by the GPH and the U.S. in Mindanao, Muslim men are depicted as enemies, and women and children are made invisible. Thus, bombings and indiscriminate strafing have been forms of attack by the militarily powerful states of the Philippines and the U.S. working together against the

---

[2] From the North African Moors that invaded Spain in the eighth century.

[3] See Abinales 2010 for a critical analysis of the dominant historical discourse on the Mindanao conflict.

[4] Known as the Corregidor massacre on 18 March 1968. Up to 68 male Moro recruits of the top-secret, government-led Operation Merdeka were allegedly killed by GPH Armed Forces when they refused to pursue the operation that would kill their kin in Sabah. The operation was part of the GPH plan to forcibly take Sabah from Malaysia.

[5] Known as Tacbil Mosque Massacre, this is the strafing and killing of 1776 civilian Muslims in a mosque on 24 September 1974 in Malisbong, Palimbang, Sultan Kudarat. The perpetrators were the 15th Infantry Battalion, Armed Forces of the Philippines.

insurgency in Marcos' martial law, Estrada's all-out-war, and Aquino's all-out-offensive policies.

The ARMM, inaugurated in 1990 as a result of negotiations with the MNLF, was described as "a failed experiment" two decades later by President Benigno Aquino III. The MILF maintains a stronghold in ARMM. Its leadership, in 2010, abandoned the separatism for an independent federal state-like autonomy of the Bangsamoro. Some grassroots MILF fighters view the collaboration as a self-defeating compromise and have supported the new militant Bangsamoro Islamic Freedom Fighters (BIFF) instead. The agreements between the GPH and the MILF further sparked renewed vigor from a faction of the MNLF that led a siege[6] in Zamboanga in 2013. Known actors in the MNLF, MILF, BIFF, and ASG are male. Except when they emerge as victims, women are usually unseen in the narrative of the Bangsamoro.

Despite the ongoing peace negotiations and a ceasefire order, the Special Action Force (SAF) of the Philippine National Police (PNP) performed operation "Oplan Exodus" in Mamasapano, Maguindanao—an MILF-controlled territory—on 25 January 2015 without coordinating with the MILF nor the Armed Forces of the Philippines. The result was 67 deaths; of these 44 were SAF men, 18 MILF men, and 5 civilians. In mainstream and alternative media sources, the widows of the SAF and the MILF fighters clamored for justice (see Kilab Multimedia, 2015). The clash in Mamasapano revealed critical aspects of the conflict in Mindanao and changed the pace and course of the peace process.

The brief historical account presented here shows emerging sources of conflict brought about by systematic land grabbing, lack of social services, and human rights violations in the form of militarisation and massacres. The war that is being waged by liberation movements in Mindanao seems to aspire for redress of the historical injustice against Muslims in the Philippines (see Jubair, 1999). Against this backdrop, I sketched the gender order in which males have taken on public roles and women the private. The expensive military solutions that the government has adopted have not solved the conflict because they failed to address the inequality and injustice. The peace processes that the GPH initiated seemed to be a more fruitful endeavour towards peace in Mindanao, a direction consistent with the long-term vision to satisfy human needs, advocated by peace psychologists (Christie, Tint, Wagner, & Winter, 2008).

Women in Southeast Asian Peace Talks

A new and affirmative aspect in the current talks between the MILF and the GPH is the participation of women. Women are actively being brought on board as negotiators and consultants. Most notably, the GPH panel is chaired by a woman and has had women members since 2004, while the MILF recently appointed two Moro

---

[6] MNLF alleged that the GPH has standing agreements made with their group that are being abandoned by way of the peace accord with MILF.

women to its Board of Consultants and Technical Working Group (Pahm, 2013). Before presenting and analysing the gender content of the BDP, I briefly situate the BDP within peace efforts that are involving women in Southeast Asia.

The low participation of women in peace negotiations relates to the marginal position of women in most societies. Only four percent of signatories to major peace agreements worldwide from 1992 to 2011 have been women, and no woman was chief negotiator in UN-brokered talks (UN Women, 2012). For instance, no woman participated in the 2007 peace meeting between the MILF predecessor, Moro National Liberation Front, and the GPH. Notably, the 2011 negotiations between the leftist National Democratic Front of the Philippines and the GPH represent a stand-out high point of 33 % women signatories and 35 % women negotiators.

A force that affirms the necessary participation of women in the prevention and resolution of conflicts is the UN Security Council Resolution 1325 (2000) on women, peace, and security. The resolution urges all parties to take measures to protect women and girls from gender-based violence, particularly rape and other forms of sexual abuse in conflict situations. As an agenda, increased women's participation is common in peace negotiations in Southeast Asia, lobbied by women's organisations and international bodies. The theory has been that women's presence in processes of negotiating would lead to more substance in the discussion of gender-related issues (UN Women, 2012). Two examples of expanding women's roles in peace are in the peace talks between Aceh separatists and the Indonesian government, and the ongoing peace process in Myanmar.

The peace talks between Aceh separatist movement and the Indonesian government was initially all male. In 2004, the Free Aceh Movement enjoined Shadia Marhaban to participate on their panel of five. The 2005 talks in Helsinki were largely considered a success, but having a woman in the panel did not translate into having a gender perspective in the negotiations (UN Women, 2012). The lone woman at the negotiating table in hindsight reflected that she was unaware of Resolution 1325 and missed the relevance of including gender issues in the peace process. "In order to secure signature to an agreement, reputable international organizations, the European Union (EU)—as the guarantor of the Helsinki MoU—and even the UN itself opted to side-line women's issues within the process", wrote Marhaban (2012, p. 20).

The role of women was also not on the agenda in the peace processes under the military regime in Myanmar. A significant feature of the current peace process is the inclusion of a few women from armed groups at the peace table and the more public nature of the peace process (Lahtaw & Raw, 2012, p. 7). In addition, women observers have been given access to the negotiations. The new space for women has made civil society actors in Myanmar hopeful that this space can be expanded as the peace process develops. However, content-wise, a 2012 opinion survey among women in top- and mid-level positions in Myanmar's civil society organisations indicates that attention to gender was negligible in previous peace processes (Lahtaw & Raw, 2012). Thus far, military offensives persist in ethnic conflict areas, even as the government talks peace, with rape and sexual assault continuing to be used as tools of war (see KWAT, 2013). Since 2010, the Women's League of Burma has documented

100 cases of sexual violence, including 47 gang rapes perpetrated by Burmese military in ethnic regions (Women's League of Burma, 2014). Furthermore, the government refuses to address the violence against Rohingya Muslims in the Rakhine State, which has displaced thousands and killed hundreds (Council on Foreign Relations, 2015), and encouraged human trafficking.

Increased participation of women in Southeast Asian peace negotiations is expected to bring more attention to gender. However, the Aceh example shows that the attention to gender may not naturally follow women's participation. The Myanmar experience, on the other hand, suggests that women's participation in the peace negotiations does not preclude the continuation of state-perpetuated gender-based violence. Thus, while the region has shown great interest in involving women in the peace process, placing gender justice on the peace agenda remains an ongoing challenge.

Gender and Development in the BDP

To examine the quality of peace envisioned in the Bangsamoro, I turn to the May 2015 BDP Integrative Report prepared by the Bangsamoro Development Authority (BDA), the development arm of the MILF, in consultation with stakeholders and government and non-government partners.[7] In this section, I present the text of the BDP as my primary data. I first describe the basic content of the BDP and then present my discourse analysis of how gender is used in the body of the development agenda.

The BDP is a blueprint for development in the Bangsamoro region, the means and an end of the Bangsamoro autonomy. The plan provides vision, strategy, and recommendations in the short (2015–2016) and medium (2016-beyond) terms. The Integrative Report is a 216-page document, with 15 chapters and seven annexes. The early chapters explain the background and analysis of the conflict in the Bangsamoro, the plan methodology and development framework, and the current situation and opportunities. The later chapter focuses on recommendations for each priority sector.

Acknowledging that the conflict in the Bangsamoro is rooted in complex security, justice, and economic drivers, the BDP moves away from the "business as usual" approach in development planning. It recognises that "enduring peace and stability can be attained through just, inclusive, equitable and highly tangible socioeconomic rehabilitation, reconstruction, and development" (BDA, 2015, p. xv). The Peacebuilding and Sustainable Human Development Framework adopted for the BDP is based on the principles of stakeholder inclusion and consideration for the drivers of conflict (see Abubakar, 2013). The plan specifically promises to ensure local participation and the delivery of basic services, two duties that are not

---

[7] The analyses and recommendations were formulated by thematic experts, validated at the ground level, and complemented by Community Visioning Exercises (BDA, 2015).

adequately met by the current government. The BDP has identified six thematic areas for developmental projects and sectoral recommendations: economy and livelihood, infrastructure, social services, environment and natural resources, culture and identity, and governance and justice as relating to goals of normalisation and development. The plan recognises that gender cuts across these themes, along with the issues of youth and peacebuilding (BDA, 2015, p. 3).

In my analysis, I test the logic of the BDP's use of "gender" and adopt a critical frame analysis, following Ron Schmidt's lead (2015). To investigate the document (see Table 11.1), I first reviewed the entire BDP and then focused on those parts that talk about gender. Column one therefore lists sentences from the body of the BDP (Vision, Chapters 1–15) original text that contain the word "gender". The second step was to consider the local context (location in the document) and properties of the text (presence and absence of crucial elements, wording, metaphors, and other devices used, if any). The second column therefore notes where the sentence is situated within the BDP and provides comments on the text properties. The third step was to bring out the logic of the text in relation to its role in the development agenda of the BDP. The third column therefore identifies the underlying assumptions and arguments that the text puts forward. The fourth step was to bring the text (column 1) in conversation with wider contexts that impede the development of the Bangsamoro. In the fourth column, I therefore pose counter-arguments that test the logic of the original text, to show how gender as used in the BDP could benefit from critical attention to meet the development goals of the Bangsamoro. Finally, based on all preceding columns, I identified the emergent "gender" framing in the last column. Framing comes from the words considered in local and wider contexts, but also produces ideologies and discourses.

The gender frames in the last column of the table are gender-equals-women (5), gender-equals-sex (2), and gender-as-social positions (2). In three cases, no particular frame emerges, since there is not enough information to draw upon any substantive conclusion. On the one hand, the BDP uses gender interchangeably with sex, and on the other, to refer to social positions. The dominant frame, however, is its reference to gender as synonymous to women. Following Schmidt, I extracted the dominant gender frame identified and consider their strengths and weaknesses in the discussion that follows. The counter-arguments I posed in the fourth column further animate my analysis in the next section.

Developing a Gender Framework

The dominant narrative on gender employed in the BDP is that "women" equals "gender" or "gender" is synonymous with "women". Most of the gender sensitivity measures presented in the Plan, when concretised, relate to women. The strength of this formulation is in the recognition that women are marginalised in the Bangsamoro and is the first step in challenging gender inequality. In this light, the BDP is progressive in many ways, certainly in its vision of enjoining women to participate in

Table 11.1 Gender in the BDP (2015)

Text	Context and comments (A)	Assumptions and argument/s (B)	Counter-argument/s (C)	Gender frame (D)
(1) Inclusiveness—guaranteeing that the benefits of economic growth and the dividends from peace process shall be shared to all stakeholders in the Bangsamoro, regardless of political or ethnic affiliation, gender, or creed (p. xv)	Cited in the Vision as the first principle of the BDP There is recognition of the widespread political and economic exclusion in the Bangsamoro Absence of equity in the text Rhetorically strong in ethos, pathos	Everyone should and will benefit from economic growth in the Bangsamoro Structures will be placed in the Bangsamoro to have inclusive sharing of economic growth and dividends	Shares from economic growth may not be equitable Those who are privileged in society based on political or ethnic affiliation, gender, or creed may benefit the most from economic growth	Gender as social positions
(2) [Theme] h. Cross-Cutting Concerns [Components] Gender, youth and other vulnerable groups, peacebuilding, food and nutrition, security [Development Partners] IOM, UN-WFP, UN-Women [Government Counterparts]—(p. 16)	Appears in Table 1: List of BDP Themes, Components, and Participating Partners, summarising the BDP Plan Methodology and Framework There is an impetus to look at these "other" concerns in the Bangsamoro. Listing of cross-cutting concerns suggests analytical sophistication, listing of partners shows credibility Absence of content—government counterparts	Throughout the BDP, gender is an important concern Partnering with IOM, UN-WFP, UN-Women will help address cross-cutting concerns of gender, youth and other vulnerable groups, peacebuilding, food and nutrition, security	(2C1) Gender is a box ticked in the BDP, a minor concern (2C2) Limited partnerships might overlook men in the BDP	Gender = women
(3) Figure 4: Population Age and Gender Projections (2010 and 2040). [Figure on Gender labelled female and male] (p. 24)	In the background chapter, the figure illustrates the human resource potential of the Bangsamoro BDP identified economic challenges as vulnerable employment of mostly men and the low participation of women and youth in the labor force Gender interchanged with sex in graph	Women and men have different contributions to the Bangsamoro (3B2) Women's participation in economic activities will be a source of future economic growth Gender = female and male	Women and men have potential for similar contributions to the Bangsamoro Women's labour has been and may continue to be exploited and invisible in the Bangsamoro Gender is a social construction	Gender = sex

(4) Promote culture-sensitive and gender-responsive health approaches (p. 36)	In Chapter 6, Strategy and Recommendations, this appears in the table presenting recommended projects and activities for Phase 1 (short-term), under the Culture and identity theme	Culture-sensitive and gender-responsive health approaches are effective	Gender-responsive approach not defined in the BDP	Gender=women
	In the next column, under Phase 2 (medium-term) is "Establish cultural centers for women"	Culture-sensitive and gender-responsive means attending to the needs of women	Gender-responsive health approaches necessarily includes men	
(5) Technical assistance is being extended to MAGELCO with respect to: … and (g) managing processes related to environmental, social, and gender impacts in investment operations (p. 69)	In Chapter 8, Infrastructure theme, this appears in the capacity building recommended towards the electric cooperative in Maguindanao, MAGELCO	There are gender impacts in investment operations that need to be managed	(5C1) The gender impacts are not specified and thus management is problematic.	?
	Listing of investment impacts levels	Non-electrification affects women in homes (?)	Non-investment in electrification would be difficult to pin down as affecting a specific gender	
(6) A.6. Gender and Development	The title of a section in Chapter 9, Social Services. The section recognises that women are marginalised based on GDI, many work in other countries, and identifies the vulnerability of women and girls as victims of GBV, that reinforces gender inequality and limits the development participation of women	Women are marginalised and vulnerable as victims of gender-based violence (GBV)	Women are not equally marginalised and vulnerable as victims of GBV	Gender=women
(7) Gender Disparity Index (GDI)				
(8) Gender-based violence			(8C) LGBT, poor young men can also be vulnerable in Bangsamoro and in other countries as migrant workers	
(9) Gender inequality (p. 79)			(9B) Gender inequality limits the participation of women and men (men in care work, etc.)	

(continued)

Table 11.1 (continued)

Text	Context and comments (A)	Assumptions and argument/s (B)	Counter-argument/s (C)	Gender frame (D)
(10) B.5. Gender	Title of a section in the Social Services chapter, specifying strategic goals in response to the issues provided in section A.6. (see above)	BDP gives gender importance	Attention to gender does more than just attend to the vulnerable in humanitarian action, but contribute to service delivery efficiency and effectivity	Gender = women
(11) Specific focus is also needed in improving prevention and response to GBV and discrimination based on gender or disability (p. 90)	The section opens with a discussion on the need for Bangsamoro humanitarian action capabilities, then says that focus on GBV and discrimination is needed	In capacity building for social services, attention to the vulnerable is crucial	(11C) That nowhere in BDP are LGBT recognized, men seen as vulnerable means these pertain to women	(GBV = VAW) (Discrimination based on gender = discrimination against women)
(12) In the short-term, the Bangsamoro will: ... b. Conduct gender training using modules that deal with sectoral issues and themes, e.g., GBV, trafficking, illegal recruitment... (p. 90)	Still in the same section, this figures in the outline of short- and medium-term strategies	The BDP shows sensitivity to the marginal position of women in the Bangsamoro	(12C) Focus on women's marginality and vulnerability may overlook women's	Gender = women
	Other than gender training modules in the short term and human rights education in the medium term, the recommendations pertain to women—such as women's access to protection mechanisms, etc	Gender in the BDP goes beyond women in terms of awareness and educational campaigns	contributions to human security	Gender as social positions
(13) The CAB's and the BBL's provisions on economy, social development, environment, governance, and justice and security are formulated in harmony with customary laws and traditions, while ensuring cultural, gender, and intergenerational inclusivity (p. 106)	In the introduction of Chapter 11, Culture and Identity	CAB and BBL are gender-inclusive	Customary laws and traditions may not be gender-inclusive	?
	CAB is the Comprehensive Agreement on the Bangsamoro, the framework for the peace negotiations		(13C2) Patriarchy is not seen as a problem in the Bangsamoro	
	Silent on traditional gender roles, patriarchy in the Bangsamoro in the entire chapter		Again, gender is a box ticked in the BDP, but gender inequality remains a minor concern in the plan	

(14) [CAB] commits the parties to cooperation for its implementation and to continuing multisector dialogues that ensure inclusivity, accountability, and gender balance to all stakeholders in the Bangsamoro (p. 132)	In Chapter 13, on Proposed Implementation Arrangements and Financial Modality, emphasising Bangsamoro leadership in planning, delivering, and monitoring socioeconomic, political, and cultural interventions in its territory. The statement is a commitment to the BDP principles	CAB commits to ensure gender balance in the Bangsamoro	The commitment to ensure gender balance in the Bangsamoro is not yet apparent in the BDP	?
(15) 9. **Inclusiveness**. All data will be disaggregated by gender, sex and, where possible, other social classifications relevant to the unique social landscape of the Bangsamoro, such as ethnicity and religion, to ensure inclusiveness (p. 146)	This is the last item in the Guiding Principles section of Chapter 15, Results-based Monitoring and Evaluation Framework	The Bangsamoro government plans to solicit gender- and sex-disaggregated data in the Bangsamoro	That gender and sex are not defined clearly in the BDP makes this task difficult	Gender = sex
	Annex G corresponding to the chapter drops sex- for gender-aggregated data (p. 175)	The content of the annex on inclusiveness evaluation reflects attention to gender roles	(15C2) Inconsistency between the chapter and the annex suggests that "gender" has been used carelessly in this section	

the building of the Bangsamoro. The flaws in this formulation are, however, significant. Firstly, it excludes other genders (Table 11.1, 8C; 11C). In adding women into
the development agenda, it presumes that this satisfactorily covers concerns on gender. Gender is a social construction of the sexes, whereas "women" is but a category
of gender (Sardenberg, 2007); thus, "women" does not capture the entirety of gendered lives. Gender goes beyond the genitalia and should include non-
heteronormative genders in the Bangsamoro. Secondly, it universalises Bangsamoro
women's experience, as if all women experience the same level of marginalisation
and discrimination. In the same manner, there is an implicit assumption that men are
invincible. Lastly, it fails to criticise the historical patriarchal arrangements in the
Bangsamoro. In this section, I will discuss the last two points in more detail, revisiting the gender order I have sketched in the Moro history and counter-arguments I
have proffered in the table above to show why an improved framing of gender in the
BDP is necessary to meet its goals of sustainable peace and development.

Why use "gender", when the BDP means "women"? "Gender" has been appro-
priated by mainstream aid institutions and good governance discourses to the point
of paying lip service (Elson, 1995). Top-down, externally imposed gender mainstreaming (Mukhopadhyay, 2007) reduces gender and development to a legitimate
technical fix. In short, the term has been hijacked by institutions in ways that forward their different agendas without justice as an objective (see Cornwall, Harrison,
& Whitehead, 2007). The BDP (see Table 11.1, 2C1; 5C1; 15C2) seems to have
fallen in what a Filipino radical feminist organisation, Makibaka, warned as a "gender trap" (Baden & Goetz, 1998). This could explain why the BDP does not define
gender-impacts clearly and uses gender interchangeably with women.

Differentiating Experiences of Women and Men

The framing of women-equals-gender universalises women and overlooks class
divisions in society that differentiates their level of marginalisation and discrimination. The universalisation is reminiscent of the women in development (WID)
approach of the 1970s that focuses on women's access to economic development
and argues for integration (Boserup, 1970) and political involvement. Building on
these gains, the gender and development (GAD) approach reflects the goal of gender equality, as addressed by the women's movement in the 1980s (Baden & Goetz,
1998). While underscoring women's potential contribution to the labor force
(Table 11.1, 3B2; 9B), the BDP formulation appears to construct "gender", as was
fashionable in mainstream international institutions of the 1990s, with an emphasis
on gender awareness but without an emancipatory aim (Table 11.1, 13C2).

In a patriarchal society such as the Bangsamoro, women and girls are likely to be
abused more than men and boys. However, poor young men are also at great risk in
conflicts organised by elites, including clan wars (Table 11.1, 8C). In wars abroad,
male combatants have been documented to be vulnerable in the hands of adversaries
and are also victims of sexual violence (Zarkov, 2007). When the BDP says that

interventions must be crafted with a gendered and peacebuilding lens, it necessitates an understanding of class, ethnicity, and gender to socially locate women, girls, men, and boys in a web of power relations. While there is a need to be vigilant that "gender" is not used as a backdoor to locate men front and centre, "gender" makes visible the relationship between people of varying identities and sexualities and the shared responsibility of creating an equitable world.

Patriarchy as Structural Violence

A crucial element that is missing in the women-equal-gender framework is to identify and criticise an established patriarchal order in the formal and informal institutions within the Bangsamoro (Table 11.1, 13C2). Gender inequality in the Bangsamoro prevents marginalised women and men from developing themselves and contributing to the development of their communities. Peace researcher Johan Galtung described conflict in seemingly peaceful situations as structural violence (Galtung, 1969). While direct violence harms or kills people swiftly, structural violence is a chronic harming or killing slowly, through normalised social arrangements that privilege a group and deprive the basic needs of another. Gender inequality can be seen as a form of structural violence that is a consequence of the normalised gender order in societies that privileges men in history. In Mindanao, this means that conflict can exist after direct violence has ceased.

Understanding the operation of a patriarchal arrangement in the Bangsamoro history helps define what roles men can take and avoids the trap of affording absolute symmetry in support and protection between sexes based on "impartiality". In the historical background I presented to foreground the conflict in the Bangsamoro, war has been shaped by the roles men took to defend themselves, their families, and communities. The gender order that shaped the conflict needs subversion to build peace. Stereotypes such as that household issues concern women and public issues concern men must obviously be avoided and men must be allowed to take on various roles in peacebuilding. As new roles are being cast for men to contribute to peace, the hero role men play in the narrative of war espoused by the MILF needs to be thoughtfully considered as should their lead in clan wars. The notion that women need to be saved follows suit, as this misses the opportunity to make women active partners in peacebuilding (Table 11.1, 12C). The changes in roles change the story. Since narratives aid in mobilisation through identification and production of a community (Fine, 1995), these narratives could be revised towards directions such as equality and justice. Other narratives are possible (Bergeron, 2004) in circumstances where the Moro people determine their unique peaceful future.

Galtung (1975) suggests that peacebuilding as a peace activity is a proactive attempt aimed at healing and reducing structural violence in an effort to prevent conflict in the future. Galtung (1985) and Wagner (1988) refer to the promotion of equitable social arrangements as positive peace. Seen in this light, addressing the gender gap in the DBP is a crucial part of peacebuilding in the Bangsamoro and an investment towards a more stable peace. The benefit of a holistic peace agenda that considers gender in its entirety is that it becomes a vehicle for the social change that is needed to keep peace. This is a difficult but worthy project because it requires a change in the dominant culture. For instance, the vision of equality and justice espoused by the BDP entails the transformation of religious and public institutions to dismantle patriarchy. Peace in this sense is not only an absence of war, but works towards an absence of conflict through cooperation.

Words, Frames, Ideologies, and Discourses

Words do matter, especially in power-laden documents such as plans and policies. Ferree and Merrill observe that, "language often carries masculinist assumptions and normative judgments that pass as neutral concepts" (2004, p. 247). Let us take as illustration the BDP's first core value of vicegerency, elucidated as the following:

> Man, according to the teachings of Islam, is the representative and vicegerent of Almighty Allah on Earth. This world is a trust and man is its trustee. Prophet Mohammad (peace be with him) also said: "All of you are shepherds and all of you are responsible for your herds: The leader is a shepherd and is responsible for his subjects (BDA, 2015, p. 13).

The original Quranic texts from which the BDP quotes refer to vicegerents as humans, men and women. As a core value that informs all interventions, vicegerency could have been described in a gender-neutral formulation ("all", "each person") used in expounding other core values. Instead, the translation of the original excerpt contains a discourse on gender that is presented as normal, yet enacts and reproduces male dominance as it influences minds (Van Dijk, 1993). What is interesting is that vicegerency does not appear in an earlier draft of the BDP. In the drafting process, the BDA consulted a variety of stakeholders, including feminist scholars and advocate groups, and the progression of its versions demonstrates an ongoing struggle within the MILF. This dynamism is crucial, but what emerges in the final policy underscores the dominant narrative in the BDP.

Words can be viewed as frames in which ideologies and discourses are manifested and themselves produce ideologies and discourses. Gender discourses comprise debates on privilege and difference and are fundamentally *political* (Ferree & Merrill, 2004) discourses relating to the use and distribution of power and its underlying values and mobilisations. The language of a development plan such as the BDP is crucial in that it shows speech acts that reflect wider attitudes forged in the peace process. In a policy, language can be observed as "thinking in operation", and a force that will translate into action, and thus has methodological implication (Billig, 1995). In the same light, carefully crafting concepts used in a peace agenda can help foster conditions that attract peace. Naturally, gender should figure not only on the level of language, but in the content of the peace process. For example, when the BDP says that the promotion of gender-responsive health approaches is in the first phase of the plan, it should engage men in reproductive health programmes.

Learning from criticisms of the international family planning programme, interventions should take gender relations into account to enhance women's status and involve men in equal and supportive domestic partnerships (Greene, 2000).

In this section, I illustrated that gender, as framed in the BDP as synonymous to women, has shortcomings that need to be addressed in order to build sustainable peace and development in the Bangsamoro. Framing gender more broadly and critically is crucial in formulating policies that address the social inequalities that perpetuate conflict. In the absence hereof, we may reinforce old problems of male privilege or marginalise the queer identities in the Bangsamoro. The language and content of the BDP is important because it determines what is at stake for the Bangsamoro people in their struggle for autonomy.

Peace in Gender Justice

Gender and power actively construct the history of the Bangsamoro. Recognising the legitimate claims of the Moro people, peace processes have been embarked upon, the latest of which is the current negotiations between the MILF and the GPH. I presented in this chapter the gender content of the BDP, which aims to address sources of conflict in the Bangsamoro through an autonomous Bangsamoro government. Like the Free Aceh Movement, the MILF has broken ground with the inclusion of women in the peace panels. Unlike the Free Aceh Movement and Government of Indonesia peace talks, aspects of Resolution 1325 have been woven into the agenda of the negotiations. However, having women participate at the negotiating tables is one aspect and having gender on the agenda is another. A former member of the GPH panel negotiating with the MILF observed, "Although there are many women active in the peace movement, many of them are reluctant to advocate gender issues" (Santiago, 2011, p. 31). Muslim secular feminism that advocates for gender equity and Islamic feminism that raises the issue of equality in private and public spaces are already stirring debates in Mindanao (Brecht-Drouart, 2015). Just as activists in Myanmar are concerned with the shaping of their peace process, women and men in vibrant civil society in the Philippines could define the gender discourse in the BDP in both invited and invented spaces.

The framing of gender in the BDP is crucial because "gender" has been used as a technical fix in development agendas. As already indicated, through discourse analysis, I found that gender is used in a way that it is synonymous with women. If women's issues are assumed to be the only gender issues, then the BDP fails to appreciate how gender operates. Empowering Moro women is an important step towards gender equity, but it would be presumptuous to assume that women will always speak for all genders, and on all aspects of gender-based oppression.

Understanding that women and men experience conflict differently because of the gender roles and opportunities afforded them, deeper research on Moro women's and men's various experiences of conflict would benefit the peace policies of the BDA. The universalisation of the experiences of women is not just misleading, but also spells failure for policies. The differences of experience among women and men show a large variety within a specific group. With equity in mind, gender is rewardingly considered in relation to power lines such as class, and where relevant, like in Mindanao, ethnicity, generation, and geographic location. Recognising the diversity of the Moro people requires policies to be closer to reality in order to be effective. In the end, it is the quality of the discourse on gender that will make a difference to the lives of everyday women and men after the conflict.

Taking up gender in the BDP is an opportunity to commit to gender justice; that is, if gender is used in the BDP, it should do gender some justice. In its current formulation, the BDP does not do so in its silence on the patriarchal arrangements within the Bangsamoro. Peace psychology researchers prescribe contribution towards positive peace in the form of equitable social relations, including gender relations. There is no shortcut; painstaking changes in power relations are requisite. Addressing structural violence in the form of social and gender justice builds and keeps the peace. How this central issue can be practically addressed in peace negotiations and post-conflict development must be subject of future research.

While the BDP talks equality, justice, and peace, its commitment to gender equality is not yet reflected in the current language and content of the plan. Disadvantaged women and men will continue to suffer from structural violence within the Bangsamoro if a careful, gender-inclusive, anti-patriarchal perspective is missing in the BDP. In this chapter, I underscored the relevance of women's participation in peace processes and critically framing gender on peace agendas. Attending to the quality of gender discourse by (re)politicising "gender" to bring back its emancipatory aim, in addition to the increased participation of women in peace and development programmes, is an aspect of a sustainable peace.

Acknowledgements The author thanks Tyrell Haberkorn, Tamara Jacka, three anonymous reviewers, and fellows at the 14th International Symposium on the Contributions of Psychology to Peace for their helpful comments on earlier versions.

References

Abinales, P. N. (2010). *Orthodoxy and History in the Muslim-Mindanao Narrative*. Metro Manila, Philippines: Ateneo de Manila University Press.

Abubakar, C. A. (1983). The Islamization of Southern Philippines: An overview. In F. L. Jocano (Ed.), *Filipino Muslims: Their social institutions and cultural achievements*. Quezon City, Philippines: Asian Center, University of the Philippines.

Abubakar, A. (2013). *Building peace in conflict affected communities through the sustainable human development framework: A case study of Mindanao*. Penang, Malaysia: Universiti Sains Malaysia.

Baden, S., & Goetz, A. M. (1998). Who needs [sex] when you can have [gender]? Conflicting discourses on gender at Beijing. In C. Jackson & R. Pearson (Eds.), *Feminist visions of development: Gender analysis and policy*. London, UK: Routledge.

Bangsamoro Development Agency. (2015). *Bangsamoro development plan integral report*. Retrieved from http://bangsamorodevelopment.org/wp-content/uploads/2015/05/BDP-IR.pdf

Bergeron, S. (2004). *Fragments of development: Nation, gender, and the space of modernity*. Ann Arbor, MI: University of Michigan Press.

Billig, M. (1995). Rhetorical Psychology, Ideological Thinking, and Imagining Nationhood. In H. Johnston and B. Klandermans (Eds.) *Social Movements and Culture*, Minneapolis: University of Minnesota Press, 64–82.

Boserup, E. (1970). *Women's role in economic development*. London, UK: George Allen & Unwin.

Brecht-Drouart, B. (2015). The influence of the national question on gender issues in the Muslim areas of the Southern Philippines: Maranao Muslim women between retraditionalization and Islamic resurgence. In H. Ahmed-Ghosh (Ed.), *Contesting feminisms: Gender and Islam in Asia*. New York: SUNY Press.

Christie, D. J., Tint, B. S., Wagner, R. V., & Winter, D. D. (2008). Peace psychology for a *peaceful* world. *American Psychologist, 63*(6), 540–552.

Cornwall, A., Harrison, E., & Whitehead, A. (2007). *Feminisms in development: Contradictions, contestations & challenges*. London, UK: Zed Books.

Council on Foreign Relations. (2015, June). *The Rohingya Migrant Crisis*. Retrieved from http://www.cfr.org/burmamyanmar/rohingya-migrantcrisis/p36651.

Dwyer, L. K., & Cagoco-Guiam, R. (2012). *Gender and conflict in Mindanao*. The Asia Foundation. Retrieved from https://asiafoundation.org/resources/pdfs/GenderConflictinMindanao.pdf

Elson, D. (1995). Male bias in the development process: An overview. In D. Elson (Ed.), *Male bias in the development process* (2nd ed.). Manchester, UK: Manchester University Press.

Fairclough, N. (1995). *Critical discourse analysis: The critical study of language*. London, UK: Longman.

Ferree, M. M., & Merrill, D. A. (2004). Hot movements, cold cognition: Thinking about social movements in gendered frames. In J. Goodwin & J. M. Jasper (Eds.), *Rethinking social movements: Structure, meaning and emotion*. Lanham, MD: Rowman & Littlefield.

Fine, G. A. (1995). Public Narration and Group Culture: Discerning Discourse in Social Movements. In H. Johnston and B. Klandermans (Eds.) *Social Movements and Culture*, Minneapolis: University of Minnesota Press, 127–143.

Galtung, J. (1969). Violence, peace and peace research. *Journal of Peace Research, 3*, 176–191.

Galtung, J. (1975). Three approaches to peace: Peacekeeping, peacemaking and peacebuilding. In J. Galtung (Ed.), *Peace, war and defence—Essays in peace research* (Vol. 2, pp. 282–304). Copenhagen, Denmark: Christian Ejlers.

Galtung, J. (1985). Twenty-five years of peace research: Ten challenges and some responses. *Journal of Peace Research, 22*, 141–158.

Greene, M. E. (2000). Changing women and avoiding men: Gender stereotypes and reproductive health programmes. *IDS Bulletin, 31*(2), 49–59.

Jubair, S. (1999). *Bangsamoro: A nation under endless tyranny* (2nd ed.). Ann Arbor, MI: University of Michigan Press.

Kachin Women's Association Thailand. (2013, October). *Undermining the peace process: Burmese Army atrocities against civilians in Putao, Northern Kachin State, report*. Retrieved from http://womenofburma.org/kwat-oct-2013-undermining-the-peace-process/

Kilab Multimedia. (2015, February 26). The widows of Mamasapano [video]. *YouTube*. Retrieved from https://www.youtube.com/watch?v=mfYYWhZnevs

Lahtaw, J. N., & Raw, N. (2012). *Myanmar's current peace process: A new role for women?* Center for Humanitarian Dialogue, Opinion. Retrieved from http://athenaconsortium-s3.studiocou-cou.com/uploads/document/file/15/Myanmar_OP_FINAL.pdf

Lontoc, J. F. (2006, February). Professor traces historical roots of Muslim struggle in the Philippines. *UP Newsletter, 27*(2).

Macapado, H. (2015, March 5). *Tinig ng Kabataang Muslim (Voice of Muslim Youth)*. Speech delivered at Mamasapano: Media, at Wika ng Digmaan (Mamasapano: Media and the Language of War), College of Mass Communication, University of the Philippines, Diliman, Quezon City, Philippines.

Macasalong, M. S. (2013). *The liberation movements in Mindanao: Root causes and prospects for peace*. Dissertation, International Institute of Islamic Thought and Civilization, International Islamic University, Malaysia.

Majul, C. A. (1999). *Muslims in the Philippines* (2nd ed.). Quezon City, Philippines: University of the Philippines Press.

Marhaban, S. (2012). The sole woman at the negotiation table. In S. Willoughby, R. Behouria, & N. Williams (Eds.), *Women's perspectives of peace and security* (Vol. 1). N-Peace. Retrieved from http://n-peace.net/uploads/default/publications/files/4e95f818bec4cc1a4bad375467dbcb1b.pdf

Mukhopadhyay, M. (2007). Mainstreaming gender or 'streaming gender away: Feminists marooned in the development business. In A. Cornwall, E. Harrison, & A. Whitehead (Eds.), *Feminisms in development: Contradictions, contestations & challenges*. London, UK: Zed Books.

Pahm, S. (2013). Filipino women peace makers in Mindanao. In R. Behouria & N. Williams (Eds.), *Women's perspectives of peace and security* (Vol. 2). N-Peace. Retrieved from http://n-peace.net/uploads/default/publications/files/edbb0e75e24d6c58106e1f49625f9048.pdf

Santiago, I. M. (2011). Mindanao. In *Peacemaking in Asia and the Pacific: Women's participation, perspectives and priorities*. Center for Humanitarian Dialogue. Retrieved from http://athena-consortium-s3.studiocoucou.com/uploads/document/file/9/57WomenatthePeaceTableAsiaPacificreportMarch2011.pdf

Sardenberg, C. M. B. (2007). Back to women? Translations, resignifications and myths of gender in policy and practice in Brazil. In A. Cornwall, E. Harrison, & A. Whitehead (Eds.), *Feminisms in development: Contradictions, contestations & challenges*. London, UK: Zed Books.

Schmidt, R., Sr. (2015). Framing immigration. *Migration and Citizenship, 3*(1), 10–15.

Tan, S. K. (1987). *A history of the Philippines*. Quezon City, Philippines: University of the Philippines Press.

UN Women. (2012). *Women's participation in peace negotiations: Connections between presence and influence*. Retrieved from http://reliefweb.int/sites/reliefweb.int/files/resources/03AWomenPeaceNeg.pdf

Van Dijk, T. A. (1993). Principles of critical discourse analysis. *Discourse & Society, 4*, 249–283.

Wagner, R. V. (1988). Distinguishing between positive and negative approaches to peace. *Journal of Social Issues, 44*(2), 1–15.

Women's League of Burma. (2014). *Same impunity, same patterns: Sexual abuses by the Burma Army will not stop until there is a genuine civilian government*. Retrieved from http://womenofburma.org/same-impunity-same-pattern-report-of-systematic-sexual-violence-in-burmas-ethnic-areas/

Zarkov, D. (2007). *The body of war: Media, ethnicity, and gender in the break-up of Yugoslavia*. Durham, NC: Duke University Press.

Chapter 12
Social Cohesion, Violence, and Education in South Africa

Yusuf Sayed, Azeem Badroodien, Akiko Hanaya, and Diana Rodríguez

Public education institutions are arguably the primary institutions through which social solidarity in most societies may be promoted (Durkheim, 1964; Merton, 1968; Tawil & Harley, 2004). They are also the main sites where values and social norms can best be developed and where future citizens may be taught to better communicate with each other (Feinberg & Soltis, 2009). It is also within educational institutions that engagements with past injustices, historical memory, transitional justice processes, and better communal interaction in the social arena can bring communities together and encourage processes of forgiveness and healing (Hamber, 2007).

In this chapter, we examine how education and teachers are conceptualised within policymaking related to building social cohesion in South Africa. More specifically, we consider the intended educational goals of social cohesion, its value in schools in reducing societal conflict, and its objective to foster enduring forms of social justice and peace in everyday life. We argue that in providing educational opportunities to learners, teachers are the determinants both of education quality in schools (Mourshed, Chijioke, & Barber, 2010; Sayed & Ahmed, 2015; Barrett, Chawla-Duggan, Lowe, Nikel, & Ukpo, 2006) and of effecting nation-building, identity construction, and peace and reconciliation in classrooms. Furthermore, as the main

Y. Sayed (✉)
Center for International Teacher Education, Cape Peninsula University of Technology, Cape Town, South Africa

University of Sussex, UK
e-mail: Sayed.cite@gmail.com

A. Badroodien • A. Hanaya
Centre for International Teacher Education, Cape Peninsula University of Technology, Cape Town, South Africa
e-mail: BadroodienA@cput.ac.za; akiko.hanaya@gmail.com; A.Hanaya@sussex.ac.uk

D. Rodríguez
Teachers College, Columbia University, New York, NY, USA
e-mail: dmr2164@tc.columbia.edu

© Springer International Publishing AG 2017
M. Seedat et al. (eds.), *Enlarging the Scope of Peace Psychology*,
Peace Psychology Book Series, DOI 10.1007/978-3-319-45289-0_12

239

drivers and symptoms of conflict and fragility in society can inevitably be traced back to structural inequalities, including the distribution of education opportunities, this provision of equal access to quality education can encourage and promote social cohesion and peace (Rose & Greeley, 2006). We argue that in order to do so, education policies and programmes need to visibly promote redistribution (equity), recognition (of diversity), representation (engagement), and reconciliation (dealing with grievances, injustice, and legacies of conflict) (Fraser, 1995, 2005; Hamber & Kelly, 2004; Novelli, Lopes Cardozo, & Smith, 2014).

The chapter is structured around two main threads. It begins by defining social cohesion as reflected in a variety of international policy documents and policies, and argues that if social justice is to be truly promoted then the structural factors that militate against equality need to be addressed. In this regard, a more nuanced view of the relationship between social cohesion and violence is also needed if the concept of peace and solidarity is to be embedded in society. The second thread explores the state-level components that give form to how social cohesion is conceived and operationalised within state-level thinking (Green & Janmaat, 2011). In this section, we explore social cohesion in relation to education policies post-1994 that have sought to realise central values in South African education that are based on the country's constitution, concentrating on violence in the school environment, and examining its implications for teachers and for the provision of quality education in South Africa.

Defining Social Cohesion Within Policy

In recent times policymakers have begun to take a keener interest in a social cohesion agenda, due to increasing social inequality, poverty, and crime across the world. Within policy documents, international organisations like the Organization for Economic Cooperation and Development (OECD), the World Bank, the United Nations Development Programme (UNDP), and the UN Department of Economic and Social Affairs (UN DESA) conceive of and define social cohesion in a variety of ways. What is notable in each of their definitions is that they all regard social cohesion as the loose bonds that bring individuals together and that influence their behaviour, and the equivalent of building solidarity and trust, inclusion, social capital, and reducing poverty in society. Social cohesion, they suggest, is promoted when a sense of belonging and a willingness to help are inculcated amongst citizens, and when all heterogeneous groups have a sense of belonging, participation, inclusion, recognition, and legitimacy (Chan, To, & Chan, 2006; UNESCO-IIEP, 2006; UNDP, 2014; OECD, 2011; World Education Forum, 2015).

We argue that definitions of social cohesion that focus on the above also need to include key structural factors that militate against equality. In that regard, we advocate for a inclusion of a conception of social justice that is historically informed, relational, place-based in nature, that takes into account the experiences and claims of marginalised groups in society, and that includes a systematic analysis of the social, cultural, and political conditions that underlie unequal distributions in society (Zwarteveen & Boelens, 2014; Marc, Willman, Aslam, Rebosio, & Balasuriy,

2012). Along with Osler (2011), we assert with regard to education that social cohesion initiatives aimed at achieving social justice have to always equip learners with the capacity to transform society, and education provision thus needs to be constantly enriched to promote this transformative end.

In line with Fraser's (2005) work, we contend that a socially just society requires full participation, and as such mere social interaction with others is insufficient to ensure the economic *redistribution* of resources and opportunities. Policies must thus always also include sociocultural remedies for better *recognition* and political *representation* (Fraser, 2005; also see Novelli et al., 2014) (see Fig. 12.1 below). Additionally, there is also an important need for processes of *reconciliation* in societies affected by conflict and emerging from histories of division, processes that "promote an encounter between the open expression of the painful past" and the search for "a long-term, interdependent future" (Hamber & Kelly, 2004, p. 10). This would address historic and present tensions, and grievances and injustices in ways that build a more sustainable peaceful society (Fraser, 1995).

This conceptualisation can be likened to Galtung's (1976) seminal references to how to build positive peace, where spaces are cultivated that include a focus on social justice, a direct response to the causes of violence, and the elimination of structural violence (Smith, McCandless, Paulson, & Wheaton, 2011). We argue that, for this, the provision of quality education would play a key role in fostering positive peace and greater social solidarity, as well as instilling forms of justice that directly address the root causes of conflict (Keddie, 2012; Sayed & Ahmed, 2015; Tikly & Barrett, 2011). In the rest of the chapter, we explore the role of education policy, education provision, and teachers (as one such provision) in building this kind of environment.

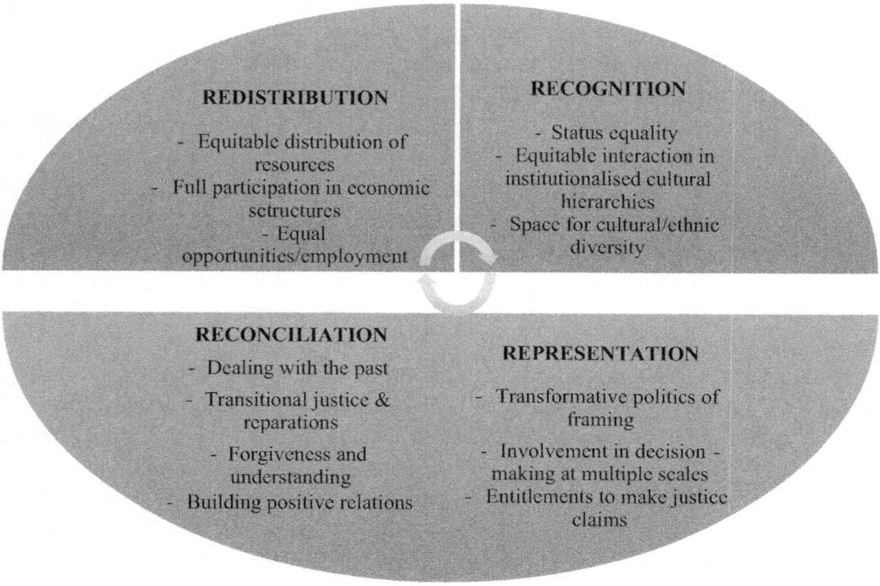

REDISTRIBUTION

- Equitable distribution of resources
- Full participation in economic setructures
- Equal opportunities/employment

RECOGNITION

- Status equality
- Equitable interaction in institutionalised cultural hierarchies
- Space for cultural/ethnic diversity

RECONCILIATION

- Dealing with the past
- Transitional justice & reparations
- Forgiveness and understanding
- Building positive relations

REPRESENTATION

- Transformative politics of framing
- Involvement in decision - making at multiple scales
- Entitlements to make justice claims

Fig. 12.1 The four Rs (adapted from Fraser, 2005 and Novelli et al., 2014)

In doing so, we accentuate four key points about conflict and violence in society and in schools:

1. The root of most social tensions and forms of violence in society can be found in sociocultural, political, and economic inequality.
2. Not only do different forms of violence and tensions limit the capacity to provide access to quality services, but they also contribute to a deep divide between individual daily experiences of violence and overall broader social and political structures (Salmi, 2000; Seitz, 2004).
3. Conflict and violence is most acutely felt when individuals are dehumanised in the ways they interact with one another, and when institutions and societies are correspondingly structured to support this.
4. Social disharmony is promoted when different manifestations of violence become intertwined in relationships between individuals and broader social and political structures and processes (Scheper-Hughes & Bourgois, 2004).

Education Policies and Social Cohesion

A key challenge with regard to the above is how to better understand the conflicting demands on educational institutions, and teachers, as peacebuilders in protracted and post-conflict contexts. We contend that a starting point would be to explore the implications of teaching amidst conflict and violence, and the policies attached thereto.

Besides national policies, curricula, and school-level factors, we recognise that social relationships shape, constrain, and challenge the daily actions of teachers in the classroom. In contexts where different forms of violence criss-cross individual and collective notions of belonging, the role of teachers is invariably interconnected to the broader network of relationships in which they participate. As individuals, teachers are bound up in a network of social interactions that are shaped by, and shape, the context in which they work. Their capacities to engage in peacebuilding are thus constrained by the levels of violence, social cohesion, and social justice within the environments in which they operate. Their capacity to engage is also influenced by the kinds of education policies and processes initiated, what the policies are meant to achieve, and what they prescribe in their operational texts.

Notably for South Africa, despite undergoing democratic elections in 1994, followed by a proliferation of education policies and a particular viewpoint of how teachers could facilitate change, meaningful change for the majority of its citizens has not been forthcoming. As such, while processes of policy development post-1994 in South Africa have tried to harness social cohesion initiatives to engage with a variety of socio-economic inequalities, it is how violence has become imbricated within social relationships in schools that has probably most influenced how teachers have set about fulfilling their key roles. This is explored below.

Education Policies and Social Change in South Africa After 1994

The period 1994–1999 was arguably the most significant period in terms of policy formulation in recent South African history. This is because the period after 1994 required the development of frameworks to completely restructure the education sector and to build a unified and democratic education system that redressed past injustices. The task to inscribe in law the framework and vision of the new democratic Constitution of 1996—3 Green Papers, 4 White Papers, 6 Bills, and 20 Acts—was immense (Sayed, Kanjee, & Nkomo, 2013). The implied changes may be described as an extreme form of "transformative remedies" to past injustices, given the focus on restructuring the underlying generative narrative of the country (Fraser, 1995, p. 86). Reforms immediately after 1994 were directed at the focus on and promotion of equality, and the eradication of all forms of discriminatory practices and structures. For example, one of the first undertakings after 1994 was to replace the previously fragmented and racially stratified education system with a single system.

The South African Schools Act (SASA) of 1996 (South Africa, 1996) thereafter sought to ensure that all children had the right of access to quality education, and thus made schooling compulsory along with trying to provide an equitable allocation of state funding for education (*Redistribution*).

Also, redressing past injustices was one of the most articulated principles of reform, with the Constitution as well as the South African Schools Act forbidding all forms of discrimination based on race. Redress was particularly aimed at correcting past education injustices that was based on racial inequality and segregation (*Reconciliation*), and forbade all schools, including private schools, from using race to discriminate against learners at admission. Ironically, the Act was mostly silent on how forms of discrimination affecting teachers would be addressed.

Moreover, the Constitution Section 29 (2) assured all learners the right to receive education in the official language(s) of their choice in public schools (*Recognition*). Broad-based participation in decision-making processes was recognised as essential for the democratic movement and social change, and the SASA devolved significant powers to school governing bodies. Governing bodies were composed of the school principal and elected representatives of parents, educators, non-teaching staff, and (in secondary schools) learners, and they could also co-opt non-voting members. Furthermore, parents were set up to have a majority stake in education governance in order to ensure that previously marginalised constituencies had a greater voice (*Representation*).

Finally, with regard to later education policies aimed at transformation, the Amended National Norms and Standards for School Funding and the amended South African Schools Act after 1999 sought to directly address issues of inequality in schools by recognising that funding provisions in the SASA of 1996 had worked mainly to the advantage of public schools that were patronised by middle-class and wealthy parents, and served to imitate past discriminatory investment in schooling and highlight vast disparities in the income of parents (*Reconciliation*). To address these inequalities, a progressive pro-poor funding policy was introduced in the period 2004–2009 where 40% of schools, namely the poorest two-fifths as determined by poverty indicators, were made "no-fee" schools. This was extended in 2010 to include the three lowest fee quintiles.

Education and the Focus on Values

In terms of the policy process as it related to social cohesion, the most significant education policy occurred in the period 1999–2004 under Minister Kader Asmal with his *Values in Education Initiative*. This initiative sought to identify, realise, and embed some of the central values in South African education based on the Constitution, and led to the formation of key policies like the *Manifesto on Values, Education, and Democracy of 2001* and the *National Policy on Religion and Education of 2003* (Sayed et al., 2013).

The *Manifesto on Values, Education, and Democracy* (Department of Education (DoE), 2001) identified key values that it considered necessary to underpin social change and solidarity. The Manifesto identified ten fundamental values (as contained in the Constitution): democracy; social justice and equity; equality; non-racism and non-sexism; Ubuntu (human dignity); an open society; accountability (responsibility); the rule of law; respect; and reconciliation, that it regarded as key to compelling social transformation. This was supported by 16 strategic actions that were believed would help in instilling democratic values in young South Africans in schools, such as nurturing a culture of communication and participation in schools, role modelling and promoting commitment, as well as competence among educators, making arts and culture part of the curriculum, making schools safe to learn and teach in, and ensuring the rules of law. Aware of teachers' transformative role towards social cohesion, the Manifesto denounced the many forms of violence, including sexual abuse and harassment, manifested in South African schools. To counteract this reality, the document reiterated the idea of teachers as role models. According to the Manifesto, teachers had to exhibit at all times the values of competence and commitment.

To build on this, the South African History Project was also initiated shortly thereafter. One of the Project's key publications included a 6-volume series, *Turning Points in South African History*, in which it collaborated with the Institute for Justice and Reconciliation (IJR). The aim of the project was for it to be used in teaching South African History in the National Curriculum Statement Grades 10–12 (General), to lay the basis for learners to have a common outlook on the history of South Africa and about living together.

In sketching the above policy developments, we acknowledge that many of the policies related to social cohesion have generally *said* all the right things. This, of course, does not mean that the policies and their rationales have been actively implemented or pursued. We note, however, that the overall goal in the chapter is to broadly sketch the trajectory of policies (and their logic) associated with social cohesion, as a way of locating the role assigned to education and teachers within them.

Education Polices After 2009 Amidst Policy Discourses of Social Cohesion

As a concept, it was only after 2009 that the term "social cohesion" really started to appear more frequently within official policy statements, and took a decidedly firmer form. In this regard, three policies have relevance, namely the National Development Plan (NDP) of 2012, the Mid-term Strategic Framework (MTSF) of 2014–2019, and the Department of Education's Five-year Strategic Plan (2015/2016–2019/2020).

The problem statements of each of the above documents returned to the legacies of apartheid and South Africa's divided and unequal society in terms of race, gender, disability, space, and class, and accentuated the dire need to directly address these. As such, the documents identified the Department of Arts and Culture (DAC) to be mainly responsible for coordinating this focus. In that regard, the *National Strategy for Developing an Inclusive and a Cohesive South African Society* (DAC, 2012) was specifically developed in 2012 to provide an overall definitional and operational view of social cohesion, captured as:

> Social cohesion is defined as the degree of social integration and inclusion in communities and society at large, and the extent to which mutual solidarity finds expression itself among individuals and communities (DAC, 2012, p. 30).

A cohesive society, according to the DAC, could only be achieved if there was a reduction or elimination of inequalities and exclusions within South African society, as well as close cooperation between citizens to develop shared goals that would improve the living conditions for all.

This view, in the form of nation-building, was seen as a process whereby a society of people with diverse origins, histories, languages, cultures, and religions could come together as equals within the boundaries of a sovereign state with a unified constitutional and legal dispensation, a national public education system, an integrated national economy, and shared symbols and values. The focus on a "society of people" was to work towards eradicating the divisions and injustices of the past, to foster unity, and to promote a countrywide conscious sense of being proudly South African where everyone was committed to the country, and open to the continent and the world (DAC, 2012, p. 30).

In relation to social cohesion, it was asserted that this approach to building the nation was in essence the practical actualisation of democracy based on the unity and equality of its members. Thus, while social cohesion could be thought of as community-based, targeted at the micro-social level and underpinned by an overall sense of belonging, it needed to be embedded in and had to operate at the national macro level. Ironically, given the firm focus on being inclusive, the *National Strategy for Developing an Inclusive and a Cohesive South African Society* did not comment or elaborate on how the relationship between teachers and social cohesion was understood.

In this regard, the NDP, in outlining the long-term macro socio-economic policy of South Africa, devoted an entire chapter to nation-building and social cohesion (Chap. 15). In this, it identified the following as factors that would promote social cohesion: sport and art; interaction across race and class; learning history, heritage, and culture; and learning each other's language, and noted a number of actions that would better achieve social cohesion in society, and within education. This included enabling learners to read the Preamble of the Constitution in different languages at school assemblies, ensuring representation through the sharing of common spaces across race and class, and encouraging citizens to actively partake in different local committees, boards, and forums (National Planning Commission, 2013).

Subsequent to the above, the MTSF of 2014–2019 listed 14 priority outcomes that it felt would enhance nation-building and social cohesion. For example, Outcome 1 on basic education suggested that the introduction of African languages in schools would foster social cohesion, while with Outcome 4, the focus on public employment schemes was meant to increase or add value to social cohesion initiatives.

Finally, as outlined in the MTSF, the NDP, and DAC documents, the Department of Basic Education (DBE) had historically always been seen as playing perhaps the main role in effecting social cohesion. This was most visible in the re-establishment of the Directorate for Social Cohesion and Equity in Education in 2011, which was a readjustment of the previous Directorate for Race and Values within DBE. This shift evidenced a transition to a more broad understanding of the intersections between race, class, and gender as means to social exclusion.

Moreover, the role of the DBE in the promotion of social cohesion is also visible within the DBE's long-term plan, two mid-term plans, and annual sector plans. *Action Plan to 2019: Towards the Realisation of Schooling 2030,* for example, details the overall direction of the basic education sector to achieve the goals set out in the NDP, in the MTSF, *Five-year Strategic Plan (2015/2016–2019/2020),* and in the *Annual Performance Plan (2015–2016).* The latter DBE plans are closely aligned to the NDP and MTSF priorities for the education sector.

This alignment is represented in Table 12.1 below. It highlights how the various policy papers have expressed the priority roles of education for social cohesion, and the tasks that the MSTF allocated to the DBE in achieving outcome 14.

Furthermore, as is noted in the DBE's *Five-year Strategic Plan (2015/2016–2019/2020),* the term social cohesion has been used at least 12 times in relation to the introduction of African languages in schools and to other school social cohesion programmes. To operationalise this, the DBE piloted in 2014 the incremental introduction of African language (IIAL) programme in schools, as well as the drafting of a Social Cohesion Programme handbook focusing on how to improve social cohesion in schools, foster human rights and responsibilities, encourage parental and community involvement, and create a culture of excellence using local history.

This fits into the characterisation of Freemantle (2012) who notes that the fundamental characteristic of social cohesion initiatives within state policy processes is that they are mainly "integrated into an existing and long-standing discourse of nation building" (Freemantle, 2012, p. 2) where they are used either synonymously or as an addition to nation-building. Freemantle (2012) observes that in such a situation social cohesion would only then be seen as ways of promoting citizenship, patriotism, and nationhood, and as the main or only denominator that bonds citizens.

Table 12.1 Excerpts from MTSF—tasks of the DBE for outcome 14

Actions	Indicators
Promote the bill of responsibility, constitutional values and national symbols amongst children in schools	National stakeholder forum established and the quarterly reporting on the different roles they perform in schools
	Printing and distributing the bill of responsibilities booklets, posters, and flyers, together with values in action manuals
	Activities that show engagement with the bill of responsibilities, with regions responsible for reporting
	Number of learners that participate in moot court and other Democracy Programmes
	Number of schools reciting the preamble of the constitution at school assemblies
	Percentage of schools flying the national flag
	Percentage of schools that have booklets and posters of national symbols and orders
Increase multilingualism in the school environment	Percentage of schools where one African language is taught
Promote social cohesion in schools	Number of schools which offer art
	Schools where oral history programme is part of the national curricula
	Schools where National Action Plan against Racism, Xenophobia, Sexism, and Related Intolerances is implemented
Provide mass participation opportunities	Mass participation sport events that are inclusive of social cohesion programmes
Improve participation in school governing bodies' elections	Number of programmes and interventions that focus on increasing voter turnout in schools run from the DBE
	Percentage of parents who participate in elections of school governing bodies

However, Shuayb (2012) cautions that this kind of positioning in relation to nationhood rarely translates into acceptable forms of social justice. In contextualising developments within overall international trends, she notes that social cohesion initiatives in instances like that described above generally only focus on how to better foster stability and consensus when escalating inequalities are seen to threaten the economic market system. Citing Osberg, Shuayb (2012) argues that using social cohesion and the building of a common citizenry in addressing inequalities can easily be seen as simply trying to develop a positive correlation between economic development and social well-being and, as such, is simply be an agenda for distribution, complacency, and consensus.

Social Cohesion and Violence in South Africa

Along with the ways in which social cohesion is characterised within policy documents in South Africa, as noted above, understandings of social cohesion in South African policies are also often impugned by the belief that widespread violence in schools undermines the environment necessary for effective teaching and learning. There are two approaches to this.

On the one hand, school-based violence is conceptualised in its physical manifestation and is seen to start and end in schools that socially and historically were disadvantaged. Some argue that this pervasiveness of continued violence is intimately tied to South Africa's legacy of apartheid. On the other hand, violence is also viewed with regard to its symbolic manifestation, in its overall threat to social solidarity in South Africa. It is argued that social solidarity and community interaction is irreparably undermined when "physical violence becomes the first line strategy for resolving conflict and gaining ascendancy" (Abrahams, 2004, p. 4).

In South African schools, multidimensional school-based violence takes on various forms, such as bullying, theft, sexual and gender-based violence, assault and fighting, gang-related violence, cyber-bullying, xenophobia, corporal punishment, and homophobia (Burton & Leoschut, 2013; Mncube & Harber, 2013; Buckland, 2005). This means that students and teachers must cope with violence as a routine. Over time, its main overall consequence has been that it has changed the kinds of ways learners interact with each other and their communities. A study by the Centre for Justice and Crime Prevention (CJCP), for example, found that one in five secondary school learners—a total of 22.2%—had experienced one or more form of violence while at school in the 12 months between August 2011 and August 2012 (Burton & Leoschut, 2013). This translated to over a million secondary school learners (1,020,597) across the country struggling directly with how to overcome visible conflict.

In the above regard, various treaties were ratified by South Africa from 1994 that obliged the South African government to ensure the safety of learners and educators in schools and protect their human rights. These treaties included international and regional human rights commitments attached to the Convention of the Rights of the Child (CRC, ratified in 1995), the Convention on the Elimination of All Forms of Discrimination against Women (CEDAW, ratified in 1995), the International Covenant on Civil and Political Rights (ICCPR, ratified in 1998), and the Convention Against Torture (CAT, ratified in 1998). They were further tied to regional laws and treaties dealing with violence and safety that included the African Charter on Human and Peoples' Rights (ACHPR, ratified in 1996), the African Charter on the Rights and Welfare of the Child (ACRWC, ratified in 2000), and the Protocol to the African Charter on Human and Peoples' Rights on the Rights of Women in Africa (Maputo Protocol, ratified in 2004). The above treaties after 1994 were seemingly put in place to provide all the necessary sanctuaries to protect the rights of South African citizens.

However, a key concern with the above policies and treaties has been that they have mainly focused on protecting the human rights of learners and educators and not tried to address the psychological effects of violence and conflict on learners. This approach has been mainly based on the belief that the ways learners interact with each other in schools, as well as with their communities, are keenly influenced by levels of violence in their schools and communities. Policies since 2008 have thus primarily focused on providing safe school environments. One clear example is the signing of an implementation protocol between the DBE and the

South African Police Service in 2011 that "aimed to promote safer schools and prevent the involvement of young people in crime" (Department of Basic Education (DBE), 2011, p. 1). In this agreement, each school was linked to local police stations and local reporting systems on school-based crime and violence were established. Safe School Committees were also established that worked in partnership with local non-governmental organisations, local police, and district officials to implement crime prevention programmes in schools and community mobilisation interventions. This was followed by the initiation of the National School Violence Prevention Framework (NSVPF) in 2013 that sought to integrate existing school safety strategies and policies and provide a simplistic, yet comprehensive, approach to addressing the violence prevention needs of schools. The framework outlined roles and responsibilities of the DBE, provincial departments of education, and schools and school communities, and stipulated that provincial departments ensure that all schools were trained and implemented the framework, ensured a reporting system that linked school to national, and ensured that school-level role players were properly equipped to deal with the challenges related to safety. The framework included practical manuals for the diagnosis and identification of problems, with actual dealings and interventions planned according to the specific situations of schools.

As is clear from the above, by prioritising the physical manifestations of violence to the neglect of addressing other normalised and symbolic forms of violence in schools, policies after 2008 tended to securitise violence and, in so doing, closed down opportunities for alternative social cohesion initiatives to gain traction in schools. This is most evident in schools where legalistic support was provided to learners to protect them from violence at schools, but were not followed by the necessary capacity of school governing bodies and provincial departments to implement school safety measures nor to ensure safe learning environments for teachers and learners. There was also an absence of the necessary resources, skills, and training for school governing bodies and teachers to fulfil their duties (Squelch, 2001).

We contend that by focusing mainly on the physical dimensions of violence, and not adequately attending to the needs of victims of school-based violence, schooling policies have in fact contributed to the escalation of violence in schools. It is an added drawback that it is mostly learners in impoverished areas, where there are high levels of violence and little resources available to deal with it, that suffer as a result of this approach.

Teachers and Violence

A further challenge to social cohesion in South African schools, that has strengthened the resolve of the above security-framed approach, has been the level of sexual abuse of learners by educators, and the large numbers of inappropriate relationships between educators and learners. According to the above-cited study of CJCP in 2013, 4.7 % of secondary school learners were sexually assaulted or raped while at school in the 12-month period. It also found that female learners (7.6%) were more prone to be victims of sexual assault than their male counterparts (1.4%), and that a great number of learners were re-victimised. The extent of the abuse has placed enormous pressure on government policy since 1994, given that it is government that is accountable for what happens to learners in schools, and given that teachers are meant to be the legal and moral arbiters of the state's *In Loco Parentis Responsibility.*

Policies such as the Employment of Educators Act (1998) that regulate the conditions of service, discipline, retirement, and discharge of educators, have focused on developing better processes that force provincial departments of education to dismiss educators found guilty of committing acts of sexual assault on learners, or for having a sexual relationship with a learner of the school where he or she was employed. It is expected in new amendments that the South African Council for Educators Act (2000) would further assist by ensuring that an educator is removed from the South African Council for Educators (SACE) register if he or she was "found guilty of a breach of the code of professional ethics" (Unilever Ethics Centre, 2002, p. 1). The SACE Code of Professional Ethics outlines the conduct that is expected between educators and learners, namely that educators have to refrain from "any form of abuse physical or psychological (section 3.6)", "improper physical contact with learners (section 3.5)", "any form of sexual harassment (physical or otherwise) of learners (section 3.7)", and "any form of sexual relationship with learners at a school (section 3.8)" (Unilever Ethics Centre, 2002, pp. 136–137).

On the side of learner rights, the Criminal Law (Sexual Offences and Related Matters) Amendment Act (2007, section 54) and the Children's Act (2005, section 1) have also attempted to set better processes in place to deal with the problem, such as making it a crime for an educator to fail to report a sexual offence against a child, especially if that educator knows or reasonably believes that a child was being sexually abused.

Again, notwithstanding the policies and processes noted above, the over-emphasis of a legal framework approach has meant that teachers and schools have invariably not been able to tackle the other dimensions of sexual violence that linger within schools, nor insert an approach that engages with the root of the phenomenon. These efforts have also not been helped by most educators who sexually abuse learners not facing meaningful consequences for their actions, nor government departments not being held accountable for their failure to protect, prevent, and respond to such abuse (University of Witwatersrand, 2014).

Teachers, Social Cohesion, and Social Justice

If the goal of social cohesion is to develop a bond that brings individuals together and influences their behaviour (Shuayb, 2012), how can state policies best realise this? If social cohesion initiatives are meant to generate feelings of trust, a common sense of belonging, and a willingness to cooperate with others in contexts of social justice, how can policies address the kinds of structural issues and factors that perpetuate inequalities and increase disunity? A key challenge in respect of the above is how to simultaneously address the micro issues of teacher and learner protection and the macro-level challenge of tackling the social, cultural, and political conditions that contribute to unequal distribution within society. Social cohesion initiatives can only provide social meaning and respect for all citizens when policies ensure the kinds of participation that places everyone on par with each other as full partners in social interaction (Fraser, 2005).

Part of the solution, we imagine, lies in how different kinds of violence are identified and addressed within the schooling lives of teachers and learners, and how these are addressed in meaningful ways through the explicit and hidden curriculum. Social cohesion initiatives will only be able to contribute to forms of positive peace in schools, and provide the kinds of social justice necessary to transform the root causes of violence in schools when there is meaningful schooling participation and when "marginalised learners" start achieving better schooling outcomes (Keddie, 2012, p. 15; UN DESA, 2015). In that regard, the recent 2030 Global Education Agenda has one clear goal or overarching vision, namely to "*Ensure inclusive and equitable quality education and promote life-long learning opportunities for all*". The policy recommendations in the 2030 Incheon Declaration and Education Framework for Action (UNESCO, 2015, pp. 8–9) highlight the central role of teachers as:

> Teacher policies and regulations should be in place to ensure that teachers and educators are empowered, adequately recruited and remunerated, well trained, professionally qualified, motivated, equitably and efficiently deployed across the whole education system, and supported within well-resourced, efficient and effectively governed systems. Relevant learning outcomes must be well defined in cognitive and non-cognitive domains, and continually assessed as an integral part of the teaching.

While there are many debates about targets and indicators relating to education quality and teachers, it is clear that teachers matter. Good quality education and teaching is particularly vital in societies emerging from and affected by conflict. However, whilst teachers are obviously important, there is an added need to develop a contextualised and clear understanding of what pedagogical processes are needed in schools to generate quality learning that is able to effect social solidarity and change. This also applies to how teacher agency is understood with regard to teachers working with learners in creative and dynamic ways, noting that this relationship is never a straightforward causal connection (Fenstermacher & Richardson, 2005). Disconcertingly in current policy texts, teacher agency is often reduced to a variety of audit trails that underplays their ability to enact generative learning in classrooms with pupils (Robertson, 2012).

In terms of what roles teachers could play in relation to social cohesion, this chapter thus concludes with three key viewpoints. First, we point out that there are currently far too many expectations being placed on teachers. They have to engage with transferring subject knowledge, life skills, citizenship and peace education, moral and ethical education, child protection, human rights, skills for sustainable livelihoods, challenging gender inequalities, and the practice of learner-centeredness, to name but a few (Sinclair, 2002; UNESCO-IIEP, 2006). While these are important dimensions in the lives of learners and schools, such an ambitious variety of responsibilities runs the real risk of overstating the potential of schools and their teachers to effect broad social transformation. This chapter cautions, as Davies (2010) does, about being over-optimistic about education's impact on society. In this context, it is sobering to note that in a survey of ten countries, only 23 % of teachers thought they had influence over policy and practice (UNESCO, 2013). As such, teacher agency is not a realistic possibility, nor is agency possible, when faced with multiple and conflicting demands in environments focused on narrow accountability measures.

Second, we argue that the current trend to focus teacher energies on mainly knowledge and content needs to be rebalanced to accommodate firmer relationships with learners and the communities from which they come. There is an urgent need for more joined-up actions with sectors and services outside of schools in order for social cohesion initiatives to gain traction in schools.

Thirdly, teachers cannot be expected to be change agents in schools if their capacities to engage in social cohesion initiatives continue to be constrained by the approaches of policies, the ways in which policies conceptualise key concepts (like violence) that shape school environments, and the structures with which they interact. Social cohesion initiatives must recognise that the roles and lives of teachers are firmly interconnected within the broader networks of relationships and structures in which they participate, and that teachers can only play productive roles within these networks of relationships if the policies and violence that define their everyday life are better problematised.

We conclude by noting that the actions proposed above are only possible in the South African context by ensuring that the education policy landscape foregrounds a more transformative understanding of social cohesion, that teacher education providers and others involved in teacher professional development offer an enriched learning experience for trainee and practicing teachers to capacitate them to act as agents of social cohesion, and that public schools and their governance mechanisms and procedures are (re)designed such that they can create a positive environment for redressing inequity and effecting social cohesion. Only by these changes and more, can South Africa overcome the deep historic and structural inequities of a society fractured along the fault lines of race, class, and gender to create the conditions for just and durable peace and social cohesion.

References

Abrahams, N. (2004). Sexual violence against women in South Africa. *Sexuality in Africa Magazine, 1*(3), 4–6.

Barrett, A. M., Chawla-Duggan, R., Lowe, J., Nikel, J., & Ukpo, E. (2006). *Review of the international literature on the concept of quality in education*. Bristol: EdQual.

Buckland, P. (2005). *Reshaping the future: Education and postconflict reconstruction*. Washington, DC: World Bank.

Burton, P., & Leoschut, L. (2013). *School violence in South Africa*. Retrieved from http://www.fedsas.org.za/downloads/15_18_12_Monograph12-School-violence-in-South%20Africa.pdf

Chan, J., To, H. P., & Chan, E. (2006). Reconsidering social cohesion: Developing a definition and analytical framework for empirical research. *Social Indicators Research, 75*(2), 273–302.

Davies, L. (2010). The different faces of education in conflict. *Development, 53*(4), 491–497.

Department of Arts and Culture (DAC). (2012). *A national strategy for developing an inclusive and a cohesive South African society*. Pretoria: Department of Arts and Culture.

Department of Basic Education (DBE). (2011). *Implementation protocol between the DBE and the South African police service on the prevention of crime and violence in all schools*. Pretoria: Department of Basic Education. Retrieved from http://www.gbf.org.za/?dl_id=752

Department of Education (DoE). (2001). *Manifesto on values, education and democracy*. Pretoria: Department of Education.

Durkheim, E. (1964). *The division of labor in society*. New York, NY: The Free Press.

Feinberg, W., & Soltis, J. F. (2009). *School and society*. New York, NY: Teacher College Press 5th edition.

Fenstermacher, G., & Richardson, V. (2005). On making determinations of quality in teaching. *The Teachers College Record, 107*(1), 186–213.

Fraser, N. (1995, July–August). From redistribution to recognition? Dilemmas of justice in a 'post-socialist' age. *New Left Review, 1*(212), 68–93.

Fraser, N. (2005). Reframing justice in a globalizing world. *New Left Review, 36*, 69–88.

Freemantle, I. (2012). *Addressing the division of whom? South Africa's fault lines and trends in social cohesion policy*. Johannesburg, South Africa: African Centre for Migration and Society.

Galtung, J. (1976). Three approaches to peace: Peacekeeping, peacemaking and peacebuilding. In J. Galtung & C. Ejlers (Eds.), *Peace, war and defence: Essays in peace research* (pp. 282–304). Copenhagen: Christian Ejlers.

Green, A., & Janmaat, J. G. (2011). *Regimes of social cohesion: Societies and the crisis of globalization*. London, UK: Palgrave Macmillan.

Hamber, B. (2007). Forgiveness and reconciliation: Paradise lost or pragmatism? *Peace and Conflict, 13*(1), 115–125.

Hamber, B., & Kelly, G. (2004). *A working definition of reconciliation*. Occasional paper published by Democratic Dialogue, Belfast. Retrieved from http://www.ark.ac.uk/orb/summaries/Hamber04.doc

Keddie, A. (2012). Schooling and social justice through the lenses of Nancy Fraser. *Critical Studies in Education, 53*(3), 263–279.

Marc, A., Willman, A., Aslam, G., Rebosio, M., & Balasuriy, K. (2012). *Societal dynamics and fragility: Engaging societies in responding to fragile situations*. Washington, DC: World Bank.

Merton, R. K. (1968). *Social theory and social structure*. New York, NY: Free Press.

Mncube, V., & Harber, C. (2013). *The dynamics of violence in South African schools*. Pretoria, South Africa: University of South Africa.

Mourshed, M., Chijioke, C., & Barber, M. (2010). *How the world's most improved school systems keep getting better*. London, UK: McKinsey & Company.

National Planning Commission. (2013). *National Development Plan 2030: Our future—Make it work*. Pretoria: Government Printer. ISBN 978-0-621-41180-5.

Novelli, M., Lopes Cardozo, M., & Smith, A. (2014). *A theoretical framework for analysing the contribution of education to sustainable peacebuilding: 4rs in conflict-affected contexts*. Retrieved from http://learningforpeace.unicef.org/wp-content/uploads/2015/05/Theoretical-Framework-Jan15.pdf

Organization for Economic Cooperation and Development (OECD). (2011). *Perspectives on global development 2012: Social cohesion in a shifting world*. Paris, France: OECD Publishing.

Osler, A. (2011). Education policy, social cohesion, and citizenship. In P. Ratcliffe & I. Newman (Eds.), *Promoting social cohesion: Implications for policy and evaluation* (pp. 185–206). Bristol, UK: Policy Press.

Robertson, S. L. (2012). Placing teachers in global governance agendas. *Comparative Education Review, 56*(4), 584–607.

Rose, P., & Greeley, M. (2006). *Education in fragile states: Capturing lessons and identifying good practice*. Draft Paper prepared for the Development Assistance Committee Fragile States Working

Groups, Service Delivery Workstream, Subteam for Education Services. Retrieved from http://tool-kit.ineesite.org/resources/ineecms/uploads/1096/Educ_Fragile_States_Capturing_Lessons.PDF

Salmi, J. (2000). *Violence, democracy, and education: An analytic framework* (LCSHD Paper Series No. 56). Washington, DC: World Bank.

Sayed, Y., & Ahmed, R. (2015). Education quality, and teaching and learning in the post-2015 education agenda. *International Journal of Educational Development, 40*, 330–338.

Sayed, Y., Kanjee, A., & Nkomo, M. (2013). *The search for quality education in post-apartheid South Africa*. Cape Town, South Africa: HSRC Press.

Scheper-Hughes, N., & Bourgois, P. (2004). *Violence in war and peace: An anthology*. Oxford, UK: Blackwell.

Seitz, K. (2004). *Education and conflict: The role of education in the creation, prevention and resolution of societal crises-consequences for development cooperation*. Eschborn, Germany: Deutsche Gesellschaft für Technische Zusammenarbeit (GTZ). Retrieved from http://relief-web.int/sites/reliefweb.int/files/resources/1F610940FB2A51B749256FFE001BD784-EDandConflict-GTZ.pdf

Shuayb, M. (Ed.). (2012). *Rethinking education for social cohesion: International case studies*. Basingstoke, UK: Palgrave Macmillan.

Sinclair, M. (2002). *Planning education in and after emergencies*. Paris: UNESCO, International Institute for Educational Planning. Retrieved from http://toolkit.ineesite.org/resources/ineecms/uploads/1091/Planning_Education_in_and_After_Emergencies_EN.pdf

Smith, A., McCandless, E., Paulson, J., & Wheaton, W. (2011). *The role of education in peace-building: Literature review*. New York, NY: UNICEF.

South Africa. (1996). *South African Schools Act 84 of 1996*. Pretoria, South Africa: Government Printer.

South Africa. (1998). *Employment of Educators Act No.76 of 1998*. Pretoria, South Africa: Government Printer.

Squelch, J. (2001). Do school governing bodies have a duty to create safe schools? An education law perspective: current issues in education law and policy. *Perspectives in Education, 19*, 137–149.

Tawil, S., & Harley, A. (2004). *Education, conflict, and social cohesion*. Geneva, Switzerland: UNESCO, International Bureau of Education.

Tikly, L., & Barrett, A. M. (2011). Social justice, capabilities and the quality of education in low income countries. *International Journal of Educational Development, 31*(1), 3–14.

UN DESA. (2015). *Transforming our world: The 2030 agenda for sustainable development A/RES/70/1*. Paris, France: United Nations Department of Economic and Social Affairs.

UNESCO. (2013). Education for All Global Monitoring Report 2013/4 Teaching and Learning: Achieving Quality for All. Paris: UNESCO.

UNESCO. (2015). *Education 2030 Incheon declaration and framework for action: Towards inclusive and equitable quality education and lifelong learning for all*. Paris, France: UNESCO.

UNESCO-IIEP. (2006). *Guidebook for planning education in emergencies and reconstruction*. Paris, France: UNESCO International Institute for Educational Planning.

Unilever Ethics Centre. (2002). *South African Council for Educators: Handbook for the code of professional ethics*. Durban, South Africa: University of Natal.

United Nations Development Plan (UNDP). (2014). *Human development report 2014. Sustaining human progress: Reducing vulnerabilities and building resilience*. Retrieved from http:/hdr.undp.org/en/2014-report

University of Witwatersrand, School of Law: Centre for Applied Legal Studies and Cornell Law School: Avon Global Center for Women and Justice and International Human Rights Clinic. (2014). *Sexual violence by educators in South African schools: Gaps in accountability*. Washington, DC: Avon Foundation for Women and the Ford Foundation.

World Education Forum. (2015). *Incheon declaration: Education 2030—Towards inclusive and equitable quality education and lifelong learning for all*. Paris, France: UNESCO.

Zwarteveen, M. Z., & Boelens, R. (2014). Defining, researching and struggling for water justice: Some conceptual building blocks for research and action. *Water International, 39*(2), 143–158.

Chapter 13
Political Emotions During Democratic Transitions in the Global South

Cristina Jayme Montiel and Arvin Boller

Democratic transitions or democratisations are changes in governments of states or countries with the end goal of establishing a more open and pluralistic governance system (Hadenius & Teorell, 2006; Stojanov, 2012; Welzel & Inglehart, 2008). In the last 100 years, the world has seen two democratisation tsunamis in the Global South's political diaspora. These featured a series of social movements spread across regions in the periods between the Second World War and the end of the Cold War. The first wave of democratisation movements occurred post-World War II. This period was marked by a succession of anti-colonial movements and struggles for independence against the Allied colonial powers.

The second wave of democratisation, on the other hand, arose as the Cold War tottered toward the close of the twentieth century. During this period the wave of democratisation movements took the form of collective action against oppression, corruption, and social injustices that had been characteristic of postcolonial autocracies. More specifically, this more recent series of power shifts were fueled by politicised civilian-based movements that struggled against domestic militarised dictatorships. Such people-powered movements claimed democracy in several regions, most notably in Latin America, Asia, Africa, and Eastern Europe, toppling multiple dictators in Latin America, Asia, and Africa, dissolving the United States and Soviet superpower hegemony, and establishing more pluralistic governments. Among the more recent democratisation movements within the Global South was a series of uprisings and armed rebellions that spread across the Arab world, mainly with the aim of ending oppressive Arab dictatorships. This episode of democratisation movements is otherwise known as the Arab Spring.

Multiple social psychological similarities can be gleaned across post-Cold War democratic shifts. First, such political changes involve an asymmetrical relationship between the state and the rest of society, with the state normally yielding exceedingly

C.J. Montiel (✉) • A. Boller
Ateneo de Manila University, Quezon, Philippines
e-mail: cmontiel@ateneo.edu; Arvin.boller@yahoo.com

© Springer International Publishing AG 2017
M. Seedat et al. (eds.), *Enlarging the Scope of Peace Psychology*,
Peace Psychology Book Series, DOI 10.1007/978-3-319-45289-0_13

disproportionate power over the civilian population. Second, these democratisations feature a kind of psychological struggle between the powerful state and the growing forces of People Power. Third, these transitions hold two goals: a short-term goal to topple an authoritarian ruler, and a more long-term goal of democratic consolidation by strengthening an open, civilian-based type of government. And lastly, such compelling power shifts arise alongside large-scale and intense collective emotions among millions of local people engulfed by the wave of political change.

As long as domestic nuances are taken into account, these four similarities allow us to fit the democratisation process into a relatively unitary psychological analysis of politicised interactions between the state and People Power movements. This chapter first describes the features of democratic transition, namely, political and psychological asymmetries, and stages of transition. The second part of this chapter then pinpoints salient collective emotions that accompany intrastate political shifts.

Psychology of an Asymmetric Struggle: Authoritarian Structure Versus Democratic Change Agents

During a dictatorship, as in the eras of colonial rule, the relationship between those who control the political structure and change agents is acutely asymmetrical. Such a one-sided power relationship is mirrored in the psychological diaspora, in what Hegel calls a lord-bondage dialectic. Hegel, in his work *The Phenomenology of Spirit*, talked about the struggle between two consciousnesses. He described how two dialectic consciousnesses impose their own image onto the other, leading to one subduing the other and starting an asymmetrical relationship, with the lord dictating all the actions of the bondsman. The most important elements here are the lord and the bondsman, and their asymmetrical relationship with each other. Giddens (1984) aptly explains how such a rigid sociological asymmetry can be transformed by agentic individuals and organisations embedded in the asymmetric system. The structuration process in an authoritarian system reveals that democratisation is about the political and psychological struggles of prodemocracy agents, to change the authoritarian structure and allow greater freedom.

Giddens's (1984) structuration theory pivots around two interactive elements— the agent and the structure. An agent is described by Giddens as a being that can act purposively and can reason out his/her actions. This intentional agentic action is dependent on but not fully determined by the structure. The structure, on the other hand, consists of rules and institutions that restrict the otherwise indefinite freedom of the agent. Transformative actions of the agents reshape the structure, which in turn influences anew the actions of the agents (Giddens, 1984).

Bandura posits a similar interactive perspective in his social cognitive theory, where he highlights the importance of the environment shaping the behaviour of human beings and likewise emphasises the role of agency in human action (Bandura, 2001, 2006). Bandura (2001) goes beyond the idea of individual agency and introduces the notion of collective agency. He emphasises cognitive features of collective agency, claiming that "People's shared belief in their collective power to produce desired results is a key ingredient of collective agency" (Bandura, 2001, p. 14). We further posit affective characteristics of collective agency in this chapter and discuss collective emotions as features of the agentic production of new democratic structures. The notion of collective agency is pivotal in understanding democratic transitions since structural changes cannot be effected by single-person interventions. Democratisation involves the process of multiple agents forming a vast and heterogeneous united front in order to topple an autocratic regime.

A political restructuration process depends not just on the vertical interaction between the structure and the agents, but also on the horizontal interactions between the individual and collective change agents in the prodemocracy united front. Hence the process of democratisation can be disaggregated into two simultaneous subprocesses—an upward process whereby the agents change the structure and a lateral process whereby the agents act in relation to other agents. These subprocesses cut across varying analytical layers, namely a national structure, social movements, and individual change agents; and bidirectional relationships among these three layers. In many cases, a fourth global layer may be added. Although social structures are often seen as domestically embedded, a number of liberation movements frame oppression as a global phenomenon between the colonial world and its former colonies. For example, Franz Fanon's (1963) *The Wretched of the Earth* pushed for mass armed struggles by African nations against their colonisers.

Although both vertical and lateral dialectical forces operate simultaneously during a transition, one force tends to come to the fore at particular stages of power shifts. The start of the transition is marked by vertical dialectics, as People Power confronts and topples a strong authoritarian state. During democratic consolidation, lateral dialectics take centre stage, as the once united front cracks up in the grab for personal and organisational power. We posit that various collective emotions permeate the different stages of democratic shifts, and that collective violence and non-violence among agentic forces are associated with differing collective emotions and emotional narratives among the change agents.

Collective Anger Against a Repressive State Unifies and Directs Prodemocracy Movements

The main purpose of social movements is to remove a perceived injustice in a society (Rodgers, 2010). Anger is an emotion that stems from indignation, a consequence of the injustice and threat by another entity (Albert, 2013; Woods, Anderson, Guilbert, & Watkin, 2012). This feeling of indignation can arise from different sources. It can be personal (e.g. torture), collective (e.g. genocide), or vicarious (e.g. observed persecution of others) (Albert, 2013). Nevertheless, the indignation that a person experiences arouses the emotion of anger and this emotion fuels a *need* to act. The need to act can stem from the related need of releasing pent-up pressure, or catharsis (Al-Saleh, 2015; Clore & Centerbar, 2004; Stürmer & Simon, 2009).

Anger is a pervasive emotion that can be found across the different stages of democratic transition. Anger transforms from an individual affective state to a collective emotion that fuels the actions of social movements (Stürmer & Simon, 2009). Individual angers are shaped by personal histories and physiological conditions of a person. On the other hand, collective anger finds their roots in group-shared histories of oppression, and is expressed through synchronised acts of mass movements.

Anger is not only psychologically cathartic. In asymmetric political dialectics, as People Power confronts a strong state, anger places large numbers of people in the same posture to act together against a dictatorship, creating a single purpose for unified action (Rodgers, 2010). Prodemocracy mobilisers agitate and produce collective anger by purposively communicating to the citizenry conditions of state torture, persecution, and repression. Social movements then harness political rage to create direction and force for their actions. Hence, collective anger allows a normally heterogenous group to find a unifying anti-state cause.

Anger is an emotion that interacts with the other emotions of democratic transitions. In particular, anger needs courage in order to express defiance towards authority, especially in authoritarian regimes that have no reservations in retaliating against activists (Albert, 2013). Truly, angry mobilisations are only strengthened by oppressive actions by the regime. This can be observed in different democratic transitions. Several examples come to mind. In the Philippines, the assassination of Ninoy Aquino triggered a wide powerful reaction from the people (Lentz, 1988). The killing of Oscar Romero led to the bloody civil war that saw an end to the Salvadoran military leadership (Peterson & Peterson, 2008). The self-immolation of Mohamed Bouazizi sparked the Jasmine revolution, leading to the democratisation of Tunisia and triggered the Arab Spring in various parts of the Arab world (Stepan, 2012). In particular, the leaders of the Arab Spring only sought to redirect the anger of the protesters, eventually leading to the toppling of dictatorial regimes in Tunisia, Egypt, Libya, and Yemen (Al-Saleh, 2015).

During the dialectics of democratic transition, particularly during the initial phase, collective anger is experienced alongside other related political emotions. An upward dialectical process is marked by courage to overcome the fear and terror perpetuated by a downward pushing autocratic regime. On the other hand, a lateral dialectical process within the initial phase of democratic transition, is marked with co-respect among comrades and social movements, and mutual tolerance from multiple agents struggling together in a heterogenous and centrifugal political front.

Whereas during the toppling of the regime, anger facilitates social action, in the turmoil following the shift in power, anger can become a destructive force by causing a rift between former allies. During democratic consolidation, when the anti-dictatorship fervour subsides, anger may arise between former allies who now find themselves competing for personal and organisational power in the newly established democratic space. The contest for scarce resources, political office, and representation may produce division among former allies, thus leading to the emergence of negative emotions such as anger. Such emotional outcome is distinctly possible especially where there is an absence of an inclusive process of governance. Angry conflicts may emerge among individual prodemocracy leaders; between leaders and followers; and among political organisations. As change agents position themselves in the new government, others are left out in the cold. Anger springs forth due to this selective lack of recognition (Albert, 2013). These feelings of injustice could lead to anger toward whoever causes the asymmetrical relationships between otherwise equal agents (Woods et al., 2012). This anger could eventually lead to a divide between agents, with the offended side taking action to correct the injustice, and the other side retaliating. During this time period in a democratic transition, unbridled anger, as mentioned, may play a destructive role.

Emotions During Asymmetric Dialectics: State Control by Fear Versus the Agentic Counter-Emotion of Courage

One of the main characteristics of autocratic regimes is the fact that political action is available only to a small number of people associated with the regime (Way, 2005). Any attempt at political action by ordinary citizens may cause retaliation from the regime, hindering prodemocracy agentic actions. Oppression can be seen as a separation of the political sphere from the public sphere by means of fear. Democracy, on the other hand, allows the public to engage in political action without fear of retaliation from the government.

Individual Fears and State Terror

We distinguish between fear and terror as arising on two interrelated analytical layers, the individual and an entire nation under authoritarian rule, respectively. Although triggered by elements in the political context, the experience of fear is largely personalised and private. On the other hand, terror is politicised collective fear located within a society rather than a person. It is produced by a terrifying episode that is mass communicated to the public through conventional and social media. The effects of terrorising episodes on individual fears vary according to the intensity of the episode and the social psychological conditions of the person.

The production of state terrorism and their consequential individual fears are the primary weapons of authoritarian regimes (Keane, 2002; Suu Kyi, 1991). Across the different authoritarian regimes, reports of violence are not uncommon, from Africa (Bartholomew, 2012), Latin America (Macias, 2012; Peterson & Peterson, 2008), Europe (Alver, 2013), Middle East (Ghalioun & Costopoulos, 2004), to Asia (Han, 2005). In Namibia, the citizens reported continuous harassment from apartheid South African in order to impose their superiority over the Namibians (Bartholomew, 2012). Torture was a common practice in Chile until the end of the Pinochet era in 1990 (Macias, 2012) and in the dictatorship in Argentina during the 70s (Steger, 2007).

Assassinations and political detention are also commonly used by the regimes in order to control the threat of the opposition, with examples including Bishop Oscar Romero of El Salvador (Peterson & Peterson, 2008), Benigno Aquino Jr. of the Philippines (Lentz, 1988), Aung San Suu Kyi of Myanmar (Hlaing, 2012), the killing fields of Khmer Rouge (Montiel, 2006), and the significant abuses of security forces in several Arab Spring countries (Yom, 2005).

These terror tactics aim to curb political action on the part of the citizens by retributive or punitive means (Feldman & Stenner, 1997). When Suu Kyi said that the "the fear of the scourge of power corrupts those who are subject to it" (Suu Kyi, 1991, p. 1), she correctly describes how the perpetuation of the authoritarian regime is supported by the citizens' fear produced by these terror tactics. In Hegel's dialectic, the bond servant comes into bondage because of fear of death at the hands of the lord. By instilling this fear, the master is able to subdue and subordinate the bondsman.

What is the agentic emotional antidote to individual fears and state terrorism? Courage. The interplay of collective fear and courage arises as prodemocracy movements struggle to topple an authoritarian regime.

The Centrality of Domestic Courage in Democratic Power Shifts

Courage among agentic individuals and organisations stands as a liberating emotion that counters the silencing powers of state fear. It is a collective and domestic courage that primarily relies on the human strength of one's own people, rather than on the power of militarised force or foreign support. Examples from successful democratisations reveal how local courage inspired People Power to rally against a terrifying state.

Acts of individual courage can be found in most stories of democratisations. In her essay called freedom from fear, prodemocratic icon Aung San Suu Kyi urged the people of Burma to develop their courage, challenging citizens who wanted to be free to continue fighting for themselves fearlessly (Suu Kyi, 1991). Ninoy Aquino's decided to go back to the Philippines despite threats to his life (Lentz, 1988). Oscar Romero's assassination was a response to his bold challenge to the government (Peterson & Peterson, 2008). While not part of the third wave of democracy, Gandhi's story and legacy of courage and peaceful protest in the face of heavily armed opponents has influenced much of that era's democratic leaders, such as Nelson Mandela and Vaclav Havel, especially in their own show of courage and practice of non-violent political action.

The imperative of collective rather than individual courage. However, these individual acts of courage cannot change the structure of the state by themselves. Restructuration requires unified collective action. Individual acts of courage affect the process of democratisation by working through the collective entity. Bunce and Wolchik (2010) noted in their study of the post-Soviet bloc that the countries that underwent successful democratisation featured united opposition fronts and collective action. Similarly, many other asymmetric power shifts have been implemented through collective political action, mainly in South Europe, South America, the post-communist bloc (Linz & Stepan, 1996), Southeast Asia (Montiel, 2006), and Middle East (Tessler, Jamal, & Robbins, 2012).

Seen through the lens of social learning, symbolic protest acts of courage provide inspiration and are imitated by publics in large swaths of collective courage. Religious scripts provide another avenue for collective courage, with narratives about divine protection (*God is on our side*) and the interpretation of extreme self-sacrifices through religious martyrdom storylines. Finally the lowering of public fear and rise of collective courage accompanies positive changes in the political environment, as democratic institutions stabilise.

Symbolic individual courage inspires collective courage. Bandura's social cognitive theory asserts that experience does not only come from one's own work (Bandura, 2001, 2006). Rather, experiences of other people are also sources of one's self-efficacy. Hence, we posit that individual acts of courage work through the collective by means of social learning. The citizens, upon observing the experience of another person performing an act of courage, could learn from that experience and perform an act of courage themselves.

For example, when Argentina was ruled by an authoritarian regime, the actions of the Mothers of Plaza De Mayo drew vast amounts of support from numerous people, culminating in the downfall of the regime in 1982 (Steger, 2007). This democratic group featured the widows and mothers of those abducted and tortured by the Argentinian government. They wore white shawls to symbolise the innocence of the missing, and protested peacefully and arm-in-arm against the police, despite their inexperience in conflict (Steger, 2007). Similarly, the Kurdish mothers in Turkey inspired collective action with their perseverance in perpetuating the Kurdish culture despite repression from the state. They studied how to learn and write to help propagate the cultural events the Kurdish people hold. This demonstrated how social learning helps spread resistance to much larger groups of people (Kucukaydin, 2010).

Another example is the action of the Tunisian vendor before the Jasmine revolution. Protesting the regime's repression, the vendor committed self-immolation (Chomiak, 2011; Stepan, 2012). Such a publicised act confronted the fear of death not only in the vendor, but also among the collective citizenry of repressed Tunisia, triggering the Jasmine revolution (Chomiak, 2011; Stepan, 2012). In South Africa, Steve Biko served as the symbol of Black Resistance and his persecution and eventual death in the hands of the apartheid state inspired thousands of young students to stake their lives in protest rallies that led to the eventual fall of the apartheid government (Wilson, 2009).

Omnipotent God and post-death salvation as social narratives for collective courage. When religious narratives frame struggle and suffering, fear of the oppressor can be overcome. Such religious storylines contribute to a phenomenal rise in collective courage by providing vicarious strength through an almighty God, and inspiring martyred political deaths with post-death salvific narratives.

The process of democratisation highlights the religious aspect of self-sacrifice. Martyrdom can be seen as the supreme self-sacrifice accessible to nonpowerful protesters who want to restore justice among the oppressed (Braver & Rohrer, 1975). Former studies have seen acts of self-sacrifice as actions intended to promote worldly goals (Alshech, 2008). However, by drawing from their religious beliefs of spiritual faith, followers of religious groups are able to discursively change self-sacrifice into religious martyrdom. Religious martyrdom leads to the belief that a divine force was acting on human history, as was the interpretation of the state murder of El Salvador's Catholic Bishop Oscar Romero (Peterson & Peterson, 2008). In contrast to the worldly advocacies of self-sacrifice, religious martyrdom emphasises that the goal of one's sacrifice is to get to heaven (Alshech, 2008; Brkich, 2011).

Studies on religious martyrdom in particular reveal the mechanism by which individual actions inspire collective actions. With the belief that life on earth is insignificant compared to life in heaven, the martyrs devalue earthly life and willingly give themselves up to attain paradise or eternal life. Such notions appear to be salient in martyrologies within various religions, such as Christianity and Islam (Alshech, 2008; Brkich, 2011). Both faiths provide storylines of martyrdom that inspire courage during oppression and suffering. Both faiths likewise associate a martyr's death with heroic piety and post-death salvation.

For example, Islamic self-immolating actions validate the beliefs of the collective group, thus further convincing others to become martyrs also (Alshech, 2008; Maarouf, 2013). Likewise, both Christian and Islamic martyred deaths become part of human history and collective memory (Alver, 2013), inspiring others beyond the lifetimes of those who gave up their lives for freedom.

Christian religious martyrdom can be found in narratives of those persecuted for their Christian faith, such as the early Christians who were executed during the Roman period. Christian faith highlights that life on earth is merely temporary, whereas life after death is dignified and eternal. Several scholars have noted that early Christian martyrs believed that their choice to die instead of capitulate to the Roman empire permitted them an honourable and heroic death that guaranteed salvation while exalting both God and themselves (Brkich, 2011). Droge and Tabor (1992) also wrote that some Christians took the idea of "following" Jesus more literally, in that they believed that salvation could only be guaranteed through the reenactment of Jesus' sacrifice or the voluntary offering up of oneself to death.

Brkich (2011) explains that the construction of martyrology or the reinterpretation of Christian executions by early Christians was motivated by the need to give meaning to the deaths of their fellowmen, and refuse the notion that the deaths and sufferings they had experienced were meaningless. Christian texts, according to Brkich (2011), provided a framework for them to understand such executions. An example of such Biblical text is found in the Gospel of Mark: "If any want to become my followers, let them deny themselves and take up their cross and follow me. For those who want to save their life will lose it, and those who lose their life for my sake, and for the sake of the gospel will save it".

The reinterpretation of execution into religious martyrdom provided early Christians an opportunity to gain a distinct group identity as a suffering community. Thus, it led to a change in their social identity resulting in a more cohesive collective with moral power and fueling resistance against and revulsion toward the Roman Empire (Brkich, 2011).

Similar to Christianity, Islam carries its own narratives of martyrdom. In Islam, the seven blessings of God on a martyr are enumerated as follows:

> (1) he is forgiven from the moment his blood is first shed; (2) he will be shown his place in paradise; (3) he will be spared the trial of the grave; (4) he will be secure on the Day of the Greatest Terror (the Day of Judgment); (5) there will be placed on his head a crown of dignity, one ruby of which is better than this world and all that is in it; (6) he will be married to seventy-two of al-hur al-'in (virgins); and (7) he will be permitted to intercede for seventy of his relatives (narrated by al-Miqdaam Ibn Ma'di Karb, reported in Sunan Tarmdi). (Maarouf, 2013, p. 18)

As argued by Alshech (2008), the Second *Intifada* (uprising/resistance or to "get rid of invaders") between Israel and Hamas ("The Islamic Resistance Movement") particularly highlights this transformation of self-immolation of Hamas members, from an act intended to promote worldly goals (or more specifically patriotic goals such as liberating Islamic land) to one intended towards more eschatological goals (such as the attainment of eternal life). Instead of being called *suicide*, the fighters saw themselves as committing *shahada* (martyrdom) (Maarouf, 2013).

By turning self-sacrifice into an act of heavenly honour, Hamas was able to resist the superior Israeli military, as well as gain more support from the Muslim population (Alshech, 2008). It is critical to note, however, that some Muslim scholars object to suicidal acts recognised as acts of martyrdom—claiming specifically that such acts of suicide are forbidden by Islamic law (Alshech, 2008).

Emotions During Democratic Consolidation

During authoritarian regimes, agent-to-agent relations can be described as divergent, where prejudices, racism, and discrimination abound (Altemeyer & Hunsberger, 1992; Geddes & Zaller, 1989). However, intragroup cohesion prevails when there is a common goal of dismantling oppressive structures. For example, the experience of Namibians reveals the divergence not only between South Africans and Namibians, but also between Namibians where the groups are divided between those supporting armed rebellion, and those who want change via political means (Bartholomew, 2012). Feminist studies also have shown that differing perspectives of women in regard to gender discrimination during revolutions are minimised when the larger goal of toppling the dictator is salient (Boldt, 2011; Borren, 2013), that is, fracturing tendencies are minimised by a superordinate goal of toppling the dictator.

The divisive forces of a united front turn more problematic when the dictator falls, and there is no common enemy to unite the democratic front. As multiple agents relate to each other during the process of democratic consolidation, the dialectical narratives of respect versus competitive intolerance arise in lateral motions of democratisation. This divergence in emotional overtones of inter-agentic relations becomes a crucial feature of post-transition peace and conflict. Insightfully, Fanon (1963) warns against local elites grabbing power "to corner the positions formerly kept for foreigners" (p. 126).

During this stage of democratisation, open political space shared by prodemocracy forces can turn intolerant and competitive—even violent, rather than respectfully cooperative, as ideological orientation and contestation may shape post-autocratic social relations. For example, the next 10 years after a successful Philippine People Power in 1986, saw the national state grappling with a dozen serious coup attempts, instigated by militarised forces that originally belonged to the anti-dictatorship movement. In Egypt, the victory of the Muslim Brotherhood came with their aim to "islamise" Egypt; however, this stands in contrast to the efforts of Tunisia to delineate state from religious interests despite having a religious party win the elections (Fadel, 2011; Stepan, 2012). Such contentions and contestations between secularist and religious political thought and movements are not only evident within the Arab region but across regions and continents as well.

Other democratically consolidating states demonstrated more collective respect in lateral relations among change agents. For example, the transition in Albania showed how teachers helped fix intrastate intolerances and discrimination, in order to create a more egalitarian country (Gardinier, 2012). South Africa's power shift in the 1990s did not deteriorate into post-transition intra-black violence due to the skillful negotiating skills of Nelson Mandela and other peacemakers like Cyril Ramaphosa. Further, Nepal and the newly democratised Namibia were found to have more effective democracies, with civil society contributing more to the societal democratisation because of the lack of local elites who usually dominate the political scene (Ignatow et al., 2012).

Conclusion

This chapter looks into the large-scale collective emotions at play within democratic transitions, particularly in the Global South. Collective anger, courage, fear, terror, respect, and competitive intolerance are among the emotions that arise in the vertical and lateral political relationships in the course of democratic transition.

Anger is found to be evoked by leaders to mobilise collective action and a sense of unity among the excluded in situations of struggle for liberation and social justice. However, anger features quite differently in post-authoritarian situations, especially when there is a contest for political and economic resources. The mobilisation and expression of collective anger is shaped by context, political ideology, and social actor motives.

Narratives of martyrdom produced through references to religious texts provide meaning and rationale for the enactment of collective anger directed at oppressive structures. Thus, the enactment of collective anger assumes transcendental meaning and dimensions.

While the enactment of collective anger may be important in the struggle for social justice, the attainment of social justice is ultimately contingent on the establishment of inclusive social and political structures as well as processes of decision-making in governance. Exclusions in post-authoritarian situations create a climate for ongoing anger which in turn fuels polarisation and the re-inscription of non-participatory social structures.

References

Albert, S. P. (2013). Philosophy, recognition, and indignation. *Peace Review, 25*(3), 336–342. doi: 10.1080/10402659.2013.816550.

Al-Saleh, A. (2015). *Voices of the Arab spring: Personal stories from the Arab revolutions.* New York: Columbia University Press.

Alshech, E. (2008). Egoistic martyrdom and Hamās' success in the 2005 municipal elections: A study of Hamās martyrs' ethical wills, biographies, and eulogies. *Die Welt Des Islams, 48*(1), 23–49. doi:10.1163/157006008X294918.

Altemeyer, B., & Hunsberger, B. (1992). Authoritarianism, religious fundamentalism, quest, and prejudice. *International Journal for the Psychology of Religion.* doi:10.1207/s15327582ijpr0202_5.

Alver, A. (2013). Cultural memory of 1970's Turkish political history: The question of state-sanctioned torture and imprisonment in the March 12th novel "Yaralsin." *Turkish Studies, 8,* 81–102. Retrieved from http://search.ebscohost.com/login.aspx?direct=true&profile=ehost&scope=site&authtype=crawler&jrnl=13082140&AN=91655030&h=DcAHAPmz4R9b1JavzZR.i1jUhiU8jUEZpnPOdpfiKIAxV5uygG%2FuHOEFa8xU9Xq1fdxsWWiTaOH3GBzQfGQQe9w%3D%3D&crl=c

Bandura, A. (2001). Social cognitive theory: An agentic perspective. *Annual Review of Psychology, 52,* 1–26. doi:10.1146/annurev.psych.52.1.1.

Bandura, A. (2006). Perspectives on psychological science toward a psychology of human agency. *Perspectives on Psychological Science, 1*(2), 164–180. doi:10.1111/j.1745-6916.2006.00011.x.

Bartholomew, T. T. (2012). A human being is free: The phenomenological experience of liberation in Namibia. *International Perspectives in Psychology: Research, Practice, Consultation, 1*(2), 94–109. doi:10.1037/a0028823.

Boldt, K. (2011). Chilean women and democratization: Entering politics through resistance as Arpilleristas. *Asian Journal of Latin American Studies, 24*(2), 27–44. Retrieved from http://www.ajlas.org/v2006/paper/2011vol24no202.pdf.

Borren, M. (2013). Feminism as revolutionary practice: From justice and the politics of recognition to freedom. *Hypatia, 28*(1), 197–214. doi:10.1111/j.1527-2001.2011.01260.x.

Braver, S. L., & Rohrer, V. (1975). When martyrdom pays: The Effects of information concerning the opponents' past game behavior. *Journal of Conflict Resolution, 19*(4), 652–662. doi:10.1177/002200277501900407.

Brkich, A. (2011). Death, martyrdom and the reconstruction of social identity. *Journal of Religion and Culture.* Retrieved from https://artsciweb.concordia.ca/Ojs/index.php/jrc/article/viewFile/68/30.

Bunce, V. J., & Wolchik, S. L. (2010). Defeating dictators: Electoral change and stability in competitive authoritarian regimes. *World Politics, 62*(1), 43–86. doi:10.1353/wp.0.0043.

Chomiak, L. (2011). The making of a revolution in Tunisia. *Middle East Law and Governance, 3*(1), 68–83. doi:10.1163/187633711X591431.

Clore, G. L., & Centerbar, D. B. (2004). Analyzing anger: How to make people mad. *Emotion, 4*(2), 139–144. doi:10.1037/1528-3542.4.2.139.

Droge, A. J., & Tabor, J. D. (1992). *A noble death: Suicide and martyrdom among Christians and Jews in antiquity.* San Francisco: HarperSanFrancisco.

Fadel, M. (2011). Modernist Islamic political thought and the Egyptian and Tunisian revolutions of 2011. *Middle East Law and Governance, 3*(1), 94–104. doi:10.1163/187633711X591459.

Fanon, F. (1963). *The wretched of the Earth*. New York: Grove.

Feldman, S., & Stenner, K. (1997). Perceived threat and authoritarianism. *Political Psychology, 18*, 741–770. doi:10.1111/0162-895X.00077.

Gardinier, M. P. (2012). Agents of change and continuity: The pivotal role of teachers in Albanian educational reform and democratization. *Comparative Education Review, 56*(4), 659–683. doi:10.1086/667396.

Geddes, B., & Zaller, J. (1989). Sources of popular support for authoritarian regimes. *American Journal of Political Science, 33*, 319–347. doi:10.2307/2111150.

Ghalioun, B., & Costopoulos, P. J. (2004). The persistence of Arab authoritarianism. *Journal of Democracy, 15*(4), 126–132. doi:10.1353/jod.2004.0062.

Giddens, A. (1984). Elements of the theory of structuration. In *The constitution of society. Outline of the theory of structuration* (pp. 1–28). Cambridge: Polity.

Hadenius, A., & Teorell, J. (2006). *Authoritarian regimes: stability, change, and pathways to democracy, 1972-2003*. The Kellog Institute (pp. 1–35). Retrieved from http://scholar.googleusercontent.com/scholar?q=cache:DqBB31VNUosJ:scholar.google.com/&hl=en&as_sdt=0,5&as_vis=1

Han, I. (2005). Kwangju and beyond: Coping with past state atrocities in South Korea. *Human Rights Quarterly, 27*(3), 998–1045. doi:10.1353/hrq.2005.0037.

Hlaing, K. Y. (2012). Understanding recent political changes in Myanmar. *Contemporary Southeast Asia, 34*(2), 197–216. doi:10.1355/cs34-2c.

Ignatow, G., Webb, S. M., Poulin, M., Parajuli, R., Fleming, P., Batra, S., et al. (2012). Public libraries and democratization in three developing countries: Exploring the role of Social Capital. *Libri, 62*(1), 67–80. doi:10.1515/libri-2012-0005.

Keane, J. (2002). Fear and democracy. In K. Worcester, S. A. Bermanzohn, & M. Ungar (Eds.), *Violence and politics: Globalization's paradox* (pp. 226–244). New York: Routledge.

Kucukaydin, I. (2010). Counter-learning under oppression. *Adult Education Quarterly, 60*(3), 215–232. Retrieved from http://aeq.sagepub.com/content/60/3/215.short.

Lentz, H. (1988). *Assassinations and executions: An encyclopedia of political violence, 1865-1986*. Jefferson: McFarland.

Linz, J. J., & Stepan, A. (1996). Problems of democratic transition and consolidation: Southern Europe, South America, and Post-Communist Europe. In *Problems of democratic transition and consolidation: Southern Europe, South America, and Post-Communist Europe* (pp. 38–54). doi:10.2307/20047958.

Maarouf, M. (2013). Suicide bombing: The cultural foundations of Morocco's new version of martyrdom. *Journal of Religion and Popular Culture, 25*(1), 1–33. doi:10.3138/jrpc.25.1.1.

Macias, T. (2012). "Tortured bodies": The biopolitics of torture and truth in Chile. *The International Journal of Human Rights*. doi:10.1080/13642987.2012.701912.

Montiel, C. J. (2006). Political psychology of nonviolent democratic transitions in Southeast Asia. *Journal of Social Issues, 62*, 173–190. doi:10.1111/j.1540-4560.2006.00445.x.

Peterson, A., & Peterson, B. (2008). Martyrdom, sacrifice, and political memory in El Salvador. *Social Research, 75*(2). Retrieved from http://socialresearch.metapress.com/index/870n350548107376.pdf

Rodgers, K. (2010). "Anger is why we're all here": Mobilizing and managing emotions in a professional activist organization. *Social Movement Studies, 9*(3), 273–291. doi:10.1080/14742837.2010.493660.

Steger, M. B. (2007). Peacebuilding and nonviolence: Gandhi's perspective on power. In D. J. Christie, R. V. Wagner, & D. A. Winter (Eds.), *Peace, conflict, and violence: Peace psychology for the 21st century* (pp. 1–18). New Jersey: Prentice-Hall.

Stepan, A. (2012). Tunisia's transition and the twin tolerations. *Journal of Democracy, 23*(2), 89–103. doi:10.1353/jod.2012.0034.

Stojanov, K. (2012). The post-socialist transition as a process of biographical learning: On the contradiction between democratization and political alienation in Eastern Europe. *Constellations, 19*(1), 121–134. doi:10.1111/j.1467-8675.2011.00669.x.

Stürmer, S., & Simon, B. (2009). Pathways to collective protest: Calculation, identification, or emotion? A critical analysis of the role of group-based anger in social movement participation. *Journal of Social Issues, 65*(4), 681–705. doi:10.1111/j.1540-4560.2009.01620.x.

Suu Kyi, A. S. (1991). Freedom from fear. *Midwifery Today with International Midwife*. Retrieved from http://www.ncbi.nlm.nih.gov/pubmed/21584963.

Tessler, M., Jamal, A., & Robbins, M. (2012). New findings on Arabs and democracy. *Journal of Democracy, 23*(4), 89–103.

Way, L. A. (2005). Authoritarian state building and the sources of regime competitiveness in the fourth wave: The cases of Belarus, Moldova, Russia, and Ukraine. *World Politics*. doi:10.1353/wp.2005.0018

Welzel, C., & Inglehart, R. (2008). The role of ordinary people in democratization. *Journal of Democracy*. doi:10.1353/jod.2008.0009.

Wilson, F. (2009). *Dinosaurs, Diamonds and democracy: A short, short history of South Africa*. Cape Town, South Africa: Random House Struik.

Woods, M., Anderson, J., Guilbert, S., & Watkin, S. (2012). "The country(side) is angry": Emotion and explanation in protest mobilization. *Social & Cultural Geography, 13*(6), 567–585. doi:10.1080/14649365.2012.704643.

Yom, S. (2005). Civil society and democratization in the Arab world. *Middle East Review of International Affairs, 9*(4), 14–33. Retrieved from http://www.eden.rutgers.edu/~spath/351/Readings/Yom-CivilSocietyandDemocratizationinArabWorld.pdf.

Chapter 14
Do No Harm? How Psychologists Have Supported Torture and What to Do About It

Michael Wessells, Nora Sveaass, Donald Foster, and Andrew Dawes

Among the many forms of human violence, torture surely ranks among the most contemptible. Not only does it cause deep psychological wounds (Basoglu, Jaranson, Mollica, & Kastrup, 2001, 2007, Basoglu, Livanou, & Crnobaric, 2007; Stover & Nightingale, 1985), but it is also an imminent threat to peace. Indeed it is frequently used to support dictatorial regimes that have little regard for human rights and that seek to shatter political opposition. Because it leaves searing memories and may generate powerful desires for revenge, torture can enable cycles of violence.

Diverse human rights standards, beginning with the Universal Declaration of Human Rights (1948), prohibit torture and support the dignity and rights of all people. In these and other respects, human rights standards are fundamental components of global efforts to build peace. The main human rights standard pertaining to torture is the UN Convention Against Torture and Other Cruel, Inhuman or Degrading Treatment or Punishment (UNCAT; see Brownlie, 1992), which entered into force June 26, 1987. The UNCAT prohibits states from using torture, which is defined as "any act by which severe pain or suffering, whether physical or mental, is intentionally inflicted on a person for such purposes as obtaining from him or a third person information or a confession, punishing him for an act he or a third person has committed or is suspected of having committed or intimidating or coercing him or a third person…" (Article 1). It expressly prohibits torture under all circumstances,

M. Wessells (✉)
Mailman School of Public Health, Columbia University, New York, NY, USA
e-mail: mikewessells@gmail.com

N. Sveaass
Department of Psychology, University of Oslo, Oslo, Norway
e-mail: nora.sveaass@psykologi.uio.no

D. Foster • A. Dawes
Department of Psychology, University of Cape Town, Cape Town, South Africa
e-mail: Donald.Foster@uct.ac.za; adkinloch1@gmail.com

© Springer International Publishing AG 2017
M. Seedat et al. (eds.), *Enlarging the Scope of Peace Psychology*,
Peace Psychology Book Series, DOI 10.1007/978-3-319-45289-0_14

including settings of war, political violence, or public emergencies. Orders from a superior officer or public authority may never be invoked as a justification of torture (Article 2). The Optional Protocol to the UNCAT (OPCAT), that was adopted on December 18, 2002 and entered into force June 22, 2006, provides for regular visits by independent, international and national bodies to sites where people are deprived of their liberty in order to prevent torture or cruel, inhuman or degrading treatment or punishment.

The prohibition against torture today is considered a peremptory norm, also called *jus cogens*, meaning that it binds all states regardless of whether they have signed the specific treaties or not. The movement to end torture must therefore be considered a universal obligation. A legal cornerstone of anti-torture efforts is the Geneva Conventions and its Added Protocols, which call for the humane treatment of prisoners of war, among other things. Similarly, the International Criminal Court considers torture to be a crime against humanity when it is part of a systematic attack against civilian populations.

Despite these prohibitions, torture has become deeply entrenched in global systems of war and political violence. Although torture has a long history related to religious persecution, it has in contemporary times become a frequently used tool by both state and non-state actors. The global reach of torture has been well documented for decades by organisations such as the International Committee of the Red Cross, Amnesty International, and Human Rights Watch. These and other groups have shown that torture has been used regularly in efforts to repress and silence political opposition; extract or coerce disclosure of information about the activities of real or perceived adversaries; terrorise populations, gain revenge for real or perceived transgressions; or degrade, humiliate, or punish members of demonised out-groups.

A growing body of evidence indicates that psychologists and psychiatrists, too, have been involved in torture. In countries such as the former Soviet Union, psychiatrists contributed to torture and cruel, inhumane treatment by helping to diagnose political dissidents as mentally ill people, who were then locked away in psychiatric wards (Ougrin, Gluzman, & Dratcu, 2006; Targum, Chaban, & Mykhnyak, 2013; Yankovsky, 2013). The recently released report by the U. S. Senate Select Committee on Intelligence (2014; also see Eban, 2007), for example, documented how two psychologists hired by the CIA interrogated and tortured presumably high value detainees in the post-9/11 efforts by the US government to control terrorism.

The documented role of psychologists involved in torture raises profound issues of professional ethics and the roles and responsibilities of psychologists in regard to torture. Discussions of these questions typically focus on horrendous acts or direct support for torture by psychologists working in national security settings. Yet some of the strongest support for torture comes from inaction in forms such as not blowing the whistle in the face of human rights violations, not investigating fully the activities of psychologists in settings of mistreatment, or not holding psychologists accountable for their actions, among many others. The responsibility of psychologists to blow the whistle relates to any situation where there is reasonable ground to believe that an act of torture has been committed. Being silent when there are signs or evidence of wrongdoing contributes to norms of silence and inaction and is a form of complicity. It is important, then, that discussions of psychologists and torture focus not only on what psychologists have done but also on what they and their professional organisations have not done.

The purpose of this chapter is to examine how psychologists have enabled torture and abuse through a mixture of action and inaction, and to suggest how psychologists can do their part to end the use of torture and other cruel, inhuman, or degrading treatment or punishment.

Using the cases of the apartheid era in South Africa and the US case of the post-9/11 response to terrorism, it examines how both individual psychologists and professional psychological organisations have supported torture directly or indirectly and the ethical implications thereof. Recognising the urgency of strengthening the international regime against torture, the chapter also identifies concrete steps that psychologists in different countries can take as a means of helping to end and prevent the use of torture. Direct action to prevent torture and ill-treatment must be considered a basic aspect of the role of psychologists.

How Psychologists Enable or Contribute to Torture

The globalised nature of torture and the use of torture by many different governments and non-state actors make it important to view torture in international perspective. It would be self-serving and inaccurate to say that highly dictatorial regimes such as that of Robert Mugabe in Zimbabwe have a monopoly on torture. In fact, systematic torture occurs also in states that have made strong claims to democracy and freedom and ratified international treaties forbidding torture. With these points in mind, we examine two cases of state approved and led torture—South Africa during the apartheid era and the US post-9/11. Both cases illustrate how most psychologists looked the other way even when wrongdoing was widely alleged or known, thereby contributing to the conspiracy of silence that enabled torture. Of necessity, both cases draw on a limited body of evidence, as torture programmes nearly always operate in secrecy and are cloaked in denial. In both cases, there is need of ongoing investigation and more complete evidence regarding how psychologists contributed to or enabled torture.

Case 1: South African Psychology in the Context of Political Repression and Torture

From its origins in second decade of the twentieth century, South African psychology has been shaped by a political and ideological context characterised by segregation, racism, and oppression of the black majority (Foster, 2008; Seedat &

MacKenzie, 2008). Psychologists were divided in the early years between those who championed the essential nature of race differences in psychological traits (often through the production of "evidence" of black racial inferiority in IQ) and those of more critical (and liberal) bent (Foster, 2008).

Psychologists of both persuasions came together in 1948—ironically the birth date of the Apartheid system—to form the first professional body, the *South African Psychological Association* (SAPA). Relations between members supportive of Apartheid and those opposed came to a head and eventually split on the issue of race and membership. In 1962, some members of SAPA, mostly Afrikaans and conservative, left SAPA to form the whites only and apartheid supporting *Psychological Institute of the Republic of South Africa* (PIRSA). Members of PIRSA were responsible for a number of research projects that sought to provide scientific justification for aspects of Apartheid policy including the development of separate residential areas for black South Africans (Dawes, 1985; Long, 2013). Twenty-one years later, in a climate of intensified political repression and resistance, the two organisations came together to form the non-racial *Psychological Association of South Africa* (PASA). And 10 years on in 1994, following the first non-racial democratic elections in the country's history, the current body, the Psychological Society of South Africa (PsySSA) was established and included those who had rejected membership in PASA.

As the spate of political detentions increased in the early 1980s, groups of young psychologists based in the liberal universities became increasingly active in opposing human rights abuses by the apartheid state. They wrote letters to the press critical of detention without trial and highlighted psychological aspects of torture. Detentions, torture, and deaths in police detention paralleled the nationwide upsurge in resistance to the regime in the 1970s. Steven Biko's murder at the hands of the security police in 1977 is perhaps the best known of many cases. On February 5, 1982, news of Biko's death after 70 days in detention and of Dr. Neil Aggett, a physician and trade union activist, sparked a nationwide outcry, though not in professional psychology.

Progressive university-based psychologists and their graduate students realised the need for new organisational structures if they were to contribute effectively to services for people affected by state violence, and to advance the cause of political transformation. The tipping point came in 1983 when the South African Institute of Family and Marital Therapy hosted an international Family Therapy conference at a casino hotel in one of South Africa's impoverished so-called independent black Homelands (Bophuthatswana). A small group of young psychology lecturers and their students based at the University of the Witwatersrand were arrested as they protested against this event (demonstrations were illegal throughout the 1980s). Their main position was that it was unacceptable and unethical to hold a meeting on the healing of families in a part of South Africa to which thousands of blacks had been forcibly relocated and which served as a migrant labour reserve for men to work apart from their families in mining and other industries located in white South Africa. They also sought to draw the attention of international visitors to these facts and indicate to them that one could not conduct academic business as usual in apartheid South Africa in violation of the international academic boycott. Shortly after these events the *Organisation for Appropriate Social Services in South Africa* (OASSSA) was launched in Johannesburg with membership open to all mental health workers who endorsed its progressive anti-apartheid stance and alignment with the broad movement toward the liberation of the country (Long, 2013). By 1985, OASSSA had a national footprint (Vogelman, 1987). Yet another progressive grouping—the *Apartheid and Psychology Committee*—was formed in the late 1980s by psychologists based in the University of the Western Cape who saw the need for a Black Consciousness aligned structure (Cooper, Nicholas, Seedat, & Statman, 1990; Long, 2013). Founding member, Saths Cooper, had himself spent time in detention, and was sentenced to 10 years imprisonment in 1976 for his political activities (including a spell on Robben Island with Nelson Mandela). And also in 1983, the publication *Psychology in Society* (PINS) was launched (Foster, 2014). Established in opposition to the mainstream South African Journal of Psychology, and run by an editorial collective of psychologists affiliated to OASSSA, PINS was intended as a forum for critical voices in the profession. It is still in print 30 years on.

Between 1981 and 1994, when the first democratic elections were held, members of these progressive organisations became increasingly active in opposing human rights abuses by the apartheid state. Members of the progressive mental health groups, in association with their medical colleagues, provided psychological services to torture survivors and their families. Some gave expert psychological testimony in court challenging the admissibility of confessions made in detention by those accused of political offences. It was invariably difficult to prove that physical torture had been administered as this was always denied by the police. Also, there was no way of corroborating the story of a detainee held incommunicado without legal representation. Knowing this, psychologists argued that solitary confinement alone was known to have deleterious effects on mental states and would likely induce the prisoner to make a "confession" that would satisfy her captors and result in being brought to trial. This testimony was rejected by the courts (Foster, 1990). Among their reasons was that the evidence for deleterious effects was based on research conducted in other countries. In short, there was no independent South African data on the effects of detention and none on detainees' experiences.

To address this gap and in the hope of strengthening the ability to present plausible locally gathered evidence, Foster and his colleagues embarked on a study of men and women who had been held in detention to establish the techniques used by the security services and to examine the physical and psychological consequences. In fact, the study was illegal as the Police Prisons Acts of the day made it an offence to write about conditions in detention. To avoid detection, the data and emerging report had to be in a secure place in the University of Cape Town known to only four people. The result of this groundbreaking undertaking was a report released to the public in September 1985 (Foster & Sandler, 1985). It revealed the many torture techniques used, including isolation, sleep deprivation, beatings, and a form of "waterboarding". It also showed how the practice was institutionalised among the security services throughout the country and not the business of a few rotten apples.

Not surprising, the authors were roundly condemned and the report was criticised as political agitation and poor in methodology by the government of the day. The authors were even asked to provide the names of participants so they could be followed up independently!

Foster went on to deliver a paper on his findings at the 1985 PASA national conference. Apart from interested psychologists, members of the audience included a bevy of hostile security police and the talk caused a furore at the meeting. It remains a question as to how they knew about the research. Foster was branded a traitor in the Afrikaans daily papers reporting on the meeting. The following year, Amnesty International invited Foster on a speaking tour of the UK and the USA where he presented the findings to a number of institutions, including the American Psychological Association. The report of his interview with Kathleen Fisher is published in the Social Issues section of the *APA Monitor* of November 1986. The study was published as a monograph 2 years after its release (Foster, Davis, & Sandler, 1987).

Other publications and presentations at international meetings gave attention to the plight of children and adolescents, including those affected by township violence and imprisonment (Burman & Reynolds, 1986; Dawes, 1987a, 1987b; Dawes, Tredoux, & Feinstein, 1989; Straker, Moosa, & Team, 1988). These studies provided all the evidence needed for organised psychology to take up a position on the mental health consequences of government policy, detention without trial (affecting thousands), and torture. However, at no point did PASA make a statement. One does not know what went on behind closed doors in committees (we note that minutes are not available). But perhaps the silence was not surprising given a mix of influences including: the fragile union of recently conjoined conservative and more liberal members; a professional ethos that demanded the separation of the discipline from political issues on the grounds that it should be a value free and "disinterested" science and profession (Dawes, 1985); and finally, the fact that a number of members were police and military personnel.

Do we know whether South Africa had its own *psychologists of the dark side* to advise its interrogators? No evidence of this was brought before the Truth and Reconciliation Commission. South Africa did (and still does) have a Military Psychological Institute that during the apartheid years was mainly involved in psychological testing. There is no knowledge of their involvement in such activities. However, we do know that South Africa had close relations with Latin American regimes known for their torture and murder of dissidents and detainees, and also strong military ties to Israel. Bell and Ntsebeza (2001) remark:

> South Africa became a useful laboratory for torture and interrogation techniques. Over the years, there were established exchanges of information with Chile and Argentina during their bloody dictatorships, and with Taiwan as well as France and US military interrogators. (p. 37)

It is perhaps of some interest that the Argentinian naval officer Alfredo Astiz, notorious for his reputation as a torturer and death squad commander, was assistant military attaché to South Africa in the late 1970s and early 1980s.

The point of all this is that we do not have evidence of involvement of psychologists in the architecture of South African interrogation techniques. However, the record, murky as it inevitably is, points to the strong probability that security personnel learnt at least some of their trade from their counterparts elsewhere. Were the US interrogation experts referred to by Bell and Ntsebeza apprised of the many psychological studies of the effects of sensory deprivation and other literature such as that on learned helplessness? This seems very likely given the significant body of relevant research conducted in the USA over many years. Did they have contact with British interrogators operating in Northern Ireland and who used similar techniques (Shallice, 1972)? Another Pandora's box awaits opening.

What we do know is that by the mid-1980s, South African organised professional psychology (PASA) knew very well what was going on. They chose to do nothing.

Case 2: US Psychologists in the Post-9/11 Era

Nowhere is the case of psychologists' direct participation in and support for torture more evident than in the case of the US post-9/11. Before discussing psychologists' roles, however, it is useful to outline the national and international context for their activities.

The Post-9/11 Context. The September 11, 2001 attacks on the USA caused mass deaths and destruction on US soil and ignited widespread public fear. Taking a hard line, then President George W. Bush declared a "war on terror" against al-Qaeda and related groups. To stir patriotic sentiment and bring international allies on board, he depicted the situation in black and white terms by announcing "you're either for us or against us". The public media ramped up public fears by repeatedly referring to or replaying images of the horrors of the attacks and discussing the likelihood of future attacks. Public discussions of "ticking time bomb" scenarios amplified hysteria and likely helped to reduce any moral concerns about the mistreatment of suspected terrorists.

Behind the scenes, then Vice President Dick Cheney and CIA colleagues led the charge to deny prisoner of war (POW) status to captured members of al-Qaeda or Taliban groups. The classification as detainees rather than POWs who would have been protected against mistreatment by the Geneva Conventions opened the door legally for mistreatment. The legal path toward mistreatment was carved by Bush's signing of the still secret 2001 Memorandum of Notification, followed by numerous "torture memos" issued by the Department of Justice (Danner & Eakin, 2015). An essential part of Bush's legal manoeuvres involved the redefinition of "torture". An August 1, 2002 memo from Assistant Attorney General Bybee to Alberto Gonzalez, Counsel to the President, argued that activities count as torture only if they inflict pain "equivalent in intensity to the pain accompanying serious physical injury, such as organ failure, impairment of bodily function, or even death". Furthermore as early as during the time of ratification of the UNCAT, the US government lodged a restrictive interpretation of the provisions of the convention, limiting acts of psychological torture to "prolonged mental harm". Psychological torture, as defined by the convention, "constitute a wider category of acts, which cause severe mental suffering, irrespective of their prolongation or its duration" (UN, 2006, para 13, p. 3). This point was reiterated during the consideration of the U. S. periodic report by the UNCAT in 2014 with the following recommendation. "In particular, it (the State) should ensure that acts of psychological torture are not qualified as 'prolonged mental harm'" (UN, 2014, para 9, p. 3). It further noted that "serious discrepancies between the Convention's definition and that incorporated into domestic law create actual or potential loopholes for impunity" (UN, 2014, para 9, p. 3).

Another serious discrepancy between the UNCAT and the U. S. policy is the State party's insistence on the Convention not being applicable in times and in the context of armed conflict, on the basis of the argument that the "law of armed conflict" serves as and is applicable as an exclusive *lex specialis*. This extremist redefinition of torture was antithetical to the UNCAT and international law, and these positions were criticised by the Committee Against Torture in 2006 as well as in 2014 as being in nonconformity with the convention (UNCAT, 2006, 2014). The redefinition of torture was subsequently rejected by the U. S. Supreme Court and overturned by the Obama administration. For a time, though, it invited interrogators to "take the gloves off" and to begin systematic torture and mistreatment, which were marked by euphemisms such as "coercive or enhanced interrogations" and "torture lite" methods. Coupled with these legal machinations was an expansive programme of rendition that moved detainees to international "black sites" in countries such as Afghanistan, Thailand, Iraq, and Lithuania (Risen, 2014) that were well hidden and in places that had fewer restrictions against torture and mistreatment.

By July, 2003, Amnesty International had published reports of mistreatment of detainees in sites such as Abu Ghraib prison and the Bagram Air Force base in Afghanistan. These reports and the subsequent release of photographs showed the use of hooding, forced nudity, prolonged stress positions, prolonged sleep deprivation, physical beatings, loud noise, exposure to attack dogs and freezing temperatures, and sexual and cultural humiliation, deprivation of comfort items, and restricted access to the Quran, among other abuses (Danner, 2004). In the following years, a steady stream of reports from organisations such as Human Rights Watch, Amnesty International, and even the US Government itself documented the use of similar mistreatment of detainees held at Guantanamo Bay and other sites. Over time, the documented array of methods expanded to include waterboarding, wall slamming, sleep deprivation, threats against detainees' family members, close confinement (e.g. in coffins), and rectal rehydration, among others (U. S. Senate Select Committee on Intelligence, 2014). These methods are conspicuously psychological and aim to break people down without leaving evidence of physical wounds and harm (Physicians for Human Rights, 2007). It was only during the Obama administration that these methods were prohibited, and steps are still under way to make them illegal under U. S. law.

One of the worst aspects of survivors' ordeal was their lack of access to procedural justice. Indeed, detainees had no right to habeas corpus and had (and still have) no right to public trial, only to military tribunal. Significant numbers of detainees at Guantanamo Bay turned out not to be terrorists (Danner & Eakin, 2015; Risen, 2014).

Psychologists' Active Participation. It is now certain that some US psychologists played a direct role in torture and mistreatment of detainees. Starting in mid-2002, the US military formed Behavioral Science Consultation Teams (BSCTs) that advised on the interrogations of detainees held at Guantanamo Bay. The BSCTs were designed initially to be led by a psychiatrist with two subordinate psychologists, as typical of Medical Corps teams. Subsequently, BSCTs were led by a PhD psychologist with mental health assistants (Master's degree level). The presence of a psychologist would legally ensure that an interrogation session met the non-torture standard of the US government "torture memos". Operationally, the idea was that psychologists could identify weaknesses such as particular fears that interrogators could exploit. Also, psychologists who observed interrogations could potentially calibrate the intensity of the mistreatment, depending on the responses and condition of the detainee.

Psychologists who ought to have had moral reservations about such activities could say that they were following orders and obeying military regulations. Under the US military regulations of the time, such actions were viewed as legal. In addition, they could point to the APA Code of Ethics for support. In 2002, the APA Ethics Code was amended to read: "If psychologists' ethical responsibilities conflict with law, regulations, or other governing legal authority, psychologists make known their commitment to the Ethics Code and take steps to resolve the conflict. If the conflict is unresolvable via such means, psychologists may adhere to the requirements of the law, regulations, or other governing legal authority". The latter clause, like the failed attempt of Nazi perpetrators to defend themselves at the Nuremburg trials by saying they had only followed orders, placed national law above international law and human rights standards. This objectionable clause was not removed by the APA until 2010, well after the period in which the damage had been done, some 60 years after the adoption of the Nuremburg Principles by the International Law Commission of the United Nations. These principles were based on the Nuremburg Tribunal General Assembly resolution 95, (I) from 11 December 1946 (Casese, 2009).

The active roles played by psychologists extended well beyond the US military into the global, highly secretive work of the CIA. Recently, the 2014 Senate Intelligence Committee Report on Torture shed new light on the scope and nature of these activities. The report documents how the CIA contracted two former military psychologists—James Mitchell and Bruce Jessen—to help interrogate presumably high value detainees. Both had been trainers in the US military programme to help prepare US pilots and other knowledgeable personnel to withstand torture if they were captured. The programme—called SERE (Survival, Evasion, Resistance, and Escape)—exposed key personnel to harsh techniques, including waterboarding in a minority of cases. By reverse engineering the SERE methods, Mitchell and Jessen aimed to create methods that, when applied to detainees, would produce a state of "learned helplessness" and lead them to disclose actionable information. To quiet ethical concerns and enable them to market their approach effectively, Mitchell and Jessen argued that the methods were not torture because they were already used by the US military to train its own soldiers. Further, they claimed that the use of the techniques would lead detainees to tell the truth (Risen, 2014). Some of the SERE methods were variations on torture methods that had been used against US soldiers by China and North Korea during the Korean War. The purpose of the methods had not been to obtain accurate information but to break people down, force them to sign false confessions, and eliminate them as political threats.

Having been contracted by the CIA, Mitchell and Jessen directly interrogated Abu Zubaydah in 2002. Abu Zubaydah had been captured in Pakistan and taken to a CIA-run black site in Thailand. There he was interviewed by Arabic-speaking FBI interrogators using traditional methods of information gathering, including rapport building. Initially, the CIA had doubted the detainee's identity. But they came to believe that he was one of the leaders of al-Qaeda, although it subsequently emerged that he was not a member of al-Qaeda but had served in essence as a travel agent (Danner & Eakin, 2015). The CIA handed him to Mitchell and Jessen, who personally conducted the interrogation. Ultimately, Abu Zubaydah was water-boarded 83 times and deprived of sleep for 180 h before the interrogators concluded that he had no additional useful information to give.

The irony was that the torture of Abu Zubaydah led by Mitchell and Jessen yielded no new useful information (Senate Intelligence Committee Report, 2014). Although torture supporters claimed that he had divulged useful information that had likely helped to stop other mass attacks on the USA, the Senate Committee Report concluded the opposite. Abu Zubaydah did disclose that Khalid Sheikh Mohammed had masterminded the 9/11 attacks and that a plot to use dirty bombs was afoot, but FBI interrogators had collected this information without using torture and before Abu Zubaydah had been tortured by the CIA (Eban, 2007; Danner & Eakin, 2015; Senate Intelligence Committee Report, 2014). That the torture techniques did not yield new information came as no surprise to experienced interrogators, who pointed out that torture most often yields false information since the person who is being tortured will say nearly anything to stop the pain or even use the opportunity to tell strategic lies. The Senate Intelligence Committee Report also documented how the CIA had used cases of presumed "success" such as that of Abu Zubaydah, to garner support for ongoing coercive interrogations and additional funding. Despite attempts at justifying torture as part of intelligence work, the absolute prohibition of torture is crystal clear, and that no "exceptional circumstances whatsoever, whether a state of war or a threat of war, internal political instability or any other public emergency, may be invoked as a justification of torture" (art. 2, see Brownlie, 1992).

The Role of the American Psychological Association. As an organisation that has a stated commitment to supporting well-being and human rights, the APA should have taken a strong, proactive position against psychologists' participation in the abuse and mistreatment of detainees. One might have expected at least that the APA would have held early, open, transparent debates about the roles of psychologists and how to conceptualise and manage the complex ethical issues involved. And it should have spoken out against attempts to undermine binding obligations, including attempts at redefining torture and allowing detainees to be held in illegal places of detention, where detainees were stripped of all rights and legal safeguards.

But that is not what happened. APA was silent with respect to the policy changes and instead of preventing abuse and involvement, the APA helped to legitimate psychologists' support for torture (while vociferously proclaiming their anti-torture stance) and in the key years of 2001–2007, created cover for objectionable, unethical practices. Further, as documented in the recent Hoffman report (Hoffman et al., 2015), which was the product of an inquiry initiated by the APA Board of Directors, APA officials systematically colluded with the Department of Defense (DoD), taking a deliberately tailored and general stance which allowed mistreatment within the limits set by the DoD. In addition, the APA Ethics Director (Steven Behnke) intentionally manipulated the Council of Representatives and took steps behind the scenes to prevent or limit the passage of motions or the establishment of policies that were out of line with the DoD policy. Other APA officials, notably the Communications Director (Rhea Faberman), gave ethics a backseat relative to the public image of the APA and engaged in a pattern of denial, duplicity, and feigned commitment to human rights.

To understand how this happened, one must appreciate not only the public mood of fear and patriotism but also the long history of involvement of the APA with the US military and the desire of APA officials to curry influence with them. In short, the US military has repeatedly helped the APA to boost the prestige and standing of psychology, which for a long time had suffered "physics envy" and operated in the shadow of more mature, empirically strong natural sciences. Psychologists achieved greater stature when at the time of World War I, the Department of War asked the APA to develop tests to help select the most trainable recruits (Cattell, cited in Samelson, 1979, p. 106). Subsequently, psychologists contributed much to US military efforts in World War II (Capshew & Hilgard, 1992). Having greater stature and access to military leaders, many US psychologists have received extensive funding for their research from the (renamed) Department of Defense. Long before the establishment of a Division of Peace Psychology in the APA in 1990, the APA has had a Division of Military Psychology, founded in 1945–1946 (Gade & Drucker, 2000). When in the latter part of the twentieth century psychologists sought to obtain prescription privileges, which the medical profession opposed, the APA turned to the US military. The US military provided fertile ground for tests that subsequently led to psychologists gaining lucrative privileges to prescribe medications in numerous states.

Following the 9/11 attacks, APA officials had numerous secret meetings with officials from the DoD and the CIA (Risen, 2014). These meetings are believed to have been about the roles of psychologists in the new security environment and about professional ethics. To have limited the discussions of professional ethics to intelligence and DoD officials was a bad option that was part of the wider pattern of APA-DoD collusion (Hoffman et al., 2015). That same approach characterised much of APA's subsequent work on the issue. The primary example of this was the establishment in 2005 of a special Presidential initiative—the Psychological Ethics and National Security (PENS) Task Force—to take stock of whether the APA Ethics Code applied in the post-9/11 national security settings and provided appropriate guidance. The 2005 PENS Report decried torture and the use of cruel, inhumane, or degrading treatment, even citing UNCAT to support its case. Yet it legitimated psychologists' participation in interrogations and other national security activities, stating that "a central role for psychologists working in the area of national security investigations is to assist in ensuring that processes are safe, legal, and ethical for all participants" (p. 2). This was stated even in light of the fact that many of the detainees were held in secret detention (UN, 2014). The report provided a convenient cover for the use of the harsh techniques, which did not count as torture under the Bush administration's redefinition and were legal under the then current military regulations. It took a pro forma stance against torture, without even noting the problematic Bush redefinitions. The PENS Report embraced the view that U. S. law—even the extreme versions that the Bush administration had put in place—trumped international human rights standards.

The flaws with the PENS process were many (Olson, Soldz, & Davis, 2008). The Task Force was a stacked deck, as six of its ten appointed members either currently worked or had worked for the US government in the national security sector, including the intelligence sector. The selection of the PENS members was guided by DoD and national security personnel and was itself part of the APA-DoD collusion (Hoffman et al., 2015). The initial appointments to the Task Force (including only two peace psychologists—J. M. Arrigo and M. Wessells, who subsequently resigned from the Task Force) were made in secret, and the Task Force required that no notes or records be kept of its discussions. Over the weekend in which it conducted its work, numerous APA leaders participated and controlled the process. A particularly controlling presence was Russ Newman, whose wife was a BSCT psychologist. Also invited in were numerous psychologists who had been involved in discussions with the White House and the CIA. Notably lacking were rich, nuanced discussions of complex ethical issues (Arrigo, 2006). Most Task Force members voiced or accepted the necessity of using harsh methods to obtain actionable information and adhered to the patriotic view (which Hitler had used) that one's highest ethical obligation is to protect one's country against attacks. Repeatedly, the current or former national security workers stated, without evidence or argument, that psychologists' presence helped to guard against severe mistreatment. Psychologists were portrayed as the "Good Us" who could not only help to protect the country against the Evil Other but also blow the whistle if outright torture occurred. This was argued even in a situation where the "good" and the "bad" guys were playing on the same team. It is an understatement to describe these discussions as self-serving. In an unusual move, the deeply flawed PENS Task Force Report was accepted quickly and directly by the APA Board of Directors before it had even been shared with the representative governing body, the APA Council of Representatives (Olson et al., 2008).

The PENS discussions and report were intentionally non-specific in regard to what was permitted, and key language in the report was either drafted by DoD officials or written with an eye toward not constraining DoD actions (Hoffman et al., 2015). Of the many grey areas that had been left open for further discussion were questions such as how much sleep deprivation could be used before it was counted as cruel or inhumane? The then current Army Regulations permitted sleep deprivation in limited amounts per night but did not spell out how many nights the deprivation regime could be continued. Nor did the regulations limit the combination of various methods, when it was obvious that the severity of impact stemmed from the concurrent use of multiple methods. The Task Force took no steps to add clarity, though it recommended (probably as a means of appeasing two wary peace psychologists) the development of a document ("case book") that would subsequently clarify the grey areas. A credible case book was never developed, as only a thin, unsubstantive commentary document was placed quietly on the APA website in 2011 (Hoffman et al., 2015).

The post-PENS period was characterised by ongoing collusion between the APA and DoD, systematic manipulation of the APA democratic governance process, and APA communications subterfuge (Hoffman et al., 2015). The APA Ethics Director, Steven Behnke, manipulated the policy development process in coordination with the DoD. Whenever a new Council resolution on torture or interrogations was under development, he checked behind the scenes with DoD to make sure the wording was agreeable to DoD. Quite often, he urged wording of the resolutions that were either compatible with DoD wishes or, seeking compromise, were less out of alignment with the DoD than were alternate wordings or resolutions. In 2006, he manipulated the process by enabling joint work on a resolution by Division 48 (Peace Psychology) and Division 19 (Military Psychology). On receiving the draft resolution, he immediately checked it with DoD, the contact for which said it was "acceptable". However, seeing that the resolution might not be received well if it had come from Division 19 as critics of the military and its interrogation posture were vociferous at the moment, he had the resolution brought forward only by Division 48. He even drafted himself the note that was sent from the Chair of the APA Ethics Committee (who had chaired the PENS Task Force and supported its report) indicating that the resolution had no inconsistencies with the APA Ethics Code.

To help insure Council's approval of the resolution at the 2006 annual APA Convention, he organised in advance a staged discussion on issues of psychologists' involvement. The speakers were Surgeon General Kevin Kiley, Ethics Committee Chair Olivia Moorehead-Slaughter, and dissenter Steven Reisner. Far from being an "open discussion", it was carefully orchestrated by sandwiching Reisner between two PENS supporters, both of whom were provided with carefully honed talking points. Its intent was to build support for psychologists' continued involvement in interrogations, reduce the public pressure on the APA, and give the appearance of democratic process. The immediate outcome of this intensive orchestration by APA staff was the Council's approval of the resolution.

Over a longer term, these clandestine activities likely contributed to the failure of the APA Council of Representatives to exercise leadership on the issues and draw a bright line that limited psychologists' involvement in interrogations and mistreatment. At best, the APA took slow, modest steps, many of which contained loopholes that allowed continued human rights violations. In 2007, the APA Council of Representatives passed a resolution prohibiting psychologists use of or support for specific harmful interrogation techniques such as those that had been used at Abu Ghraib and Guantanamo Bay. Also that year, the APA enabled public discussion of the issues at its programme on "Ethics and Interrogations" at its annual convention.

Subsequently, as US fears subsided and as groups such as the Coalition for an Ethical Psychology (ethicalpsychology.org), Psychologists for Social Responsibility (www.psysr.org), and Withhold APA Dues (withholdapadues.com) decried APA actions and inaction on the issue, the APA took a number of additional steps. In a 2008 letter to President Bush, the APA presented a new policy that limited psychologists' involvement in interrogations. In 2009, the Council of Representatives had approved a new Vision Statement that called for APA to promote human rights, health, well-being, and dignity. In 2010, the APA Ethics Code was amended and deleted the objectionable clause that placed national law above international law and human rights standards.

Alongside these modest improvements was an ongoing pattern of APA duplicity that was evident in its refusal to prosecute member psychologists who had participated in or been involved in the mistreatment of detainees. APA officials stated repeatedly that violations of the APA Code of Ethics would lead to investigation and, if warranted, prosecution and action. Yet the APA did very little on this front, probably as a means of continuing good relations with the DoD and limiting bad press for the profession. Psychologist Trudy Bond filed a complaint to the APA charging that one of its members, John Leso, had participated in the torture of Mohammed Al-Qautani, who was alleged to be one of the 9/11 hijackers. Although the evidence against Leso is believed to be convincing (Eidelson, 2015; Miles, 2006), the APA closed the case without normal adjudication (Eidelson, 2015). In addition, a complaint against James Mitchell, one of the psychologists who had led CIA funded interrogations and torture, was filed in 2005. But the APA Ethics Office took no action, and Mitchell eventually resigned from the APA in June, 2006 (Hoffman et al., 2015). The APA unwillingness to prosecute people such as Mitchell and Leso created an environment of impunity for military psychologists who violated professional ethics in their national security work.

APA duplicity was evident also in the fact that it supported Behnke to travel around the world to speak on ethics at international psychology conferences. He also contributed in central publications on ethics for psychologists (e.g. Leach, Stevens, Lindsay, Ferrero, & Korkut, 2012). As late as July, 2015 he was an invited speaker to symposia on ethics, including a symposia sponsored by the European Federation of Psychology Associations (EFPA). Fortunately, psychologists protested his participation in the symposium, and he did not attend. Nevertheless, the day the Hoffman report was made public, the APA Ethics Director's name appeared in the scientific programme as the convenor on invited symposia on ethics and social justice.

The Hoffman report (2015) concluded that APA authorities approved of or did not speak out against psychologists' participation in interrogations because they wanted to curry favour with DoD, maintain good public relations, and keep up the growth of psychology. APA officials tend to want to position psychology well with the Government, and to maintain cosy relations with the DoD, which has, over the years, yielded significant advantages. DoD is one of the largest employers of psychologists and has given large amounts of grant money to psychologists. APA officials may also have wanted to avoid the negative press that would have resulted had they disagreed publicly with the Bush administration policies. In addition,

PENS Task Force members expressed strong patriotic sentiments that may have made them want to align with the position of the President and the DoD. APA officials may have been influenced by similar sentiments.

Of course, this does not excuse the APA for not having taken a strong leadership stance against torture and psychologists' involvement in torture and mistreatment. From the beginning, the APA should have denounced publicly the Bush administration's inappropriate redefinition of torture and also its policy of inflicting mental suffering on people in detention. It should also have called for adherence to human rights standards and the UNCAT, even if doing so would have put it at odds with the administration and the military regulations of the day. It should have taken immediate steps to remove the objectionable clause in its ethics code, and it should have taken a strong position against all forms of mistreatment, including the sleep deprivation and "torture light" methods that the PENS report had failed to address adequately. In many ways, the APA became not a passive bystander but an active enabler of mistreatment. As the Hoffman report details, it consistently denied wrongdoing, made duplicitous statements about how it was upholding professional ethics, and placed the maintenance of its image far above considerations of professional ethics. As a result, it made a mockery of professional ethics and badly tarnished the image of psychology.

It would be a mistake, however, to think that the APA spoke for all psychologists. At APA Conventions between 2005 and 2009, a vocal, highly energetic group of peace psychologists such as Jean Maria Arrigo, Trudy Bond, Roy Eidelson, Brad Olson, Steven Reisner, and Stephen Soldz put forward strong and unanswered criticisms of the APA's position. Also, organisations such as the Coalition for an Ethical Psychology (www.ethicalpsychology.org) and Psychologists for Social Responsibility (www.psysr.org) spoke strongly against psychologists' participation in interrogations and denounced the presence of psychologists at Guantanamo Bay, which operated outside the boundaries of the Geneva Conventions. Dissident psychologists from other countries also put pressure on the APA. At one point, the Psychological Associations in Scandinavia expressed deep concern with APA policy on these matters, both in writing and in meetings. As mentioned earlier, the APA position on psychological participation in enhanced interrogation had been questioned at international conferences and meetings. These criticisms, however, tended to elicit defences of the APA position. Even when confronted with psychologists engaged in secret places of detention, the conference organisers denied that this was a problem or dilemma, let alone human rights violation.

The work of dissident psychologists was likely important in identifying the problems in the APA and US government positions, enabling some corrective steps to be taken, and stirring the conscience of many psychologists. It also built critical momentum that set the stage for three works to have momentous impact and turn the tide against the APA positions. Those works consisted of the U. S. Senate Committee on Intelligence report (2014), which disclosed greater, more concerning roles played by psychologists in torture; the book *Pay any price*, in which former New York Times reporter James Risen accused the APA of collusion with the DoD and CIA based in part on access to emails of a deceased former CIA contractor; and the

Hoffman report, which was the product of an APA Board commissioned investigation regarding possible APA collusion.

Although dissident psychologists' efforts were highly valuable and large numbers of psychologists did oppose the APA positions and activities, the majority of US psychologists did not speak out against psychologists' involvement in national security interrogations and torture. This silence likely helped to undermine the ethical orientation and actions of psychologists at a key moment in US history. In other words, the APA was a huge obstacle to ethical practice of psychology, but it was not the only obstacle. Why the majority of psychologists remained silent is unknown but may have reflected lack of critical thinking, fear of the enemy, patriotism, unwillingness to take a controversial stand against the President, and, of course, the legitimation by the APA of psychologists' roles in interrogations. Brewster Smith (1986), a former APA President who was long regarded as the "conscience of the APA", pointed out that US psychologists tend to reflect the wider US public mood and values. A recent national survey (Pew Research Center, 2014) indicated that 51 % of US citizens view the CIA interrogation methods as "appropriate". This is no excuse but a reminder that the paucity of appropriate ethical reasoning and action that was visible in the USA in the post-9/11 era may have deep roots in US society and culture.

A bright spot in this otherwise sordid case of professional ethics gone awry is that the APA Council of Representatives passed, on August 8, 2015, a resolution stating that "psychologists shall not conduct, supervise, be in the presence of, or otherwise assist any national security interrogation for any military or intelligence entities, including private contractors working on their behalf, nor advise on conditions of confinement insofar as these might facilitate such an interrogation". Although the Hoffman report was the proximal stimulus for this action, the APA resolution and change of course owed much to the work of dissident psychologists.

Reflection

Both the South African and the US cases serve as poignant reminders that torture is not the province of a few rogue individuals. Often, states are the perpetrators of torture, and they bring their vast resources, bureaucracy, and secret intelligence operations to bear in their justification and their attempts to hide their practices of torture. Both cases also illustrate how torture can be enabled by a mixture of collective and individual courses of action and inaction. Professional psychology organisations and their members may reflect the dominant views within the society and may support the use of mistreatment of prisoners out of desire for good relations with the government, patriotism, concerns over loss of status, power, or image, or a combination of these. The implication is that the transformation of professional psychology organisations is an important part of efforts to end the use of torture. At the same time, it is essential to recognise that the inaction of individual psychologists can help to enable the use of torture. With these points in mind, we now turn to the key tasks of prevention.

Prevention

In regard to torture and other human rights violations, prevention is a high priority. Psychologists' responsibility to help prevent torture relates to the fact that the profession of psychology aims to promote human well-being, which is shattered by regimes and practices of torture. In addition, psychologists have specialised knowledge and skills that relate to prevention. Through research and clinical practice, they have documented the enormity of the damage caused by torture, traumatic stress, isolation, and the adverse effects of discrimination, marginalisation, humiliation, and deprivation of individual freedoms and respect. They also have developed intervention skills and approaches that support healing, recovery, and well-being. Because psychologists work in prisons, psychiatric facilities, military settings, and other places where human rights violations may occur, they are often "on the front lines" and more likely to witness or to become aware of abuses. Psychologists have professional credibility and position that bestows the power to intervene. This credibility relates to the fact that professional psychology organisations generally have ethics codes that oblige their members to promote well-being, avoid causing harm, and report violations that they witness or know about. For all these reasons, it is in all ways inappropriate for psychologists to sit by while abuses are occurring or to hold that abuses would likely be worse if psychologists were not present.

How psychologists can fulfil their responsibilities to prevent torture is best conceptualised holistically. It would be a mistake to focus only on reporting violations when the conditions that lead to the violations are preventable. Such a holistic approach is offered by the familiar framework of primary, secondary, and tertiary prevention (Caplan, 1964). Primary prevention of torture includes preventive steps taken before mistreatment has occurred. Secondary prevention efforts are directed toward containing the mistreatment once it has begun and reducing the risks of further mistreatment. Tertiary prevention efforts include immediate steps to protect and treat the people who have been abused.

A holistic, systemic approach also requires extensive engagement with and efforts by government and international bodies. Governments have the power to hold professional organisations accountable in a way that could not be achieved by individuals acting alone. A key part of preventing torture is to help government bodies enact legislation and policies that not only prohibit torture but that take corrective steps against civil society agencies or groups whose policies or actions tacitly or explicitly support torture. If the government is the perpetrator of torture, it is likely to suppress, undermine, or even attack whistle-blowers and people who work to publicise and prevent torture. In such settings, it is important to carefully think through how to develop contextualised approaches that face these hard realities and limit the harm done to those who in fact blow the whistle and engage in preventing torture.

Primary Prevention

Education about human rights is part of the foundation of primary prevention. In countries such as the USA and South Africa, human rights education is not part of the core curriculum for psychologists, and multiple generations of psychologists go through their professional training without having read basic human rights instruments or discussed their implications for practice. Human rights education is essential for helping psychologists understand that, under the UNCAT and other international law, there are no circumstances under which torture is permissible, even if national law says otherwise (Sveaass, 2009). In an age of fear of terrorism, this knowledge and understanding can help psychologists to resist government calls for "taking the gloves off" or treating harshly people who are suspected of being terrorists or having information that could be used to combat terrorism. In fact, when the Bush administration attempted to redefine torture and reform national law in a way that contravened the UNCAT, there should have been instant and loud outrage on the part of the psychologists and their professional associations. Similarly, professional organisations should take a strong, immediate, and highly public stand against the presence of psychologists in situations that operate outside the realm of human rights standards.

A critical part of primary prevention is the ongoing development of codes of professional ethics that embody the primacy of human rights standards and international law over national law. A potentially useful step in regard to ethics codes is the definition of a broad set of principles and a common framework for psychological ethics in different countries. The Universal Declaration of Ethical Principles for Psychologists, adopted in Berlin in 2009, was a significant step in this respect. Its preamble states that:

> ...Psychologists are committed to placing the welfare of society and its members above the self-interest of the discipline and its members. They recognise that adherence to ethical principles in the context of their work contributes to a stable society that enhances the quality of life for all human beings.

Although such collective efforts lean in the right direction, there is a need to give greater attention to human rights. All professional ethics codes for psychologists should pass the litmus test of consistency with international human rights standards, regardless of whether they mention them specifically. When a professional organisation's ethics code, policies, or guidelines fail this litmus test, international and national bodies should take punitive action. In particular, the UN should withdraw NGO consultative status (which APA had in most of the pos-9/11 era), and the national government should withdraw the organisation's non-profit status. Within psychology, the International Union of Psychological Science, the members of which are national psychology organisations, should bar and publicly reprimand national psychology organisations whose ethics codes are not fully consistent with international human rights standards.

Education about which means of interrogation are in compliance with human rights standards and which are not is also important for psychologists who may be present at or involved in interrogations. The weight of evidence and practical experience of intelligence workers is that methods of torture and harsh treatment are ineffective means of obtaining accurate information (Soufan & Freedman, 2011). As was true in the case of Abu Zubaydah, one is more likely to obtain useful information through more traditional, "softer", methods such as relationship building. Psychologists who are somehow involved in settings of information gathering and questioning individuals, including interrogation in relation to terrorism, should be willing to use and further develop these more relational skills and methods that respect the rights of those being questioned.

The definition of torture is also a matter of primary prevention that relates to psychologists' knowledge and expertise. The Bush administration's redefinition included the view referred to above that something was considered torture only when it led to "prolonged mental harm". This view contradicted not only human rights standards but also psychological knowledge. The fact that two torture survivors recover at different rates—one relatively fast and one relatively slow—would not indicate that only the latter had been tortured. Psychologists and psychological organisations should be at the forefront of efforts to help governments and the wider public understand that torture includes all acts that are inflicted to cause severe mental suffering, regardless of the duration of suffering. Psychologists should work toward primary prevention by building psychologically informed definitions of torture into national laws and policies and by criticising and working to correct revisionist efforts that would enable torture.

The need to clarify and identify responsibility for implementing human rights standards as well as responsibility for violating such principles is a high priority. To prevent violations, it is critical to implement monitoring systems that can detect the risks for violations, and situations where violations are likely or are actually occurring. Effective monitoring systems must be more than fancy diagrams and should include steps to ensure that psychologists working in relevant settings know about them, understand how to document violations, and are willing to assess and report violations. The willingness to use monitoring systems is often the weak link. Organisations should provide incentives for professionals engaged in such monitoring work and aim at reducing the culture of fear that often surrounds reporting. Workers may fear that if they report a violation (whistle-blowing), they will be ostracised by their peers and superiors and their careers will suffer. Further, if whistle-blowing does not lead to action and discernible improvements, then workers will be less likely to report.

Monitoring systems must avoid arrangements that metaphorically have the fox watching over the chicken house. Particularly when a government is the perpetrator of torture and is likely to suppress, discredit, attack, or otherwise harm the whistle-blower or potential whistle-blower, it is crucial to include monitoring by independent national and international bodies. Under the Optional Protocol to the UNCAT, there are national preventive mechanisms (NPM) that consist of professionals from different areas who, as part of an independent but state established body, perform regular visits to places where there are persons who have been deprived of their liberty. These professionals work in close collaboration with the treaty body established by the Protocol, namely the Sub-committee for the prevention of torture (SPT) (OPCAT, 2014). In addition, human rights monitoring organisations such as Amnesty International and Human Rights Watch may be engaged with as a means of naming and shaming governments that mistreat whistle-blowers or engage in torture. Also, support for those who raise their voices may be provided by others who understand the tactics the government will likely use, the struggles that whistle-blowers face, and the best means of coping with the situation. These steps illustrate how psychologists will need to work beyond the borders of psychology and engage with government realities if they are to be effective in helping to prevent torture.

More broadly, psychologists may contribute to primary prevention by taking steps to prevent violence and mistreatment at levels such as the family and community levels. Although interpersonal violence may seem far removed from politically motivated torture, norms that support violence in everyday settings such as households, schools, workplaces, and the local streets can create an enabling environment for cruelty, abuse, and mistreatment of other kinds. It is important to bear in mind that the state has the responsibility to protect against violence and take proper measures when such acts occur. Failure to show due diligence and failure to protect are considered as violations (UN, 2012). Similarly, the oppression and derogation of particular out-groups in local communities can indirectly support the mistreatment of the out-group members by police and the military. Further, the mistreatment of people in prisons or people who are being held by the police or other authorities can help to create a societal norm that regards abusive treatment as acceptable.

Secondary Prevention

If mistreatment is occurring, for example in prisons or other places where individuals are deprived of liberty, the immediate responsibility of psychologists is to blow the whistle and provide relevant documentation of the mistreatment and the suffering it has created so that steps can be taken to minimise the harms or end the mistreatment. Protective steps for detainees could include psychologists identifying the harm that is being done and recommending that the detainees be shifted to areas where their rights can be better protected. If abuse were occurring because of overzealous interrogators or lower level officials, one could enhance the presence of monitors or even give them the ability to report to officers higher in the chain of command. Steps should also be taken to comfort the detainee and provide appropriate therapy and psychosocial support. Psychological organisations should support these efforts by using their knowledge, networks, and credibility to help define appropriate steps to limit and correct the mistreatment.

This approach, however, will not work unless attention is given to the real dangers and enormous psychological, legal, and financial stress that most whistle-blowers face. For example, psychologists who worked at Guantanamo Bay in 2004 and who reported abuses such as sleep deprivation and loud noises would have been out of step with the military regulations and laws of that time. They would likely have been reprimanded by their commanding officers, raising concerns about their ongoing ability to support their families and to have a military career. They may also have suffered from the knowledge that they were disobeying their Commander in Chief or avoiding doing what most people saw as their patriotic duty. In many countries in which the government has been the perpetrator of torture and wanted to hide it, whistle-blowers have been harassed, left unemployed and unemployable, beaten, threatened, or even tortured or disappeared. In such situations, it is vital to provide appropriate psychosocial, economic, and legal support for those who in fact take action to report and denounce acts of torture or ill-treatment. In principle, national psychology associations could help to provide this support, although as discussed above, it would need to be guided by and collaborate with networks of former whistle-blowers.

A key part of ending mistreatment once it has begun is to take steps against the perpetrators. If psychologists are suspected of having been involved in mistreatment, they must be held accountable for their actions lest there develops a culture of silence and impunity that gives comfort to perpetrators and enables abuse to continue. Militaries, police, and prisons all have their mechanisms for dealing with perpetrators in their own ranks, although these typically do far too little to hold perpetrators accountable. Our focus, however, is on psychologists' organisations. To encourage prevention, professional organisations need to take concerted, decisive action to investigate suspected infractions and, in the case of actual violations, impose significant penalties such as barring them from practice that will help to deter others from committing violations.

In addition to conducting investigations and taking action against psychologist members who have been involved in torture and mistreatment, professional psychological organisations need to speak early and loudly and to exercise leadership in denouncing torture immediately following its occurrence. Those responsible for the organisations should send notices to their members reminding them of their ethical obligations, denouncing specific forms of mistreatment, and drawing a bright line that one cannot step across. Even if their own members have not been involved in the mistreatment, they should call strongly for independent investigations that will help to end impunity for psychologists' involvement.

To do their part to prevent torture, psychologists must be willing to engage with governments. Where there is evidence of torture, from whatever source, national psychological associations and their international counterparts (e.g. the IUPsyS) must confront the responsible governments to express their concern and demand full and independent investigations of the alleged practices. We recommend that these must be conducted by investigators appointed by the national psychological association, and should include a member of the legal profession who is not in the employ of the state.

Tertiary Prevention

Rehabilitation is a core part of tertiary prevention. For persons who have suffered serious human rights violations, rehabilitation is not only a matter of tertiary prevention but also a right (Van Bowen, 2009). The UNCAT, for example, obliges states to provide redress following torture, with the redress being for as full a rehabilitation as possible (UNCAT, 1984, art. 14; Sveaass, 2013). Psychologists have a significant role to play in the rehabilitation process, as well as ensuring that this right in fact can be accessed and enjoyed by victims of torture (Redress, 2009).

Ending impunity for human rights violations is essential and the claim for justice following human rights violations is a cornerstone of tertiary prevention. The focus on accountability, including the struggle against impunity for crimes against humanity, has been growing over the past several decades. Today, the international consensus is that those responsible for crimes against humanity, including torture, war crimes, and genocide, must be brought to account and be punished by "appropriate penalties which take into account their grave nature" (UNCAT, 1984, art. 4). The establishment of the International Criminal Court (ICC) as a permanent court as well as the Tribunals that dealt with the genocide in Rwanda (ICTR) and the Former Yugoslavia (ICTY) illustrates the weight given to these efforts. Their aim is not solely to punish those responsible, but also to prevent the occurrence of new crimes. ICC critics appropriately point out that the Court has been too selective and limited in regard to whom it has selected for prosecution. To date, the ICC has been unwilling to indict or hear cases against leaders such as George W. Bush for their role in torture or the mass deaths associated with the invasion and occupation of Iraq. Efforts to correct this problem are needed to help build an international system that does not condone torture.

The elimination of "safe haven" for those responsible for crimes against humanity is also a way of preventing such crimes in the future. The importance of ending impunity and claiming justice should be raised also from a psychological point of view, because justice, acknowledgement, and recognition based on the fact that injustice has been committed may help survivors to move on following severe trauma (Sveaass, Agger, Sønneland, Elsass, & Hamber, 2014). Psychologists may contribute to such efforts by supporting victims and witnesses, insuring that rights are protected throughout the legal process, and providing expert witness, among other things (Stover, 2005; Sveaass, 2013).

At every stage, the willingness to act is the criterion by which prevention efforts should be gauged. It is not enough to have human rights foundations included in one's ethics codes or to be trained in non-coercive methods of gathering information. Psychologists must speak up when the rights foundations of ethics codes are challenged, when torture has been redefined in inappropriate ways, and when their professional organisations enable mistreatment or remain quiet while mistreatment is known to be occurring. Often it can be more effective for psychologists not to speak individually only but to join with others. In the US case, many psychologists have spoken with a single voice through activist organisations such as Psychologists for Social Responsibility and the Coalition for an Ethical Psychology. The key to prevention is for each psychologist and for each professional society or organisation to do their part to actively encourage as well as take all possible steps to ensure that international obligations for the protection of human rights in fact are respected and implemented.

Conclusion

Advocates for the use of harsh methods of interrogation frequently argue that such methods are necessary when the country is faced with grave security threats. This argument, however, stands on the flawed assumption that harsh methods work and deliver actionable intelligence that helps to protect the country. The recent U. S. Senate Intelligence Committee Report (2014) provides the most compelling evidence to the contrary that is currently available. The fact that the harsh methods did not work any better than other methods, despite the enormous sums of money spent on the harsh methods, ought to urge leaders and interrogators to think twice before using harsh methods of interrogation.

The use of harsh methods may also create additional security problems. In regard to the USA, the harsh treatment of Muslim detainees may stir resentments and feelings of oppression that help to politicise young Muslims and lead them toward extremist groups such as ISIS. Also, the use of harsh interrogation methods wholly contradicts the absolute prohibition against torture and sets aside the important fact that even in the face of exceptional circumstances, the right not to be tortured is defined as a non-derogable right. Last but not least, harsh interrogation amounting to torture weakens the global efforts to create strong norms against the use of torture and undermines accountability for those responsible. A better strategy for preventing terrorism is one that is collective and that seeks to limit all forms of horrendous violence. National security concerns can never be placed above the absolute prohibition against torture, as laid down in the Convention Against Torture and other international human rights covenants, the implementation of which is fundamental for ending the most odious forms of violence.

In a dangerous world, however, it is reasonable to assume that some governments and champions of coercive interrogations will continue to create "ticking time bomb" scenarios and urge their intelligence services to use harsh methods as a means of obtaining information from terrorism suspects. In this context, strong national laws, in line with the international standards, are needed to prevent torture. A high priority is to enact national legislation that limits extended detention and requires that detainees be brought to trial within 48 h. In addition, there should be sharp legal limits on the use of prolonged solitary confinement and other forms of torture that are proscribed by the UNCAT. Also, international humanitarian authorities such as the International Committee of the Red Cross and other international human rights bodies should provide independent monitoring of sites where detentions and interrogations are underway. It would also be useful for the bodies that legally licence psychologists in particular countries or states to require that all licence holder or applicants sign a legally binding agreement that they will not conduct, participate in, or support (e.g. through training or observation) interrogations that involve harsh methods that are banned under the UNCAT. These legal measures at state and substate levels will help to prevent states from engaging in heinous violations of human rights. These legal changes must be complemented by steps to increase psychologists' understanding and knowledge of how to act when facing violations, injustice, and impunity. By themselves, legal changes will not likely occur or have their full impact unless psychologists take a concerted stand against torture.

References

American Psychological Association. (2005). *Report of the American Psychological Association Presidential Task Force on Psychological Ethics and National Security*. Washington, DC: Author.

Amnesty International. (2011). *Guantanamo: A decade of damage to human rights and 10 anti-human rights messages Guantanamo still sends*. London: Amnesty International Publications.

Arrigo, J. M. (2006). *Unofficial records of the APA PENS Task Force Meeting, June 14-16, 2005, Washington, DC*. Stanford: Hoover Institution Archives, Stanford University.

Basoglu, M., Jaranson, J. M., Mollica, R., & Kastrup, M. (2001). Torture and mental health: A research overview. In E. Gerrity, T. M. Keane, & F. Tuma (Eds.), *The mental health consequences of torture* (pp. 35–62). New York: Kluwer Academic/Plenum.

Basoglu, M. D., Livanou, M., & Crnobaric, C. (2007). Torture vs other cruel, inhuman, and degrading treatment. *Archives of General Psychiatry, 64*, 277–285.

Bell, T., & Ntsebeza, T. (2001). *Unfinished business. South Africa, apartheid and truth*. Cape Town: RedWorks.

Brownlie, I. (Ed.). (1992). *Basic documents on human rights* (3rd ed.). Oxford: Clarendon.

Burman, S., & Reynolds, P. (Eds.). (1986). *Growing up in a divided society. The contexts of childhood in South Africa*. Johannesburg: Ravan Press.

Bybee, J. S. (2002). *Memorandum for Alberto R. Gonzales, Counsel to the President*. Washington, DC: U. S. Department of Justice Office of Legal Counsel.

Caplan, G. (1964). *Principles of preventive psychiatry*. New York: Basic Books.

Capshew, J. H., & Hilgard, E. R. (1992). The power of service: World War II and professional reform in the American Psychological Association. In R. B. Evans, V. S. Sexton, & T. C. Cadwallader (Eds.), *100 years: The American Psychological Association, a historical perspective* (pp. 149–175). Washington, DC: American Psychological Association.

Casese, A. (2009). Affirmation of the principles of International Law recognized by the Charter of the Nürnberg Tribunal. *United Nations Audiovisual Library of International Law*.

Cooper, S., Nicholas, L. J., Seedat, M., & Statman, J. M. (1990). Psychology and apartheid: The struggle for psychology in South Africa. In L. J. Nicholas & S. Cooper (Eds.), *Psychology and apartheid* (pp. 1–21). Johannesburg: Vision/Madiba.

Danner, M. (2004). *Torture and truth: America, Abu Ghraib, and the war on terror*. New York: New York Review of Books.

Danner, M., & Eakin, H. (2015). The CIA: The devastating indictment. *The New York Review of Books, LXII*(2), 31–32.

Dawes, A. (1985). Politics and mental health: The position of clinical psychology in South Africa. *South African Journal of Psychology, 15*, 55–61.

Dawes, A. (1987a). Security laws and children in prison: The issue of psychological impact. *Psychology in Society, 8*, 27–47.

Dawes, A. (1987b). *Children in prison Plenary address to the International Conference on Children, Repression and the Law in Apartheid South Africa*. Harare, Zimbabwe.

Dawes, A., Tredoux, C. G., & Feinstein, A. (1989). Political violence in South Africa: Some effects on children of the violent destruction of their community. *International Journal of Mental Health, 18*(2), 16–43.

Eban, K. (2007). Rorschach and awe. *Vanity Fair*, July 17, 2007.

Eidelson, R. J. (2015). "No cause for action": Revisiting the ethics case of Dr. John Leso. *Journal of Social and Political Psychology, 3*(1), 198–212.

Foster, D. (1990). Expert testimony on collective violence. In D. Hanson & E. D. van Zyl (Eds.), *Towards justice* (pp. 154–172). Cape Town: Oxford University Press.

Foster, D. (2008). Critical psychology: A historical overview. In C. van Ommen & D. Painter (Eds.), *Interiors. A history of psychology in South Africa* (pp. 92–122). Pretoria: UNISA Press.

Foster, D. (2014). Musings and memories: 30 years of psychology in society. *Psychology in Society, 46*, 9–14.

Foster, D., Davis, D., & Sandler, D. (1987). *Detention & torture in South Africa: Psychological, legal & historical studies.* Cape Town: David Philip Publisher.

Foster, D., & Sandler, D. (1985). *A study of detention and torture in South Africa: Preliminary report.* Cape Town: Institute of Criminology, University of Cape Town.

Gade, P. A., & Drucker, A. J. (2000). A history of Division 19 (military psychology). In D. A. Dewsbury (Ed.), *Unification though division: Histories of the divisions of the American Psychological Association* (Vol. V, pp. 9–32). Washington, DC: American Psychological Association.

Hoffman, D. H., Carter, D. J., Lopez, C. R. V., Besmiller, H. L., Guo, A. X., Latifi, S. Y., et al. (2015). *Report to the Special Committee of the Board of Directors of the American Psychological Association: Independent review relating to APA ethics guidelines, national security interrogations, and torture.* Chicago: Sidley Austin LLP.

Leach, M. M., Stevens, M. J., Lindsay, G., Ferrero, J., & Korkut, Y. (Eds.). (2012). *The Oxford handbook of international psychological ethics.* New York: Oxford University Press.

Long, W. (2013). Rethinking "relevance": South African psychology in context. *History of Psychology, 16*(1), 19–35.

Miles, S. (2006). Medical oaths betrayed. *Washington Post*, July 9.

Olson, B., Soldz, S., & Davis, M. (2008). The ethics of interrogation and the American Psychological Association: A critique of policy and process. *Philosophy, Ethics, and Humanities in Medicine, 3*(3). doi:10.1186/1747-5341-3-3.

UN Convention Against Torture and Other Cruel, Inhuman or Degrading Treatment or Punishment. (1984). (Reprinted in I. Brownlie (Ed.). (1992) *Basic documents on human rights* (3rd ed., pp. 38–51). Oxford: Clarendon Press). Retrieved from http://www.ohchr.org/EN/ProfessionalInterest/Pages/CAT.aspx.

Ougrin, D., Gluzman, S., & Dratcu, L. (2006). Psychiatry in post-communist Ukraine: Dismantling the past, paving the way for the future. *Psychiatric Bulletin, 30*, 456–459.

Pew Research Center. (2014). *About half see CIA interrogation methods as justified.* Washington, DC: Author.

Physicians for Human Rights. (2007). *Leave no marks: Enhanced interrogation techniques and the risk of criminality.* Washington, DC: Author.

Redress. (2009). *Rehabilitation as a form of reparation under international law.* London: Redress.

Risen, J. (2014). *Pay any price: Greed, power, and endless war.* New York: Houghton Mifflin Harcourt.

Samelson, F. (1979). Putting psychology on the map: Ideology and technology in intelligence testing. In A. R. Buss (Ed.), *Psychology in social context* (pp. 103–168). New York: Irvington.

Seedat, M., & MacKenzie, S. (2008). The triangulated development of South African Psychology. In C. van Ommen & D. Painter (Eds.), *Interiors. A history of psychology in South Africa* (pp. 63–91). Pretoria: UNISA Press.

Senate Select Committee. (2015). *The Senate Intelligence Committee Report on Torture: Committee Study of the Central Intelligence Agency's Detention and Interrogation Program.* New York: Melville House.

Shallice, T. (1972). The Ulster depth interrogation techniques and their relation to sensory deprivation research. *Cognition, 1*(4), 385–405.

Smith, M. B. (1986). War, peace and psychology. *Journal of Social Issues, 42*(4), 23–38.

Soufan, A., & Freedman, D. (2011). *The black banners: The inside story of 9/11 and the war against al-Qaeda.* New York: Norton.

Stover, E. (2005). *The witnesses. War crimes and the promise of justice in The Hague*. Philadelphia: University of Pennsylvania Press.

Stover, E., & Nightingale, M. D. (Eds.). (1985). *The breaking of bodies and minds*. New York: W. H. Freeman.

Straker, G., Moosa, F., & Team, S. C. (1988). Post-traumatic stress disorder: A reaction to state-supported child abuse and neglect. *Child Abuse & Neglect, 12*(3), 383–395.

Sveaass, N. (2009). Destroying minds: Psychological pain and the crime of torture. *New York City Law Review, 11*(2), 303–324.

Sveaass, N. (2013). Gross human rights violations and reparation under international law: Approaching rehabilitation as a form of reparation. *European Journal of Psychotraumatology, 4*, 17191. Retrieved from http://www.eurojnlofpsychotraumatol.net/index.php/ejpt/article/view/17191'\t'_blank.

Sveaass, N., Agger, I., Sønneland, A. M., Elsass, P., & Hamber, B. (2014). Surviving gross human rights violations: Exploring survivors' experience of justice and reparation. In S. Cooper & K. Ratele (Eds.), *Psychology Serving Humanity. Proceedings of the 30th International Congress of Psychology* (Western Psychology, Vol. II, pp. 66–84). New York: Psychology Press.

Targum, S. D., Chaban, O., & Mykhnyak, S. (2013). Psychiatry in the Ukraine. *Innovations in Clinical Neuroscience, 10*, 41–46.

U. S. Senate Select Committee on Intelligence. (2014). *The Senate Intelligence Committee report on torture: Committee study of the Central Intelligence Agency's detention and interrogation program*. New York: Melville House.

UN CAT. (2006). *Conclusions and recommendations of the Committee against Torture to report submitted by United States of America, CAT/C/USA/CO/2*. Retrieved from http://tbinternet. ohchr.org/_layouts/treatybodyexternal/Download.aspx?symbolno=CAT%2fC%2fUSA%2fCO%2f2&Lang=en.

UN OPCAT. (2014). *Optional protocol to the convention against torture and other cruel, in human or degrading treatment or punishment*. Retrieved from www.un.org/law/avl, http://www.ohchr.org/EN/HRBodies/OPCAT/Pages/OPCATIndex.aspx.

UN CAT. (2014). *Conclusions and recommendations of the Committee against Torture to report submitted by United States of America, CAT/C/USA/CO/3-5/*. http://tbinternet.ohchr.org/_layouts/treatybodyexternal/Download.aspx?symbolno=CAT%2fC%2fUSA%2fCO%2f3-5&Lang=en.

Universal Declaration of Ethical Principles for Psychologists, adopted in Berlin in 2009.

Universal Declaration of Human Rights. (1948). Reprinted in I. Brownlie (Ed.). (1992). *Basic documents on human rights* (3rd ed., pp. 21–27). Oxford: Clarendon Press.

Van Bowen, T. (2009). Victims' rights to a remedy and reparation. The United Nations basic principles and guidelines. In C. Ferstman, M. Goetz, & A. Stephens (Eds.), *Reparations for victims of genocide, war crimes and crimes against humanity* (pp. 19–41). Leiden, The Netherlands: Martinus Nijoff.

Vogelman, L. (1987). The development of an appropriate psychology: The work of the Organisation of Appropriate Social Services in South Africa. *Psychology in Society, 7*, 24–35.

Yankovsky, S. A. (2013). *Medicalizing suffering: Postsocialist reforms of the mental health system in Ukraine*. PhD dissertation, University of Tennessee. http://trace.tennessee.edu/utk_graddiss/1798.

Part IV
Conclusion

Chapter 15
Interrogating the Structure of Knowledge: Some Concluding Thoughts

Shahnaaz Suffla, Mohamed Seedat, and Daniel J. Christie

Through its thematic focus on *Engaging Invited and Invented Spaces for Peace*, the 14th International Symposium on the Contributions of Psychology to Peace sought to privilege voices from cultures and situations that are typically not included in dominant peace discourses and interrogate the hegemonic position of Western scholars as the principal architects of knowledge in peace psychology.

The Symposium opened with a reflection on the state of violence and peace across the world. Suffla and Seedat (2015) drew on available figures on homicide, reports on conflict, war, and human rights, and indices of conflict intensity, global peace, human development, and world happiness to illustrate that despite global advances in democratic traditions and human rights successes, violence and conflict remain intractable concerns. At the time that the Symposium was held, Africa's estimated homicide rate was reported to be highest among the regions of the world; the majority of countries in Africa were shown to have experienced violent conflict, with nation states that witnessed civil wars and wars of the liberation in recent decades having suffered a grave human and social toll; and enduring peace was found to be restricted to only a handful of African countries, or privileged groups within countries. Suffla and Seedat

S. Suffla • M. Seedat (✉)
Institute for Social and Health Sciences, University of South Africa, Johannesburg, South Africa

South African Medical Research Council-University of South Africa Violence, Injury and Peace Research Unit, Cape Town, South Africa
e-mail: ssuffla@mrc.ac.za; Seedama@unisa.ac.za

D.J. Christie
Institute for Social and Health Sciences, University of South Africa, Johannesburg, South Africa

Department of Psychology, The Ohio State University, Columbus, OH, USA
e-mail: christie.1@osu.edu

© Springer International Publishing AG 2017
M. Seedat et al. (eds.), *Enlarging the Scope of Peace Psychology*,
Peace Psychology Book Series, DOI 10.1007/978-3-319-45289-0_15

(2015) argued that while the submitted evidence did not represent an exhaustive set of factors and discourses that might be considered as relevant to the portrait of violence and peace across the African region and the rest of the world, the data clearly demonstrate that peace is contingent on a number of factors, including human development, socio-economic equity, subjective well-being, and human rights.

The opening reflections of the Symposium also considered the case of South Africa as an example of the doing of violence and the doing of peace. Suffla and Seedat (2015) traced the country's halting and at times uncertain journey towards democracy and described the various policies, structures, mechanisms, and instruments intended to serve the country's conflict transformation agenda, as well as the civil society initiatives directed at healing, dialogue, and community-building. In examining South Africa as an instance of incomplete peacebuilding and reconciliation, they raised critical questions about the role and scope of peace psychology in the host country, but also globally, as it occurs on the continuum between invited and invented spaces.

Against this context-setting for the Symposium, and reading the collection of chapters that represent the proceedings of the Symposium, we accordingly offer five observations.

Invited and invented spaces for participation in knowledge construction. To return to the notion of invited and invented spaces, as drawn from the work of Andrea Cornwall (2002) on citizenship, first we suggest that the enactment of peace psychology traverses both invited and invented spaces. As referenced in the Introduction to the volume, Cornwall (2002) invokes the concept of space as a frame through which to consider, conceptualise, and construct practices of participation; in this text, deployed specifically to refer to participation in knowledge construction. In particular, she interrogates the architecture of power and difference in the crafting and sculpting of spaces for engagement in institutionalised and non-institutionalised spaces, both where participation is invited and where spaces are more organically created (Cornwall, 2002). From this perspective, as efforts are directed at enlarging participation opportunities, new spaces are created into which people are invited to participate by various kinds of authorities, such as government. Such spaces tend to be regularised. Invented spaces, on the other hand, are claimed or designed by less powerful actors, such as the contributors to this volume, frequently as a consequence of common concerns or pursuits that are identified through processes of mobilisation or concourse. The claimed and created realm is often where social actors counter hegemony through debate, dialogue, and resistance.

Spaces are of course inhabited by power, power that is visible, hidden, and invisible. Power may be at once visible in the formal rules, structures, social actors, institutions, and processes of decision-making, and yet also concealed in the setting of political agendas that operate to exclude or devalue the concerns and representation of less powerful groups. Invisible power is likely the most insidious of its derivatives to the extent that it shapes the psychological and ideological boundaries of participation. In this instance, not only are significant problems and issues withheld in spaces of participation, but equally from the consciousness of individuals and communities.

Reflexivity. The movement in and out of invited and invented spaces is often messy and punctuated by contradictions and tensions, obliging a critical examination of the assumptions, values, discourses, and practices that we deploy to portray reality and create knowledge, as well as the influence of the intersubjective context on knowledge construction. Nonetheless, the chapters in this volume represent socially conscious efforts to claim and create a participatory space that is defined by common concerns and common pursuits, that is characterised by mobilisation and activism, and that is distinguished by an imagination and a vision of change and justice. We would like to believe that in invented spaces such as the one represented by this volume, we can participate in dialogues, deepen conversations, and raise questions, relatively free of the constraints of bureaucracies, state discourses, the pressures of dominance, and the injurious influences of visible, hidden, and invisible power. Simultaneously, it is in the dynamic process of enlarging the scope of peace psychology that peace psychologists are observed to develop relationships of solidarity and engagement while engaging reflexively on issues of power and inequality, and the reproduction of dominance even in claimed and created spaces.

Emancipatory discourses and transformational practices. We suggest that peace psychologists, like other groups of intellectuals and practitioners concerned with matters of human welfare, need to consider carefully our roles and social and ethical responsibilities in invited and invented spaces. The corpus of work contained in this volume succeeds then in encouraging conversations about how best to deepen peace psychology's enactments across invited and invented spaces. Collectively, the chapters contribute to surfacing new perspectives about the devices of visible, hidden, and invisible power and demonstrate enactments of how to claim and construct spaces fashioned towards emancipatory discourses and transformatory practices.

Hope. This collection of chapters may also be read an attempt at reflecting on work that seeks to intervene to support hope and hopefulness when globally citizens seem to be in despair about the capacities and decisions of governments and organised state structures; at a time when religion is misappropriated and extracted as a commodity to support violence and wreak terror; at a time when governments in the name of security spend billions on military to kill people in distant lands; and when the technologies of death are sterilised and sanitised to conduct targeted killings and drone strikes. The work is the efforts of groups of peace psychologists to visibilise the importance of hope-related work and to encourage optimism for ourselves as peace scholars and practitioners.

Epistemic violence. Sustaining efforts to support hope and hopefulness call for a serious look at epistemic violence, or the violence of knowledge production, where the 'non-Western' ways of perceiving, understanding, and knowing the world are consigned to the margins and Western-centric hegemonic knowledge is universalised. Those of us who may feel disillusioned by psychological orthodoxy may want to think about ways of breaking the cycle of epistemic violence so evident in psychology and the wider body of work in peace and conflict studies. We suggest that it is no longer adequate to point out the importance of the inclusion of multiple voices and local meaning-making, but to change the very architecture of knowledge production. This presents an exciting opportunity for a new wave of peace scholarship focused on developing the conceptual and analytical tools, and methodologies and forms of engagement that reduce the influences of visible, hidden, and invisible power, and grows and strengthens critical and inclusive forms of peace psychology.

To conclude, the chapters appear to encourage dialogue and conversations about issues that go to the heart of peace psychology, including its characterisation as a sub-discipline of psychology and its possible roles at the macro-level of society with respect to conflict resolution, conflict management, and conflict transformation. Importantly, the contributions to the volume underscore the value of arriving at a new architecture of knowledge in peace psychology, through emancipatory agendas that offer alternatives to militarisation, military expenditure, state-sponsored violence, and the like. We suggest that peace psychology has much work to do on how to support the expanded roles suggested here.

References

Cornwall, A. (2002). *Making spaces, changing places: Situating participation in development, IDS Working Paper 170*. Brighton, UK: Institute of Development Studies.

Suffla, S., & Seedat, M. (2015). *Engaging invited and invented spaces for peace: Setting the context*. Unpublished manuscript, Johannesburg, South Africa: Institute for Social and Health Sciences, University of South Africa & South African Medical Research Council-University of South Africa Violence, Injury and Peace Research Unit.

Index

© Springer International Publishing AG 2017
M. Seedat et al. (eds.), *Enlarging the Scope of Peace Psychology*,
Peace Psychology Book Series, DOI 10.1007/978-3-319-45289-0

Printed in Great Britain
by Amazon

29508526R00183